# SUMMER SOLDIERS

*A Survey & Index of
Revolutionary War
Courts-Martial*

# SUMMER SOLDIERS

## A Survey & Index of Revolutionary War Courts-Martial

### By James C. Neagles

Ancestry Incorporated
Salt Lake City, Utah
1986

Library of Congress Catalog Card Number 85-073273
ISBN Number 0-916489-05-1

First Printing 1986
10 9 8 7 6 5 4 3 2 1

Printed in the United States of America

# Contents

# Foreword

T hough we might say that this is the best summary volume of its type on Revolutionary War courts-martial, I can hear the genealogist or family historian questioning, "Who needs it? My ancestors can't be there, for I don't have ancestors who could get themselves court-martialed!" Perhaps. But let's see.

The historian will like *Summer Soldiers: A Survey & Index of Revolutionary War Courts-Martial,* for it reveals the little-known fact that a relatively large number of courts-martial were necessary during the Revolution, and also gives both the forests and the trees in presenting sound overall conclusions drawn from its presentation of detailed abstracts of the individual cases. The book is thorough, covering all the cases obtained after much research by the author into all the unit orderly books to which he could get access. It is documented, showing the repository where information was obtained for each item, and, because the items are abstracts, giving the reader who requires more information a cited source for each. It is enlightening, for it gives us a new insight into General Washington's heroic task of conducting a war under the most frustrating of circumstances, and, by showing us the most common offenses, it gives an eloquent description of some of these circumstances.

The Revolutionary War buff will like *Summer Soldiers,* for it adds color to one's knowledge of one of the truly most interesting of mankind's numerous armed struggles. It was not just the private who found himself in front of a court-martial. The general, too, had to answer for his actions, and sometimes even at his own request, to clear himself of unofficial charges whispered behind his back. General "Mad Anthony" Wayne insisted on his own court-martial, and he was acquitted with honor. Benedict Arnold was court-martialed, and was acquitted of some charges, but sentenced for others to receive a reprimand from Washington—but keep in mind that this was before his infamous betrayal, and the author builds a case to show that his court-martial might have been a significant factor in leading Arnold to the treason path. General Charles Lee was court-martialed and permanently dismissed from the army (Washington in a style of language now lost to us once called him a "dastardly poltroon," but today's commanders could probably not think up anything more original than "S.O.B."). We also learn of a plot to assassinate Washington, and in other cases we learn much of Washington's compassion, and his overriding common sense in endorsing or commuting the death penalty in accordance with the greater issue of whether it would aid or hinder the overall war effort.

The sociologist will like this book, for in these court-martial records we see men uprooted from a customary manner of living and suddenly thrust into the temptation of being made custodians of scarce goods, or demoralized by defeat, or corrupted into deserting by the prospect of being able to collect another enlistment bonus by joining some other unit. We see the punishments by being drummed out of the service, whipped with a cat-o'-nine tails, or made to run the gauntlet. We see men "biting the bullet," and the bullet is a real one.

The librarian will like *Summer Soldiers*, for, in my estimation, no type of book belongs in a public library more than that category which might encourage history-ignorant generations to learn something about our national heritage. This is an American history book compiled from authentic contemporary sources, illustrating vividly a facet of what went on before us, saying something new, and presenting it in an interesting and readable way. Our libraries need all of this type of book that they can get.

And what about the genealogist-family historian? Except perhaps for that type of family historian who insists on being allowed to choose only those ancestors he or she thinks sufficiently suitable to one's pride, this book could be of considerable value, for it puts a bit of flesh on what might otherwise be just a bare statistic. Our very human ancestors were capable of all the glories and all the frailties that "flesh is heir to," and to accept one while rejecting the other would be to paint a false picture. Mind you, not every court-martial revealed the baser side of human nature, and some actually gave detailed portraits of highly commendable courage, but base or courageous, if they are our ancestors, we should want to know every detail about their lives that we can. In many cases, an abstract presented here, once identified positively or tentatively as relating to a given ancestor, can lead to much additional information in the original files. The facility given by this book in allowing us to determine quickly and easily whether a given ancestor appears in court-martial records can save much time and labor. Even if we should not have an ancestor in this book, if we had any ancestor at all in the Revolutionary War, it is interesting to read about a very real and prevalent aspect of their environment. Mr. Neagles's book should appeal to a large audience.

*Eugene A. Stratton, C.G., F.A.S.G.*
*Salt Lake City, Utah*
*January 1986*

# Introduction

*These are the times that try men's souls. The summer soldier and the sunshine patriot will, in this crisis, shrink from the service of their country . . .*

Thomas Paine

M any of the officers and soldiers of the American Revolution were not patient, courageous, upright, or heroic. As Paine feared, some were summer soldiers who shrank from duty. Some were impatient, cowardly, trouble-making scalawags; others were generally honorable and idealistic by nature but simply unable to withstand pressures or resist the temptations which confronted them as members of the Revolutionary War fighting force. This book is an attempt to describe and document the behavior of these various individuals as they ran afoul of George Washington's rules and the Articles of War. The primary purpose is to present an account and an alphabetized listing of cases, with source documentation, of the courts-martial listed in the Revolutionary War orderly books. This, it is hoped, will prove beneficial both to historians and genealogists.

This is not strictly a social analysis of the character of the Revolutionary War soldier or officer. Various historians have leapt into that arena and have produced some probing investigations—often disagreeing with one another.[1] Rather, this is a presentation of the types of offenses committed and the punishments meted out in cases which went to trial by court-martial. The reader will find the offenses and punishments interesting when contrasted to accounts of modern day military justice. From statistical or empirical analyses of this material, social historians may make or revise their own conclusions relative to the military personality and character of the revolutionary soldier or officer.

the entries of 3,315 court-martial records in 168 sets of orderly books for units serving under Washington's command or under his generals or other commanding officers. This collection should spare historians the time-consuming and laborious task of reading the orderly books themselves. Likewise, historians who wish to go directly to the original orderly books can utilize the source documentation found here.

Genealogists wishing to write their family histories in more complete detail may find one of their Revolutionary War ancestors listed as a defendant in a court-martial. He may have been found guilty and punished or perhaps wrongly accused and released or pardoned. Thus, a family history may be enhanced by such interesting facts. Although the ancestor may have been overlooked in a local history "hometown heroes" list and never included in pension records, the mention of his name in an orderly book provides a primary source and is considered proof of military service at a definite time and place. The name or number of his military unit also provides opportunity for further research into his full service career.

During the course of gathering material for this book, the author felt it necessary, as a secondary purpose, to make some interpretation of the causes and conditions which formed a basis for the nonconformist behavior of some Revolutionary War soldiers and officers. Much has been written about the motivations underlying a colonist's decision to enlist in the militia or the Continental Army.[2] Among others, there was the need to earn some money (albeit not very much). Enlistees received a cash bounty at the time of enlistment and were awarded a grant of land after the fighting ceased. On the other hand, there was sometimes an idealistic willingness to fight for independence from Britain. Undoubtedly, some were influenced by hometown pressures or the recognition gained from donning a military uniform.

During the early phase of the war, many soldiers were volunteers or militiamen representing middle-class landowners impatient with the oppression of the hated "Redcoats." Later on, the ranks were increasingly filled with less affluent men who hoped to profit somehow by enlisting or were merely eager to change their humdrum existence. The officer corps was comprised of persons from the higher and better educated classes. Even these men, with more opportunity than others, often succumbed to temptations to enlarge their financial fortunes, and they, too, were court-martialed in substantial numbers.

None of the varying backgrounds seemed to dictate whether a specific individual would commit a military transgression and end up a court-martial defendant, desert from the service, or join a band of mutineers. Rather, individuals seemed only to react to the unique situations in which they happened to find themselves. The author has set forth his own theory of "situational crime" which might explain such improper actions. In support of his theory, he has briefly described a succession of losing battles and the attendant heavy loss of life, the scarcity of pay and its depreciating value, the inadequate clothing and food provided, the pressures of mob action in a fomenting mutiny, and the comparative ease of deserting from a military unit. Also evident were many financial temptations which arose from the situational circumstances of being an officer or civilian trading with the army. The author attributes most military violations to the fact that violators simply found themselves at a certain place at a certain time when they were provoked by one or more difficult situations or tempted by perceived opportunities. At this point, bad judgment was often used in reacting. The details of offenses resulting from these faulty reactions and the ensuing punishments meted out by military tribunals are described herein without further analysis.

# CHAPTER 1

# Military Justice

*Thursday, July 6th, 1775. Headquarters, Cambridge.*
*GENERAL ORDERS: A general court-martial is ordered to sit tomorrow, at ten o'clock a.m., for the trial of John Seymour, John Batchelor, and Wm. Groston, all of Colonel Gridley's regiment, charged with desertion and theft . . .*
*Notice is to be given to the prisoners today.*

## RULES AND ARTICLES OF WAR

T he British system of laws and regulations governing its military forces, including the process of court-martial, provided the background for the American military justice system. Until the Revolution, everyone who lived in the colonies, except aliens from countries such as France, Spain, Germany, etc., was a British subject, and a colonial soldier technically was part of the British army. In the French and Indian War, American colonists served as British soldiers and officers attempting to control or curtail the advancing French adventurers and their Indian allies. During this war, a young George Washington and an even younger Anthony Wayne, among others, began their lessons in warfare. Thus, when the Continental Congress, two months after Lexington and Concord, adopted Rules and Articles of War to govern the Continental Army, they were very similar to those which governed the British soldier, except that American punishment was noticeably less severe.

The Articles of War adopted 30 June 1775, with a few additions on 7 November 1775, served the new American military forces until a new set was adopted by congressional resolution on 20 September 1776. Except for a few amendments, these regulations remained in effect until the close of the American Revolution and beyond. They described the procedure for establishing and conducting courts-martial, and they contained a schedule of offenses with appropriate punishments for violators. This document was organized into sections, each comprised of two to several numbered articles as subheadings. They provided for general, brigade, and garrison (or detachment) courts-martial, based primarily upon the administrative realities at any given time as well as the severity of the offense charged or rank of the accused. In cases of high-ranking officers, Congress reserved the right to review and affirm or disapprove the findings of the court-martial. The commanding general was authorized to establish a court-martial and appoint officers to serve on the court, designating one as president of the body. A general court-martial required thirteen members, and the judge advocate general was authorized to prosecute in the name of the United States. The method for taking oaths, the testimony of witnesses, and other legal procedures were set out in detail. A death sentence could not be imposed without agreement by two-thirds of the court's members.

There is some confusion relative to the court's authority over personnel of state militia units. However, when militiamen were assigned to and became part of the Continental Army, the Articles of War also covered them. Still, many militiamen were paid solely by and served only in their own states or counties and were, therefore, subject to no penalty more severe than a fine.

Violators were arrested and confined pending their trials, but confinement was not frequently a mode of punishment following a conviction. Legal limits were set on the length of time a defendant could be confined prior to trial. Submission of daily reports of prisoners' names and numbers was required. Washington, at Valley Forge, once became concerned over a large number of men being held for trial and issued the following order: "Great numbers of prisoners are now in the Provost suffering severely from the severity of the season. Brigade court-martials are to be appointed tomorrow and sit every day until all the men who belong to the respective brigades are tried."[3]

Following a trial, the court issued a finding and published it in the unit's orderly book for all to read. The finding had to be approved by the commanding general and the sentence could be executed only by that general's order. In the units immediately attached to Washington's command, review responsibility generally fell on the commander-in-chief himself. In some cases, the commanding general did not agree with the court, especially regarding sentences. By amendment to the Articles of War on 14 April 1777 Congress empowered a commanding general to pardon or mitigate all punishments authorized by a court-martial, except that death sentences had to first be reported to Congress. The next month, on 27 May 1777, Congress had second thoughts and permitted the general or the commander-in-chief to pardon or mitigate all punishments, including death. A further refinement, by amendment of 18 June 1777 allowed: "That a general officer commanding a separate department, be empowered to grant pardons to, or order execution of, persons condemned to suffer death by general courts-martial, without being obliged to report the matter to Congress or the commander-in-chief." [4]

The orderly books indicate that Washington spent an inordinate amount of time reviewing court-martial proceedings and issuing related orders. He was careful to see that legal procedures were followed and was known to invalidate a court-martial finding where improper proceedings had taken place. For instance, in 1782, after a James Brown of the Second Regiment of Artillery was sentenced to death after being found guilty of desertion and attempting to side with the enemy, Washington disapproved the sentence because the court had not been created either by himself or by a commanding general as required by the Articles of War. By such action, Washington let it be known that no unauthorized officer could ever set up a semi-legal court and administer his own brand of justice.

Various sections of the Articles of War dealt with specific categories of behavior required of the officers and soldiers. For example, section one described the proper holding of and deportment at divine services. It imposed penalties for profanity and penalized chaplains for undue absences. A group of sections dealt with crimes such as treason, mutiny, desertion, cowardice, absence without leave, and enlistment irregularities. Another group dealt with violations against persons, such as fighting, dueling, robbery, and plundering. Still another group dealt with violations against property or administrative matters, including embezzlement, improper use of money entrusted to an officer, theft, fraud by a civilian who had business with the military, and improper requisitioning or use of military clothing or supplies.

## SUPPLEMENTAL ORDERS

Expanding upon the official Rules and Articles of War, Washington and his generals issued supplemental field orders to maintain efficiency and to ensure the health and safety of their troops. Washington, acutely aware that his soldiers were far from disciplined, and knowing that they were by nature suspicious and hostile toward any threat of regimentation, attempted with difficulty to instill some semblance of order and standardization among them. He used persuasion, appeal to personal honor, castigation of the enemy, threat of corporal punishment, and even death, to enforce his edicts. Samples of such orders are reproduced below for illustration.

### Gambling

Congress had outlawed gambling by civilians as well as soldiers during the Revolution. Washington personally considered it to be a vice which would cause dissension among his troops and railed against it constantly.

> The commander-in-chief is informed that gaming is again creeping into the army; in a more especial manner among the lower staff in the environs of the camp. Therefore, in the most solemn terms declare, this vice in either officer or soldier, shall not when detected, escape exemplary punishment. And to avoid discrimination between playing and gaming, forbid cards and dice under any pretense whatsoever.[5]

## Use of Alcohol

Washington also realized the dangers of excessive use of alcohol and tried to limit unauthorized use. In the tradition of British military practices, however, and recognizing the morale benefits of permitting drink in moderate amounts as a reward, he and his commanding generals issued rum at appropriate times, such as during a holiday season or when the weather made it a welcome treat. On 12 August 1779 Washington ordered: "In consequence of the extreme bad weather last night and this morning, the general orders one-half gill of rum to be issued to every man in camp."[6] One wonders what sort of bad weather occurred in the middle of August—heavy rain or wind, perhaps: "As the troops at Providence are miles distant from the enemy, and not necessary to be under arms before day, the guards and the fatigue parties only, to receive one-half gill of rum daily, in wet weather or other extraordinary occasions."[7]

## Absenteeism

A particularly frustrating practice of the soldiers was absenteeism or straggling away from camp or a march. They simply wandered into the countryside or nearby towns. Because of this tendency, it was impossible for an officer to report accurately how many of his men could be counted on for duty at any one time. He did not know if his men were merely roaming the countryside or had deserted permanently. Many men were listed as "deserters" on monthly personnel returns only to show up a few days later. Despite orders forbidding it, soldiers disappeared for varying lengths of time to be free of military restrictions, or to find food, firewood, or female companionship. The camps were often subject to the marauding of hostile Indians either under British hire or merely bent on personal thievery or assault on an unwary solder. In this regard, one general issued the following statement: "It being beyond a doubt that parties of savages are hovering around the camp, the troops are reminded of the orders against straggling . . . . Those who are detected in a breach of this order are to receive 20 lashes upon the spot."[8] In contrast, less serious infractions were also dealt with: "The major was astonished and mortified to learn that some of the soldiers were wearing their regimental hats when they were not on parade duty, contrary to orders."[9]

## Personal Appearance

Washington was concerned with the appearance of his troops despite their almost universal lack of adequate uniforms. Sometimes they had neither shoes nor coats to protect themselves from the cold. The officially approved uniform was basically blue, but there were many variations among the units. Many individual soldiers had only part of a uniform or none at all. In an attempt to standardize and differentiate between units, Washington resorted to the traditional European usage of various colored ribbons, feathers, or hair to be placed in the hat for identification purposes. In an attempt to create an *esprit de corps*, as well as a feeling of individual self-worth, he exhorted his troops to maintain their personal appearance as best they could. As was the custom of the day, the hair was to be greased with tallow and powdered.

### Individual Misbehavior

Washington became righteously exercised when the reputation of the army was sullied by the misbehavior of his soldiers. He constantly issued stern warnings against going into the countryside to plunder, steal, or otherwise molest the citizenry. Many were court-martialed and punished severely for such behavior. An example of his severe tone is evident in the following:

> Notwithstanding all the cautions, the earnest requests and the positive orders of the commander-in-chief to prevent our army from plundering our own friends and fellow citizens, yet to his astonishment and grief, fresh complaints are made to him that so wicked, infamous, and cruel a practice is still continued, and . . .
>
> We complain of the cruelty and barbarity of our enemies – but does it equal ours? – they sometimes spare the property of their friends, but some amongst us beyond expression barbarous, rob even them – Why did we assemble in arms, was it not to defend the property of our countrymen? Shall we then to our eternal shame and reproach be the first to pillage and destroy it?
>
> At the same time the commander-in-chief most solemnly assures all, that he will have no mercy on offenders against these orders – their lives shall pay the forfeit of their crimes. Pity under such circumstances would be the height of cruelty.[10]

Another instance of misbehavior by his troops was denounced in no uncertain terms:

> Complaint having been made by the inhabitants situated near the Mill Pond that some of the soldiers come there to go into swimming in the open view of the women and that they come out of the water and run to the houses naked with a design to insult and wound the modesty of female decency. 'Tis with concern that the general finds himself under the disagreeable necessity of expressing his disapprobation of such a beastly conduct, whoever has been so void of shame as to act such an infamous part, let them well veil their past disgrace by their future good behavior, for they may depend upon it any new instances of such scandalous conduct will be punished with the utmost severity. This is not meant to prohibit the troops from going into the water to bathe, but from going in, in improper places . . .[11]

## ORDERLY BOOKS

The distribution of orders from the commander-in-chief or from any of the generals commanding a unit was done through a series of books maintained on a daily basis. These are often referred to as "order books" since they contained orders, but are more properly called "orderly books," as they were usually kept by an "orderly sergeant."

To relieve Washington of many of his administrative chores, a "major-general-of-the-day" was appointed daily. It was the duty of the officer, through the adjutant general, to formulate daily orders, including the password (called the "parole") and the countersign for the day, and to name subordinate officers-of-the-day. He also issued instructions for the day's activities, be they routine camp duties or broad plans for a battle as set forth by Washington or a commanding field general. The court-martial proceedings at headquarters also were noted, as well as any special instructions emanating from the commander-in-chief.

Every morning a major representing each general of the brigade came to headquarters to receive the orders from Washington's adjutant general. The majors then went back to their own regimental adjutants and passed on the orders. Each regimental adjutant in turn relayed the orders to the first sergeant or the orderly sergeant of each company. At each level the adjutant or the sergeant recorded in his unit's orderly book the general orders from headquarters and added the special orders of his own commanding officer. He also entered the results of any court-martial held at headquarters which involved his own men and of courts-martial held by his own unit. Accordingly, each orderly book was unique but also contained material found frequently in other orderly books. Entries differed from book to book, and accuracy often suffered, especially regarding names.

The following is not an exact copy of any particular day's entries in any particular orderly book, but is a composite of several typical and actual entries found in various books. These entries illustrate the more common types of information to be found in these books. For ease of reading, abbreviations, spelling, and punctuation have been updated where reasonable; not only in the following abstracts but throughout this book where material is abstracted from orderly books. Readers are urged to inspect the actual copies of the books, if practical to do so, to obtain the flavor of the absolutely precise wording and spelling used by the orderlies.

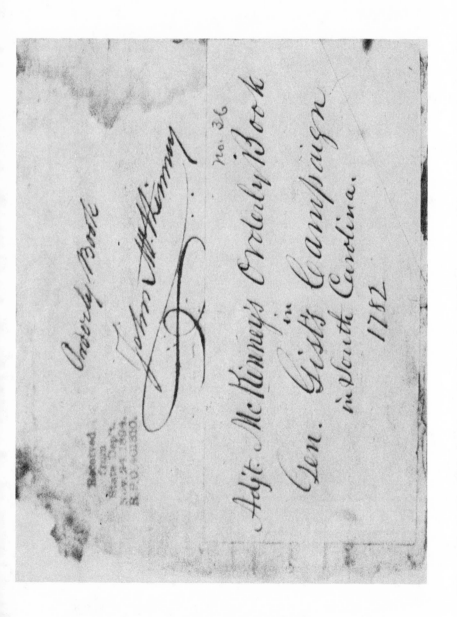

*Figure 1:1*. Adjutant McKinney's Orderly Book.

***Figure 1:2***. Orderly book page from Valley Forge.

Head Quarters, Wilmington,
6th September 1777

Major General tomorrow ............................Lord Stirling
Brigadier General tomorrow .........................Scott
Field Generals tomorrow ...........................Col. Park &
                                                    Maj. Ford
B. Maj .............................................Jones

Parole, "HALIFAX": Countersign, "GENEVA"

The general has no doubt every man who has a due sense of the importance of the cause he has undertaken to defend and who has regard for his own honour and the reputation of a soldier will, if called to action behave like one, contending for every thing valuable, but if contrary to his expectation, there shall be found any officer or soldier so far lost to all shame as basely to quit their posts without orders, or shall skulk from danger or offer to retreat before order is given for so doing by proper authority from a superior officer they are to be instantly shot, as a just punishment to themselves and for example to others. This order, those in the rear and the corps of reserve are to see duly executed to prevent the cowardly from making a sacrifice of the brave and by their ill example and groundless tales, calculated to cover their own shameful conduct, spreading horror as they go.

That this order may be well known and duly impressed upon the army the general orders that the commanding officers of every regiment to assemble his men and have it read to them to prevent the plea of ignorance.

The general begs that every officer be attentive to all strange faces and suspicious characters which may be discovered in camp, and if upon examination, no good account can be given why they are there, they are then to carry them to the major-general-of-the-day for further examination. This, as it is only a necessary precaution is to be done in a manner least offensive.

The general officers are to meet at five o'clock this afternoon at the brick house at White Clay Creek and fix upon proper piquets for the security of the camp.

Jno. Laurance and Peter P. Thornton, Esq. are appointed extra A. D. Camps [*sic*] of the commander-in-chief. All orders therefore through them in writing or otherways are to be regarded in the same light as if proceeding from any of his A.D. Camps [*sic*].

A general court-martial to be convened tomorrow to try the following persons . . . ., with the following officers as members of the court, Colonel Worthington to act as president . . . .

All chaplains are to perform divine services tomorrow and every Sunday with their respective brigades and regiments, where their situation will possibly admit; and commanding officers of Corps are to see that they attend themselves with officers of all ranks, setting an example.

Captain Christopher Gardiner, of Colonel Varnum's Regiment, in the Rhode Island Brigade, tried by court-martial whereof Colonal Thomas Church was president, for deserting his post is found guilty of the crime, and unanimously sentenced to be cashiered, as incapable of serving his country in any military capacity.

# CHAPTER 2

# Situational Crime

*. . . men accustomed to unbounded freedom, and no control, cannot brook the restraint which is indispensably necessary to the good order and government of any army; without which licentiousness, and every kind of disorder will triumphantly reign.*

George Washington

U ltra-conservative colonials of 1775 were apt to remain loyal to the Crown and behave in the accepted manner of true British subjects, which they were. They tended to join local Tory groups or at least attempted to remain neutral of the conflicts swirling about them. They resented the unsettling influence of the hot-headed rebels who met secretly and declared that violent action soon would become necessary to restore the inherent rights and privileges of British citizens. Some even talked of complete independence – an unthinkable and fearful concept to loyal Englishmen who had been trained from childhood to revere the monarchy and mother country.

By contrast, the emboldened and impatient rebels circulated petitions and demanded all citizens sign under threat of loss of business, social ostracism, and sometimes physical harm. These rebels commanded such respect that eventually they were placed in leadership positions. From this impetuous class of citizens, the American army soon drew volunteers. They were by nature rebellious and independent in thought. Indeed, their bold and nonconformist traits may have been inherited from ancestors who had fled from European oppression, both civil and religious, hoping they could make a better life elsewhere. Relatives and friends who did not emigrate may have been the meeker and more compliant persons. It was the sons and grandsons of these independent and individualistic pioneers who made up most of the soldiery in 1776.

Such men were not prone to exchange one yoke for another imposed by a military establishment, even their own. The local militia and state volunteers often followed only their own chosen officers rather than the Continental Army officers. They knew their militia officers personally, and it was these officers who handed them their enlistment bounty. On the other hand, the Continental Army officer was a stranger from another colony and was a person of whom to be wary. If conditions in camp became too difficult, the individual soldier (and occasionally even his entire unit) felt he was exercising a fundamental right when he simply walked away and went home. Leaving an intolerable situation and going home to one's family to plant a crop or otherwise tend to personal needs or desires was not looked upon as a crime, except by the higher echelons. If denied such privilege, soldiers often took the matter into their own hands by deserting or displaying aggressive behavior against either the military system itself or fellow soldiers or officers.

Offenses against the law, either civilian or military, seldom occur in a vacuum. Rather, they tend to be committed directly out of circumstances which provide opportunity to improve one's lot. When one suffers sufficiently from personal pressures brought about by peers, superiors, or the environment, he is prone to do something—anything—to relieve the pressure. Even when one is not suffering particularly, he is sometimes tempted to improve his financial situation should a favorable opportunity present itself. Of course, depending on an individual's personality and moral character, the pressure need not always be intense or the opportunity overwhelming to result in a criminal act. The majority of persons, those with acceptable moral standards and with realistic recognition that an illegal act may lead to serious consequences, seldom or never violate the law. Even with those persons, however, the pressure or opportunity might be so powerful that a normally law-abiding person will violate the law. This might occur when one is placed in an unusual situation where the potential for crime is not only possible but plausible. If one is not placed in such a situation, he might never entertain the notion of an illegal act, but the reverse can happen under various sets of circumstances; when it does, the "situational offender" is created.

During the American Revolution an abundance of situational crime occurred—crime which would not have taken place had the offenders been at home on their farms with their families. Finding themselves in uniform as rebel soldiers; calculating their personal odds of meeting death by gunshot, bayonet, disease; being crippled in battle; suffering from a scarcity of decent food or clothing; subject to intense weather without adequate shelter; and growing irritable at the pettiness and jealousies of leaders and fellow soldiers, they were ripe for any suggestion which would relieve their frustrations or improve their lots. These were the soldiers whose behavior eventually resulted in a military court-martial. These persons would not otherwise have broken any law except for the peculiar situation in which they found themselves.

Basically, there were two conditions underlying most violations of the Rules and Articles of War. The first was a soldier's fear and feeling of desperation growing out of the reality of battle and the miserable camps in which he lived. The second was the opportunity to improve oneself financially which grew out of the unique position in, or affiliation with, the army. Such opportunities included: chances to steal military supplies or another's possessions for resale, plundering and robbing inhabitants living near camp, withholding or misusing funds entrusted to an officer, falsifying requisitions for supplies and using them for personal gain, and conniving to make oneself eligible for multiple enlistment bonuses. Also included were the opportunities for fraud and embezzlement by civilians doing business either with the Continental Army or the British.

The major purpose of this book, after highlighting the typical military offenses growing out of the conditions prevalent during the American Revolution and the usual punishments meted out, is to provide a listing of names of soldiers and officers, and sometimes civilians, who were court-martialed. As a prelude, however, it will be helpful to understand the background relating to the offenses committed. Using the above-stated two basic conditions existing as the primary background to situational crime, this chapter will briefly describe some of those conditions.

## FEAR AND DESPERATION

### The Battles

Fear of death or crippling for a potentially losing cause was a major factor influencing the behavior of the American soldier. It was normal to try to escape such a fate if possible. Years before the American victory at Yorktown, Virginia in 1781, it often appeared that the war would be lost to the superior British forces. Time after time, only poor leadership decisions by British commanders or some fortunate happenstance saved the Americans from total defeat in a major battle. Precious few battles encouraged the American soldier that the ultimate goal of freedom would be gained on the battlefield. Rather, he hoped to survive a losing cause, or that diplomatic negotiations might soon end the impasse between the two armies. It is understandable that given such a philosophy, a soldier might take advantage of any opportunity to extract himself from the fighting. He was, however, a natural born fighter, who, when pressed into action, brought forth his best effort and deported himself proudly. This saving spirit probably enabled the colonists to persevere and attain victory—assisted by the sometimes reluctant and tardy French nation. Some of the worst battles are summarized in chronological order below. Though not necessarily terrible from a tactical point of view, they served to create feelings of fear and desperation in the minds of the soldiers who bore the brunt of the fighting. Many numbers of casualties are estimates, since it is difficult for historians to know the exact number of killed, wounded, or captured from old or nonexistent records.[12]

## Bunker Hill (Breed's Hill)

Although claimed as a British victory, the new American army demonstrated that it could withstand a major attack despite its unreadiness for battle. The famous phrase, "Don't fire until you see the whites of their eyes," was coined because of the scarcity of American ammunition and to ensure accuracy and concentrate firepower.

## Quebec, Canada

To reach Quebec, Americans led by General Benedict Arnold, spent two months marching and boating through Maine in snow and bitter cold. Large numbers died of starvation or froze to death; others deserted *en masse*, stealing food and supplies. After failing to take Quebec by siege and frontal attack, the Americans retreated. Heading southwards, hundreds more died of smallpox, malaria, and dysentery, as well as by murder at the hands of Indians and revengeful Canadian citizens. After several months, they escaped from Canada for good—badly beaten and crippled. They were the luckier ones—the few who survived.

## Long Island, New York

British armies landed on Long Island and pushed the Americans back toward the mainland. Fifteen hundred Americans died before the remainder were secretly evacuated across the East River under cover of night and fog. Washington then led the survivors in a retreat northward through Manhattan, to White Plains, and then westward across New Jersey.

## Fort Washington, New York

After heavy bombardment, Fort Washington, at the northern end of Manhattan, was surrendered to the British. There were 150 Americans killed and wounded, and 2,600 to 2,700 taken prisoner—to languish or die on British prison ships in the harbor.

## Oriskany, New York

New York militia, accompanied by some friendly Indians and led by Nicholas Herkimer, marched to relieve Fort Stanwix which had been under British fire. They were ambushed by a group of Tories and Indians leaving 150 to 200 dead and fifty wounded.

## Brandywine, Pennsylvania

The battle at Brandywine was an attempt to prevent the British from marching on Philadelphia, then serving as the new nation's capitol. The Americans had a force of 10,000 to 15,000 men. After approximately 700 were killed or wounded and 400 captured, the Americans retreated leaving the British to occupy Philadelphia.

### Germantown, Pennsylvania

Following the British victory at Brandywine and occupation of Philadelphia, Washington planned an attack attempting to recapture it. The attack stalled at nearby Germantown and was turned back. At one point, two groups of Americans, confused by a heavy fog, mistakenly fired on each other. In a British counterattack, approximately 152 were killed, 521 wounded, and 400 missing. Washington's army was then forced to spend the winter at Valley Forge, Pennsylvania, coping with severe cold and shortages of supplies, clothing, and food.

### Monmouth, New Jersey

When the British decided to abandon Philadelphia, Washington's army followed them eastward across New Jersey. American forces occasionally harrassed the British, but avoided a major confrontation until they reached Monmouth Courthouse, where Washington decided to attack in force. When the British counterattacked, the American General Charles Lee retreated in confusion. Washington personally stopped the disastrous retreat and rallied the men. They then fought off the British attack and mounted their own counterattack forcing the British to withdraw and escape to New York. General Lee was subsequently court-martialed for disobedience and misbehavior during the battle (see chapter four).

### Savannah, Georgia

The British capture of Savannah resulted in the loss of more than 100 Americans, many of whom died while fleeing through the swamps outside the city.

### Stono Ferry, South Carolina

British soldiers stationed outside Charleston decided to retreat after learning that an American force was on the way. However, the British left a rear guard at Stono Ferry on James Island. The battle that ensued claimed the lives of 150 Americans and 130 British.

### Minisink, New York

A New York militia unit pursued a raiding party of Tories and Indians but were ambushed and lost 120 of their 150 men.

### Savannah, Georgia

A combined French and American force failed in an attempt to retake Savannah by siege. During the engagement, over 800 allied soldiers were killed.

### Charleston, South Carolina

After holding out for a month against British siege, the Americans surrendered the city. More than 5,000 troops, including several generals, were taken prisoner, and 250 were left dead or wounded. Earlier, during a British attack on an American supply depot at Monck's Corner, north of Charleston, another 100 Americans lost their lives.

### Waxhaws, South Carolina

The British overtook a group of Americans retreating to North Carolina, leaving 113 of them dead. Of the 203 wounded, half later died.

### Camden, South Carolina

In a major engagement, the British attacked with bayonets, causing the inexperienced Americans to flee in terror. Even experienced soldiers were forced to retreat or surrender. Approximately 800 to 1,000 Americans died and several hundred others were captured.

### Fishing Creek, South Carolina

Resting Americans were surprised by the British, leaving 150 dead and 300 captured.

### King's Mountain, South Carolina

This was a battle between Americans of opposing idealogies and resulted in the deaths of 157 Tories and twenty-eight rebels.

### Cowpens, South Carolina

In one of the few clear-cut major victories by the Americans, over 900 British soldiers were killed, wounded, or captured (compared to only eighty Americans). This battle featured attack and counterattack, using cavalry and bayonet charges.

### Guilford Courthouse, North Carolina

In a battle similar to that at Cowpens, the British General Cornwallis resorted to firing artillery grape shot at his retreating troops as well as at the advancing Americans to stop a complete rout. Eventually, after British bayonet attacks, the Americans retreated, leaving seventy-eight dead and 183 wounded. The British losses, however, were much higher.

### Eutaw Springs, South Carolina

A major battle ending in a draw between two exhausted forces left 500 American and 700 British casualties. The next morning the British withdrew to Charleston.

### Yorktown, Virginia

The last major battle of the war, resulting in a crucial and stunning victory for allied French and American forces, left eighty-three allied troops dead and 250 wounded. There were 500 British dead and wounded and more than 8,000 taken prisoner, constituting the bulk of the British army in America.

## LIVING CONDITIONS

While on the march to or from actual engagements with the enemy or to join with other units, the troops usually were obliged to withstand deplorable conditions which produced despair to the point of desertion or equally irrational behavior. They slept on the ground and carried small backpacks, if they were fortunate enough to have one—or to have anything to put into them. Food was often obtained by foraging the farms and orchards in the vicinity of the march. In winter, and when the inhabitants of the countryside could not supply them, they were dependent upon food and supplies brought to them sporadically by the quartermaster corps. During the two month trek to Quebec in the middle of winter, soldiers were reduced to boiling and eating their shot pouches or any other scrap of leather they could find. There is one story of a group falling upon their dog and making a feast of him, leaving not a trace. After the losses in Canada, and during the retreat southward, they not only starved and died of smallpox, malaria, typhus, and dysentery, but also were ravaged by "musketoes [sic] of a monstrous size."

By contrast, in 1778, at the time of the Monmouth battle, the area was gripped by a heat wave with temperatures at or near 100 degrees every day causing thirty-seven Americans to die of sunstroke. Scattered thunderstorms only served to intensify the mugginess caused by high humidity. During campaigns in the South, soldiers engaging in the battle at Camden, South Carolina, were short of food and marched or struggled over sandy roads and swamps. Their primary food was green corn and green peaches, and being forced to drink only tainted water caused many to experience severe gastric problems.[13]

In camp at Valley Forge, Washington once had to include the following in his daily orders:

> Complaints having been made with respect to the bread, as being sour and unwholesome, the quarter-master-general is hereby directed to inquire into the matter, and report upon it; at the same time, to inform the bakers that if any more complaints are made, and they shall be found just, they will be most severely punished.[14]

By culling bits of information from various sources it is possible to envision a typical camp used as winter quarters or in other seasons when troops waited in readiness for marching orders. Originally there would be only tents for shelter. If a unit from a state was supplied by its home state with good quality tents, they were comfortable; if not, they did the best they could. Eventually, after a longer stay, huts were constructed out of hewn logs, the cracks being daubed with clay or mud to keep out the wind and rain. At times the daubing was scratched out so the outside air could get in to relieve the foul atmosphere inside created by smoke from the fires and the sick and unwashed inhabitants. Any houses taken over by the military were used by the officers. At Valley Forge for instance, Washington slept in a canvas marquee until all of his men were under some type of shelter. Only then did he move into a nearby large brick home, to be joined later by his wife Martha.

One such house was slated for Baron Frederick Von Steuben, who arrived from Europe with the rank of major general to teach and drill the men in a manual of arms. During a temporary absence by the Baron, a Captain Lipscomb moved into his house. Von Steuben filed charges forcing the captain to undergo a court-martial. After a finding of not guilty, Washington tried to mollify the Baron with these words, "Captain Lipscomb did not intend that disrespect to Baron DeSteuben which the Baron apprehended; at the same time, he must observe that there was impropriety in Captain Lipscomb's taking quarters in a house destined for the general commanding the division."

Wives or other women were more or less permitted in camp, their presence excused as being a helpful method of getting the wash done or the meals cooked. At times, such women actually were prostitutes from nearby towns, and Washington harangued his troops about the dangers of venereal disease and especially against women coming to camp to entice the soldiers to desert to the enemy. While the army was in Manhattan, the soldiers frequented an area known as the Holy Ground, so called because it was owned by the Trinity Church. This was a high prostitution area said to be responsible for infecting as many as forty soldiers of each regiment. A story is told that two soldiers had been killed and a third castrated by the prostitutes there. This resulted in retaliation by other soldiers who wrecked the houses where the crimes had been committed.

Tradesmen, known as sutlers, were permitted to engage in business within the boundaries of a camp. They sold various articles to soldiers and usually provided a legitimate service to them. Illegal behavior by such sutlers subjected them to the military code of justice and some were court-martialed. Among other things, they sold liquor. In one general order, Washington ordered them to sell no more than one-half pint of spirits per day to any soldier. Obviously, such an order could hardly be enforced. He also denounced the "gin shops" operating just outside camp and forbade them to sell any liquor to a soldier under penalty of having their premises vacated and used to house the troops—a threat which he carried out.

Within each camp, probably near the tent or hut area, there was a parade ground. Probably on a daily basis, weather permitting, each unit was ordered to "fall out" of its quarters and assemble in a military manner on "the parade." Inspections of a sort were held, and orders were read aloud after a muster roll had been called. At some of these assemblies the troops donned their best uniforms, including regimental hats, properly feathered or ribboned for review by the commanding officer. Failure, either by officers or soldiers to report to the parade at the appointed time could result in a court-martial.

At a distance from the sleeping area there was a slaughterhouse where beef, pork, or other meat was butchered and prepared for the cooks. Supply tents or houses were established to store the unissued foodstuff and other military gear, including clothes, blankets, guns, and ammunition. Members of the quartermaster corps were in charge of such storehouses.

During the miserable winter spent in quarters at Morristown, New Jersey, under conditions closely akin to Valley Forge the previous winter, Washington divided the state of New Jersey into eleven districts, instructing each district to allot grain and cattle to the army. Washington had been angered the year before when, retreating across that state trying to defend it, he had difficulty convincing New Jersey men to serve in the defense of their own state. Despite his diplomatically worded instructions, Washington probably felt little remorse in imposing upon that particular state for sustenance. He sent his troops to the districts to collect the allotments. They contacted local magistrates and followed Washington's orders to "delicately let them know you are instructed, in case they do not take up the business immediately, to begin to impress the articles called for. This you will do with as much tenderness as possible to the inhabitants."

Trenches were dug at various locations in camp to serve as latrines, or, as they were called at the time, "vaults." Among his many orders, Washington at least once had to insist upon the use of the vaults in lieu of the open ground.

Water was always a problem, and many fell ill because of impure drinking water. Glancing at the mortality rates of the battles summarized earlier, it is seen that thousands were killed from gun and cannon fire, thousands more were killed or laid low by disease. It was estimated that 3,000 died of disease during the Valley Forge encampment alone. Bad water and spoiled food kept the army in a weakened condition because of dysentery, referred to as the "soldier's flux," or "camp distemper."

Smallpox was a primary killer, and it took hundreds and thousands from the active rolls for long periods of time even when it did not kill. Innoculation was engaged in on a wholesale scale, but even that practice was still not perfected, and it debilitated those innoculated for several days after they received the treatment. Soldiers had to be segregated according to whether they had already lived through a smallpox infection and thus were immune, or whether they were still susceptible to the disease. Other segregation was made according to those who had or had not received the innoculation. During a retreat from Canada, A Dr. Beebe wrote, "If ever I had a compassionate feeling for my fellow creatures, I think it was this day, to see large barns filled with men in the very height of the smallpox and not the least thing to make them comfortable."

## FINANCIAL OPPORTUNITY

Although the vast majority of the courts-martial grew out of infractions traceable to the fears of battle and the desperations of camp life, more than a few arose out of persons being placed in a position where they could profit personally. Some of those situations and a few examples of taking illegal advantage are set out below. Contributing to a decision to commit an offense involving money or goods which could be used or sold for cash were the failures of Congress and its army to remunerate soldiers as promised. The standard pay for a private was six and two-thirds dollars per month. Usually it came late, often by several months. During the New York campaign, soldiers were asked to fight even though their pay was two months in arrears. During the southern campaigns, they often fought without any pay at all and with little hope for any in the future. Washington once wrote about this discouraging situation as follows:

> . . . my situation is inexpressibly distressing to see the winter fast approaching upon so naked an army, the time of their services within a few weeks of expiring, and no provision yet made for such important events. Added to this the military chest is totally exhausted. The paymaster has not a single dollar in hand. The commissary general assures me he has strained his credit to the utmost for the subsistence of the army. The quarter master general is precisely in the same situation, and the greater part of the army in a state not far from mutiny, upon the deduction from their stated allowances. I know not to whom to impute this failure, but I am of the opinion, if the evil is not immediately remedied, and more punctuality observed in the future, the army must absolutely break up.[15]

Pay was in Continental currency which depreciated during the war period until it became almost worthless. To correct this development, Congress made additional payments to help make up the difference, but this was done only after the war ended. Pennsylvania, for one, granted "depreciation lands" in its westerly areas to those who served to the end of the war. Such postwar payments, however, did not help during the time the soldier was actually fighting and wishing for the means to buy some necessity for himself or to send money home to his poor family.

### Plundering and Theft

When Washington was forced to obtain food directly from the citizenry, he was careful to pay or to issue bills of credit for all such supplies. He deplored the concept of plundering the American citizens as being worthy only of the enemy. There were instances, however, where plundering and living off the countryside was an officially approved way of staving off starvation during a grueling march. The individual soldier often had no hesitation to plunder a town his unit had just overwhelmed. He considered the treasures to be found there the spoils of war. His officers often condoned that philosophy—and even encouraged it. An example is found in a soldier's diary preserved for posterity. It stated that a Sergeant Amaziah Blackmore, accompanied by a lieutenant and a fifer, went to East Chester among the deserted houses to plunder them. They were captured by a patrol of Hessians on a similar mission, but Sergeant Blackmore escaped. When he reported to his commanding officer that evening, "Captain Baley and Lieutenant Richmond went down and plundered some houses at East Chester of furniture of the value of $400 and one colt." Upon learning of this, Brigadier General John Nixon thought "this was such fine work that he made a present of the colt to Captain Baley."

Washington once stated in a letter:

> I have ordered instant corporal punishment upon every man who passes our lines, or is seen with plunder, that the offenders might be punished for disobedience of orders; and inclose (sic) you the proceedings of a court-martial held upon an officer, who with a party of men had robbed a house a little beyond our line of a number of valuable goods; among which (to shew that nothing escapes) were four large pier looking glasses, women's cloathes, and other articles which one would think could be of no earthly use to him. He was met by a Major of Brigade, who ordered him to return the goods, as taken contrary to genl. orders, which he not only premptorily refused to do, but drew up his party and swore he would defend them at the hazard of his life; on which I ordered him to be arrested, and tryed for the plundering, disobedience of orders, and mutiny; for the result to the proceedings of the court; whose judgement appeared so exceedingly extraordinary that I ordered a reconsideration of the matter, upon which, and with the assistance of fresh evidence, they made shift to cashier him.[16]

There was also stealing from the army itself. A Lieutenant McDonald of the Third Pennsylvania Regiment was court-martialed for "taking two mares and a barrel of carpenter's tools, which mares he conveyed away, and sold the tools at a private sale." A man named Windsor Fry was sentenced to death after being found guilty of "plundering the commissary store and stealing a quantity of beef, candles, and rum; and breaking open two windmills and stealing a quantity of meal."

Theft of another soldier's property was usually infrequent and of a petty nature. Articles stolen most commonly were hats, boots, and other pieces of clothing, probably taken out of desperation for one's own needs.

### Fraud and Embezzlement

Officers were charged with the responsibility of enlisting recruits and were furnished with public money for that purpose. It was sometimes possible for an officer to report a hypothetical enlistment, falsely carry a name on his monthly returns, and pocket the money himself. In a few instances, a man could be recruited and then immediately assigned as a laborer at either the officer's own farm or that of a friend, while being reported present in camp. Officers placed in charge of army supplies were especially vulnerable to the temptation of embezzlement of goods in their possession. Captain Oliver Parker, of Colonel Prescott's Regiment, for instance, was "cashiered" after being found guilty of "defrauding his men of their wages by false returns, imposing on the commissary and drawing supplies for more men than were in his company, and for selling these." A foragemaster named Hugh Baker was also dismissed from the service for "keeping a horse without permission, and not returning it until a complaint was made against him." Israel Davis was found guilty of "detaining about sixty pounds of Massachusetts currency, the property of five soldiers, for money due them from the town of Newbury." Incidentally, this man was acquitted of a charge of detaining for two months pay drawn by him belonging to a soldier in his unit.

A highly coveted discharge from the army was worth paying for, if a soldier had the means to buy it from an unscrupulous officer with the authority to issue one. Such an officer, knowing that the soldier might well desert anyway, could figure to profit from the man's decision to go home regardless. One such officer was Captain Thomas Lucas of Colonel Varnum's Regiment, who was dismissed from the service after it was revealed that he had illegally "discharged a soldier and received a sum of money for so doing; returning the soldier's name on the muster roll after discharging him." Also, a Captain Thomas Beall of the Maryland Independent Corps, was dismissed for "discharging a soldier after having been duly enlisted, and for receiving his regimental clothing; for defrauding the United States."

**Trading with the Enemy**

In comparison with the paltry treasury of the Continental Army, the British army was well-off and paid its suppliers in British pound sterling rather than with paper money, printed to excess by the United States and its individual colonies. Thus, it was tempting for any high officer or a civilian to sell or engage in deals with the British. Congress, by resolution on 8 October 1777, and by general order from Washington on 12 December 1779, forbade any transactions with the enemy. This practice by army personnel was not a common danger except during the New York campaigns when most of the state and city officials as well as the citizenry were Tories, and when the British were making open offers to the American soldiers and civilians. A young soldier named Jones traded with the enemy in New York, and Washington said that he "got bewitched after hard money." A high-ranking officer, John Beatty, the Commissary General of Prisoners, dealt with the British, but received only a reprimand. He submitted his resignation the next day, however.

During the time that the British occupied Philadelphia, Washington was given almost dictatorial powers over the citizens. He was given authority over those who dared to negotiate a better price—in hard money—for delivering goods to the British. He went so far as to forbid anyone even to enter the city of Philadelphia while the British occupied it, and some were court-martialed for disobedience of that order. A Loyalist or anyone else possessed of excessive greed who sold anything to the enemy was judged and punished by the army. An example is Joseph Edwards, an inhabitant of Pennsylvania, who attempted to drive cattle to the enemy. He was fined £100 and confined in the provost guard until the sum was paid. Also, "$20 of the sum was to be paid to each of the Light Horsemen who apprehended the prisoner as an encouragement of their activity and their good conduct. The residue of the sum to be applied for the use of the sick at camp." Another example is an inhabitant, Thomas Ryan, who was fined fifty crowns and confined in the guard house till the sum was paid. His offense was the taking of eight quarters of mutton and a bull beef into Philadelphia.

CHAPTER 3

# Offenses and Punishments

*There is a radical evil in our army—the lack of officers . . . . a parcel of stu-
pid men who might make tolerable soldiers, but are bad officers . . . . As the army
now stands, it is only a receptacle for ragamuffins.*

Henry Knox

## OFFICERS

George Washington, in his orders and statements, generally praised
the valiant efforts of his Continental Line officers, saying they
tried, against great odds, to keep troops in line and ready for battle.
Contrary to the philosophy of some generals and politicians,
Washington had little use for the militia, which came and went at
distressing frequency. Speaking of militia officers, he said, ". . . there
is no such thing as getting officers of this stamp to exert themselves
in carrying orders into execution—to curry favor with the men (by whom
they are chosen, and on whose smiles possibly they may think they may
again rely), seems to be one of the principal objects of their
attention."[17]

One out of every six courts-martial listed in this book were trials
of officers, accounting for 593 of the total 3,315 cases. The charges against
officers were brought by fellow officers simply to revenge slights and
insults, or for jealousy of those who had received earlier and suppos-
edly unmerited promotions. Toward the end of the war, when he was
trying to reduce the number of such types of courts-martial, Washington hoped, ". . . for the honor of the service there will be no instances
where vexatious charges will be exhibited by one officer against another
through petulance or personal animosity."[18]

In England, as well as in America, the term "gentleman" was used
to designate a person of the landed class and served to denote a social
distinction from the unlettered yeoman farmer, mechanic, or merchant.
The officer staff consisted almost entirely of persons who, in civilian life,
were classified as "gentlemen." The army phrase, "officer and gentleman," became standard usage. It followed, thus, that when an officer
behaved in an "ungentlemanly manner," he was also acting in an

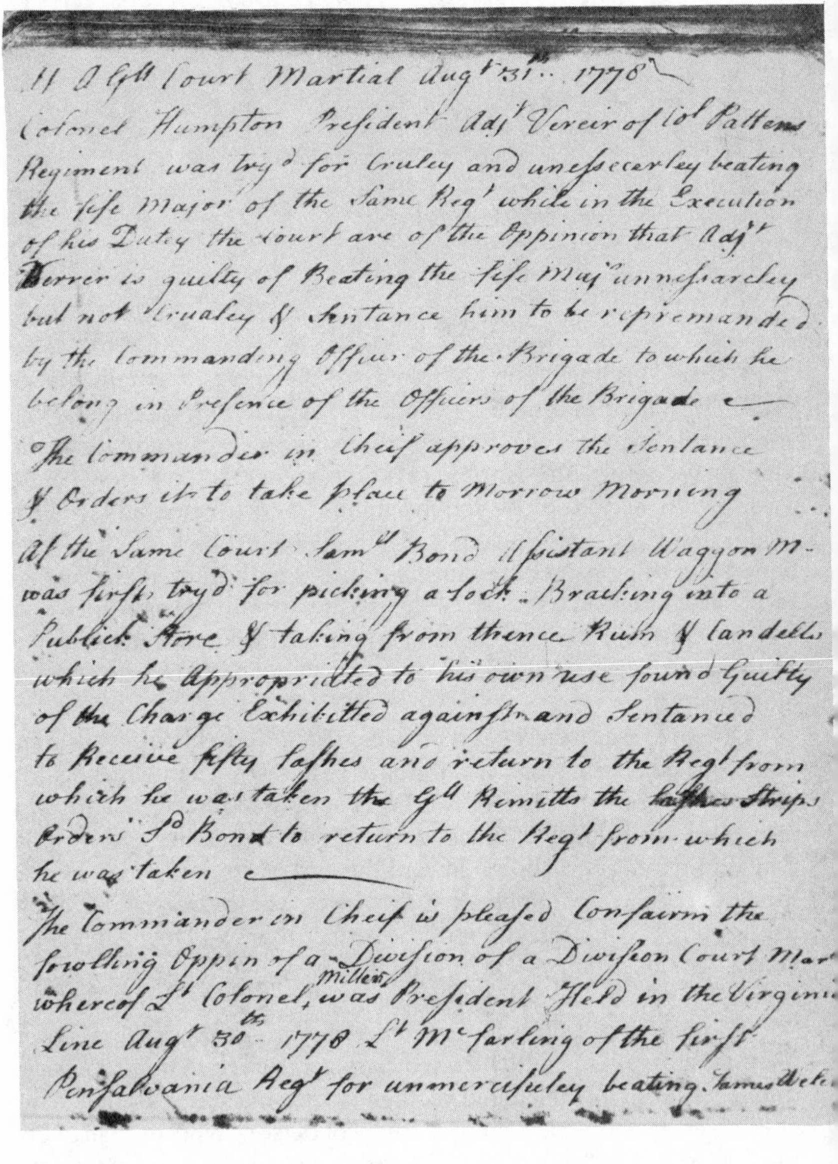

At a Gl Court Martial Aug 31. 1778
Colonel Hampton President Adj Verier of Col Pattens
Regiment was tryd for Cruley and unessearley beating
the fife major of the Same Reg while in the Execution
of his Duty the court are of the Oppinion that Adj
Verrer is guilty of Beating the fife maj unnessearsley
but not Cruley & Sentance him to be repremanded
by the Commanding Officer of the Brigade to which he
belong in Presence of the Officers of the Brigade
The Commander in Cheif approves the Sentance
& Orders it to take place to Morrow Morning

At the Same Court Sam Bond Assistant Waggon m
was first tryd for picking a lock. Braking into a
Publick Store & taking from thence Rum & Candells
which he Appropriated to his own use found Guilty
of the Charge Exhibitted against and Sentanced
to Receive fifty lashes and return to the Regt from
which he was taken the Gl Remitts the lashes Strips
Orders Sd Bond to return to the Regt from which
he was taken

The Commander in Cheif is pleased Confairm the
fowlling Oppin of a Division of a Division Court Mar
whereof Lt Colonel, Miller was President Held in the Virginia
Line Augt 30th 1778 Lt McFarling of the first
Pensalvania Regt for unmercifuley beating James Wes

*Figure 3:1.* Orderly book recording of an officer's court-martial.

"unofficerlike manner." Often a formal statement of charges against an officer was preceded by the general charge of acting in "an unofficerlike and ungentlemanlike manner." The details of his alleged transgressions would then follow. In chapter six, listings of charges against officers usually are restricted to details of the offense, but one may assume that the original writing of the orderly books included the general charges cited above.

Types of offenses committed by officers were closely related to the financial or administrative nature of their positions. When an officer drew more clothing, supplies, or rations than permitted for his unit, he was either treating his men to a larger share than regulations permitted, or he was selling the excess for profit. A less severe offense included an officer's failure to bring his unit to the parade ground as required. Some were tried for not adequately supervising enlisted men being held in the post guardhouse awaiting trial. Officers were forbidden to associate freely with enlisted men and were sometimes court-martialed for so doing, especially if they engaged with them in the vice of playing cards.

Like enlisted men, officers sometimes left camp without permission and stayed for extraordinary lengths of time. Generally, they escaped punishment unless the absence was excessively long or took place just before an impending battle. For instance, Lieutenant Josia Fuller was charged with "being absent for more than a month . . . ." He was acquitted, but Lieutenant John Powers was not so fortunate. Powers was found guilty and dismissed from the service after a trial for "not returning to his regiment at the expiration of his furlough, and not rejoining his unit when ordered to do so."

More serious offenses involved an officer's behavior in action against the enemy. Many officers were accused of cowardice, using gross bad judgment, or being negligent during a battle. For instance, Captain Zane, of the Thirteenth Virginia Regiment, was convicted of "acting in a cowardly manner when sent on a scouting party, by ordering his men to retreat when he had a considerable advantage over the enemy." The court ordered him dismissed from the service. By contrast, Captain Thomas Jackson of the Third Regiment of Artillery, was acquitted after being charged with "cowardice and misbehavior before the enemy at Germantown, by relinquishing his command, and by being drunk on duty."

The usual punishment for a convicted officer was a reprimand from the commanding general or, if the offense was more serious, dismissal from the service, sometimes with a statement that he was "unfit ever again to serve as an officer in the Continental Army." A reprimand was normally given at the head of the massed regiment or written up in the day's "general orders," or both. Regardless of whether an officer received a reprimand or dismissal, the end result was humiliation before his fellow officers, troops, and associates and family back home. To ensure humiliation, a dismissal action was frequently published in the newspapers circulated near the camp as well as around the culprit's residence.

In summary, officers' offenses were primarily of a financial type and punishment was designed to impose disgrace upon the offender. The procedures of dismissal ceremonies were humiliating in themselves, but sometimes the officer's sword would also be broken—occasionally over his head. He would then be forced to march slowly before the assembled troops on the parade ground as the drummer beat a slow cadence, "drumming him out of the army."

## SOLDIERS

. . . they are strolling through the country to their respective homes, a conduct so dastardly in itself, and fraught with the greatest mischief to the Publick Cause, by disheartening the brave who are left in the field to face the enemy, deserted by their comrades, calls for immediate and exemplary punishments.

William Heath

Soldiers, in contrast to officers, usually committed a wholly different type of offense, and received a wholly different type of punishment. If ever there was a difference in treatment between officers and enlisted men, it was in the area of military justice. In a word, the most common offense committed by soldiers was desertion. They left by the thousands and continued to do so year after year. New enlistments were necessary merely to fill scores of vacancies created by desertions as well as by deaths and expiration of short enlistments. Washington seldom could predict how many men he could count on from one month to another. Part of the problem was alleviated when he convinced Congress to provide for enlistment terms of three years, or the duration of the war. He could never prevent large-scale desertions, however, and this plagued him to the final day of demobilization. Washington fully understood that the desertion pattern was largely traceable to the wretched living conditions in camp and on the march. He once said, by way of explanation, " . . . they bore it with a most heroic patience, but sufferings like these accompanied by the want of cloathes, blankets, etc. will produce frequent desertions in all Armies."[19]

Poor living conditions were not the complete reason for deserting however. There were three basic types of desertions, with motives varying considerably. Admittedly, the leading reason for desertion as simply to escape the horrible conditions under which a soldier lived, and return to his family and home. At times, the alternative to rampant disease and death in camp was to pack up and walk home. In such cases, the move to desert was simply a logical and understandable action necessary for self-survival — at least from a soldier's rationalization.

A more insidious desertion, but also understandable to some degree, was leaving with an intent to reenlist in order to receive a second enlistment bonus, as well as to be placed on a second eligibility list for postwar bounty land. Most states paid bonuses and gave bounties of varying amounts. Although the Continental Congress eventually saw fit to increase its own enlistment bonus of twenty dollars to ten times that amount, it was seldom able to compete successfully with some of the states which were under pressure to recruit forces to protect their own homes or shorelines, or to meet the quotas set by Congress as their share of the fighting force. For example, New Jersey and Virginia added substantial amounts of cash to the federal bonus and promised additional land plus a suit of clothes to seal the bargain. This situation was tempting to the soldier who earlier had enlisted for only twenty dollars while the more recent recruits were being paid much more. Desertion of this type was frequent, judging from the court-martial records, and those records reflect only those caught at the game.

The third type of deserter was the one who went directly to the enemy and became a British soldier. Throughout the war, British spies and Loyalist agents in the community dangled promises of high pay and rewards to any soldier who would "turn his coat" and enlist in the British army which, they were told, would most certainly prevail in the end anyway. This treasonous desertion was a means not only to escape the high risk of death or injury in a losing cause but also to reap financial gains. This type of desertion was especially high among Americans who had only recently emigrated from Europe, particularly from England. To further encourage them, the British offered escalating rewards to the deserting soldier if he brought his arms and military accoutrements with him.

The table below illustrates the high incidence of desertion as the basis for court-martial of enlisted men.

Extensive means were used to find and bring back deserters. Recruiting officers were told to be alert to those enlisting again after a previous discharge. They were instructed to make sure a valid discharge certificate was presented before signing up an ex-soldier. Congress authorized a five dollar reward to any civilian or any military officer who brought in a deserter. Although the reward was later raised to eight dollars and then to ten dollars, this incentive resulted in few deserters being apprehended. At least twice, Washington issued statements of amnesty for any deserter who chose to come back within a stated time period. This device also was only marginally successful. Many areas of the country were known havens for army deserters. The Republic of Vermont, for instance, was not yet a state, and deserters flocked there to escape apprehension as well as federal taxation. North Carolina took in deserters by droves, and Georgia and Virginia deserters headed there to hide out. The frontier lands of Kentucky, Tennessee, and the western mountains of North Carolina also were welcome retreats.[20] British deserters often joined American deserters in those frontier areas, and they later became American citizens. A state legislature would sometimes take official steps to round up deserters within its borders and would advertise in its newspapers for a particular deserter if a name and description were provided, but generally the states were deficient in their attempts to stem the tide of mass desertion.

---

### REVOLUTIONARY WAR COURTS-MARTIAL BY CATEGORY OF DEFENDANTS, AND OFFENSES CHARGED AGAINST ENLISTED MEN; FROM RECORDS IN A SAMPLE OF ORDERLY BOOKS*

| OFFENSE | NUMBER OF COURTS-MARTIAL | PERCENT |
|---|---|---|
| ENLISTED MEN | | |
| Desertion: | 1,162 | 43.5 |
|    Simple desertion – 837 | | |
|    Desertion to the enemy – 209 | | |
|    Desertion with fraudulent | | |
|      reenlistment – 116 | | |
| Violation of military regulations** | 706 | 26.4 |
| Theft from the army or army | | |
|    personnel | 288 | 10.8 |
| Plunder or theft from civilians | 194 | 7.3 |
| Mutiny or riotous behavior | 155 | 5.8 |
| Assault or robbery | 94 | 3.5 |
| Offense unidentified | 67 | 2.7 |
|    Total – enlisted men: | 2,666 (80.5%) | 100.0 |
| COMMISSIONED OFFICERS | 593 (17.8%) | |
| CIVILIANS | 56 ( 1.7%) | |
|    Grand Total: | 3,315 (100.0%) | |

\*  Includes trials which led to acquittal or which resulted in clemency or a pardon, as well as those which led to a finding of guilt which resulted in punishment.

\*\*  Includes such offenses as absent without leave, drunkenness, failure on sentry post, threatening, improper action in battle, etc.

In addition to desertion, there were other groups of offenses typical of the soldier and not the officer. They consisted of theft, plunder of homes located near camp, insolence to or striking an officer, and refusal to obey orders. Articles stolen from homes normally included clothing, food, or household goods which could be sold. The list of offenses committed by soldiers in chapter six reveals many atypical offenses and will be of interest for general reading, notwithstanding that, an ancestor's name may or may not be found there.

Unlike the disgrace heaped upon a miscreant officer, a soldier's punishment was designed to inflict bodily pain in the form of flogging or, in the extreme, death. Confinement was infrequently used as punishment, although a number of the more dangerous persons were sent to civilian jails for safekeeping. The New Gate Prison in Connecticut housed many prisoners of war, but only rarely American prisoners. It originally was a copper mine and consisted of a maze of tunnels carved out of rock sixty feet below the surface. Washington used it only for prisoners "deemed to be such flagrant and atrocious villains that they cannot by any means be set at large." In a few cases, confinement took the form of service aboard a war vessel. Such a sentence usually specified that the criminal was "not to set his foot on American soil till the end of the war." Such a sentence not only provided punishment, it also served as a naval recruitment device.

Flogging was accomplished by using a "cat-o'-nine-tails," a whip with knotted cords on the many flayed ends of the rope. These ends cut stripes on a prisoner's back, and the practice was described as giving a certain number of "stripes" or "lashes." The original Articles of War limited the number of lashes for any offense at thirty-nine. At that time, almost every guilty soldier who was flogged received the maximum number of lashes. By contrast, the British military code permitted up to 1,000 lashes. Washington, realizing the futility of deterring lawbreakers with a maximum penalty of only thirty-nine lashes, pleaded that the revised Articles of War, being prepared in 1776, provide a higher maximum. He justified his request by stating:

> For the most atrocious offense (one or two instances only excepted), a man receives no more than thirty-nine lashes; and these perhaps (thro the collusion of the officer who is to see it inflicted) are given in such a manner as to become a matter of sport than punishment; but when inflicted as they ought, many hardened fellows who have been the subjects, have declared that for a bottle of rum they would undergo a second operation; it is evident, therefore, that this punishment is inadequate to many crimes it is assigned to, as proof of it, thirty and forty soldiers will desert at a time . . . .[21]

The new Articles of War raised the limit to 100 lashes and quickly became the standard for all but less serious offenses which justified a flogging. An observer of the day, in his journal, recorded the practice of flogging:

> The law of Moses prescribes forty stripes save one, but this number has often been exceeded in our camp. In aggravated cases, and with old offenders, the culprit is sentenced to receive one hundred lashes, or more. It is always the duty of the drummers and fifers to inflict the chastisement, and the drum-major must attend and see that the duty is faithfully performed. The culprit, being securely tied to a tree, or post, receives on his naked back the number of lashes assigned him, by a whip formed of several small knotted cords, which sometimes cut through the skin at every stroke. However strange it may appear, a soldier will often receive the severest stripes without uttering a groan, or once shrinking from the lash, even while the blood flows freely from his lacerated wounds. They have adopted a method which they say mitigates the anquish in some measure: it is by putting between the teeth a leaden bullet, on which they chew while under the lash, till it is made quite flat and jagged. In some instances of incorrigible villans [sic], it is adjudged by the court that the culprit receive his punishment at several different times, a certain number of stripes repeated at intervals of two or three days, in which case the wounds are in a state of inflammation, and the skin rendered more sensibly tender; and the terror is greatly aggravated.
> Thacher's Journal, January 1, 1780.

That the drummer, under an officer's supervision, wielded the whip was a historical practice. Traditionally, military trials were held with the unit's drum serving as a centerpiece of the proceedings, and the drummer executed the sentence. Thus, the term "drum-head justice" came into being and was still used though only in a ceremonial sense, during the American Revolution. Members of the provost marshal department were also often responsible specifically for the execution of the death sentence, except when the commanding officer selected his own firing squad and administered a quicker form of retribution. Although the court-martial process was standard, in times of emergency, a commanding officer was given, or assumed, the authority to administer immediate justice on the spot. Washington even spelled out this authority in his orders as he expressed concern for particularly revolting or troublesome types of offenses. Accordingly, the literature shows instances when an officer whipped or even shot to death a man for desertion or sometimes a lesser crime.

In some instances, a whipping was not received in a static position, but rather during a run between a "gauntalope" or "gauntlet" of soldiers lined up in parallel rows. A sergeant was assigned to lead the prisoner, at the sergeant's pace, while the flanked soldiers beat the guilty one with sticks or other implements as he passed by. Despite the frequent use of this punishment, one commanding general disapproved of the practice. When two of his soldiers, Elaha (Elijah) Meach and Justice Machem, were convicted of desertion and sentenced to run the gauntlet, the general said in his order: "The running of the gauntlet being an undetermined mode of punishment not authorized by any Article of War, and (contrary) to the spirit, if not to the letter of the Third Article, 18th Section, of the Articles of War, the General disapproves the foregoing sentence."[22]

As with officers, enlisted men were also dismissed from the service, but their dismissals were usually accompanied by 100 or so lashes before they were "drummed out." The sentence to dismiss, for either soldier or officer, was sometimes augmented by a declaration that the dismissal be done "with infamy," as the offense merited in the eyes of the court.

The ultimate punishment was death, and many Revolutionary War soldiers ended their careers in this fashion. The most common mode of execution was to hang a soldier from a scaffold erected by the quartermaster corps, under the supervision of the provost marshal. A rifle or musket squad was also used, but not as often. Members of a firing squad generally were soldiers of the condemned man's own unit—to serve as a stronger deterrent for the others. The soldier who deserted merely to go home usually was let off with 100 lashes, but the repeat offender and the soldier attempting to side with the enemy oftentimes was put to death immediately.

Washington used the death sentence primarily as an example to the others and philosophically believed that deterrence was the exclusive reason for any punishment. He seemed to despair of taking the life of a soldier, but was quick to do so if it might serve as a lesson. He pardoned several soldiers after they had received a death sentence, but only after the affair had served its deterrent purpose. A pardon often came only at the last moment—after the condemned had confessed his errors and sins to a chaplain in front of the soldiers in witness and as the rope was being tightened around his neck. In those instances, Washington felt the purpose of the death sentence had been sufficiently served, and the actual taking of life could then be suspended. In some cases of multiple execution, he would permit some of the unlucky ones to go ahead and pay the supreme penalty and then pardon the remainder who waited their turn at the foot of the scaffold.

In one notorious case, Washington pardoned a man from death to avoid confrontation. A soldier named Leffingwell was condemned to death after being convicted of cowardice, following an arrest by Adjutant General Reed of Pennsylvania. Leffingwell's case developed into a celebrated cause, and his comrades, believing that an injustice was

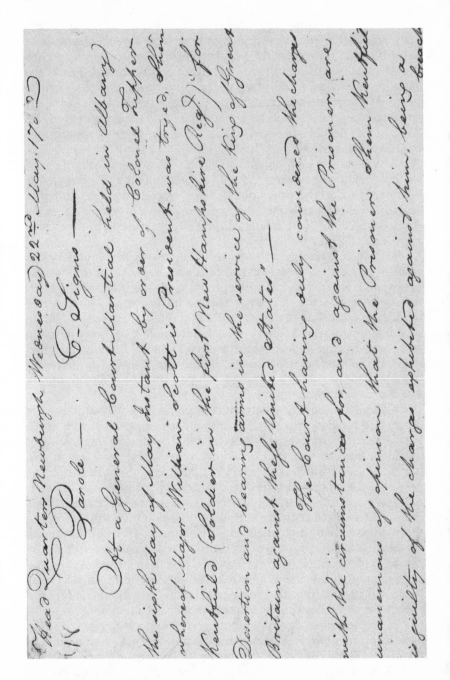

*Figure 3:2*. An orderly book recording of a death sentence.

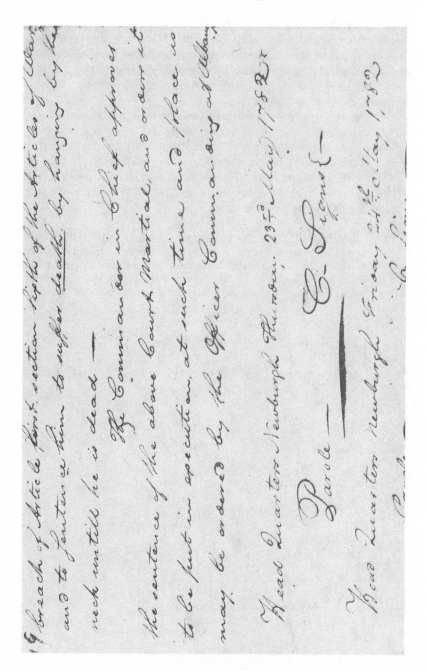

*Figure 3:3.* An orderly book recording of a death sentence.

being done, declared that if their comrade was executed, his would not "be the only blood that would (be) spilt." The officers of Leffingwell's unit (a Connecticut unit) intervened and convinced Reed to reconsider and ask Washington to pardon Leffingwell. Washington was only too happy to agree to the forthcoming request and thus avert a major confrontation within the ranks.

The selection process for a pardon, however, was seldom clear in most cases. A favorable word from a commanding officer on behalf of one about to die was often sufficient ground for a pardon from the commander-in-chief—but not always.

Some fortunate persons who had been sentenced to death, but not yet executed, were granted a reprieve on 4 July 1778 when Washington issued the following proclamation:

> This day being the anniversary of our glorious INDEPENDENCE . . . . will be commemorated by the firing of thirteen cannons from West Point at one o'clock, P.M. The Commander-in-Chief thinks it proper to grant a GENERAL PARDON to all prisoners in the army, now under sentence of death. They are to be released from confinement accordingly.

# CHAPTER 4

# High-level Courts-martial

*. . . I cannot but think it extremely cruel, when I have sacrificed my ease, health, and a great part of my private property in the cause of my country, to be calumniated as a robber and a thief.*

Benedict Arnold

S ome commanding officers, most of them generals, were also subjected to the court-martial process. Blame was sometimes leveled at them by their junior officers following a losing engagement with the enemy. Some were found guilty; others were exonerated, often with honor, after they successfully defended themselves against the accusations of men they had recently led into, or retreating from, battle.

An example is the case of General Anthony Wayne, implicated in a disastrous incident near Paoli's Tavern, just outside Brandywine, Pennsylvania, as the British readied their march into Philadelphia. Wayne, assigned to attack enemy supply lines, bivouacked his troops and set out sentries as the men slept around their campfires. Wayne and some of his officers then fell to drinking and relaxing. Without warning, and in complete silence, the Hessian General Charles Grey and his troops swarmed into the camp. There is a dispute over whether shots were fired during the attack, but it is agreed that this was, by and large, a bayonet attack as they hacked away at the American soldiers. From 100 to 150 Americans were killed and seventy-one taken prisoner. Wayne later said in a letter to Washington that " . . . we were not more than Ten Yards Distant—a well directed fire *mutually* took Place."[23]

Wayne's men saved the cannon, but lost 1,000 muskets and two wagons loaded with supplies. Wayne's accuser claimed the general had received advance notice of the enemy's attack and should have been ready. Wayne demanded a court-martial to clear his reputation and erase the charge of negligence. At the trial, he was acquitted with honor after all the facts were revealed.

Before turning to courts-martial of other high-ranking officers, attention will be paid to the trial of Private Hickey—the dupe of a large and highly organized Tory conspiracy. This conspiracy included a scheme to assassinate George Washington.

## Thomas Hickey

In 1776, New York's provisional government and the people of that colony were still ambivalent and reluctant to join their sister colonies in open rebellion against England. The British sought to exploit that Loyalist feeling by enhancing the climate in which wavering citizens could rise up against the rebels and be ready to join the British at the time of their impending invasion. Individuals who had already thrown in their lot with the American army were approached by British spies and sympathizers to defect to the other side with a promise of higher pay in British currency.

Fearing personal harm, the royal governor, Lord Tryon, took refuge aboard a British ship lying in the harbor. He kept a continuous correspondence with his accomplices on the mainland, chiefly the mayor of the city, David Matthews. One of Matthews's henchmen was a gunsmith named Gilbert Forbes. Forbes was provided with sizeable amounts of money to enlist young men, including American soldiers, to stand ready to join in when the British invaded Manhattan by way of the King's Bridge. The conspiracy included counterfeiting money authorized by the colony of Connecticut. At least five members of George Washington's own respected and trusted Commander-in-Chief's Guard even became enmeshed in the plot. A letter written after the event by a relative of one of the traitorous soldiers, said, "The drummer (Green) of ye Guard was to have stabbed ye General." During Green's testimony, he admitted enlisting the others, principally Thomas Hickey, a trusted member of the guard.

Hickey, a likeable Irishman and well thought of by Washington had been chosen by the conspirators to assassinate the general. He was on good terms with Washington's housekeeper and approached her for assistance to carry out the scheme. She pretended to go along with him but actually reported immediately to Washington. The plan was that Hickey would place poison in a portion of green peas which the housekeeper would then serve to Washington. The general played out his part up to the time that he refused the peas and had the dish taken away. Shortly thereafter, on 15 June, Hickey and Private Michael Lynch, also of the Commander-in-Chief's Guard, were arrested and confined. They weren't charged for attempting assassination, but rather for violating the civil law of passing a counterfeit bill.[24]

The two were confined for two days at which time it was determined that since the New York court was an instrumentality of Great Britain, it had no authority to prosecute the men. This was legally correct since the Declaration of Independence had not yet been signed and the United States was not yet a legal entity. The men were then turned over to the military for court-martial. There is no record that Michael Lynch was ever tried, nor is there any record of the dispositions of the other traitorous members of the Commander-in-Chief's Guard. All of them may well have been executed later, judging from a letter by Doctor William Eustis, who was active in the ensuing round-up of Tory conspirators. He wrote, "We are hanging them as fast as we find them out." The other members of the guard who were caught up in the British schemes were the drummer, William Green, the fifer, Johnson, and a Private Barnes.

On 22 June, Washington was fearful of a general uprising by New York citizens incited by the machinations of Mayor Matthews and his fellow conspirators. Seeking to dampen the public fervor, Washington ordered the mayor's arrest. Although Matthews was immediately taken away for safekeeping, he was never convicted of any wrong-doing. On that same day, Washington ordered Hickey to face a court-martial, charged with "exciting and joining in a Mutiny and Sedition, and of treacherously corresponding with, inlisting among, and receiving Pay from the enemies of the united American Colonies." Hickey pleaded not guilty. Both actions by Washington served to discourage any further escalation of British and Loyalist espionage.

On 26 June, Hickey faced thirteen officers and listened to the testimony of some of his fellow conspirators, William Green, Forbes, Isaac Ketchum, and William Welch. Ketchum testified:

> Last Saturday week the Prison (Hickey) was committed to Goal [sic] on suspicion of counterfeiting the Continental currency, and seeing me in Goal [sic], inquired the Reason for it. I told him because I was a Tory. On this conversation ensued upon Politicks. In different conversations he informed me that the army was become damnably corrupted. That the Fleet was soon expected, and that he and a number of others were in a Choir to turn against the American Army when the King's Troops should arrive, and ask'd me to be one of them . . . .

Hickey produced no evidence of his innocence, but said in his own defense that he:

> . . . engaged in the Scheme at first for the Sake of cheating the Tories and getting some money from them; and afterwards consented to have his Name sent on Board the Man of War, in order that if the Enemy should arrive and defeat the Army here, and he should be taken prisoner, he might be safe.[25]

Following the trial, the court concluded that Hickey was guilty and sentenced him to be "hanged by the Neck till he is dead." Washington confirmed the sentence the following morning and ordered Hickey into execution. The order read, in part:

Headquarters, New York, July 27, 1776

The General approves the sentence, and orders that he be hanged tomorrow morning at eleven o'clock. All the officers and men off duty belonging to General Spencer's and Lord Stirling's encampment to attend the execution of the above sentence. The Provost Marshal immediately to make the necessary preparations and to attend on that duty tomorrow.

More than 20,000 people gathered the next morning to witness the affair, which was culminated from a tree limb in a field near Bowery Lane, close to where the present Grand and Christie Streets now intersect. In attendance was the above-mentioned Doctor William Eustis.

Immediately after the execution, Washington determined that because this was the first soldier to suffer death by execution since the establishment of the Continental Army, and because there was a need to furnish an example not only to the Loyalist citizenry, but also to his own troops, he issued the following statement:

The unhappy fate of Thomas Hickey, executed this day for mutiny, sedition and treachery, the General hopes will be a warning to every soldier in the army to avoid these crimes, and all others, so disgraceful to the character of a soldier and pernicious to his country, whose pay he receives and bread he eats. And in order to avoid those crimes the most certain method is to keep out of the temptation of them, and particularly to avoid lewd women, who, by the dying confession of this poor criminal, first led him into practices which ended in an untimely and ignominious death.

## Major General Benedict Arnold

Possibly the prime factor in Benedict Arnold's decision to become a traitor to America was his own court-martial. General Arnold was one of Washington's more daring and skilled commanding officers. He gloried in the attack and sought opportunities to lead men into battle. He fought bravely in the Canadian campaigns where he was wounded and crippled in the leg. He built a navy of sorts and fought on Lake Champlain. He served at Saratoga and in many other battles. A personal friend of Washington, he was respected by him as a military leader. Unfortunately, Arnold was a vain man, impetuous and imprudent in speech. His overbearing personality and aggressiveness led to disagreements with some of his fellow generals, most of whom he characterized as too cautious in nature. He became unpopular with Congress which promoted several other brigadier generals with less seniority to the rank of major general before they eventually gave that rank to Arnold. While stationed in Philadelphia after the British had evacuated that city, he incurred the displeasure of many civilian officials there; and the Executive Council of Pennsylvania, distrusting military leaders anyway, filed charges against him—charges which led to a military court-martial.

During the subsequent long wait for his trial date, Arnold suffered financially, partially because of his taste for high living and partially because Congress delayed interminably payment of his necessarily complex claims for his yet unremunerated services on behalf of the army, which included advancements of his own money to pay some of his troops.[26]

Even before the charges against Arnold were filed by Pennsylvania officials, he had talked with Washington about his plans to resign from the army and retire to an acreage he owned in New York after he married a young girl named Peggy Shippen. Miss Shippen was from one of the leading families of Philadelphia, but she had Tory leanings and contacts. He married her in 1779, his first wife having died during the early part of the war. At one point in his career, Arnold did, in fact, submit a resignation, but hastily withdrew it when Washington offered him an important command opportunity which he did not wish to miss.[27]

When the Pennsylvania Council sent their charges against Arnold to Congress they took the precaution to furnish a copy to the newspapers. Washington advised Arnold that, to obtain an opportunity to clear his name and present his side of the controversy, he should ask for a court-martial. The request was made and Congress set 1 May 1779 as the trial date. Only four of the eight charges placed by the Pennsylvania group were deemed appropriate for a military court-martial. They were:

1. Granting an unauthorized pass to a vessel belonging to Tories (*The Charming Nancy*) with the purpose of enabling them to leave Philadelphia to enter a port of the U.S. without the knowledge or consent of the Commander-in-Chief.

2. On taking possession of the city, he had closed the shops and stores, preventing the public from purchasing, while he (Arnold) is alleged to have made considerable purchases for his own benefit.

3. Imposing menial offices upon the militia when called into service and defending his right to do so.

4. Using public wagons of the State of Pennsylvania to transport property of the Tories for his own use.

The trial was postponed to 1 June as a result of a letter from Joseph Reed, president of the Pennsylvania Council, who insisted that the charge relating to improper use of public wagons not be dropped or minimized. Anxious to have his day in court, Arnold fumed at the delay. He wrote to Washington in anger:

If your Excellency thinks me criminal, for Heaven's sake let me be immediately tried and, if found guilty, executed. I want no favour; I ask only justice. If this is denied me by your Excellency, I have no where [*sic*] to seek it but from the candid public, before whom I shall be under the necessity of laying the whole matter . . . . I have nothing left but the little reputation I have gained in the army. Delay in the present case is worse than death . . . .[28]

The British had earlier talked with Arnold (who first initiated the conversations has never been proved) and suggested that he transfer his loyalties to their side. Arnold, like many others in high places at that time, was pessimistic that the American army would ever prevail over mighty England. He confided his fears and feelings of being slighted by Congress to his new bride. She sympathized with him and perhaps was instrumental in his decision to at least confer with British emissaries while he fretted over the delays in his pending court-martial.[29]

Not until 21 January 1780 was Arnold able to present his impressive and courageous defense. At the trial, he even insinuated that some members of the court itself might have at one time or another been guilty of some types of shady behavior, similar to those for which he was accused. On 26 January the court acquitted him of charges two and three, but found him guilty of charges one and four—the granting of a permit for *The Charming Nancy* and the personal use of the public wagons. The court sentenced him to receive a reprimand from the commander-in-chief.[30]

The sentence had to be sent to Congress for confirmation, and it was not until 6 April 1780, more than a year after the charges had originally been placed by Pennsylvania, that Washington could finally issue the officially mandated reprimand. The previous month, Arnold had asked to command a naval expedition to the West Indies to plunder on behalf of the American army, a project which he had personally urged two years earlier. After much deliberation by Congress, the project was cancelled. After exhausting this possibility for loyal service to the American cause, he began to consider the offers made by the British. He had not finally made up his mind, however, until after he received Washington's reprimand. Although it was written in a conciliatory tone and seen by many as a mere "tap on the wrist," it angered Arnold who saw it as a betrayal from both Washington and Congress. The reprimand, dated 6 April 1780, was as follows:

> The Commander-in-Chief would have been much happier in an occasion of bestowing commendations on an officer who had rendered such distinguished services to his country as Major General Arnold; but in the

present case a sense of duty and a regard to candour oblige him to declare that he considers his conduct reprehensible, both in the civil and military view, and in the affair of the wagons as imprudent and improper.

The rest of the Arnold saga is well-known history and will not be repeated here. In summary, though, Arnold was given, at his insistent request, the command of West Point. Thereupon, the British adjutant-general, Major Andre, officially promised Arnold a sum of £20,000 and the rank of major-general in the British army if West Point were turned over to the British and payment of his expenses and a brigadier-generalcy if the plan did not succeed. Before Andre could get back to his ship, he was captured by some American soldiers and incriminating evidence was found on him. Upon learning from a courier of Andre's arrest, Arnold, just in the nick of time, fled from a dinner with some other American officers, at which Washington himself was shortly expected. Andre was court-martialed and executed as an enemy spy. Arnold served the British until the end of war and later led a raid on his home state of Connecticut in reprisal against the enemy which he felt had betrayed him—not the other way around.

### Colonel Moses Hazen

Colonel Hazen was a Canadian who at first wavered between loyalty to England and America. He chose America and was active in its behalf during the battle at Montreal. His commanding officer, Benedict Arnold, did not like him and claimed that he had been lax in his handling of goods plundered by the army from Montreal merchants. When the goods disappeared, Arnold blamed Hazen for letting it happen. Hazen countercharged that Arnold had profited personally from the missing plunder. Eventually, Hazen asked for a court-martial to vindicate himself.

During the trial, Arnold became upset and extremely discourteous to the officers of the court when they refused to permit his principal witness to testify against Hazen. The result was that Hazen was exonerated, and the court went so far as to demand that Arnold himself be arrested. Higher up, an agency of Congress, the Board of War, looked into the court's suspicion of personal profiteering by Arnold but exonerated him. As for the demand that Arnold be arrested, General Horatio Gates, then in command of the northern department of the army, simply dissolved the court, stating, "The United States must not be deprived of that excellent officer's services at this important moment."

Months later, Hazen got back at Arnold when he contended that Arnold had slandered him. In a subsequent second court-martial, Hazen was again supported by the court, but nothing else of significance came of the affair.

**Major General Charles Lee**

During a portion of the war, Washington's second in command was General Charles Lee, a former British colonel, who foolishly allowed himself to be captured in December 1776. He remained in British custody on a ship or in New York until he was released in April 1778. It was learned many years later that during his imprisonment he advised the British how they might conquer the American forces. His release was part of a prison exchange after the Americans had captured a British general and offered him for the release of Lee. General Lee was a small man with a large ego. He is reputed to have been excessively thin, ugly of face, uncouth in personal habits, and foul-mouthed. Washington might have chosen some other general as his second in command, but traditions of seniority compelled him to stick with Lee. To his credit, Lee deported himself well in most instances and early in the war had ably led the southern forces.[31]

During the American defeats in New York and the subsequent retreat across New Jersey, Lee became increasingly recalcitrant and hedged on following anything but directly worded orders from Washington. He probably believed that Washington's mistakes in leadership during those trying times would eventually lead to his recall, with himself being given the post of commander-in-chief.

Lee was one of the generals who accompanied Washington in the march eastward across New Jersey following the British withdrawal from Philadelphia. The American plan was to avoid a full-scale attack and follow and annoy the British whenever possible. Lee decided to hew to the original plan even in the face of a conflicting decision by Washington on 27 July 1778 to attack in force at Monmouth Courthouse, New Jersey. When ordered to attack the British as they rested from the terrible heat of that summer, Lee made no move to carry out the order. Many have theorized the reason for his lack of action—some suggesting actual treason. Others speculated that he simply did not trust Washington's judgment of the situation and, feeling that the British were a far superior force anyway, tried to save his men from a retreat already beginning by other units before his own troops fell back.[32] The fact is that Lee's troops engaged in a disorderly retreat on their own, allowing the British to launch a counterattack at the weak point.

Upon discovering this development, Washington confronted Lee in the field and demanded an explanation. One observer of the day described Washington's rage at the confrontation as being a "terrific eloquence of unprintable scorn." Washington is said to have then taken personal command on the spot, reforming the troops and stopping their retreat. Lee was placed in minimal charge of a covering reserve unit, but was ignored and issued no further commands during the engagement. The battle went on all day, and at midnight, after the fighting had ceased, the British marched away under cover of darkness.

A few days later, as Washington contemplated how to deal with Lee, he received a letter from him demanding an apology for the language used against him. Washington replied that Lee would be given an opportunity to explain "to the army, to Congress, to America and to the world in general his reasons for not attacking . . . as (he) had been directed and in making an unnecessary, disorderly and shameful retreat." Upon receipt of this reply, Lee first demanded permission to retire from the army and then changed his mind and asked instead for an inquiry or a court-martial. Washington consented immediately and promptly sent his adjutant general to arrest him and hold him for trial.

The court-martial, with Major General Lord Stirling presiding, began on 4 July 1778. Four other generals and eight colonels were on the tribunal sitting at Brunswick, New Jersey. Lee was charged:

1. For disobedience of orders, in not attacking the enemy on the 28th of June, agreeable to repeated instructions.

2. For misbehavior before the enemy on the same day, by making an unnecessary, disorderly, and shameful retreat.

3. For disrespect to the Commander-in-Chief, in two letters dated 1 July and 28 June.

A transcript of this lengthy and notorious court-martial is available and may be read with interest in the publication, *Proceedings of a General Court-Martial — for the Trial of Major General Lee,* privately printed in New York in 1864. On 12 August the court was ready to hand down its judgment. Lee was found guilty on all three counts. The conclusion of the court was:

> The Court do sentence Major General Lee to be suspended from any command in the armies of the United States of America, for the term of twelve months.

Congress approved the verdict and the sentence. Before the twelve month term had expired, Lee had written an insulting letter to Congress, and was thereupon dismissed from the army permanently. His career was at an end.

### Major General Phillip Schuyler

In July 1777, Fort Ticonderoga, once wrested from the British, was retaken by a far superior force of 7,000 British and German troops. Major General Schuyler was in command of the forces in that area but was not present during the attack on the fort, having left Major General Arthur St. Clair in command. When the attack came, St. Clair accurately realized that his meager force of 3,000 men could not hold the fort and

*Figure 4:1.* Orderly book page recording General Lee's court-martial.

*Figure 4:2*. Orderly book page recording General Lee's court-martial.

retreated under cover of night without any attempt to defend it. His decision permitted part of the American army to retain its strength to fight again another day. Washington later said the decision had been a sound one. The retreat was a debacle and there was inadequate control over the militiamen who fled in disorganized panic.[33]

On 12 July, St. Clair united with Schuyler, and they retreated together, with Schuyler leaving a burnt countryside behind him to make it difficult for the British to survive their pursuit. Trees were chopped down across the roads and bridges were ripped out to delay the pursuers. Farmers along the route burned their crops and killed their cattle as they fled so the enemy could not use them. During the flight, Schuyler hoped to pick up recruits and make a stand somewhere, but it did not happen. Instead, he was relieved of command and replaced by General Gates.

Because of the criticism that he was not personally present at the fall of Fort Ticonderoga, Schuyler requested a court-martial to clear his name. The trial took place at Pawling, New York, on 1 October 1777. The verdict, affirmed by Congress, was :

> The Court having considered the charge against Major General Schuyler, the evidence and his defense, are unanimously of the opinion that he is not guilty of any neglect of duty in not being at Ticonderoga as charged, and the Court do acquit him with highest honor.

The following spring, Schuyler resigned from the army but continued to support and assist Washington as a civilian.

### Major General Arthur St. Clair

At White Plains, New York, General St. Clair was tried on the following charges:

1. For neglect of duty . . .
2. For cowardice, with treachery, with incompacity as a general. . .
3. For treachery . . .
4. For inattention to the progress of the enemy, with treachery, with incompacity as a general . . .
5. With shamefully abandoning the posts of Ticonderoga and Mt. Independence, in his charge . . . .

The court ruled, and Congress approved, as follows:

> The Court, having duly considered the charges against Major General St. Clair, and the evidence against him, do unanimously acquit him of all and every one of them with the highest honor.

## Brigadier General Alexander McDougall

General McDougall was with Washington during most of the campaigns in the middle states and once commanded the camp at the Highlands. He was a loyal and trusted general, liked by Washington. He was charged, however, with several administrative errors, with converting army material to his own use, and for uncomplimentary remarks about other officers. The charges were:

1. Ordering the distribution of a quantity of boards, said to be about 1,300, which were brought to West Point in a sloop to be used for the troops at West Point only, when they should have been used at other places.

2. Not reporting to the commanding general the escapes of upwards of thirty prisoners from the Provost, and thus preventing measures to intercept them.

3. Drawing orders on the clothing store at Newburgh on several dates.

4. Writing a letter to the commanding general injurious to the command and unbecoming an officer.

5. Directing Colonel Crane and his regiment of artillery to deliver their arms and accoutrements; and threatening, upon refusal to do so, to send him to the Provost Marshal.

6. Speaking to the officers stationed at West Point to abuse other officers and accusing them of unmilitary conduct; for criticising General Heath's orders in front of other officers at the post; and for criticizing the General for several actions which he had taken.

7. Pulling down two buildings and moving them to West Point without the knowledge of the commanding general.

The court found the general not guilty of all but the last charge. He was ordered to receive a reprimand for that finding. Washington, in issuing the reprimand, took the occasion to criticize those who brought the charges in the first place. He praised the general and chided those who had brought the charges:

> It is with extreme reluctance the Commander-in-Chief finds himself under the necessaity [sic] of carrying out the sentence of the court upon the 7th charge into execution, more especially as it concerns an officer of high rank of generally accepted merit, the ill consequences from the too free censure of the conduct of officers of superior, by those of inferior ranks, are too obvious to need enumerating . . . .

## Colonel Henry Livingston

One of General McDougall's accusers was himself brought up before a court-martial. The charges were:

1. Traducing the conduct of Brigadier General McDougall in ordering a retreat of the Continental Troops on the 23rd March, last.

2. Neglecting to bring down his regiment on time on that day although ordered in time, when the enemy was near the town, and it then was unprovided with ammunition.

3. Ordering Mr. Smith doing the duty of major of brigade for his brigade, not to turn parties out of it unless the orders were directed to him, which is contrary to the usage of the army, by which he has embarrassed the service.

4. Delaying the returns of his regiment and brigade by orders and whims of his own, contrary to the known rules of the army.

5. Abusive language to General MacDougall at his own quarters.

The colonel was found to be innocent of the first three charges but guilty of the fourth and fifth. He was sentenced to receive a reprimand in the general orders.

## Colonel Samuel Gerrish

Colonel Gerrish was one of the early commanding officers in charge of the Massachusetts forces. It is not known exactly what he did to suffer a court-martial, but the charges were "behavior unworthy of an officer." He was found guilty and dismissed from the service. In the unit's orderly book, some unidentified person, on the page setting out his conviction, wrote in the words, "So much for cowardice," and that gives us some clue to Gerrish's problems.

## Colonel Joseph Vose

Colonel Vose, commanding the Fourteenth Massachusetts Regiment, was tried "upon complaint of a number of his officers" of the following lengthy list of charges—all of which resulted in an acquittal, and his being restored to take charge of his regiment:

1. Taking rum drawn from the regiment for his own use.

2. Defrauding the United States of a number of shirts out of Major Sheppard's store at Albany.

3. Selling a horse belonging to the United States to an inhabitant near Valley Forge.

4. Drawing pay for being on command while on furlough.

5. Keeping the . . . employed by the United States, to work for the army, and allowed extra pay and rations therefor.

6. Drawing pay for a sergeant doing quartermaster duty and keeping all the money but seven and a half dollars for months in his own hands and converting it to his own use.

7. . . . some blankets drawn from the store for the regiment.

8. Using cloth drawn for the regiment to make his hired man clothes.

9. General ungentlemanlike behavior to the officers of the regiment.

### Provost Marshal of the Army, William Hutton

This officer was tried at least two times. The first time he was acquitted after being tried for assisting one Samuel Harris to escape from the provost guard where he was confined for counterfeiting bills of credit.

He must have lost his appointment and then been reappointed to a lesser post since he was again tried by court-martial. On the second occasion, he was found guilty of refusing to perform the office of post marshal in the execution of John Walker, alias Robert Maples. He stated that he had been appointed to his post only the day before and did not want to execute the prisoner. He was, therefore, dismissed from the service. Incidentally, Walker (or Maples) had been found guilty of enlisting in a regiment, deserting from it, using another name, taking another bounty, and reenlisting; only to desert again. For those crimes he had been sentenced to death. It is assumed that whoever replaced Hutton performed the execution.

### Deputy Commissioner of Military Stores, John Collins

Collins was found guilty of:

1. Defrauding the public of a quantity of salt petre.

2. Employing a person to receive the same as his own property and selling it.

3. Breaking his arrest and deserting from his quarters and endeavoring to make his escape from justice by trying to obtain a berth on some vessel to go to sea.

4. Robbing another person of some public papers for his own purposes.

The court must have determined that he should have his wish concerning the sea voyage since they sentenced him to "serve on board a Continental ship of war during the present war, without permission to set his foot on shore; that his name, crime and punishment be published in the public prints."

### Doctor Charles McKnight, Surgeon and Physician in the General Hospital

The doctor was charged with converting to his own use some fatted oxen as well as a large quantity of Indian meal which had been obtained for the hospital. He was also charged with using public horses and wagons to work on his own farm. Further, he was accused of drawing large quantities of wood for the hospital but using it for his own purposes. He was acquitted of all the charges.

**Lieutenant Colonel Smith, Deputy Quartermaster**

This officer was charged with "supplying Captain Pyncheon's house and family with their necessary firewood, amounting sometimes to three fires, in unlimited quantity from the public stores." He was said to have laid out large sums of public money to build boats without orders and established a Continental ferry across the Connecticut River despite the fact that "the country ferry had been there for ages." He was also charged with enlisting a number of men for a year with Continental pay and rations at great expense while the country ferryman offered to supply the Continental ferry for the sum of £200 per year.

At the trial, the court found that although Smith had indeed built three scows and a batteau, it had been done by order of General Greene, that he had manned them at his own discretion, which was also approved by the general, and that furnishing the firewood was in the public business. He was, therefore, acquitted of all charges.

# CHAPTER 5

# Mutinies

*I am happy to inform your Excellency that every officer was present and exerted themselves to the utmost to prevent the extreme of mutiny.*

Anthony Wayne

The conditions described in chapter two led not only to individual violations of the Articles of War, but occasionally to group violations as well. Wholesale desertions were a major concern to Washington and his generals, and the fear of mutiny by entire units also kept them tense. He often pleaded with and warned the Continental Congress concerning the need for funds to provide more humane and just treatment for the troops and, accordingly, pointed out the probability of mass desertions or uprisings. It is to Washington's credit that he persevered in keeping a whole army in the field rather than making matters worse by exploiting the soldiers' fears and grievances by identifying with them. Instead, he begged for their patience and appealed to their honor, stressing the importance of remaining steadfast in opposition to the common enemy. Lacking that approach, the army might well have dissolved several times, something Washington predicted as a real possibility.[34]

Several threats of large-scale mutiny were resolved by coercion or a show of force, with little or no further resistance. In a few instances, however, things got completely out of hand and a full-blown mutiny erupted. In this chapter, brief references will be made to some of the insurrections which died aborning, as well as some which became more widespread.

The first threat to established military control appeared in September 1775, not long after the battle at Bunker Hill. It was near headquarters at Cambridge, Massachusetts, specifically at Prospect Hill, that a group of Pennsylvania riflemen, known as "shirtmen," decided to break into a guardhouse and release one of their comrades. The threat demanded the attention of General Charles Lee, General Nathanael Greene, and Washington himself. The guardhouse was reinforced to 500 men, and an entire Pennsylvania regiment was used to encircle and subdue the troublemakers, after which they were marched back to camp and court-martialed. Thirty-three men were found guilty and fined twenty shillings each. The ringleader, John Leamon, was confined for six days in addition to the fine.

Early in 1777 at Ticonderoga, when a New York militia company announced that it was going home, General Anthony Wayne quelled the incipient mutiny by pointing a pistol at a rebellious sergeant and arresting a captain deemed to be a sympathizer. In November of that year, a captain in Enoch Poor's Brigade was killed by a soldier after the captain shot another soldier to death for refusing to march to join the Continental Army stationed in Pennsylvania. Order was restored after the killings.

Late in 1778, there were two small mutinies at Providence, Rhode Island, and two more the following spring. The first instance was caused by a lack of pay, the second by a lack of flour. A similar uprising by Virginia troops at Charlottesville, Virginia, was also blamed on a lack of supplies.

1 January 1780 brought a threat from sixty Massachusetts men stationed at West Point, New York, who marched to see the governor about their grievances, in particular the lack of adequate food. They were brought back with no violence.

In May 1780, two regiments of the Connecticut Line were in winter quarters at Morristown, New Jersey. They had not received pay for five months and were close to starvation. On 25 May, orders were given to execute eleven men who had been court-martialed earlier for desertion and sentenced to death by hanging or firing squad. Men from various units had been detailed to dig the graves in advance of the executions set for the next day.

Although none of those slated for death were from the Connecticut Line, two Connecticut regiments in camp assembled on the parade and, accompanied by their drummers, prepared to leave to find much needed supplies—things they felt their commissary personnel were withholding from them. Their commanding officer, Col. R. Jonathan Meigs, was struck by one of the soldiers during a confrontation, but there was no further violence. After the colonel finished an impassioned speech to the troops, they agreed to return to their huts. A few of the more aggressive ones were arrested by soldiers of an armed unit of the Pennsylvania Line which had remained loyal and patient despite suffering in the same manner as the Connecticut unit. That marked the end of the potential mutiny, and the execution proceedings took place the next day as scheduled—although seven of the eleven men were pardoned at the very last minute.

A group in Col. Moses Hazen's regiment and another group in General John Stark's First New York Regiment mutinied in 1781. In both cases there had been either failure to pay or clothe the men adequately to survive the winter blizzards. In Stark's regiment there was some minor violence but the affair was quickly put down by the officers.

Later, during the southern campaigns, General Nathanael Greene experienced an uprising after some Pennsylvania and Maryland troops joined his southern men who had been patiently awaiting pay from their home states, especially South Carolina. To eliminate the troublemakers, Greene ordered the execution of a Pennsylvania sergeant named George Gornell (or Goznall) for inciting a mutiny. He also confined or transferred to other posts several other Pennsylvania and Maryland soldiers. In 1783, he could not prevent 100 Virginia and Maryland cavalrymen camping at the Congaree River from leaving as a group, intent upon marching to Virginia. They had not been paid and did not have enough food for themselves or their horses. They picked up supporters enroute and serious trouble was narrowly averted before the situation was controlled. It is noteworthy that this episode took place just before the war ended. Restless soldiers, anxious to be sent home after the fighting had ended, often refused to wait any longer and left without permission. The situation did not improve until complete demobilization took place later in the year.

The more serious mutinies of the war are described below.

### Pennsylvania Line

This mutiny was the most serious and best documented rebellion of the war. It began 1 January 1781 and involved the Pennsylvania Line of the Continental Army stationed near Morristown, New Jersey. The line was commanded by General Anthony Wayne and numbered approximately 2,500 men, divided into ten regiments of infantry and one regiment of artillery. The men had enlisted early in the war "for three years or during the war," and therein lay part of the misunderstanding. It was not clear by the language of most of the recruitment papers that an enlistment was or was not completed after service of three years even though the war had continued past that time.

Although as many as 1,500 men participated in this mutiny and public demonstration (more than half of those in the line), the names of only three participants are documented. Two of the men were William Bowser (Bowzar), who held the title of secretary of a twelve-man "board of sergeants," and Daniel Connell, whose signature was placed on a communication of that board. The third name, John Williams, a former British deserter, appears as the president of the board of sergeants, but it is believed he was not the ringleader despite his title. For example, he clapped two British spies into confinement for infiltrating the group of mutineers with the intention of exploiting the soldiers' uprising into a mass desertion.

Disputes over the length of enlistment and lack of back pay were causes for joining the rebellion. At 10:00 p.m., the mutineers assembled under arms and carrying field equipment, prepared to march away from camp. They waited about an hour to listen to General Wayne who, promising to bring their demands to Congress, tried to dissuade them from leaving. During that tense period, there was some serious accidental and incidental violence. Two officers, Lt. Francis White and Capt. Samuel Tolbert, were shot but recovered. Capt. Adam Bettin was killed by a soldier who mistook him for Lt. Col. William Butler, whom the soldier was chasing. Another soldier was accidentally killed by a fellow soldier. Undoubtedly, several other undocumented casualties occurred judging from Wayne's letter quoted below. After the fruitless negotiations, the mutineers picked up supporters or ordered whole units to accompany them under threat of being fired upon. Capt. Joseph Campbell ordered part of his Fourth Regiment to recapture the artillery regiment, but his men refused to obey him. The Second Regiment, led by Col. Walter Stewart, was forced at bayonet point to go along on the march. Other soldiers hid and did not participate.

The next day, General Wayne wrote a hurried letter to the commander-in-chief stationed at New Windsor on the Hudson. Because of sudden developments the following days, he never sent the letter, but it survived for posterity.

> It's with inexpressible pain that I now inform your Excellency of the general mutiny and defection which suddenly took place in the Pennsylvania Line, between the hours of nine and ten o'clock last evening. Every possible exertion was made by the officers to suppress it in its rise, but the torrent was too potent to be stemmed. Captain Bettin has fallen a victim to his zeal and duty. Captain Tolbert and Lieutenant White are reported mortally wounded. A very considerable number of the field and other officers are much injured by strokes from muskets, bayonets, and stones. Nor have the revolters escaped with impunity. Many of their bodies lay under our horses' feet, and others will retain with existence the traces of our swords and espontoons.
>
> They finally moved from the ground at eleven o'clock at night, scouring the grand parade with round and grape shot from four field-pieces, the troops advancing in a solid column with fixed bayonets, producing a diffusive fire of musketry in front, flank, and rear.
>
> During this horrid scene a few officers with myself were carried by the tide to the fork of the roads at Mount Kemble. But placing ourselves on that leading to Elizabethtown and producing a conviction to the soldiery that they could not advance upon that route but over our dead bodies, they fortunately turned towards Princeton.
>
> I have been induced to issue the enclosed order from the ideas advanced last evening by many of the noncommissioned officers and privates, and hope it may have a happy effect.

Colonels Butler and Stewart, to whose spirited exertions I am much indebted, will accompany me to Vealtown where the troops now are. We had our escapes last night. Should we not be equally fortunate today our friends will have this consolation: that we did not commit the honor of the United States or our own on this unfortunate occasion.[35]

As the mutineers marched off, they sent emissaries to Philadelphia to present their demands to Congress. The general march was closely followed by General Wayne and Colonels Stewart and Butler. On the afternoon of 3 January, the group encamped at Princeton, New Jersey, took control of the town, and waited for a reply from Philadelphia. They refused to negotiate with Wayne and his colonels but treated them with respect, even sending a personal guard to watch over them, not only on the march but also when they quartered themselves in a nearby house for the night of 3 January. The next day, Wayne spoke with representatives of the group and sent word to the Pennsylvania Executive Council that it should send a representative to negotiate with the group.

Congress had by that time established a committee to deal with the matter and had also talked with the Pennsylvania officials. A joint delegation, representing both bodies, was formed to go to Princeton to meet with the soldiers. The delegation was headed by Joseph Reed of the Pennsylvania Executive Council, and he played a major role in the negotiations from that point forward. He and his delegation journeyed two days before arriving at Trenton. Meanwhile, the mutineers at Princeton continued to talk with Wayne and his colonels, while rejecting audiences requested by other highly placed officers sent by Congress. Troops led by officers of other military units coming for action were ordered by Wayne to stay out of town and let the negotiations proceed without possibility of violence. One of those hastily organized groups was a force of eighty armed officers from Morristown.

After many exchanges of notes and the helpful groundwork by Wayne, Reed's group finally entered Princeton, riding between formal lines of mutineers who stood and saluted them as they passed. Two British infiltrators, arrested and confined by the mutineers, were shuttled back and forth between Reed's delegation and the board of sergeants. Eventually, on 10 January both were hanged as spies.

The final agreement between Reed's delegation and the soldiers was a victory for the soldiers. A promise was made that any soldiers serving three years, who had not reenlisted, would be honorably discharged, giving them a choice to go home or to reenlist and take another bonus. Disputes would be handled by a separate commission, and, in the case of lost or missing enlistment papers, an oath by the soldier would be accepted. A promise was also given concerning back pay, adjustments for depreciation of the currency, and issuance of clothing.

Final papers were signed 10 January at Trenton. In subsequent weeks, about 1,300 (or approximately half of the Pennsylvania Line) were discharged. Enlistment papers found later revealed that many soldiers had clearly enlisted for the duration of the war no matter how much time elapsed; but their false statements were generously accepted, and most had already been allowed to go home. Although there was talk, none of them were ever charged or prosecuted for such wrongdoing. After the agreement was signed, all except musicians and recruitment sergeants were furloughed until 15 March, at which time they were to report for reorganization. Many of those who had been discharged under terms of the agreement decided to reenlist.[36]

In May of that year, those same Pennsylvanians, then camped at York, Pennsylvania, were ordered by Congress (which had acted without bothering to inform General Washington) to march to Virginia to join the southern army. Despite a promise by Pennsylvania that the soldiers were to receive pay in hard money, they actually received paper money recently cranked out on the state's printing presses. It, and the paper money bounties given new recruits, depreciated as fast as it was issued. The soldiers were angry and refused to march south. General Wayne, fearful of a repeat of the affair of the previous January, hurriedly spotted six of the ringleaders, took them into custody, and convened a court-martial on the spot. After a hasty finding of guilt and the imposition of a death sentence, Wayne picked firing squads from among the men's own units to carry out the execution posthaste. Upon order, at close range, the squads poured their shot into the backs of four of the six blindfolded men. Wayne then pardoned the other two mutineers but ordered the troops to file past the dead ones lying on the ground — still bleeding.

The next day, the troops marched off to Virginia as ordered, without a word — too stunned to refuse or make comment. As seen earlier though, some of those disgruntled Pennsylvanians did cause trouble among the southern soldiers after they eventually arrived in Virginia.

### New Jersey Line

Five hundred men of the New Jersey Line stationed for the winter at Pompton, New Jersey, closely followed the developments of the Pennsylvania Line mutiny because many of them had the same grievances. Indeed, many of them had already received benefits gained by the Pennsylvania group when they, too, organized into a mutinous group. Their unit had been divided into two groups, one at Pompton and the other at Chatham. On 10 January 1781, about 200 men left Pompton and headed toward Chatham where they hoped to pick up more recruits to their cause. However, word of their coming had arrived ahead of them, and the commanding officer at Chatham had dispersed most of his troops, making them unavailable for recruitment by the Pompton group. After two days, the mutineers returned to Pompton with their commanding officer who had followed along in much the same manner as Wayne had done with the Pennsylvania Line.

This time, however, Washington determined that he should intervene personally lest the situation become general throughout his army. He appointed General Robert Howe to take 500 to 600 picked men from General William Heath's Brigade and obtain an unconditional surrender from the Pompton rebels. His force included men originally from Connecticut, New Hampshire, and Massachusetts. They were joined enroute by more troops and three guns sent from the camp at the Highlands. Washington himself arrived at Pompton at midnight on 26 January and took charge. One hour later, Howe led an attack on the rebels and, by dawn, with three guns aimed at them, the mutineers surrendered.[37]

To make an example of the worst offenders, one man was selected from each regiment for trial and immediate sentencing. The three were Sergeants George Grant, David Gilmore, and John Tuttle. At the last minute, Grant received a reprieve for some reason which yet remains unclear. Historians have suggested that he was acting under the covert leadership of his commanding officer and therefore was spared the death sentence. Gilmore and Tuttle, however, were executed by a firing squad of twelve soldiers picked from among the other mutineers.[38]

### First New York Regiment

The First New York Regiment, stationed at Fort Stanwix (later Fort Schuyler) on the Mohawk River during June 1780, became disgruntled for "want of pay and the necessary clothing, particularly shirts." Thirty-one regiment soldiers marched off to turn themselves over to the British stationed at Oswegatchie on the St. Lawrence River. Lt. Abraham Hardenbergh, aided by a group of friendly Oneida Indians, gave chase, overtaking them as they crossed a river. Thirteen were shot by Indians but the others escaped and presumably went to the enemy.

### Pennsylvania Line—1783

Like their counterparts of the previous two years, eighty angry Pennsylvanians marched off on 17 June 1783 to Philadelphia to present demands to the Continental Congress. Upon arrival, they attracted enough men from troops in Philadelphia to swell their number to about 500. Congress fled to Princeton for their own safety, and citizens of the city were in panic. Most of the army had already been demobilized, but Washington sent almost all of his remaining 500 men to put down the uprising. Before his troops engaged the mutineers, officials of the Pennsylvania Executive Council met with them and peacefully brought the situation under control.

# Footnotes

1. For a character study of the Revolutionary War soldier, see the contrasting discussions in: James K. Martin and Mark E. Lender, *A Respectable Army: the Military Origins of the Republic, 1763-1789* (Arlington Heights, Illinois: Harland Davidson, 1982); Charles Royster, *A Revolutionary People at War* (Chapel Hill, North Carolina: University of North Carolina Press, 1979).

2. For representative discussion of such motives, see works cited in note 1 above.

3. *Valley Forge Orderly Book of General George Weedon* (New York: New York Times and the Arno Press, 1971), 97.

4. John F. Callan, *The Military Law of the United States* (Baltimore: John Murphy & Co., 1858), 57.

5. "Orderly Book, Valley Forge Camp, 1 January 1778," National Archives Microfilm Series M853; Roll 3, Vol. 20.

6. "Orderly Book, Providence, 20 February 1779−4 December 1779," National Archives Microfilm Series M853; Roll 5, Vol. 32.

7. Ibid.

8. "Orderly Book, General Hand's Regiment, Wyoming, 23 June 1774−23 August 1779," National Archives Microfilm Series M853; Roll 5, Vol. 36.

9. "Orderly Book, Dobbs Ferry, 3 August 1782−4 September 1782," National Archives Microfilm Series M853. Roll 10, Vol. 65.

10. *Valley Forge Orderly Book of General George Weedon*, 32-33.

11. *The Orderly Books of Colonel William Henshaw, 1 October 1775−3 October 1776* (Worcester, Massachusetts: American Antiquarian Society, 1948), 131.

12. Michael Calvert and Peter Young, *A Dictionary of Battles, 1715-1815* (New York: Mayflower Books, 1979), viii.

13. R. Ernest Dupuy and Trevor N. Dupuy, *The Compact History of the Revolutionary War* (New York: Hawthorne Books, Inc., 1963), 360.

14. *Valley Forge Orderly Book of General George Weedon*, 23.

15. John F. Fitzpatrick, ed., *The Writings of Washington*, Vol. III (Westport, Connecticut: Greenwood Press, Publishers, 1970), 512.

16. The Editors of Military Affairs, *Military Analysis of the Revolutionary War* (Millwood, New Jersey: KTO Press, 1977), 63.

17. Fitzpatrick, *The Writings of Washington*, vol. X, 450-54.

18. "Orderly Book, Newburgh, 2 August 1782 – 14 November 1782, National Archives Microfilm Series M853; Roll 10, Vol. 64.

19. Fitzpatrick, *The Writings of Washington*, vol. X, 238.

20. Allen Bowman, *The Morale of the American Revolutionary Army* (Washington, D.C.: American Council on Public Affairs, 1943), 85.

21. Fitzpatrick, *The Writings of Washington*, vol. VI, 106-15.

22. "Orderly Book, 16 February 1781 – 1 July 1781, National Archives Microfilm Series M853; Roll 8, Vol. 50.

23. Charles J. Stille, *Major General Anthony Wayne and the Pennsylvania Line in the Continental Army* (Philadelphia: J.B. Lippincott Co., 1893), 83.

24. Carlos E. Godfrey, *The Commander-in-Chief's Guard, Revolutionary War* (Washington, D.C.: Stevenson-Smith Co., 1904),

25. Ibid., 30.

26. Ray Thompson, *Benedict Arnold in Philadelphia* (Fort Washington, Pennsylvania: Bicentennial Press, 1975), 129-30.

27. Ibid., 89.

28. Ibid., 85-86.

29. Ibid.

30. Ibid., 118-22.

31. R. Ernest Dupuy and Trevor N. Dupuy, *An Outline History of the American Revolution* (New York: Harper & Row, 1975), 39-40.

32. The entire trial of General Lee is recorded in: *Lee – Proceedings of a General Court-Martial . . . for the Trial of Major General Lee* (New York: privately printed, 1864).

33. "Orderly Book, Adjutant General Scammel, Millbrook, 24 February 1778 – 2 June 1779," National Archives Microfilm Series M853; Roll 7, Vol. 28.

34. Henry S. Commager and Richard E. Morris, eds., *The Spirit of Seventy-six*, 2 vols, (New York: Bobbs-Merrill Co., Inc., 1958), 480-84.

35. Carl VanDoren, *Mutiny in January* (New York: The Viking Press, 1943), 13-14.

36. Royster, *A Revolutionary People at War*, 30.

37. Mark M. Boatner, *Encyclopedia of the American Revolution* (New York: David McKay Co., 1966), 759.

38. Ibid., 579.

# CHAPTER 6

# Court-martial Defendants

L isted in this chapter are the names, offenses, court findings, and military units (where shown) found in the 136 Revolutionary War orderly books used as source documents. The names were often spelled phonetically by the orderly sergeants or lieutenants keeping the books, and two names with similar spellings may actually refer to the same person. In this listing, only pertinent facts concerning the courts-martial are given. The researcher finding the name of an ancestor in this listing is encouraged to go directly to the source documents shown at that entry and read the entire set of charges to see if more data concerning the person may be found. Further, since records of courts-martial are often entered in two or more orderly books, it might be helpful to inspect not only the particular sources designated here, but also other orderly books which were kept at the same place and during the same time period. On occasion, one orderly book will contain data not contained in another. Generally, the sources shown here are either the first orderly book in which a court-martial was observed by the author, or the ones which were written and preserved in a more decipherable manner.

The reference to the source documents for each entry will be found in parentheses at the conclusion of that entry. These numbers designate either certain rolls of microfilm at the National Archives; orderly books (originals and copies) housed in the Manuscript Division, James Madison Building, Library of Congress; or published copies of orderly books found elsewhere.

The language used in these listings closely follows the original records, but in many cases it has been paraphrased for easy reading, and the spelling and punctuation is often corrected. Inspection of the orderly books themselves will provide the precise expressions of that day. The terms, "cashiered" and "dismissed from the service," are used here synonymously. Actually, the courts used many forms of expression for this particular sentence. Also, a reprimand, stated simply as that here, may well have been embellished in the actual court finding to show the type of reprimand, the manner it was to be given, and by whom. When the records show that a sentence was remitted or the prisoner was pardoned, that fact is noted, sometimes with the reason for such action. Many remitted sentences were not entered into the orderly books, and because of this, one's ancestor may well have survived a sentence of death despite the court's finding. The type of execution of a death sentence (by shooting or hanging) is shown here where specified in the original records.

The first sixty-six sources listed may be found in the eleven rolls of microfilm in Microfilm Series M853—*Numbered Record Books* at the National Archives, Washington, D.C. These are orderly books kept by Washington's units or by units closely associated with his command headquarters. Sources marked 67 to 130 are orderly books found in the Manuscript Division of the Library of Congress, Washington, D.C. Sources marked 131 to 136 are published orderly books inspected at the Library of Congress, but which may be found in other libraries as well. In several instances, more than one source number will be found after an entry in order to show at least one source from two or more locations. The key to the source numbers and their corresponding orderly books may be found on pages 281-85.

## Defendants, Offenses, Punishments

AAMS (AARNS), William. Colonel Wisson's Regiment. Absenting himself from camp without leave: thirty lashes. (75)

ABBE, Nicholas. Mutiny, riot, and disobedience to orders: fine of twenty shillings. (135)

ABBOT,_____, Ensign. Tenth Massachusetts Regiment. Casting reflections on a late regimental court-martial, contending that a prisoner recently brought before it would have been punished if the members had not acted in a partial manner: reprimand. (56)

ABRAM, James, Lt. Col. Massachusetts Regiment. Killing a cow and geese: seventy-five lashes. (61) *See* Brayton, Carliss, Cook, Cowell, Gardner, Jinks, Shea, Wood.

ACKERMAN, Benjamin. Colonel McDougall's Regiment. Desertion: released from confinement for lack of prosecution. (79)

ADAM,_____, Lieutenant. Propagating a report that an officer in Tenth Pennsylvania Regiment had behaved cowardly in action at Germantown, and refusing to name the officer: dismissed from the service. (16)

ADAMS,_____. Eighth Massachusetts Regiment. 100 lashes. (124)

ADAMS, Asa. Commander-in-Chief's Guard. Going out armed, with others, to do harm to other soldiers: acquitted. (125)

ADAMS, John. Deputy Commissioner of Prisoners. Released when no one appeared to prosecute him. (44)

ADAMS, Samuel. Mutiny: twenty lashes. (84)

ADAMS, Samuel. Attempting to desert to the enemy: acquitted. (9)

ADAMS, Stephen. First Company. Neglect of duty when on sentry, allowing a man to approach him without giving the right sign, letting a prisoner go for water without knowledge of the officers, other charges: eighty lashes. (43)

ADAMS, William, Lt. First Connecticut Regiment. Absenting himself from his regiment and not joining it: cashiered. (41)

ADAMS, William. Colonel Poor's Regiment. Desertion: thirty-nine lashes. (94) (117)

ADDAMS, James. Captain Patten's Company. Leaving his guard at Philadelphia: 100 lashes. (93)

ALBUY,_____, Sergeant. First Jersey Regiment. Using the state stores of liquor. (25) *See* Wilson.

ALCOT, Stephen. Sixth Massachusetts Regiment. Desertion: 100 lashes. (63)

ALCRAIN, Charles. Mutiny, riot, and disobedience to orders: thirty lashes and drummed out of the army. (135)

ALDAPPLE,_____, Sergeant. Stealing three geese: reduced to the ranks and thirty-nine lashes. (19) *See* Allen.

ALDEN, Austin, Lt. Colonel Brewer's Regiment. Taking Jacob Brown's allowance of whiskey and drinking it, then refusing to pay for it, messing frequently and drinking and sleeping with the soldiers, writing petitions for the soldiers and taking pay for the same: dismissed from the service. (14) (134)

ALDRIDGE, Stephen. Massachusetts Line. Desertion: 100 lashes. (63)

ALEXANDER, Charles, Lt. Leaving his post and absent from his guard when a flag from the army arrived and without reporting agreeable to his duty one of the guard who deserted to the enemy: reprimand. (95)

ALEXANDER, James. Colonel Nixon's Regiment. Desertion: acquitted. (88)

ALEXANDER, Joseph. German Battalion. Mutiny and desertion: death by shooting. (25) *See* Bottemer, Cook, Hoffenberger, Kurts.

ALLAWAY, Isaac. Colonel Maxwell's Regiment. Leaving the main guard without permission: thirty-nine lashes. (117)

ALLCUT, William, Lt. Colonel Chaptman's Regiment of Militia from Connecticut. Disobeying orders by not joining his regiment: cashiered. (119)

ALLEN,_____, Adjutant. Colonel Jackson's Regiment. Disobedience to orders and abusive language to Major Hull, refusing to leave his hut when ordered: dismissed from the service. (17)

ALLEN,_____, Quartermaster. Second Pennsylvania Brigade. Disobedience of orders, neglect of duty, endangering the health of the officers and men: acquitted. (72)

ALLEN, Benjamin. Colonel Malcomb's Regiment. Desertion: twenty lashes. (118)

ALLEN, Gilbert. Second New York Regiment. Not doing his duty as a sentinel, assisting and robbing a French officer's wagon: acquitted. (44)

ALLEN, Jeremiah, Drummer. Eighth Massachusetts Regiment. Stealing a number of shirts and blankets out of the store at Newburgh: 100 lashes, twenty-five administered on four successive days. (64)

ALLEN, Jeremiah, Drum Major. Eighth Massachusetts Regiment. Suffering and encouraging John Taylor, drummer in said regiment, to sell his shoe buckles and a buckle belonging to Sergeant Smith, and a silk handkerchief belonging to Josiah Jones, when under his direction and care at Danbury: acquitted. (124)

ALLEN, John. Colonel Livingston's Regiment. Purchasing a goose from Sergeant Aldapple, which he knew was stolen: cashiered with infamy. (19) *See* Aldapple.

ALLEN, John. Colonel Spencer's Regiment. Threatening the lives of two officers under pretense of authority: run the gauntlet twice. (25) *See* Donaldson.

ALLEN, John Baptist, Capt. Drunk on picquett guard: acquitted with honor. (85)

ALLEN, Nathan. Seventh Company. Absent from roll call: twenty-five lashes. (47)

ALLEN, Nathanel. Stealing apples from an orchard belonging to Robinson's farm: twenty lashes—pardoned because of his former good conduct. (56) *See* Jocelin, Penham.

ALLEN, Robert. Colonel Alden's Regiment. Selling clothing belonging to the Continental Army: released without conviction because he ignorantly sold a small quantity of clothing and because of his irreproachable behavior.

ALLEN, Robert. Ninth Regiment. Desertion: 100 lashes. (129)

ALLEN, Samuel. First New Hampshire Regiment. Desertion and forging a discharge in the name of General Poor: 100 lashes only, in consideration of some circumstances in his favor. (111) *See* Critchet, Fosgood.

ALLEN, Samuel. Colonel Elliot's Regiment of Artillery. Desertion: 100 lashes. (19)

ALLEN, William. Artillery. Theft: thirty-nine lashes. (102)

ALLMAN, Arthur. Fifth Regiment. Attempting to desert from Fort Johnston: acquitted. (95)

ALPHIN, Ransum. Desertion: fifty lashes. (102)

AMBLER, George, Baker. Exchanging good flour for bad, not returning the quantity of bread in weight: twenty-five lashes. The sentence confirmed by General Gist who was "so induced by the prisoner's late drunkenness and bad character." (23)

AMERICAN, Edward. Fourth Maryland Regiment. Desertion: make up the time lost of the three year term, to commence 11 August 1779, pay for the expenses of his apprehension. (110)

AMERMAN,_____, Corporal. Second New York Regiment. Willful disobedience to orders: reduced to a private sentinel. (64)

AMES,_____. Second Company. Absent from roll call: thirty lashes. (63)

AMOS, Abel. Maryland Line. Desertion: acquitted. (44)

AMOS (AMANAH), Obediah. Colonel Harrison's Regiment of Artillery. Conspiracy to spike the cannon at Fort Schuyler and intending to desert to the enemy: 100 lashes. (37) *See* Johnson, Stanberry, Watkins, Wright.

ANDERSON,_____, Lieutenant. Eleventh Pennsylvania Regiment. Acting in a manner unbecoming the character of an officer and gentleman: dismissed from the service. (15)

ANDERSON,_____, Corporal. Conspiring to desert: reduced to the ranks. (89)

ANDERSON, John. First South Carolina Regiment. Deserting his command and attempting to go to the enemy: death by shooting. (95)

ANDERSON, John. Maryland Line. Sodomy: not guilty of sodomy, but guilty of attempted sodomy—run the gauntlet three times. (49)

ANDERSON, Jonathan. Virginia Line. Desertion and bearing arms against the United States: acquitted, since he was sick when taken prisoner, and twice tried to escape from the enemy. (115)

ANDERSON, Robert, Wagonmaster. Selling a rifle: redeem the rifle and return it to his regiment. (17)

ANDRES, Bargill. Ninth Massachusetts Regiment. Desertion: 100 lashes. (41)

ANDRES, Barzillia (Bargill). Drunk on the parade: fifty lashes. (42)

ANDREWS,_____, Sergeant. Sleeping out of camp: reduced to the rank of private—pardoned. (23)

ANDREWS, John. Colonel Ritzema's Regiment. Plundering a house lately occupied by Daniel Donovel: acquitted. (7)

ANGEL, Dan, Capt. General Hand's Brigade. Unjustifiably and cruelly abusing Sergeant Ashley of the German Battalion. (25)

ANNIS, Jacob. Ninth Massachusetts Regiment. Stealing from an inhabitant's barn: fifty lashes and fine of ten dollars to pay his share of the rum. (47) *See* Cruett, Ford, Pense, Tucker.

ANTINEO, William, Sailor on board the sloop *Enterprise*. Mutinous behavior: acquitted. (99)

APPLEGATE, William. Desertion: released when no evidence was presented. (95)

ARMER (ARMOURS),_____, Lieutenant. First Pennsylvania Regiment. Behaving in many respects in an ungentlemanly manner: dismissed from the service. (15)

ARMOURS (ARMER),_____, Lieutenant. First Pennsylvania Regiment. Behavior unbecoming a gentleman: pardoned. (134)

ARMSBEE, William. Colonel Angell's Regiment. Desertion: 100 lashes—remitted because of his youth and former good conduct. (32)

ARMSTRONG,_____, Lieutenant. Third Pennsylvania Regiment. Disobedience to orders in not sending a prisoner to a court-martial: acquitted with honor. (21)

ARMSTRONG, James, Lt. Third Pennsylvania Regiment. Behaving in a scandalous manner, beating a number of persons, breaking windows and other abusive treatments: guilty of beating Quartermaster Bradford, but the provocation was in some degree equal to the offense, guilty of breaking cellar windows, but on the whole, his behavior was not scandalous—reprimand. (69) (103) *See* Christy, Moore.

ARMSTRONG, John, Lt. Third Pennsylvania Regiment. Attempting to impose a falsehood on Colonel Craig respecting his attendance on the regimental parade: dismissed from the service—pardoned. (26)

ARMSTRONG, John, Lt. Third Pennsylvania Regiment. Evading his duty and accusing others: acquitted with the highest honor. (64)

ARMSTRONG, John. Captain Bolland's Company of Artificers. Stealing a key, striking and giving abusive language to Lieutenant Parker: 100 lashes. (69) (103)

ARNOLD,_____, Corporal. Abusive and insulting language to Sergeant Booth: acquitted. (91)

ARNOLD, Benedict, Gen. *See* chapter four.

ARNOLD, Benjamin, Ens. Colonel Angell's Regiment. Getting drunk and acting in a disorderly and unsoldierly manner, refusing to do his duty, threatening to leave the service whether he could get a discharge or not: dismissed with infamy. (134)

ARNOLD, Jonathan. Captain Williams' Company. Neglect of duty when on sentinel and being privy to breaking open the commissary stores: 100 lashes and fine of thiry shillings. (91)

ARNOLD, Oliver. Second New York Regiment. Desertion: death by shooting. (25)

ARNOLD, Thomas, Capt. Corps of Invalids. Not joining his regiment until 21 July although he had instructions sent to him as early as 26 March: acquitted. (56)

ARNOLD, William. General Smallwood's Regiment. Plundering a house: thirty-nine lashes. (6) *See* Clark.

ARNOLD, William. Colonel Smallwood's Regiment. Plundering a house lately occupied by Lord Stirling: acquitted. (136) *See* Clark, Donavel.

ARTHUR,_____, Lieutenant. Third Maryland Regiment. Making frequent and distant excursions on parties of pleasure, returning himself unfit for duty, disobedience to orders: acquitted of all charges except disobedience—reprimand. (44)

ASHMOND, Captain. Second Pennsylvania Regiment. Drunk during an attack on Stoney Point the morning of 16 July, behaving ridiculously and unbecoming an officer at the head of his company, disobeying general orders by frequently huzzaing during the approach to the enemy's works to the prejudice of good order and military discipline, and promoting confusion among the troops at that critical juncture: not guilty of the first charge but guilty of the second – reprimand. (110)

ASHTON, Phineas. Massachusetts Line. Desertion and enlistment in a fictitious manner: 100 lashes. (63)

ASKENS (ATKINS), Joseph. Fifth Pennsylvania Regiment. Deserting twice, escaping from his guard and endeavoring to depart to the enemy: 100 lashes. (72) (113)

ASKIN, Alex. Acting in a mutinous manner, endeavoring to excite a mutiny: fifty lashes. (9)

ASPIC, Jonathan, Sgt. Light Dragoons. Dealing with the Indians by giving an Indian the buttons off his coat for two fawn skins: reduced to a private sentinel and twenty lashes – lashes remitted. (96)

ATKINSON, Stephen. First New Hampshire Regiment. Desertion and attempting to go to the enemy: 100 lashes. (44)

AUSTIN,_____, Major. Burning a house at White Plains contrary to general orders, wanton and cruel treatment of helpless women and children, not only unworthy the character of an officer but a human creature: dismissed from service. (92) (94)

AUSTIN, James. Being a spy: acquitted. (9)

BABB, James. Colonel Bigelow's Regiment. Desertion and enlisting twice and taking two bounties: 100 lashes and a fine of 20 2/3 dollars. (88)

BABCOCK, Elias. Stealing timber out of a batteau: fine of twenty-four shillings. (118)

BACCART, Peter. First North Carolina Regiment. Entering the tent of Lieutenant Richard Dickerson whilst he was in bed, disarming and striking him, acting in a disorderly manner, playing cards in camp: reprimand. (26) *See* Craven, Dickerson, Summers.

BACKEY, James. Colonel Whitcomb's Regiment. Quitting his regiment without a discharge and enlisting in another regiment: acquitted. (117)

BACON, William. 100 lashes. (122)

BADLAM,_____, Lieutenant Colonel. Eighth Massachusetts Regiment. Neglect of duty by mustering several persons who were unfit for military service: acquitted. (51) The persons wrongfully mustered were: Costellion (lately a deserter from the enemy); Sitz, Frederic (lately a deserter from the enemy); Heitt, John (deserter from the French service); Godfrey, Peter (deserter from the French service);

Avery, Richard (boy-undersized). Taylor, Benjamin (boy-undersized); Munroe, Hugh (boy-undersized); Round, Amos, (boy-undersized); West, George (idiot); Wyman, Jason (Negro, lamed in the ankle); McCart, Andres (foreigner who deserted on the road); Pelham, Samuel (reason not given); Robins, Jonathan (reason not given); and Osborne, William (reason not given).

BAGLEY, David. Desertion: 100 lashes. (39)

BAGNELL, William. Desertion: serve the time "prescribed by act of Assembly." (102)

BAILEY,_____, Major. Nonattendance on the grand parade: reprimand. (134)

BAILEY, Edward. Third Company (Eighth Company). Being a confederate with James Mosely in stealing a shirt, a pair of linen overalls, a black handkerchief belonging to another soldier, and four linen hankerchiefs: acquitted. (66) *See* Mosely.

BAILEY, Edward. Third Company (Eighth Company). Refusing to do his duty when ordered, repeatedly neglecting and absenting himself from duty without leave: fifty lashes. (65)

BAILEY, Jacob, Brig. Gen. & Dep. Quartermaster Gen. Suffering a quantity of beef to take damage through his inattention and neglect: released due to lack of evidence. (36)

BAILEY, James. Colonel Baron's Regiment. Attempting to desert to the enemy: 100 lashes–remitted and permitted to remain in the forage department. (14)

BAILEY, John, Capt. Enlisting a number of men that were previously enlisted: cashiered and return all the money he had received, which was due the men enlisted. (9)

BAILEY, John. Seventh Maryland Regiment. Desertion: 100 lashes. (69)

BAILEY, Thomas. inhabitant of Pennsylvania. Supplying the enemy with provisions: pay fifty pounds for the use of the sick at camp. (15)

BAKER, Edmund. Ninth Regiment. Stealing sheep: acquitted. (46) *See* Clemons, Perry.

BAKER, George. Colonel Harrison's Regiment of Artillery. Desertion and attempting to go to the enemy: death. (21)

BAKER, Hugh, Foragemaster. Keeping a horse without permission and not returning it until a complaint was made against him; abusing Joseph Smedley, a citizen of Chester, and confining him under guard without order or authority: dismissed from the service and pay for the horse. (16) *See* chapter two.

BAKER, Jacob. Second Pennsylvania Regiment. Attempting to go to the enemy: 100 lashes. (21)

BAKER, Reuben. Mutiny: thirty-nine lashes. (84)

BAKER, Rufus. Mutiny: thirty-nine lashes. (84)

BAKER, William. Colonel McDougall's Regiment. Absenting himself several days from camp without permission: twenty lashes — pardoned with a reprimand "on some favorable circumstances appearing." (132) (136)

BAKER, William. Colonel Parson's Regiment. Desertion: thirty-nine lashes, with thirteen lashes administered on three successive days. (72)

BALCOM, Daniel. Colonel Jackson's Regiment. Desertion: 100 lashes. (54)

BALDWIN, Thomas, Sgt. Captain Spalding's Independent Company. Stealing a horse in the woods: reduced to private and pay for the horse. (20) *See* Swift.

BALLARD,_____, Captain. Colonel Frye's Regiment. Profane swearing and beating and abusing his men: fine of four shillings for each offense. (135)

BALLARD,_____, Sergeant. General Lee's Guard. Giving a pass to a person to cross the river: acquitted since it appeared it was done more through ignorance. (106)

BALLARD, Alrich. Captain Dunsten's Company. Suffering liquor under his charge to be drawn: acquitted. (43) *See* Gladding.

BALLOCK, Benjamin. Assistant Commissary of Issues to General Paterson's Brigade. Selling flour, rum, pork, hides, tallow and other stores: dismissed from the service and pay for all the stolen goods as listed in the record of the trial, and detained until payment is made. (110)

BALLS, Jonathan. Repeated disobedience to orders, abusing the adjutant: guilty of the first charge but not guilty of the second charge — fined one month's pay. (128) *See* Goddard.

BANKS,_____, Captain. Tenth Massachusetts Regiment. Unofficerlike behavior at the siege of Yorktown in Virginia; neglect of duty, especially on the evening of 14 October last: dismissed from the service. (124)

BANKS, Richard, Boatswain, sailor on board the sloop *Enterprise*. Mutinous behavior: acquitted. (99)

BANTLY, John. Eighth Massachusetts Regiment. Desertion: 100 lashes. (53)

BAPTIST, Francis, Sgt. Colonel Greene's Regiment. Raising a mutiny and behaving in a disorderly manner: not guilty of the first charge but guilty of the second charge – suspended and reprimand. (131) *See* Luis, Peterson, Tabor.

BARBER, Robert, Matross. Third Regiment of Artillery. Desertion and attempting to go to the enemy: death – pardoned. (42)

BARCK, Michael. Fourth Regiment of Light Dragoons. Robbing the house of widow Mary Landsford of sundry valuable articles: 100 lashes. (111) *See* Hensley.

BARCLAY, John. Colonel Wyllys's Regiment. Insulting language and speaking diminishingly of Congress, etc.: 100 lashes. (85)

BARCLIFT, Samuel. Absent nineteen hours when on duty: ten stripes. (104)

BARKER, George. Colonel Harrison's Regiment of Artillery. Desertion: 100 lashes. (37)

BARNABA, Issac. Colonel Alden's Regiment. 100 lashes. (88)

BARNARD,_____, Captain. Third Connecticut Regiment. Making a false muster for a soldier in his company, the soldier being his son, Grove Barnard: acquitted. (36)

BARNES,_____, Corporal. Eighth Massachusetts Regiment. Mutinous conduct: reduced to a private and 100 lashes. (64) *See* Birch, Meadows.

BARNES, James. Colonel Vose's Regiment. Absent without leave: acquitted. (188)

BARNES, James. Third New York Regiment. Desertion and carrying off his arms: 100 lashes and pay for the arms, and then join the First Massachusetts Regiment. (111)

BARNES, Thomas, Major. Twelfth Massachusetts Regiment. Overstaying his furlough and not returning to his regiment: cashiered. (36)

BARNEY, Frederick. Seventh Regiment. Desertion: 100 lashes. (50)

BARNEY, Nathan. Colonel Jackson's Regiment. Desertion: confined in the dungeon for one month on bread and water. (26) *See* Mathews, Pierce.

BARNS, Nemiah. Colonel Sherburne's Regiment. Sleeping on his post: 100 lashes – pardoned. (119)

BARON,_____, Lieutenant. Colonel Wigglesworth's Regiment. Drinking, ungentlemanlike behavior, striking Lieutenant Paige: cashiered. (16) (17)

BARRET, Jonathan. Abuse and insolence to Sergeant Conant by calling him a damned rascal and villain: fifty lashes – pardoned because this was his first offense. (23) *See* Conant.

BARRETT,_____, Corporal. Fifth Company. Losing his arms and accouterments, insolence to Major Prescott: reduced to private and 100 lashes. (23)

BARRETT, Jonathan. Desertion and bearing arms against the United States: death. (115)

BARRETT, William. Third Pennsylvania Regiment. Desertion with his arms and accouterments: death. (26)

BARRIER, Henry. Attempting to desert to the enemy: death. (93)

BARRY,_____, Ensign. Fourth New York Regiment. Disobedience of orders on the guard parade: reprimand. (100)

BARRY, James. Colonel Weissenfells' Company, Colonel McDougall's Regiment. Cocking and presenting his firelock at Lieutenant Houston: thirty-nine lashes. (99)

BARRY, John. Colonel Ward's Regiment. Desertion: thirty-nine lashes. (123)

BARRY, Michael. Stealing a hat from Captain Waterman: twenty lashes – pardoned in consideration of his long confinement. (2)

BARRY, Robert, sailor on board the sloop *Enterprise*. Mutinous behavior: acquitted. (99)

BARTHOLOMEW, Benjamin. Mutiny, riot, and disobedience to orders: fine of twenty shillings. (135)

BARTHSICK, Lazarus. Tenth Massachusetts Regiment. Desertion: 100 lashes. (53)

BARTITS, John. Colonel Shepard's Regiment. Theft: 100 lashes. (24)

BARTLES, Asa. Absent without leave: fine of eight shillings and reprimanded. (91)

BARTLETT, Lawrence. Mutiny, riot, and disobedience to orders: fine of twenty shillings. (71)

BARTLETT, Samuel. Colonel Gridley's Regiment. Abusive behavior. (1)

BARTLEY, James. Stealing and selling a shirt: 100 lashes. (93)

BARTLY, John. Captain Moretor's Company, Train of Artillery. Drunkenness, absenting himself from guard without leave, threatening to desert and take a man's life away, abusive language: thirty-nine lashes. (68)

BARTON, Backus. Ninth Massachusetts Regiment. Stealing and killing a cow belonging to an inhabitant: 100 lashes and fine of forty shillings to pay for the cow. (48) *See* Freeman, Sweat.

BARTON, John. Colonel Bradford's Regiment. Disobedience to orders: twenty lashes. (75)

BARTON, William. Colonel Alden's Regiment. Desertion: acquitted. (9)

BASSUT,_____, Sergeant. Permitting a person to escape from the guard: acquitted. (31)

BATCHELLER, John. Desertion: 100 lashes and join the Rhode Island Regiment. (56)

BATCHELOR, John. Colonel Gridley's Regiment. Desertion, theft. (1)

BATEMAN,_____, Quartermaster. Colonel Livingston's Regiment. Threatening to burn the hospital, abusing the priest and superior of the nunnery, threatening the doctors and attendants on the sick, behaving in a riotous, disorderly, and ungentlemanlike manner: reprimand. (128) *See* Louisien.

BATES, C. Desertion: 100 lashes. (42)

BATES, Thomas. Fifteenth Virginia Regiment. Desertion: twenty lashes. (101)

BATES, William. Selling liquor contrary to orders: license forfeited. (41)

BATHERLY, Benjamin. Colonel Wind's Regiment. Desertion and enlisting in another regiment: thirty-nine lashes for each offense. (117)

BATTEN,_____, Lieutenant. Ninth Pennsylvania Regiment. Nelgect of duty in not providing a wagoner for a military unit: acquitted. (125)

BATTLES, James. Colonel Shepard's Regiment. Desertion: death by shooting. (19)

BATTLES, John. Colonel Shepard's Regiment. Desertion: death by shooting. (19)

BAUMAN, Jeremiah. Seventh Pennsylvania Regiment. Insolent language and threatening a captain: 100 lashes. (97)

BAXTER, William. Firing a gun contrary to the general orders: fatigue duty of two days and do his back duty for the time he has been confined, and to lay every other night in the guard house till the punishment is fulfilled. (104) *See* Missick.

BAY, Canaday. Delaware Regiment. Housebreaking, stealing, and beating the inhabitants: fifty lashes. (93) *See* Brown, Murphy.

BAY, John. Sixth Regiment. Neglect of duty: reprimand. (95)

BAYLEY, Leonard. Captain Sackett's Company. Stealing shirts when on guard: released when no evidence was presented. (128)

BAYLYER, William, Sgt. Virginia Line. Desertion and bearing arms against the United States: death by hanging. (115)

BEALL, Thomas, Capt. Maryland Independent Corps. Discharging a soldier after having been duly enlisted and receiving his regimental clothing, defrauding the United States: dismissed from the service. (36) *See* chapter two.

BEATTY, John, Col. & Commissary General of Prisoners. Improper intercourse with the city of New York by writing to officials of that city contrary to general orders: reprimand (resigned the next day). (26) *See* chapter two.

BEATY, John. Embezzling public stores: fine of forty dollars and run the gauntlet twice. (103)

BEBER, Edward, Batteauman. Acquitted. (111)

BECK, James, Sgt. Desertion: 100 lashes. (42)

BECKER, Phillip, inhabitant of Pennsylvania. Attempting to carry provisions to the enemy at Philadelphia: acquitted. (14)

BECKETT, Timothy. Fifth Connecticut Regiment. Desertion and attempting to go to the enemy: 100 lashes only, with twenty-five lashes administered on four successive mornings due to his youth. (57)

BECKMAN, L. Acquitted. (31)

BECKWITH,_____, Ensign. Second Connecticut Regiment. Recruiting irregularly, defrauding by enlisting a soldier who was permitted to remain at home: dismissed from the service. (58)

BECKWITH, Noah. Colonel Gallup's Regiment. Neglecting to join his company when detached for one month's duty: returned to service for one month from the date of his confinement, pay all charges, and if still obstinate to be given ten lashes also. (82)

BEERS, Joel. Captain Whiting's Company. Taking boards from the barracks and cutting them up for his own use: fine of twenty shillings to pay for the boards. (91)

BELDING, Abraham. Captain Whitney's Company. Neglect of duty when on sentinel: forty-seven lashes. (91)

BELE, Mathew. Rioting in camp at an unreasonable hour, abusing Captain Elsworth in the execution of his office: guilty of the first charge but acquitted of the second charge—fifty lashes. (111) *See* Benjamin, Ivory, White.

BELL, Mathew. Second Virginia Regiment. Attempting to desert to the enemy with the arms and accouterments of another soldier: death by shooting. (112) *See* Hanley, Lighthall.

BELL, Samuel. Tenth Pennsylvania Regiment. Plundering Mr. Bogart, an inhabitant near Paramus: death by hanging—pardoned. (26) *See* Brown, Justice, Powers.

BELLING, John. Colonel Hamilton's Company of New York Artillery. Desertion and breaking from confinement: confined six days upon bread and water. (136)

BEMMICK, John. Fourth Company. Absent from camp twenty-four hours without leave: twenty-five lashes. (53)

BEMUS, John. Colonel Vose's Regiment. Desertion and enlisting in the Maryland Line: 100 lashes, with twenty-five lashes administered on four successive mornings. (44) *See* Hawthorne.

BENJAMIN, Samuel. Rioting in camp at unreasonable hours, abusing Captain Elsworth in the execution of his office: acquitted. (111) *See* Bele, Ivory, White.

BENNET, Amos. First Connecticut Regiment. Repeated desertion, joining the enemy: guilty of the first charge but not guilty of the second charge—death. (51)

BENNETT, Thomas. Being drunk, losing a hat, absenting himself from roll call: thirty lashes. (56)

BENSON, John. Colonel Webb's Regiment. Desertion and stealing some goods: 100 lashes and sent on board the guard ships (frigate) and kept there at hard labor during the war. (131)

BENSTEAD,_____, Captain and Paymaster. Tenth Pennsylvania Regiment. Refusing to pay Captain Cox when he paid the other soldiers of the regiment: found guilty, but when it was learned that Captain Cox did not merit the pay, he was acquitted. (9)

BENWICK (FENWICK), Baptist. Colonel Jackson's Regiment. Desertion: 100 lashes and weights chained to his legs for one month, to attend all parades in that situation. (23)

BERRIAN, George, Boatman. Breaking open a box of clothing while in his care; taking a pair of leather breeches, five pairs of boots, and one pair of shoes belonging to the officers of Colonel Nixon's regiment: acquitted. (36)

BERRY, Benjamin. Colonel Hall's Regiment. Attempting to desert to the enemy: 100 lashes. (134)

BERRY, John. Colonel Ward's Regiment. Desertion: thirty-nine lashes. (118)

BERRY, Jonathan. Colonel Ward's Regiment. Desertion: thiry-nine lashes – escaped from his guard before the sentence was executed. (74)

BERRY, Timothy. Absenting himself from camp without leave: acquitted. (28)

BESOM (BOZAR), John. Mutiny, riot, and disobedience to orders: fine of twenty shillings. (135)

BETTS, Thomas, Capt. Greatly abusing Captain Gooding, neglect of duty in exposing his property and the property of the United States to the inclemency of the weather, expressing himself unbecoming an officer in the Continental service: dismissed from the service. (131)

BETTUMFORD, Benjamin. Sixth Company. Absent without leave: twenty-five lashes. (56)

BEVENS, Joseph. Third Massachusetts Regiment. Losing his arms and accouterments, endeavoring to go to the enemy: 100 lashes and fine for the lost arms and accouterments. (46)

BEVER, John. Colonel Lamb's Regiment of Artillery. Attempting to pass a counterfeit ten dollar bill: released when no evidence was presented. (83) (84)

BEYWOOD, James. Lieutenant Erwine's Company. Absent without leave: 100 lashes. (115)

BIER, Charles. Pennsylvania Line. Desertion: 100 lashes – remitted because of his former good behavior. (64)

BIGELOW, Aaron. Two day's fatigue with a log of wood of five pounds weight swinging around his neck, and ask the pardon of his officers at the head of his company. (104)

BIGNAL, George. Tenth Virginia Regiment. Desertion: acquitted. (134)

BILBO,_____, Lieutenant. Colonel Marbury's Regiment of Light Dragoons. Quitting his post without orders: dismissed from the service. (90)

BILL, Phinneas. Connecticut Line. Desertion and re-enlisting in the Massachusetts Line under the name of John Hand: 100 lashes and fine for the amount received from his illegal bounty. (46)

BILLINGS,_____, Corporal. Captain Dusten's Company. Repeated neglect of duty and disobedience to orders: reduced to rank of private sentinel. (43)

BINGHAM,_____, Lieutenant. Fifth Pennsylvania Regiment. Spending or misapplying money given to him to pay bounty to recruits: cashiered. (42)

BINGHAM, Abner. Attempting to desert to the enemy and enticing others to do the same. (42)

BIRCH, Warren. Eighth Massachusetts Regiment. Mutinous conduct: 100 lashes. (64) *See* Barnes, Meadows.

BISHOP, Silvanus. Colonel Topham's Regiment. Stealing cartridges out of the soldiers' boxes on guard and burning them under the pots of the men cooking: acquitted. (68) (98)

BLACK, Fortune. Colonel Jackson's Regiment. Desertion: thirty-nine lashes. (23)

BLACK, William. Delaware Regiment. Plundering the house of an inhabitant near Prospect Hill: fifty lashes and fine of one-half month's pay. (93)

BLACKMA, David. Captain Whiting's Company. Taking boards from the barracks and cutting them up for his own use: fine of twenty shillings to pay for the boards. (91)

BLAISDELL, John. Captain Frye's Company, New Hampshire Regiment. Breaking into a clothing store at Newburgh at night and stealing a number of shoes and boots: reduced to a private sentinel and 100 lashes, with twenty-five administered on each of four successive mornings. (62) *See* Lee.

BLACK, Christopher. Seventh Connecticut Regiment. Desertion and reenlistment in the New Hampshire Line: 100 lashes. (46)

BLAKE, Edward, Lt. Third Regiment of Artillery. Exceeding the limits of his furlough by two days: acquitted. (50)

BLAKE, John. First Massachusetts Regiment. Breaking open the home of a citizen and insulting and abusing the inhabitants, attempting to kill Captain Frye and Captain Ellis in execution of their offices, robbing them of a hat: acquitted. (64) *See* Curtis, Smith.

BLAKE, John. Giving Thomas Giles his shirt to sell: thirty lashes. (93) *See* Giles.

BLAKE, John. First Massachusetts Regiment. Killing a cow and stealing eleven geese: seventy-five lashes and pay fifteen dollars to the owner. (86)

BLAKE, John. Massachusetts Line. Desertion: acquitted. (124)

BLAKE, Jonathan. Tearing and concealing a letter written by Colonel Kosciusko to Colonel Hay; absenting himself frequently without leave; employing in a clandestine manner several of his men upon his farm while he drew provisions for them from the public stores, and returning them present and fit for duty: cashiered. (110)

BLAKE, Lawrence. Mutiny, riot, and disobedience to orders: fine of twenty shillings. (135)

BLAKE, Ned. Maryland Line. Desertion: acquitted. (44)

BLANCHARD, Benjamin. Second Rhode Island Regiment. Desertion: 100 lashes. (100)

BLANKENDORF, Lewis. Colonel Carne's Regiment. Desertion: 100 lashes. (24)

BLANFIELD, Thomas. Colonel Parsons' Regiment. Desertion: thirty-nine lashes. (106)

BLEEKER, Leonard, Capt. First New York Regiment. Striking an ensign: reprimand. (51)

BLIN, Hezekia (Abraham). General Spencer's Regiment. Desertion: ten lashes and a fine of fifteen shillings to pay for the apprehension. (105)

BLOCHAM, Levi. Ninth Virginia Regiment. Insolence and threatening to shoot Ensign Robbins of the same regiment: thirty-nine lashes. (101)

BLOOD, Ephraim. Desertion: fifty lashes. (41)

BLOODGOOD,_____, Ensign. First New York Regiment. Taking money from a drawer of a bar room of the widow Jacobus in a clandestine manner: reprimand. (58)

BLOOM, John, inhabitant of Pennsylvania. Attempting to carry flour into Philadelphia: fifty lashes and be employed in some public work for the use of the Continentals, unless he should choose to enlist in the Continental service during the war. (9)

BLOOMER. Absenting himself from the main guard: fifty lashes. (23) *See* Brown, Conoly, Fosdick.

BLOOMFIELD, Ensign. Third New Jersey Battalion. Suffering himself to be surprised by the enemy near their lines: acquitted –"far from being unofficerlike, merits applause and is worthy of immitation." (9) (12)

BLOOMFIELD, Thomas. Colonel Parson's Regiment. Desertion: thirty-nine lashes. (136)

BODEN, James. Attempting to desert to the enemy: acquitted. (112)

BOGAARDT, John. Colonel Clinton's Regiment. Desertion: fine of one month's pay–pardoned. (118)

BOGEN, Timothy. Third Massachusetts Regiment. Sleeping on his post when on sentry: acquitted. (54)

BOGLE, Christian. Captain Shoot's Corps. Desertion and taking with him a sorrell mare and a greatcoat, the property of Colonel Selim: 100 lashes and pay for the mare and the coat. (89)

BOLLING, James. Desertion: 100 lashes. (40)

BOLTON, William. Colonel Gallup's Regiment. Neglect of orders when detached for one month's duty: return to duty for one month from date of confinement. (82)

BOND, Samuel, Assistant Wagonmaster. Picking a lock and breaking into a public store, taking rum and candles: fifty lashes and returned to his regiment–the lashes were remitted. (72) (113)

BOND, Stephen. Colonel Clinton's Regiment. Desertion: fine of one month's pay–pardoned. (118)

BONHAM,_____, Lieutenant. Second New Jersey Regiment. Allowing two prisoners to escape, one being a prisoner of war: acquitted. (30)

BONYAR,_____, Adjutant. Twelfth Virginia Regiment. Furnishing two soldiers with the countersign to go into the country to buy provisions: dismissed from the service. (17)

BOROUGH, Wiley. First North Carolina Regiment. Assaulting the house of Mr. Uriah McKeel by firing several shots through it, wounding Thomas Brown and robbing him, plundering the house of several articles of wearing apparel: 200 lashes. (26) *See* Burger, Mullen, Rickets.

BOSS,_____, Lieutenant. Fourth Pennsylvania Regiment. Imposing a falsehood concerning Major Church, being frequently intoxicated, beating and abusing a soldier and related charges: acquitted with honor. (33)

BOSS, Samuel. Third Regiment of Artillery. Abusing a captain for the purpose of obtaining a horse for his own use, forging the name of his captain for a horse: dismissed from the service. (48)

BOSTWICK, Daniel. Disobedience to orders in gaming: thirty-one lashes. (91)

BOTTEMER, Jacob. German Battalion. Mutiny and desertion: death by shooting. (25) *See* Alexander, Cook, Hoffenberger, Kurts.

BOURE, Barbara. Persuading the soldiers to desert: acquitted. (93)

BOURK, Jonathan. Striking a corporal and other disorderly conduct: reprimand. (23) *See* Witton.

BOURKE, Michael. Fourth Regiment of Light Dragoons. Robbing the house of the widow Sarah Sanford: 100 lashes. (33) (129) *See* Hansley.

BOURSE, Peter. Colonel McDougall's Regiment. Desertion: thirty-nine lashes. (136)

BOUSE, Jacob. Captain Cole's Company of Batteaumen. Desertion: fine of four dollars. (83) (84)

BOWAN, James. Communicating with the city of Philadelphia: acquitted. (14)

BOWEN, Charles. Colonel Graham's Regiment. Robbery: thirty-nine lashes and twenty lashes for drunkenness, which he used as an excuse for the robbery. (123)

BOWEN, Charles. Colonel Dayton's Regiment. Desertion: thirty-nine lashes. (136)

BOWER(S), John, Lt. Leaving the camp without permission, countenancing the soldiers in disobedience to orders: guilty of the first charge but not guilty of the second charge—reprimand and a fine of four pounds. (3) (69) (136)

BOWER, Thomas, Adj. Pennsylvania Riflemen. Drawing a petition to his Excellency without the concurrence of the other officers, and thereby inciting a dangerous mutiny and encouraging the soldiers to leave the camp without leave: reprimand. (123)

BOWDEN, Levi, Ens. Colonel Brewer's Regiment. Absconding from his regiment without leave: cashiered. (135)

BOWLES,_____, Sergeant. Sleeping out of camp: reduced to private. (23)

BOWLIN (BOWDIN), Samuel. Mutiny, riot, and disobedience to orders: fine of twenty shillings. (135)

BOWMAN, Phineas, Capt. Fifth Massachusetts Regiment. Conduct unbecoming an officer: acquitted, but ordered to ask Lieutenant Colonel Newhall's pardon publicly and be suspended from the service for three months. (60) (86)

BOWMAN, Phineas, Capt. Fifth Massachusetts Regiment. Confining Mr. Joshua Land, disobedience to orders, mishandling his corporals and sergeants of his guard, sending an indecent note to Mr. Land: guilty of a portion of the charges—dismissed from the service. (124)

BOYCE, Justin. Colonel Crane's Regiment. Desertion: 100 lashes. (24)

BOZAR. *See* Besom.

BRACK, William. Speaking and acting inimical to the cause of America: thirty-nine lashes and drummed out of camp with labels on which shall be written, "Tory," pinned on his back and breast. (113)

BRADBURY, Jacob. Third Company. Stealing corn belonging to an inhabitant, absconding from camp without leave: forty lashes for each crime. (56) *See* Taylor.

BRADLEY, Charles. Colonel Ritzema's Regiment. Absenting himself and enlisting in another corps: thirty-nine lashes. (132) (136)

BRADLEY, Cornelius. Colonel Prentice's Regiment. Desertion and carrying off his gun, enlisting again in Captain Mead's regiment: 100 lashes. (131)

BRADLEY, Neal. Colonel Clinton's Regiment. Desertion: fine of one month's pay—pardoned. (118)

BRADWATER, Lewis, Lt. Tenth Virginia Regiment. Obtaining a certificate from the regiment's commanding officer that he was not indebted to the regiment, and then went to the Virginia state store and procured goods illegally: dismissed from the service and return the goods; his resignation taken away from him. (16)

BRAND, Gabriel. Maryland Line. Absence without leave, plundering inhabitants: run the gauntlet through the whole army. (115)

BRANDON, Alexander. First Virginia Regiment. Horse stealing: acquitted. (101)

BRANGAN, John. Captain Peron's Company. Stealing a gown and petticoat from William Hunt, insulting him in his own house: fifty lashes. (22)

BRAYER, John. Reenlisting: fifty lashes. (25)

BRAYTON, Robert. Light Company, Massachusetts Regiment. Killing a cow and seven geese: seventy-five lashes. (61)

BRAZIER, Benjamin. Colonel Alden's Regiment. Desertion and enlisting twice: 100 lashes for each offense and repayment of the bounty. (9)

BREADON, Jacob. Colonel Holmes' Regiment. Absconding from the guard, sleeping out of camp: fine of four shillings. (118)

BREWER,_____, Colonel. Embezzling or misapplying part of the clothing sent by the Board of War for the officers of his regiment: Dismissed from the service. (75)

BREWER, David. Ninth Regiment of Foot Soldiers. Procuring a lieutenant's commission for his son, an inexperienced boy of 16 or 17 years of age, and drawing his pay for the month of August, during which time the boy was at home in his father's service; taking men from the army and employing them on his farm: dismissed from the service. (136)

BREWER, Daniel, Sgt. Disobedience of orders in not joining the regiment: acquitted in consideration of his former good behavior and the real distress situation of his family. (91)

BREWER, Joseph. Captain Whitney's Company. Absent from his regiment for a longer time than he had leave: reprimand. (91)

BREWER, Peter. Colonel McDougall's Regiment. Desertion: released from confinement for lack of prosecution. (79)

BREWSTER, Truelove. Colonel Cotton's Regiment. Desertion: fifteen lashes—pardoned. (120)

BREZLAND, Patrick. Colonel Vose's Regiment. Getting drunk, leaving his guard: 100 lashes. (24)

BRIANT,_____, Ensign. Embezzling private property: acquitted, but found guilty of indiscrimination in permitting soldiers to take away old iron. (68) (106) (136)

BRICE, William. German Battalion. Insulting Lieutenant Colonel Wiltnor in his quarters: acquitted. (100)

BRIDE, Jeremiah. Second Virginia Regiment. Mutiny and desertion: 100 lashes. (134)

BRIDGE, Ebenezer, Col. Twenty-seventh Regiment of Foot Soldiers. Misbehavior and neglect of duty in the action at Bunker Hill: aquitted. (135)

BRIEN, William, Capt. German Battalion. Insulting and abusing a lieutenant colonel in his quarters: acquitted. (37)

BRIGGS, John, Sgt. Being privy to the crime committed by William Reed (stealing corn) and not reporting it, stealing corn himself: reduced to a matross and to duty accordingly. (91)

BRIGGS, John. Sixth Regiment. Attempting to desert to the enemy with his arms and accouterments. (112)

BRIMAS, Peter. Losing a shirt and vest: thirty lashes. (41)

BRITT, Edward. Colonel Nixon's Regiment. Desertion: thirty-nine lashes. (106)

BROCK, William. Captain Durger's Company. Speaking and acting inimical to the cause of America: thirty-nine lashes and drummed out of the camp with a label saying "Tory," and his offense published in public orders. (118)

BROOKFIELD, Joseph. "Having become a witness on behalf of the United States, is ordered to be released from confinement." (21)

BROOKS, Azariah. Mutiny: thirty-nine lashes. (84)

BROOKS, Benjamin, Capt. Third Maryland Regiment. Accusing Colonel Gumby in a very uncouth and unjustifiable manner in making known the sentence of a general court-martial before it was approved or disapproved: acquitted. (121)

BROOKS, Benjamin. Fifth Connecticut Regiment. Taking over a vessel and disposing of the cargo; guilty of holding a treasonous correspondence with the enemy of the United States: thirty-nine lashes and confined at New Gate Prison during the continuance of the war. (127)

BROOKS, Charles. Maryland Line. Absence without leave, plundering the inhabitants: run the gauntlet through the whole army. (115)

BROOKS, John. Colonel Hazen's Regiment. Desertion: acquitted. (85)

BROOKS, Joseph. Killing an ox belonging to an inhabitant: acquitted. (39) *See* Carey, Dow, Dupee, Holmes, Hunsberry, Jackson.

BROOKS, Richard. Artillery. Desertion: acquitted. (102)

BROOKS, Thomas. Stealing: seven days confinement in the dungeon. (118)

BROTHERS,_____, Sergeant. Selling his furlough to a soldier: reduced to the ranks. (122)

BROWN,_____, Captain. Colonel Jackson's Regiment. Scandalous and dangerous neglect of duty when entrusted with the command of an outpost, disobeying the orders of Lieutenant Colonel Littlefield: acquitted of the first charge but guilty of the second charge—reprimand. (75)

BROWN,_____, Doctor. Fourteenth Virginia Regiment. Going home not only without leave but against the express consent of the commanding officer, and that at a time when the distressed situation of the regiment required his particular attendance; neglecting to have a furlough which he said he obtained from Dr. Cochran: reprimand, noting that he was in a very bad state of health when he left. (103)

BROWN,_____, Ensign. Second Regiment. Leaving his guard: reprimand. (130)

BROWN,_____, Lieutenant. Colonel Wind's Regiment. Not coming on from New York with the regiment, discharging soldiers from the Continental service, receiving money from the soldiers for their dismission: acquitted. (84)

BROWN,_____, Lieutenant. Colonel Bigelow's Regiment. Neglect of duty in being asleep on guard at ten o'clock at night: reprimand. (24)

BROWN,_____, Absenting himself from the main guard: fifty lashes. (23) *See* Bloomer, Conoly, Fosdick.

BROWN, Abijah, Lt. Col. Endeavoring to defraud the Continental services by mustering two soldiers when he at the same time employed them working on his farm: fine of four pounds. (136)

BROWN, Amos. Colonel Whitcomb's Regiment. Mutinous and abusive language: acquitted. (104)

BROWN, Benjamin, Capt. Colonel Jackson's Regiment. Refusing to assist magistrates in the execution of their offices, in the apprehension, taking up, and bringing to justice a number of men belonging to his company: acquitted. (9)

BROWN, Benjamin. Neglect of duty in suffering a deserter to escape when he was a sentinel: thirty lashes—remitted. (91)

BROWN, Charles. Colonel Graham's Regiment. Robbery: thirty-nine lashes for the robbery and twenty lashes for drunkenness, used as an excuse for the robbery. (118)

BROWN, Charles. Colonel Webb's Regiment. Drawing his bayonet and theatening the lives of several of his brother soldiers: ten stripes and a fine of fifteen shillings for the benefit of the sick in his regiment—stripes remitted because of his former good behavior. (133)

BROWN, Daniel. Insolence to Sergeant Conants: pardoned. (23)

BROWN, Daniel. Seventh Maryland Regiment. Housebreaking, stealing, and beating the inhabitants: death by hanging. (93) *See* Bay, Murphy.

BROWN, Elias, Fifer. Commander-in-Chief's Guard. Twice robbing a home; taking money, clothing, and spoons: death—escaped but much later was pardoned and reinstated to duty. (74)

BROWN, Elihu. Colonel Putnam's Regiment. Desertion and forging a pass in the name of Major Newell: 100 lashes. (131)

BROWN, George. Desertion to the enemy: duty on board an armed vessel during the war. (26)

BROWN, Henry. Seventh Regiment. Mutinous language and disobedience to orders: not guilty of the first charge but guilty of the second charge—fifty lashes. (50)

BROWN, James, civilian. Communication with the city of Philadelphia: acquitted. (134)

BROWN, James. Second Regiment of Artillery. Desertion and attempting to go to the enemy: death—disapproved because the court-martial had not been legally created by the commander-in-chief or by a commanding general of New Jersey. (58)

BROWN, James. Colonel Webb's Regiment. Stealing a pocketbook: acquitted. (133)

BROWN, John. Fourth Connecticut Regiment. Stealing a boat and deserting to Long Island to join the enemy: 100 lashes. (46) *See* Landers.

BROWN, John. Colonel Wyllys's Regiment. Desertion: twenty lashes. (106)

BROWN, John. Colonel Wyllys' Regiment. Sleeping on his post: fifty lashes. (88)

BROWN, John. First North Carolina Regiment. Sleeping on his post: thirty-nine lashes. (94)

BROWN, John. First Company, New York Regiment. Desertion and attempting to go to the enemy: death. (78) (86)

BROWN, Jonathan. Desertion: run the gauntlet frontwards and backwards. (90)

BROWN, Joseph. Delaware Regiment. Plundering the house of an inhabitant near Prospect Hill: fifty lashes and fine of one-half month's pay. (93)

BROWN, Joshoa, Capt. Colonel Bigelow's Regiment. Suffering two prisoners to escape from the Provost's guard: acquitted. (13) (134)

BROWN, Josiah. Colonel Greene's Regiment. Raising a mutiny and behaving in a disorderly manner: acquitted. (131) *See* Baptist, Buck, Cary, Davis, Dunbar, Goold, Hardin, Lane, Park, Peterson, Tabor.

BROWN, Labbus. Colonel Sheldon's Corps. Pardoned. (124)

BROWN, Laurence, Sailor on board the sloop *Enterprise*. Mutinous behavior: acquitted. (99)

BROWN, Nathaniel. Colonel Webb's Regiment. Stealing sheep from Mr. Deines, an inhabitant of Bristol: thirty stripes—pardoned. (91) *See* Gay, Merrills, Olmstead.

BROWN, Nathaniel. Captain Wyllys's Company. Profane swearing, challenging his messmates to fight, abusive language, mutinous behavior: twenty-five lashes. (91)

BROWN, Peter. Colonel McDougall's Regiment. Desertion: released when no evidence was presented. (136)

BROWN, Simson. Fifth Company. Losing his arms and accouterments: acquitted. (23)

BROWN, Simson. Fifth Company. Theft of rum out of Mr. Parker's tent: twenty-five lashes. (23)

BROWN, Thomas. Seventh Pennsylvania Regiment. Plundering Mr. Bogart, an inhabitant, near Paramus: death by hanging—pardoned. (26) (73) *See* Bell, Justice, Powers.

BROWN, Thomas. Seventh Regiment. Repeated desertion: 100 lashes. (129)

BROWN, Thomas. Seventh New Jersey Regiment. Desertion: death by hanging. (28)

BROWN, Thomas. Seventh Pennsylvania Regiment. Plundering the inhabitants at Paramus, and abusing a woman: death—the court took notice that he previously had been sentenced to death but pardoned. (30)

BROWN, Thomas. Seventh New Jersey Regiment. Desertion: death by hanging—pardoned. (28)

BROWN, Thomas. Major Prentice's Company. Disobedience to orders and neglect of duty: acquitted. (105)

BROWN, Thomas. Third New Jersey Regiment. Desertion: death by hanging, since he was an old offender and guilty of repeatd desertions. (109)

BROWN, Thomas, Sailor on board the sloop *Enterprise*. Mutinous behavior: acquitted. (99)

BROWN, William. Fourth Pennsylvania Regiment. Desertion: 100 lashes. (112)

BROWN, William. Ninth Massachusetts Regiment. Desertion: 100 lashes—pardoned. (11)

BROWNELL,_____,Corporal. Colonel Topham's Regiment. Getting drunk and appearing in liquor on the parade: reduced to the ranks. (98)

BRUMLER, John. Tenth Virginia Regiment. Sleeping on his post while on sentry over prisoners: twenty lashes. (134)

BRY, John. Colonel Smith's Regiment. Leaving his guard without leave: logged for four days. (10)

BRYAN (ROZAN), John. Mutiny, riot, and disobedience to orders: thirty-nine lashes and drummed out of the army. (135)

BRYAN, Jonathan. Desertion: 100 lashes. (93)

BRYANT,_____, Ensign. *See* Briant, Ensign.

BRYANT, James. Stealing flour from the public store: 100 lashes. (89)

BRYANT, John. Sixteenth Massachusetts Regiment. Stealing rum from a soldier: acquitted. (35)

BRYANT, William. Stealing rum from the company's general stores: ten lashes. (69) (136) *See* Ingham, Lockwood, Woodburn.

BRYMER, Peter. Robbing a potato yard: acquitted. (19)

BUCK, Aaron, Sgt. Colonel Greene's Regiment. Raising a mutiny and behaving in a disorderly manner: not guilty of the first charge but guilty of the second charge—reprimand and suspended. (131) *See* Baptist, Brown, Cary, Davis, Dunbar, Goold, Hardin, Lane, Luis, Park, Peterson, Tabor.

BUCKIN, Henry, Batteauman. Disobedience of orders: thirty-nine lashes. (111)

BUCKLEY, Daniel. Second Maryland Regiment. Desertion: 100 lashes. (21)

BUCKMAN, Elijah. Second Massachusetts Regiment. Throwing stones at a lieutenant's hut and breaking the windows: acquitted. (64)

BUIZE, Peter. Colonel Haslet's Regiment. Desertion from the camp and found near the enemy's sentries: death. (74)

BULLOCK, Jonathan. Neglect of duty when on sentinel: thirty lashes. (91)

BUNCE, Jareld, Sgt. Third Connecticut Regiment. Endeavoring to excite a mutiny in the Connecticut Line, not discussing with his officers an intended mutiny when he knew a plan was laying: acquitted. (52) *See* Gaylor, Parker. *See* chapter five.

BUNCH, Warren. Desertion: 100 lashes. (42)

BURCH, Richard. Sixth Maryland Regiment. Desertion and attempting to go to the enemy: death. (103)

BURGER, Peter. First North Carolina Regiment. Assaulting the house of Mr. Uriah McKeel, firing several shots through it, wounding Thomas Brown and robbing him, plundering the house of several articles of wearing apparel: 100 lashes – pardoned. (26) *See* Borough, Mullen, Rickets.

BURGESS, Joseph. Colonel Cotton's Regiment. Desertion: fifteen lashes – pardoned. (12)

BURK, Edmund. Third New York Regiment. Attacking Andrew Garner, fife-major in said regiment, in his tent at night with an unlawful weapon; disobeying Ensign Josiah Bogley and attempting his life by knocking him down senseless with the above-mentioned weapon: death by shooting – pardoned. (26)

BURK, Joseph, Drum Major. Absent from roll call, not beating retreat: reduced to a private drummer. (66)

BURK, Michael. *See* Bourke, Michael.

BURK, Richard. Sixth Maryland Regiment. Desertion and attempting to go to the enemy: death. (69)

BURKE, Edmund. First New York Regiment. Mutiny at Albany: death. (44)

BURKE, John. Enlisting twice: Fifty stripes and return all the money he had received because of the enlistments – stripes were remitted. (9)

BURKE, Peter. Colonel McDougall's Regiment. Desertion: thirty-nine lashes. (79)

BURNBY,_____, Lieutenant. Seventh Virginia Regiment. Absenting himself from his command without leave: dismissed from the service. (17)

BURNETT,_____, Sergeant. Fifth New York Regiment. Accessory to robbing and striking William Richardson and Benjamin Brooks, soldiers in the Sixth Massachusetts Regiment: reduced to private sentinel and 100 lashes. (111) *See* Palmentier.

BURNETT (BURNET), Ebenezer. Colonel Livingston's Company. Stealing shirts when on guard: released when no evidence was presented. (128)

BURNHAM, Elija. Colonel Marshall's Regiment. Stealing a shirt and a pair of stockings: acquitted. (9)

BURNHAM, Josiah. Colonel Poor's Regiment. Desertion: thirty-nine lashes. (84) (117)

BURNHAM, Moses. Absent from roll call and drunk at the same time: twenty lashes. (43)

BURNS, James. Stealing flour from the public store: 100 lashes. (89)

BURRESS, Samuel. Colonel Lamb's Regiment of Artillery. Desertion: fifty lashes – sentence declared illegal by the commander-in-chief, and a new trial ordered. (134) *See* Coshall.

BURREST, Richard. Colonel Hazen's Regiment. Desertion: death by shooting. (93)

BURRIS, _____, Captain. Colonel Foreman's Regiment. Disobedience to orders, neglect of duty on 5 September: acquitted with honor. (72)

BURRIS (BURRESS), Samuel. Attempting to desert to the enemy: 100 lashes over a period of two days; his back to be washed with salt water after completion of each lashing. (15)

BURROWS, Giles. Colonel Nixon's Regiment. Desertion and forging a discharge from the Continenal service: thirty-nine lashes. (136)

BURROWS, John. Third New York Regiment. Neglect of duty and being asleep on his guard: reprimand only, because of his former good character. (89)

BURTON, William, sailor on board the sloop *Enterprise*. Mutinous behavior: acquitted. (99)

BUSH, Thomas. Eleventh Pennsylvania Regiment. Desertion: run the gauntlet once a week for two weeks, from right to left and left to right each time. (112)

BUSHNELL, David. Captain Harte's Company. Absent without leave: acquitted. (91)

BUSWELL, Abraham. Abusing Sergeant Haskell, threatening to break his head with the breach of his gun, refusing to obey Colonel Little and Major Collins. (136)

BUTLER, _____, Captain. Colonel Nixon's Regiment. Several charges of defrauding his company, absenting himself from his company when on the march, enlisting a man unfit for the service: acquitted. (136) *See* Walker.

BUTLER, George. Sleeping on post when on sentry: fifty lashes. (43)

BUTLER, Ignatius. Colonel Harrison's Regiment of Artillery. Desertion: 100 lashes. (37)

BUTLER, James. Colonel Prescott's Regiment. Plundering a cellar belonging to a citizen of New York: released to join his regiment. (6) *See* Knowland, McIntire, Webster.

BUTLER, John. Colonel Bailey's Regiment. Desertion: thirty-nine lashes. (136)

BUTLER, John. Third Regiment. Desertion: 100 lashes – pardoned. (95)

BUTLER, R., Colonel. Endeavoring to excite soldiers to mutiny and not to obey orders of their captain, sending Captain Ashmead under guard to West Point to wait on General Wayne: reprimand. (110)

BUTLER, Thomas, inhabitant of Pennsylvania. Attempting to carry flour to Philadelphia: 250 lashes. (134) *See* Ryan.

BUTLER, William. Colonel Harthy's Regiment. Desertion and forging a pass: 100 lashes. (101)

BUTNEY, Jonthan, Sgt. Colonel Gerrish's Regiment. Mutiny: reduced to the ranks and a fine of forty-eight shillings. (136) *See* Harwood, Laraby, North, Rawlins, (Rowllins), Williams.

BUTT, Joseph. Colonel Morrow's Regiment. Alarming the camp by firing guns: reprimand. (96)

BUTTERBICH, Benjamin. Colonel Wind's Regiment. Desertion and enlisting into another regiment: thirty-nine lashes for each of the two offenses. (84)

BUTTON, Daniel. Major Prentice's Company. Profane swearing: fine of one shilling. (105)

BYBEE, John. Desertion: punishment postponed for further evidence. (101)

BYRD,_____, Lieutenant Colonel. Countermanding the orders of Colonel Bland and disobeying his orders. (134)

BYRNE, James. Colonel Stewart's Regiment. Desertion: acquitted. (70)

CABE, Ozburn. Fifth North Carolina Battalion. Neglect of duty in letting a prisoner escape: fifty lashes – remitted. (95)

CAGGET,_____, Colonel. Leaving his post without permission from the commander-in-chief's department. (9)

CAHAGEN, Hugh, Civilian. Stealing a coat and several firelocks: thirty-nine lashes. (132) (136) *See* Kief.

CAIM,_____, Sergeant. Delaware Regiment. Abusing an inhabitant, Mr. Dennison, in his residence: reduced to the ranks and fifty lashes. (39) *See* Davis.

CALDWELL, William, a follower of the camp. Taking up and claiming a horse, abusing the wagonmaster: acquitted. (95)

CALL, Timothy. Breaking open and robbing the store: thirty-nine lashes and a fine of thirty shillings – remitted. (91)

CALLENDER, Captain Lieutenant. Third Regiment of Artillery. Exceeding his furlough six days: acquitted. (50) (124)

CALLENDER, John, Capt. Massachusetts Forces. Cowardice: cashiered. Note: This was probably the first officer to be court-martialed during the war. He was tried prior to Washington's taking command of the Continental Army. Washington, on 7 July 1775 at Cambridge, said, "It is with inexpressible concern that the General upon his arrival in the army should find an officer sentenced by a general court-martial to be cashiered for cowardice . . . Captain John Callender is accordingly cashiered, and dismissed from all further service in the Continental Army, as an officer."(1)

CALLEY, Joshua. Fifth New York Regiment. Desertion: eighty lashes. (111)

CALVIDGE, Francis. Colonel Glover's Regiment. Desertion and reenlistment: thirty-nine lashes, with thirteen lashes administered on three successive days. (68)

CALVIN, Thomas. Eleventh Pennsylvania Regiment. Attempting to desert to the enemy with his arms: death. (28)

CAMERON, Daniel. Van Kirk's Regiment. Design against the lives of the captain and others: released as no evidence was presented. (99)

CAMP, William. Colonel Prescott's Regiment. Desertion: thirty-nine lashes. (72)

CAMPBELL,_____, Sergeant. Colonel Sherburn's Regiment. Robbing a house many valuable effects: reduced to the ranks and stand under the gallows with a rope around his neck fifteen minutes; 100 lashes. (85) (113)

CAMPBELL, John, inhabitant of Pennyslvania. Supplying the enemy with provisions: pay fifty pounds for the use of the sick at camp. (15)

CAMPBELL, Joseph. Colonel Vose's Regiment. Desertion and enlisting a second time: 100 lashes for each of three offenses and turned over to some Continental ship without the privilege of coming ashore – escaped before being taken aboard ship. (9)

CAMPBELL, Thomas. Desertion: run the gauntlet frontward and backward. (80)

CAMPBELL, Thomas. Disobedience to orders: fifty lashes. (23)

CAMRON, Donald. Absenting from his company and engaging in another corps: thirty-nine lashes. (127) *See* Rock.

CANDA, Michael. Second South Carolina Regiment. Desertion from the Fifth North Carolina Regiment: 100 lashes and serve his enlistment in the Second South Carolina Regiment. (95)

CANADY, Alexander. Attempting to desert to the enemy: acquitted. (9)

CANNON,_____, Ensign. Fourth Virginia Regiment. Accusing Ensign Ford with cowardice: dismissed from the service. (93)

CANTWELL, Thomas. Colonel Evans' Regiment. Firing his gun when he was on guard: reprimand, because the firing was an accident, as proved by John Manly. (96)

CARES, J., Sgt. Colonel Topham's Regiment. Being drunk at Stoddard's Tavern: acquitted. (98)

CAREY, James. Killing an ox belonging to an inhabitant: acquitted. (39) *See* Brooks, Dow, Dupee, Holmes, Hunsberry, Jackson.

CAREY, Jonathan. Mutiny: twenty lashes. (84)

CAREY, Philip, Ensign. Tenth Massachusetts Regiment. Exceeding the limits of his furlough by ten days: reprimand and pay for the days absent. (51)

CARLISLE,_____, Captain. Colonel Bedel's Regiment. Attempting to fire upon Lieutenant Colonel Wash and abusing him: cashiered. (84)

CARLISS, Nathan. Light Company, Massachusetts Regiment. Killing a cow and seven geese: seventy-five lashes. (61) *See* Abram, Brayton, Cook, Cowell, Gardner, Jinks, Shea, Wood.

CARMAN, Francis. Third Regiment of Artillery. Desertion and attempting to go to the enemy, stealing a boat: death. (46) *See* Grant, Parsells.

CARMAN, Michael. Sixth Maryland Regiment. Desertion and attempting to go to the enemy: death. (3) (69) (103)

CARMICLE (CARMICHAEL), Daniel. Colonel Paterson's Regiment. Disobedience to orders, reenlisting, and taking money twice; drunkenness: thirty-nine lashes and dismissed from the service. (1) (135)

CARNERY, Patrick, Wagoner. Theft: 100 lashes. (3)

CARNEY, James. Colonel Wait's Regiment. Desertion: thirty-nine lashes and wear a noose around his neck for fourteen days, and if found without it, to receive 100 lashes. (84) (117)

CARNEY, Nicholas. Colonel Hand's Regiment. Leaving camp without leave and riotous drunken behavior: thirty lashes. (106)

CARNEY, Thomas. Colonel Lamb's Regiment of Artillery. Desertion: 100 lashes. (83) (84)

CARNS, John. Massachusetts Forces. Desertion: 100 lashes. (46)

CARPENTER,_____, Ensign. Absenting himself without leave, knowing that his regiment was to go immediately into action: cashiered. (13) (134)

CARPENTER, William. Fourth Georgia Continental Battalion. Desertion: ninety-nine lashes – pardoned. (80)

CARPNEL, Amos. Colonel Johnson's Regiment. Speaking disrespectfully and villifying the commander-in-chief: reduced in rank and thirty-nine lashes, with thirteen lashes administered on three successive days. (7)

CARR, Catel (CHAPPELL, Hector). Desertion: 100 lashes. (41)

CARR, Ezekial. Fifth Connecticut Regiment. Repeated desertion, the last time to the enemy when he took up arms against the United States: death. (110)

CARR, John. Seventh Massachusetts Regiment. Desertion: fifty lashes. (44)

CARR, William. Fourth Pennsylvania Regiment. Being out an unreasonable hour of the night, suspicion of plundering the tent of an officer and taking money: guilty only of the first charge – fifty lashes. (116)

CARR, William. Colonel Holmes' Regiment. Sleeping on his post: fine of four shillings – pardoned. (118)

CARRE, Edward, Sgt. Captain Moody's Company. Absent without leave: reduced to a matross. (125)

CARROLL, John. Colonel Marshall's Regiment. Absent without permission: thirty-nine lashes. (9)

CARSON, Moses, Capt. Deserting to the enemy and carrying a number of men with him in the year 1777: dismissed from the service with a halter around his neck and label pinned to him as follows – "Moses Carson, late a captain in the American Army. This I suffer for desertion to the enemy of the United States of North America." Also confined during the present war between Great Britain and America. (110)

CARSON, Thomas. Sixth Virginia Regiment. Breaking into and robbing a house: 100 lashes and death—the death sentence imposed because he was "more atrociously guilty than the others who participated in the robbery with him." (21) *See* Garnick, Hitchcock, Johnson, Lee.

CARTER,_____, Lieutenant. Colonel Bayler's Regiment of Light Dragoons. Leaving loads of supplies unguarded, by which the enemy took them: reprimand. (17)

CARTER, Abraham, Wagoner. Embezzling public stores: acquitted. (100)

CARTER, James. Third Maryland Regiment. Stealing money from Micai Dum: 500 lashes and return the stolen money to the victim. (93)

CARTER, Jonathan. Colonel Ward's Regiment. Desertion: thirty-nine lashes—remitted since he had been confined twenty days. (74)

CARTER, Prince. Second Connecticut Regiment. Desertion and re-enlisting on three different occasions: 100 lashes, at different times, one-half on the bare back and one-half on the bare breech. (76)

CARTHY, Daniel, Quartermaster of the garrison at West Point. Disobedience to orders: guilty of one of two charges placed—reprimand. (124)

CARVER, Captain Lieutenant. Colonel Elliot's Regiment of Artillery. Embezzling and selling wood belonging to the Continent: pay for the wood and dismissed from the service—reinstated to his former rank. (98)

CARY, Gideon, Drummer. Colonel Greene's Regiment. Raising a mutiny and behaving in a disorderly manner: not guilty of the first charge but guilty of the second charge—reprimand and suspended. (131) *See* Baptist, Brown, Buck, Davis, Dunbar, Goold, Hardin, Lane, Park, Peterson, Tabor.

CASAWAY,_____, Ensign. Third Maryland Regiment. Absent without leave: reprimand. (103)

CASE, Joseph. Fifth North Carolina Battalion. Neglect of duty in letting a prisoner escape: fifty lashes—remitted. (95)

CASKASCUS, Jonathan. Colonel Morrow's Regiment. Alarming the camp by firing guns: reprimand. (96)

CASS, Daniel. Colonel Stark's Regiment. Leaving his post as a sentry before he was relieved: reprimand. (84) (117)

CASS, Elijah (alias Thomson, Elijah). Fifth Connecticut Regiment. Enlisting several times in Colonel Sheldon's Regiment and deserting therefrom: death by shooting. (111)

CASSADY, Allen. Pennylsvania Regiment. Getting drunk on his post:

twenty lashes. (117)

CASSIDY, Peter. Second New York Regiment. Defrauding an inhabitant of forty Continental dollars and three "pistriens" in silver: 100 lashes and pay for the money taken. (111)

CASSON, Hartwell. Selling his shoes: thirty lashes. (43)

CASSON, Jeremiah. Overstaying his furlough forty-nine days: acquitted, because his failure to return was due to sickness. (91)

CASTEEL,_____, Sergeant. Third New York Regiment. Theft, abusive behavior: acquitted. (28)

CASTON, John. Colonel Ward's Regiment. Desertion: thirty-nine lashes. (118) (123)

CATES, Joseph. Fourth New York Regiment. Desertion: 100 lashes and serve in the regiment for as long as he was absent from it. (28)

CATO, Prince. Second Connecticut Regiment. Desertion and enlisting in the Connecticut State Troops: 200 lashes, with 100 lashes administered at two different times. (52)

CATON,_____, Lieutenant. Third Regiment of Artillery. Exceeding the limits of his furlough by six days: acquitted. (50)

CAWLEY, Jonathan. Colonel Hazlet's Regiment. Robbing Israel Ryder: acquitted. (74) (94) *See* McDaniels.

CAZER, Solomon. Plundering the inhabitants of money, and other offenses: acquitted. (33)

CHADWICK, James. Getting drunk, fighting, and making a disturbance in camp at unreasonable hours of the night: one day's fatigue – the general thought the punishment in no way adequate to the crime. (91) *See* Woodworth.

CHAMBERLAIN, Uriah. Captain Hamilton's Company, New York Artillery. Desertion: thirty-nine lashes. (136)

CHAMBERS, John. Third Maryland Regiment. Desertion: fifty lashes but leniency recommended – remitted. (21)

CHAMPION, Samuel. Twenty stripes. (105)

CHANDLER, John. Colonel Cotton's Regiment. Desertion: fifteen lashes – pardoned. (120)

CHANDONET,_____, Lieutenant, Quartermaster Corps. Refusing to sign an order for forage sent in by Captain Carter: acquitted. (72)

CHAPEL,_____, Corporal. Neglect of duty when on guard last night, refusing to deliver a watch coat designed for the use of the sentinel: reprimand. (91)

CHAPLAIN, John. Colonel Arnold's Company. Refusing to obey Colonel Arnold's orders: fine of one month's pay and immediately join Captain Smith's company according to Colonel Arnold's order. (128)

CHAPMAN,_____, Lieutenant. Colonel Webb's Regiment. Disobedience to orders, refusing to do his duty: dismissed from the service. (1)

CHAPMAN, Adino. Stealing provisions from the Third Company: thirty lashes. (91)

CHAPMAN, Albert, Maj. Embezzling public property and endeavoring to induce the quartermaster of the regiment to assist him in embezzling powder for his own private use; making up two enormous bills against Colonel Nelson, an inhabitant of Morristown; taking up a strayed horse, the property of said Nelson; giving a false certificate to a soldier: guilty of a portion of the charges—reprimand. The general disagreed with the court and felt the sentence was entirely inadequate. (36)

CHAPMAN, Cesar. Stealing rum and sugar: thirty lashes. (91)

CHAPMAN, Elias. Desertion and stealing public property from his care when on guard over it: 100 lashes. (41) *See* Haney, Phay.

CHAPMAN, Peter. Colonel Lovell's Regiment. Desertion and theft: twenty stripes and a fine of twelve dollars—stripes remitted. (73)

CHAPPEL,_____, Corporal. Colonel Webb's Regiment. Drunkenness, making disturbances in quarters at unreasonable hours: reduced to a private sentinel and reprimand—restored to his former rank. (91)

CHAPPELL, Hector. *See* Carr, Catels.

CHASE, Ebenezer. Colonel Tyler's Regiment. Taking rigging from the public boats at Bristol Ferry and selling it, taking an iron mantle from the barracks and a woolen blanket from the ferry: fifty lashes. (98)

CHASE, John, Cpl. First New York Regiment. Desertion and reenlisting in the Rhode Island Regiment: 100 lashes. (44)

CHASE, Nathaniel. Colonel Stark's Regiment. Deserting three times: thirty-nine lashes and pay all the costs of his desertion. (84) (117)

CHEAVER,_____, Corporal. Colonel Wilson's Regiment. Assisting in counterfeiting money and passing the same: reduced to a private and 100 lashes. (75)

CHENEY,_____, Lieutenant. Disobedience to orders: acquitted. (84)

CHENEY, Elijah. Third Continental Regiment. Desertion for two years and four months: 100 lashes. (31)

CHENEY, Samuel, Surgeon. Thirty-Fourth Regiment. Drawing more hospital stores than he had a right to draw, villifying the characters of Generals Lee and Putnam: cashiered. (133) (136)

CHERRY, Elijah. First Connecticut Regiment. Repeated desertion: death. (48)

CHESTER, Joseph. Colonel Malcomb's Regiment. Desertion: twenty lashes. (118)

CHILD, Benjamin. Colonel Glover's Regiment. Previous court-martial appealed: acquitted. (135)

CHILD, Samuel. Being an accomplice or privy to several soldiers throwing stones at and insulting some officers and refusing to point out the persons concerned: acquitted. (91)

CHILDS, Joseph. New York Train of Artillery. Defrauding Christopher Stelson of a dollar, drinking damnation to all Whigs and Sons of Liberty, profane cursing and swearing: drummed out of the army. (136)

CHONICK, Robert. Massachusetts Line. Fifty lashes. (63)

CHORD, John. Second Maryland Regiment. Sleeping on his post: 100 lashes. (93)

CHRISTIE (CHRISTY), James, Capt. Third Pennsylvania Regiment. Refusing to take his post and march with the detachment: reprimand. (32)

CHRISTY, James, Capt. Third Pennsylvania Regiment (Third Delaware Regiment). Beating a number of persons, breaking windows, and other abusive treatment: guilty only of abusive treatment— reprimand. (63) (103) *See* Armstrong, Moore.

CHRISTY, John. Colonel Gansevort's Regiment. Desertion and reenlisting in Colonel Van Schaack's Regiment: 100 lashes for desertion and 100 lashes for reenlisting. (83)

CHURCH,_____, Major. Fourth Pennsylvania Regiment. Discharging a man fit for duty but "returning him" as unfit for service, using soldiers to work on his farm, illegally drawing soldiers' pay: acquitted. (27)

CHURCH, Alexander, Superintendent of Horses. Supporting at public expense six or more horses which he claimed as private property, appropriating to his own use a wagon and four horses which he claimed as his own, receiving public forage for them, permitting men in his employment to purchase poor horses for the Continental Yard for thirty dollars, which was worth a thousand dollars: acquitted. (23)

CHURCHIL, John. Absent without leave, stealing from Mr. Sacket: guilty of the first charge only—fifteen lashes. (91)

CICCAS, William. First Virginia Regiment. Desertion: acquitted of desertion, but guilty of absence without leave—fifty lashes. (108)

CILLENON,_____, Captain. Fourth New York Regiment. Calling Adjutant Sackett a liar and drawing his sword on him when unarmed, insinuating that he was a coward and challenging him to a duel: guilty, but no censure merited because of the circumstances. (69)

CIUVANS (CURRANS), Timothy. North Carolina Regiment. Absent without leave, taking a public horse, attempting to dispose of the horse: dismissed from the service. (109)

CLAFFERS, Daniel. Colonel Learned's Regiment. Desertion: thirty-nine lashes. (136)

CLAIR,_____. Suspicion of murder: acquitted. (49)

CLAIR, E. B., Cpl. Partisan Legion. Impressing a horse without a legal warrant, receiving money for the horse, plundering a Negro from an inhabitant of North Carolina and encouraging such practices in soldiers under his command: guilty only of encouraging the soldiers in such practices; reduced to the ranks and 100 lashes—lashes remitted. (115)

CLAIR, Joseph. Fourth Georgia Continental Battalion. Desertion: death by shooting. (80)

CLARAGE, Levin. Plotting and persuading a soldier to desert: acquitted. (78)

CLARK,_____, Captain. General Putnam's Regiment. Neglect of duty when on guard: acquitted. (105)

CLARK, Arthur. Colonel Whitcomb's Regiment. Threatening and insulting the officers of the regiment: acquitted. (84) (117)

CLARK, George. Suffering a prisoner to escape: six days confinement in the dungeon—pardoned. (118)

CLARK, James. First Maryland Regiment. Desertion and joining the enemy: 100 lashes. (115)

CLARK, John. Third Maryland Regiment. Desertion and attempting to go to the enemy: death. (22)

CLARK, John. Disobedience to orders, forcing the guard with clubs: thirty-nine lashes. (118)

CLARK, Samuel. General Smallwood's Regiment. Plundering a house: thirty-nine lashes. (6) *See* Arnold.

CLARK, Samuel. General Smallwood's Regiment. Plundering a house lately occupied by Lord Stirling: acquitted. (136)

CLARK, Thomas. Fourth Pennsylvania Regiment. Attempting to desert to the enemy with his arms: death. (28)

CLARK, Thomas, Drummer. Delaware Regiment. Disobedience to orders: thirty-nine lashes. (93)

CLARK, Thomas. Sixth Regiment. Twenty stripes and drummed out of camp. (105)

CLARK, William. Colonel Webb's Regiment. Absenting himself from his regiment one whole day without leave, getting drunk and pawning his shoes: thirty-nine lashes. (91)

CLARK, William. First New Jersey Regiment. Sleeping on his post: death. (44)

CLARKE,_____, Captain. General Putnam's Regiment. Neglect of duty when on guard: acquitted. (114)

CLARKE, Joel, Cpl. Colonel Webb's Regiment. Absent without leave and lodging out of camp: reduced to the ranks and 100 lashes. (30) *See* Hull.

CLARKSON, George. Colonel McDougall's Regiment. Mutiny and sedition: twenty lashes. (1) (132)

CLARRIAGE, Francis. Colonel Glover's Regiment. Desertion and reenlisting in another regiment: thirty-nine lashes, with thirteen lashes administered on three successive days. (136)

CLARY, John. North Carolina Regiment. Theft: 100 lashes. (95)

CLASS, Adam. Desertion: 100 lashes. (129)

CLASTONE, Samuel. Second Connecticut Regiment. Killing, or being combined in killing, two sheep, the property of a civilian: acquitted. (124)

CLATON, John. Desertion: 100 lashes. (77)

CLEAR,_____, Corporal. Leaving his guard and going into town to sleep: acquitted. (23)

CLEMENSHAW, Dennis. Desertion: 100 lashes. (56)

CLEMENTS,_____, Sergeant. Commander-in-Chief's Guard. Remission of duty: reduced to the ranks and returned to his original regiment. (7)

CLEMENTS, Aaron. Stealing and being an accessory to stealing several articles of clothing and silver spoons from an inhabitant of Danbury: fifty lashes. (53) *See* Dunham, Perry, Wilton.

CLEMENTS, John, Sgt. Obtaining leave of absence from a captain through deception: reduced to a private sentinel. (124)

CLEMONS, Aaron. Ninth Regiment. Stealing sheep: acquitted. (46)

CLENT, Henry. Colonel McDougall's Regiment. Desertion: released with no evidence being presented. (136)

CLEVELAND,_____, Captain. Colonel Jackson's Regiment. Refusing to do his tour of duty when duly notified: acquitted. (16)

CLEVELAND, Curlip. Overstaying his furlough: acquitted. (91)

CLIBIT, Reuben. Captain Waggoner's Company. Theft: acquitted. (96)

CLIFFORD, Abraham. Second New Hampshire Regiment. Repeated desertions: death by shooting. (111)

CLINTON,_____, Corporal. Absent without leave: acquitted. (91)

CLOSE, Adam. Sixth Virginia Regiment. Desertion: acquitted. (134)

COBURN, Thomas. Cilley's Regiment. Straggling from camp, killing a number of hogs: acquitted. (10) *See* Tucker.

COCK, John. Colonel Foreman's Regiment. Breaking open a store and drawing rum, or suffering it to be done. (132) *See* Kinsey, Relsworth.

COCKE,_____, Ensign. First Virginia Regiment. Denying what he formerly and has since said he knows respecting Captain Crump's behavior thereby acting inconsistently with honour and truth: dismissed from the service. (13)

COCKE, Thomas. Colonel Tyler's Regiment. Desertion: 100 lashes and pay for the cost of his apprehension. (98)

COCKLIN, William. Sixth Maryland Regiment. Desertion and attempting to go to the enemy: death. (103)

COCORAN, Joseph. Being drunk on his guard: fifteen lashes. (101)

CODINGTON, Godfrey. Colonel Topham's Regiment. Abusing Sergeant Santon: fifteen lashes. (68)

COFFEE, Hugh. Delaware Regiment. Burning a tent: acquitted because the fire was an accident. (93)

COFFEE, Ishmael (Thomas). Third Massachusetts Regiment. Desertion: fifty lashes. (50)

COFFER, John, Lt. Tenth Virginia Regiment. Obtaining a certificate from the commanding officer of the regiment that he was not indebted to the regiment, and then went to the Virginia State Store and procured goods illegally: dismissed from the service and return the goods, his resignation taken away from him. (16)

COFFIN, John. Abusing a captain when attempting to suppress a riot: acquitted. (16)

COGSRIFF, Dennis. Colonel Vose's Regiment. Attempted desertion: 100 stripes. (88)

COHAN,_____. Sixth Massachusetts Regiment. Desertion: fifty lashes. (53)

COHORSE, Ephraim. Striking Timothy Gibbs: twenty lashes. (22)

COLBERT, N., Seaman. Mutiny, whereas the enemy might come and saying that he would not fight against them on board the vessel: seventy-eight lashes and return to duty on board – the criminals to be whipped from vessel to vessel, receiving a part of their punishment on board each. (117) *See* Hammon, Powell, Trip.

COLBERT, William. Colonel Gallup's Regiment. Neglect of orders when detached for one month's duty: return to duty for one month from the date of confinement. (82)

COLBURN.,_____. Massachusetts Line. Desertion: 100 lashes. (63)

COLBY, Samuel. Desertion: 100 lashes. (42)

COLE,_____. Captain North's Company. Stealing rum from a sergeant: thirty lashes. (23)

COLE, Ephraim. Colonel Smith's Regiment. Stealing and disobedience: thirty-nine lashes. (10) *See* Thrasher.

COLE, Gideon. General Putnam's Regiment. Sleeping on post as sentinel. (1)

COLE, John. First Virginia Regiment. Desertion: acquitted of desertion but guilty of absence without leave. (108)

COLE, William. Being a spy: acquitted. (69)

COLEMAN, John. Second Regiment of Artillery. Desertion: 100 lashes. (53)

COLEMAN, Stephen. Captain Spark's Company. Forging an order: thirty lashes. (72)

COLI, John. Commander-in-Chief's Guard. Going out, with others, with sidearms, to harm other soldiers: acquitted. (125)

COLLINS, Israel. Colonel Elliott's Regiment. Stabbing Peter File with a knife: twenty lashes. (98)

COLLINS, James. Second Maryland Regiment. Desertion: 100 lashes. (93)

COLLINS, John. Colonel Wigglesworth's Regiment. Sleeping on his post: fifty lashes. (131)

COLLINS, John, Deputy Commissary of Military Stores. Defrauding the public of a quantity of salt petre, employing a person to receive the same as his own property, selling it, breaking his arrest and deserting from his quarters, endeavoring to make his escape from justice by trying to obtain a berth on some vessel to go to sea, robbing another person of some public papers for his own purposes: serve on board a Continental ship of war during the present war without permission to set his foot on shore; and his name, crime, and punishment be published in the public prints. (41) *See* chapter four.

COLONY,_____. Colonel Hazen's Regiment. Striking and abusing Sergeant Holmes and Corporal Quinn when on duty: 100 lashes. (83) (84)

COLSON,_____. Captain Lane's Company. Stealing a pair of overalls from one of Colonel Putnam's soldiers: fifty lashes. (72)

COLSON, Hatevil. Colonel Nixon's Regiment. Plundering an inhabitant: 100 lashes. (72)

COLSTON, Nathaniel. Colonel Nixon's Regiment. Entering the house of Reuben Crosby, an inhabitant, taking by force of arms about $300 in Continental money, a musket, a pair of plaited baskets, and other articles: 100 lashes. (125)

COLTON,_____, Captain. Colonel Greaton's Regiment. Refusing to take his post: acquitted. (85)

COLVILL, Thomas. Colonel Webb's Regiment. Desertion: fifty lashes. (131)

COMPTON, William. Second Pennsylvania Regiment. Desertion and enlisting into another corps: 100 lashes, to be administered on three successive days. (50)

COMSTOCK,_____. Fourth Company. Disobedience to orders in staying from his regiment after expiration of his pass: acquitted. (91)

CONANT,_____, Sergeant. Striking a soldier: reprimand. (23) *See* Barrett.

CONE, Joseph, Lt. Colonel Livingston's Regiment. Conduct unbecoming an officer and a gentleman, very drunk when he came before the court-martial, and entirely unfit for any kind of business: cashiered. (19)

CONELY, Patrick. Beating Hugh Miller, robbery: fifty lashes and pay compensation for the robbery. (113)

CONKLING, Samuel. Colonel Clinton's Regiment. Desertion: fine of one month's pay—pardoned. (118)

CONNELL, Daniel. Colonel Graham's Regiment (Colonel Thomas's Regiment). Desertion: thirty-nine lashes and dismissed from the service. (118) (123)

CONNER, Gabriel. Colonel Elliot's Regiment. Stealing a bundle of children's clothing: fifty lashes. (98) *See* Wyman.

CONNER, William. Fifth Massachusetts Regiment. Desertion: 100 lashes. (44)

CONNOLY, George. Delaware Regiment. Drunkenness, theft: twenty-five lashes for being drunk and 150 lashes for theft of a pocket book with about twenty pounds in it. (93)

CONNOR, James, Conductor of Wagons. Insulting and abusing certain of the inhabitants of the town, and other scandalous and disorderly behavior: acquitted. (75)

CONNOR, John. Colonel Doolittle's Regiment. Stealing a cheese, the property of Isiah Campbell: thirty-nine lashes. (135)

CONNOR, William. Fourth Georgia Continental Battalion. Desertion: death by shooting. (80)

CONOLLY, Edward. Captain Harrison's Regiment of Artillery. Desertion to the enemy and reenlisting: 200 lashes. (17)

CONOLY,_____. Absenting himself from the main guard: fifty lashes. (23)

CONOLY, William. Absenting himself from his guard, getting drunk, abusing the sergeant of the guard: twenty-five lashes. (10)

CONSOLVEN, John. Sixth Virginia Regiment. Losing his arms, equipment and accouterments: reprimand. (134) *See* Sims, Talbot.

CONVERSE,_____, Ensign. Third Massachusetts Regiment. Disobedience to orders: acquitted. (124)

CONWAY,_____, Lieutenant Colonel. Disobedience to orders, beating Colonel Ogden's waiter: acquitted with honor. (35)

CONWAY, John. Colonel Marshall's Regiment. Desertion in the late retreat from Ticonderoga: returned to his regiment in irons. (9)

CONWAY, William. Colonel Van Schack's Regiment. Insulting and cutting with a hanger the head of Oliver Mann, a surgeon: fifty lashes and a fine of eight dollars. (88)

CONWELL, Patrick. Beating Hugh Miller, robbery: fifty lashes and recompense for the robbery. (85)

CONY, Phillip, Ens. Tenth Massachusetts Regiment. Exceeding his furlough by ten days: acquitted. (50)

CONYER, Solomon. General Stark's Brigade. Riding public horses, plundering: acquitted. (100)

COOK,_____, Ensign. Twelfth Pennsylvania Regiment. Leaving his guard before he was properly relieved: cashiered with infamy. (13) (134)

COOK, Abraham. First Massachusetts Regiment. Killing a cow and seven geese: seventy-five lashes and pay fifteen dollars to the owner. (86)

COOK, Abraham. Light Company, Massachusetts Regiment. Killing a cow and seven geese: seventy-five lashes. (61) *See* Abram, Brayton, Carliss, Cowell, Gardner, Jinks, Shea, Wood.

COOK, Alex. Colonel Hazen's Regiment. Desertion: fine of twenty shillings only, because he reenlisted out of ignorance and not with any evil design, and has always behaved as a good soldier. (93)

COOK, George. Second New Jersey Regiment. Desertion: death. (51)

COOK, George. Sleeping on his post: fifty lashes – pardoned, "as he had been unwell for several days, kept awake two or three nights before by distemper, was then unfit for duty, and was standing up when found asleep." (131)

COOK, Phillip. The German Battalion. Mutiny and desertion: death by shooting. (25) *See* Alexander, Bottemer, Hoffenberger, Kurts.

COOK, Samuel. Desertion: 100 lashes. (42)

COOK, Thomas. Eighth Pennsylvania Regiment. Sleeping on guard at camp: acquitted. (96)

COOK, William, Col. Twelfth Pennsylvania Regiment. Disobedience to orders in sundry instances, specifically abandoning his unit during an attack against the enemy, and not joining it for ten days, at another time absconding from camp two or three days, at another time gave leave to his officers but reported them absent without leave: guilty of the first two charges but not guilty of the last charge—reprimand. (14) (134)

COOLES, Joseph. Third Maryland Regiment. Desertion: 100 lashes. (133)

COOPER,_____, Ensign. Fifteenth Virginia Regiment. Drunk and lying in the road in a shameful manner when he ought to have been with his regiment: cashiered. (17)

COOPER, Abraham. Being drunk after being warned: twenty lashes—pardoned because of his long and faithful service and good character. (91)

COOPER, Abraham, Wagoner. Embezzling public stores when employed in carting the same to the enemy: acquitted. (36)

COOPER, Daniel. Colonel Proctor's Regiment. Desertion: acquitted, because he had recently been transferred to the Corps of Invalids, rather than having deserted. (125)

COOPER, Daniel. Colonel Washington's Detachment. Desertion and bearing arms against the United States: death by hanging. (115)

COOPER, John. Colonel McDougall's Regiment. Mutiny and sedition: thirty lashes. (1) (132)

COOPER, John. Colonel McDougall's Regiment. Mutiny: fifteen lashes. (136)

COOPER, Thomas. Colonel Tyler's Regiment. Desertion: 100 lashes and a fine of twenty-three pounds to pay the cost of his apprehension. (2) (68)

COOPER, Thomas. Colonel Tyler's Regiment. Sleeping on his post: thirty lashes. (23)

COOPER, William. Third Massachusetts Regiment. Desertion: 100 lashes. (46)

COOPER, William. Third Massachusetts Regiment. Desertion and attempting to go to the enemy: not guilty as charged, but guilty of being absent without leave—forty lashes. (54) *See* Holland.

COOSSETT, Samuel. Colonel Greaton's Regiment. Enlisting twice: fifty lashes. (88)

CORBETT, Cornelius. Tenth Massachusetts Regiment. Attempting the life of Ens. Moses Carlton: 100 lashes. (44)

COREY, Ephraim, Lt. Colonel Prescott's Regiment. Forgery and defrauding the men of their pay and of their blanket money and coat money: cashiered. (133) (136) *See* Burris.

CORKER, Thomas. Desertion: death – pardoned on condition that he enlist for the duration of the war. (80)

CORKINS, Humphrey. Colonel McDougall's Regiment. Robbing Colonel Waterbury's store of rum: fine of twenty shillings in New York money. (99)

CORMICH, James. Colonel Sargent's Regiment. Desertion and mutiny: death by hanging. (7)

CORNING, Malicha. Captain Wyllys's Company. Hiring another person to do his duty: do forty-eight hours duty in the next tour. (91)

CORNING, Malicha. Captain Wyllys's Company. Neglect of duty and suffering a prisoner to make his escape when on sentinel: picketed for ten minutes. (91)

CORNWALL,_____, Corporal. Conspiring to desert to the enemy: reduced to the ranks. (89)

CORY, Ephraim, Lt. Enlisting a Negro slave, receiving a state bounty for said Negro, repeatedly leaving the camp, joining the regiment in an unprepared manner and not attending to his duty: dismissed from the service, and his pay be stopped till the accounts concerning public money he has received is known. (88)

CORY, William. Colonel Elliot's Regiment. Desertion: 100 lashes and serve out his year from the time he joined his regiment. (68) (98)

COSHALL, Thomas. Colonel Lamb's Regiment of Artillery. Desertion: fifty lashes – sentence declared illegal and a new trial ordered by the commander-in-chief. (14) (134) *See* Burress.

COTTEN,_____, Captain. Colonel Greaton's Regiment. Refusing to take his post: acquitted. (113)

COTTON, John, Sgt. Defrauding the regiment of part of the allowance for provisions: refund fourteen pounds, six shillings, and four pence to his regiment, and disqualified to serve as a quartermaster-sergeant in the future. (135)

COUCH, Joel. Raffling: reprimand. (91)

COURCHON, John Baptist. Desertion: run the gauntlet frontward and backwards. (80)

COURTLIDGE, Daniel. Colonel Wade's Regiment. Attempting to desert to the enemy: acquitted. (9)

COURTNEY,_____, Captain. Artillery. Leaving his howitzer in the field of action at Brandywine in a cowardly manner: reprimand by General Knox in the presence of all the artillery officers – sentence disapproved by the commander-in-chief and released without censure. (13) (134)

COURTNEY,_____, Sergeant. Disobedience to orders. (111)

COURTNEY, Hercules. Colonel Proctor's Regiment of Artillery. Neglect of duty in leaving camp when officer-of-the-day, disobedience, lodging outside camp without permission: dismissed from the service. (14)

COVILL,_____, Ensign. Fourth Massachusetts Regiment. Absenting himself from his regiment in excess of his furlough: cashiered. (58)

COWDREY, John. First New Hampshire Regiment. Killing a cow and stealing eleven geese: 100 lashes and pay fifteen dollars to the owner. (86)

COWELL, Joseph. First Massachusetts Regiment. Killing a cow and stealing eleven geese: 100 lashes and pay fifteen dollars to the owner. (86)

COWELL, Joseph. Light Company, Massachusetts Regiment. Killing a cow and seven geese: 100 lashes and a fine to pay for the stolen animals. (61) *See* Abram, Brayton, Carliss, Cook, Gardner, Jinks, Shea, Wood.

COWLES, Joseph. Maryland Regiment. Desertion: 100 lashes. (72)

COX,_____, Captain. Tenth Pennsylvania Regiment. Absenting himself from duty upwards of three months without leave: reprimand. (14)

COX, William. Second Virginia Regiment. Mutiny and desertion: 100 lashes – remitted. (134)

COYLE, Hugh. First Pennsylvania Regiment. Desertion: 100 lashes. (97) (129)

CRAFT, Edward, Capt. Colonel Gridley's Regiment of Artillery. Abusive language to Colonel Gridley: reprimand. (81) (104)

CRAIG, Jonathan. Fourth Maryland Regiment. Desertion: 100 lashes. (109) (121)

CRAIGE, John. Ninth Maryland Regiment. Desertion to the enemy: death. (69)

CRAINE, William. Artillery. Theft: thirty-nine lashes. (102)

CRAMMET, Moses. Colonel Poor's Regiment. Desertion and enlisting into another regiment: fifteen lashes. (117)

CRANDALL, Edward. Fourth Company. Exceeding the limits of his furlough nine days: acquitted. (91)

CRANE,_____, Lieutenant. Fifth Virginia Regiment. Disobedience to orders, breaking his arrest: acquitted. (134)

CRANE, Ambrose, Lt. Colonel Stewart's Regiment. Breaking his former arrest and going to Philadelphia in the company of two officers of the same regiment who were likewise under arrest: cashiered. (134)

CRANE, Nathaniel. Seventh Regiment. Exciting mutiny and speaking disrespectfully of an ensign: reduced to private and ask the ensign's pardon. (125)

CRARY, James. Colonel Hand's Regiment. Leaving the camp without leave, riotous behavior: thirty-nine lashes. (38) (136) *See* Leonard.

CRARY, Richard. Colonel Hand's Regiment. Leaving the camp without leave, riotous and drunken behavior: thirty lashes. (68) (136) *See* Leonard.

CRAVEN,_____, Lieutenant. First North Carolina Regiment. Abusive language, refusing to deliver to the inhabitants their horses which had been stolen from them by persons unknown, abusing and ill-treating his landlord, expressing himself disrespectfully and contemptuously of his commanding officer when directed to give up said horses, exacting an exorbitant sum of money from said inhabitants upon delivering them their horses: acquitted. Note: Upon review, Washington disagreed violently with the judgment and believed he actually was guilty as charged. (21)

CRAVEN, James, Lt. First North Carolina Regiment. Entering the tent of Lt. Richard Dickerson whilst he was in bed, disarming and striking him, acting in a disorderly manner, playing cards in camp: dismissed from the service. (26) *See* Baccart, Dickerson, Summers.

CRAWFORD, Jason. Fifth Connecticut Regiment. Desertion: 100 lashes. (22)

CRAWFORD, John. Seventh Massachusetts Regiment. Desertion: fifty lashes only, because of his former good conduct.

CRAWFORD, John, Drummer. Third South Carolina Regiment. Desertion and attempting to make his escape to the enemy: death by hanging. (95)

CRAWFORD, Samuel. Robbery: death by hanging–remitted. (26)

CRAWNS (?), William. Colonel Poor's Regiment. Desertion: thirty-nine lashes. (84)

CREATON, Robert. First Massachusetts Regiment. Killing a cow and stealing eleven geese: seventy-five lashes and pay fifteen dollars to the owner. (86)

CREGIER, Simon, Ens. Fourth New York Battalion. Stealing and plundering inhabitants when he was sent out with a party with express orders to protect them from plundering: cashiered and confined on board ship at Fort Montgomery until restitution is made. (131)

CRESS, Jacob, inhabitant of Pennsylvania. Stealing two cows, one of which he carried into Philadelphia: 100 lashes. (14)

CRESTY, John. Colonel Humphrey's Regiment. Desertion: thirty-nine lashes. (7) (71)

CRISTEE, John, Foragemaster. General Crumpton's Brigade. Giving certificates for a number of horses more than he had to the inhabitants of Schratenberg: acquitted. (36)

CRITCHET, Benjamin. First New Hampshire Regiment. Deserting and forging a discharge in the name of General Poor: run the gauntlet through 500 men in open order with a bayonet at his breast to regulate the pace. (111) *See* Allen, Fosgood.

CRONNONET (?), Moses. Colonel Poor's Regiment. Desertion and enlisting into another regiment: fifteen lashes. (84)

CROSBY,_____, Corporal. Concealing whiskey stolen by Stephen Root: reduced to a private sentinel. (124) *See* Root.

CROSGROVE (COSGRROVE), Edward. First Maryland Regiment. Stealing: thirty lashes. (93)

CROSMAN, William, Lt. Fifteenth Massachusetts Regiment. Frequently absent from camp without leave, being very inattentive to the company of which he had the command, disregarding the general orders by absenting himself from camp for two nights and part of two days while under marching orders: not guilty of the first charge but guilty of the other two charges—dismissed from the service, despite a recommendation that he be restored to duty. (26)

CROSS, Edward, Capt. Colonel Gridley's Regiment. Defrauding his men: severe reprimand. (2)

CROSSBY, Reuben, Batteauman: acquitted. (111)

CROSTON, William. Colonel Gridley's Regiment. Desertion, theft. (1)

CROWELL, Levi. Captain Whiting's Company. Taking boards from the barracks and cutting them up for his own use: fine of twenty shillings to pay for the boards. (91)

CROWELL, William. Colonel Nixon's Regiment. Leaving a post while on sentry and attempting to desert to the enemy: "The Court is of the opinion that said Crowell is *not compos* and ought to be immediately dismiss't the army." (133)

CROWLEY, Darby. Maryland Line. Desertion: death by hanging—pardoned. (115)

CRUETT,_____, Sergeant. Assisting and concealing stolen rum: reduced to a private sentinel. (47) *See* Annis, Ford, Pense, Tucker.

CRUMP,_____, Captain. First Virginia Regiment. Wantonly ordering Lieutenant Smith under his arrest when he knew he was executing the general orders, attempting to vindicate his conduct by giving false evidence to the court. (134)

CRUMP,_____, Captain. First Virginia Regiment. Cowardice: cashiered and his name and place of abode published in and about the camp, and in the particular state he belongs to, or in which he usually resides, "after which it shall be deemed scandalous for any officer to associate with him." (134)

CRUSE, Jonathan. First New Jersey Battalion. Desertion: guilty only of overstaying his furlough—reprimand. (112)

CULP, Phillip, inhabitant of Pennsylvania. Attempting to carry flour into Philadelphia: fifty lashes and be employed in some public work for the use of the Continentals; unless he should choose to enlist in the Continental service during the war. (9)

CUMMINGS,_____, Sergeant. Drunk on his post and abusing the guard: reduced to the ranks as a private but be restored to his former rank if his future conduct merits it. (77)

CUMMINGS, Thomas, Lt. Colonel Prescott's Regiment. Misbehavior in the action at Bunker Hill: acquitted. (104) (136)

CUMMINGS, Thomas, Lt. Behaving in a scandalous and infamous manner unbecoming an officer and a gentlemen: cashiered. (136)

CUMMINS,_____, Lieutenant. Colonel Phillips' Battalion. Absent without leave at a critical time: dismissed from the service. (118) (123)

CUNBY,_____. Ninth Massachusetts Regiment. Desertion: 100 lashes. (53)

CUNNINGHAM, Henry. Second Regiment. 100 lashes. (111)

CURBY, Charles. Third Company. Desertion: acquitted. (42)

CURRANS, Timothy. *See* Ciuvans.

CURTIS, David. Stealing: acquitted. (105)

CURTIS, Nathan. First Massachusetts Regiment. Killing a cow and stealing eleven geese: seventy-five lashes and pay fifteen dollars to the owner. (86)

CURTIS, Nathan. First Massachusetts Regiment. Breaking open the house of a citizen and insulting the inhabitants, attempting to kill Captain Frye and Captain Ellis in execution of their office, robbing them of a hat: acquitted. (64) *See* Blake, Smith.

CUTING, George. Colonel McDougall's Regiment. Desertion: thirty-nine lashes. (106)

CUTTING, Francis. Captain Craft's Company. Disobedience to orders and refusing to go on guard: acquitted. (104)

CUTTLER, Samuel. Colonel Jackson's Regiment. Desertion: 100 lashes. (28)

DAGGET, Colonel. Leaving his post without permission from the Commander-in-Chief's Department. (9)

DAGO, Peter, a transient Negro. Stealing a hat and losing or confiscating his gun: thirty stripes and confined till the hat is returned. (70)

DAIL, Samuel. Third Company. Being intoxicated when on sentry: acquitted. (65)

DAILEY, Jeremiah. Mutiny, riot, and disobedience to orders: fine of twenty shillings. (135)

DAILY, Daniel. Fourth Regiment of Light Dragoons. Desertion: 100 lashes – clemency granted. (21)

DAILY, Richard. Colonel Lamb's Regiment. Desertion and enlisting in another corps: 100 lashes. (85)

DALLY, John. Seventh Maryland Regiment. Desertion: 100 lashes. (103)

DANFORTH, Jonathan, Capt. Colonel Whitcomb's Regiment. Disobedience to orders, neglect of duty, not joining his regiment upon the march from Boston to New Hampshire, keeping some privates belonging to the regiment with him: acquitted with honor. (84) (117)

DANIEL, James. Colonel Ritzema's Regiment. Desertion: thirty-nine lashes and forfeit one month's pay. (74) (94)

DANIELS,_____, Captain. Colonel Wheelock's Regiment. Neglect of duty on his post: acquitted with honor. (84)

DANIELS,_____, Captain. Colonel Nixon's Regiment. Inattention to duty while under arms: acquitted with honor. (72)

DANIELS, George, Sailor on board the sloop *Enterprise*. Mutinous behavior: acquitted. (99)

DANIELVEONS, Daniel. Colonel McDougall's Regiment. Desertion: thirty-nine lashes. (106)

DARHART, Jahn. Tenth Pennsylvania Regiment. Attempted desertion to the enemy: death. (112)

DATTON, William. Released from confinement for lack of prosecution. (81)

DAUGHERTY,_____, Lieutenant. Sixth Maryland Regiment. Sending Captain Beall a challenge to fight a duel, associating and playing ball with sergeants: cashiered. (21)

DAVIDS, William, Sgt. Colonel Holmes's Regiment. Abusing his captain: reduced to a private sentinel and a fine of one month's pay, and confined fourteen days in the dungeon. (118)

DAVIDSON, James, Quartermaster. Colonel Livingston's Regiment. Defrauding the soldiers of their provisions, embezzling Continental property and disposing of several articles belonging to the United States: cashiered. (103)

DAVIDSON, Joel. Second Massachusetts Regiment. Desertion: fifty lashes only, in consideration of his youth. (54)

DAVIDSON (DAVISON), John, Cpl. Colonel Bridges's Regiment. Quitting his post when on duty: fifteen lashes—pardoned because of his youth and ignorance of his duty. (136)

DAVIES,_____. Colonel Angell's Regiment. Cashiered with infamy. (15)

DAVIS,_____, Lieutenant. Colonel Angell's Regiment. Swearing, threatening to be sick in order not to do a tour of duty: dismissed from the service. (134)

DAVIS, Charles. Light Company. Abusing a sergeant: reprimand and beg the sergeant's pardon at the head of the regiment. (50)

DAVIS, Daniel. Captain Williams's Company. Absent without leave: seventy-five lashes. (91)

DAVIS, David. Fifth Connecticut Regiment. Quarreling, abusing, swearing, and striking his superior officers: guilty of profane swearing—fine of one shilling. Guilty of assaulting his officer—twenty-four hours confinement in the guardhouse and ask the pardon of the officer, or upon refusal to do so, ride the wooden horse one hour. (127)

DAVIS, Henry. Colonel McDougall's Regiment. Desertion: thirty lashes. (1)

DAVIS, Henry. Colonel McDougall's Regiment. Desertion: twenty lashes. (132) (136)

DAVIS, Israel, Capt. Colonel Wigglesworth's Regiment. Fraudulently detaining two months' pay drawn by him belonging to Silas Tibbets, a soldier, obtaining a sum of money of Massachusetts currency, the property of soldiers due them: not guilty of the first charge but guilty of the second charge—cashiered and refund the money. (14) (134) *See* chapter two.

DAVIS, John. First New Jersey Regiment. Marauding: death—pardoned. (44) *See* Gibbs.

DAVIS, John. Colonel Bigelow's Regiment. Stealing cloth from an inhabitant: fifty stripes and pay for the cloth. (24)

DAVIS, John. Colonel McDougall's Regiment. Mutiny and sedition: thirty-nine lashes. (1) (68)

DAVIS, John. Captain Hamilton's Company. Desertion: thirty-nine lashes. (6)

DAVIS, Jonathan. Colonel Ritzema's Regiment. Desertion: thirty-nine lashes. (132) (136)

DAVIS, Jonathan. Plundering the inhabitants of money, and other offenses: acquitted. (33)

DAVIS, Patrick. Insolence to Lieutenant Morris of the Seventh Maryland Regiment: 100 lashes. (93)

DAVIS, Patrick. Delaware Regiment. Abusing Sergeant Jordan in his duty: fifty lashes.

DAVIS, Patt. Delaware Regiment. Abusing an inhabitant, Mr. Dennison, in his residence: 100 lashes. (93) *See* Caim.

DAVIS, Peter. Ninth Virginia Regiment. Desertion: death. (36)

DAVIS, Samuel, Lt. Third Massachusetts Regiment. Exceeding the limits of his furlough by thirty days: reprimand and a fine for the time he was absent in excess of his furlough. (50)

DAVIS, William, Drummer. Colonel Greene's Regiment. Raising a mutiny and behaving in a disorderly manner: not guilty of the first charge but guilty of the second charge—suspended and reprimanded. (131) *See* Baptist, Brown, Buck, Cary, Dunbar, Goold, Hardin, Lane, Luis, Park, Peterson, Tabor.

DAVIS, William. Colonel Swift's Regiment. Stealing for a third time: 100 lashes and sent on board one of the Continental guard ships in the

North River at Fort Montgomery, there to be kept at hard labor during the war. (131)

DAVIS, William. Sixth South Carolina Regiment. Desertion: 100 lashes. (5)

DAWNEY, Timothy. Colonel Learned's Regiment. Attempting to stab Joseph Lafflin, assaulting John Phipps, snapping a loaded musket at Luther Brouty: thirty-nine lashes and drummed out of the army. (136)

DAWS, William. Colonel Jackson's Regiment. Disobedience to orders, refusing to give a tent to cover the soldiers who were exposed to the severity of the storm, he being alone in the tent with sufficient room for another officer: reprimand. (104)

DAWSON, John. Third Regiment of Artillery. Desertion, and also desertion from the Tenth Massachusetts Regiment in 1777: 100 lashes. (124)

DAY, David. Captain Whiting's Company. Taking boards from the barracks and cutting them up for his own use: fine of twenty shillings to pay for the boards. (91)

DAY, Jonathan. Second Regiment of Light Dragoons. Desertion and enlisting in the York Levies: 100 lashes. (44) *See* Dodge.

DEAMES, Joseph. Desertion: 100 lashes. (42)

DeAMMONS (DEARMONT), John. Colonel Angell's Regiment. Attempting to pass the sentries of General Hand's Brigade, endeavoring to persuade the sentinel who stopped him to leave his post and go off with him: death. (30)

DEARLOVE, William. Fourth Pennsylvania Battalion. Stealing money from Fred Buzzard: 100 lashes. (134)

DEBOS, Luke. Desertion: 100 lashes. (101)

DEER, John. General Stark's Brigade. Riding public horses, plundering: acquitted. (100)

DeERMON, John. Colonel Angell's Regiment. Gravely abusing Katherine Stover, an inhabitant of Morristown, threatening to set her house afire: 100 lashes. (29)

DEETZ, Peter. Colonel Proctor's Regiment. Desertion: 100 lashes. (12)

DeFLORIS, Anthony. Killing a hog: fifty lashes. (91)

DeHARD, John. Colonel Nichols' Regiment. Desertion: twenty lashes. (118)

DeHAVEN, Joseph, inhabitant of Pennsylvania. Attempting to carry provisions to the enemy at Philadelphia: acquitted. (14)

DELAND, Barney. Sixth Pennsylvania Regiment. Attempting to desert and persuading a number of others to desert with him: not guilty of the first charge but guilty of the second charge – 100 lashes. (14) *See* Kennedy.

DELAND, Jacob, Cpl. Captain Cogswell's Company. Absent without leave at unreasonable hours of the night: reduced to a private sentinel. (124)

DELANO, Amosa. Colonel Cotton's Regiment. Desertion: fifteen lashes – pardoned. (120)

DELENO, Aaron. Absenting himself from camp four days without leave: fifty lashes – remitted. (66)

DELEY, John. Captain Sackett's Company. Stealing shirts when on guard: released when no evidence was presented. (128)

DELMONT, Jewell. Second Regiment of Artillery. Desertion: 100 lashes. (42)

DEMPSEY, John. Eleventh Pennsylvania Regiment. Desertion: run the brigade gauntlet once a week for two weeks, from right to left and left to right each time. (112)

DEMPSEY, Luke. Maryland Line. Desertion and joining the enemy: death by hanging – pardoned. (115)

DENNIS, Basil. Desertion: 100 lashes only, because he was in liquor and over-persuaded by Phillips. (93) *See* Phillips.

DENNIS, John. Colonel Graham's Regiment. Desertion from the advance guard, getting drunk: twenty-four lashes for the first offense and twenty lashes for the second offense. (123) *See* Young.

DENNIS, Joseph. Colonel Topham's Regiment. Playing cards while on guard: reduced to a private sentry. (68)

DENNIS, Joseph. Colonel Lash's Regiment. Joining in mutiny and sedition: thirty-nine lashes, with thirteen lashes administered on three successive days, and confined for one month. (132) (136)

DENNISTON,_____, Lieutenant. Second New York Regiment. Absenting himself from camp without permission: reprimand. (58)

DENSLOW, M., Lieutenant. Third Connecticut Regiment. Exceeding the terms of his furlough by seven days: acquitted. (50)

DERRAH, Commissary. Beating a soldier belonging to Colonel Hall's Regiment: reprimand. (93)

DESHART, Henry. Commander-in-Chief's Guard. Going out with others, with sidearms, to do harm to other soldiers: acquitted. (125)

DESIHES, John. Desertion: 100 lashes with switches. (95)

DeTRAVILLE,_____, Captain. Corps of Artillery. Fraud and other charges: acquitted. (90)

DeVALLEILLE,_____, Lieutenant. Quitting his post without leave: acquitted. (90)

DEVANCE, Hugh. Colonel Livingston's Regiment. Desertion and forging a pass: 500 lashes. (83) (84)

DEVANE,_____, Sergeant. Neglect of duty: reprimand. (27)

DEVANE, John. Colonel Angell's Regiment. Desertion to the enemy and carrying with him a guard boat: death. (23)

DeVERNESURE,_____, Captain. Light Horse. Disobedience to orders and insulting Colonel Stone in the execution of his duty: ask the colonel's pardon. (93)

DEVINS, Joseph. Third Massachusetts Regiment. Desertion: 100 lashes. (54)

DEVORS,_____, Lieutenant. Third Maryland Regiment. Disobedience to orders and absent without leave: reprimand. (69)

DeWITT,_____, Captain. Colonel Humphries' Regiment. Liberating James McCormick, a soldier in Colonel Sargent's Regiment, from the main guard, who was under sentence of death: acquitted because no crime had been lodged against the prisoner on the captain's list. (74)

DEXTER, Oliver, Lt. Colonel Angell's Regiment. Refusing to do his duty: dismissed from the service with infamy. (19)

DEXTER, Thomas. Colonel Angell's Regiment. Desertion to the enemy: 100 lashes and make up the time he lost. (33)

DIAMONT, John, Capt. Third New Hampshire Regiment. Disobedience to orders and neglect of duty in not going to Amherst in New Hampshire and doing the duty he was ordered to do: acquitted. (116)

DICKERSON,_____, Lieutenant. Infamous and scandalous behavior: dismissed from the service and the sentence be published in the newspapers of Pennsylvania. (14)

DICKERSON,_____, Corporal. Fourth Pennsylvania Regiment. Disobedience to orders: acquitted. (112)

DICKERSON, Richard, Lt. Clandestinely searching an officer's book of accounts and publishing part of the contents; taking an oath of First Lieutenant, when he actually was a Second Lieutenant; ordering soldiers to arm for his own personal safety without just cause; refusing to give his evidence when called before a court-martial; engaging to mind a soldier's watch, for which he was to receive a reward; deviating from the truth in a court-martial: guilty of a portion of the charges – dismissed from the service. (26) *See* Baccart, Craven, Summers.

DICKINSON, Nemiah. Absent from camp without leave: thirty lashes. (43)

DICKSON, John. Third Massachusetts Regiment. Desertion: 100 lashes. (52)

DIETY, Lewis. Second Regiment of Artillery. Repeated desertion: death – pardoned. (42)

DIGGS, William. Colonel Baldwin's Regiment. Desertion: twenty lashes. (132) (136)

DILWORTH, James. Colonel Moyland's Regiment of Light Dragoons. Desertion and attempting to go to the enemy: acquitted. (93)

DINGLEY, Levi. Colonel Cotton's Regiment. Desertion: fifteen lashes – pardoned. (120)

DITCH, Mathia. Maryland Line. Plundering: acquitted. (49)

DIVIER, Timothy. Colonel Vose's Regiment. Desertion and enlisting twice and taking two bounties: eighty lashes and refund the second bounty. (88)

DODGE, _____, Sergeant. Losing his arms and accouterments: ordered to a re-trial. (27)

DODGE, Nathan. General Spencer's Regiment. Desertion: ten lashes and a fine of fifty-two shillings to pay for the cost of his apprehension. (105)

DODGE, Stephen. Second Regiment of Light Dragoons. Desertion and reenlisting in the York Levies: 100 lashes. (44) *See* Day.

DODSON, John, Sgt. South Carolina Regiment. Threatening to kill Lieutenant Lewis: acquitted. (95)

DOLLY, Jeremiah. Second Massachusetts Regiment. Desertion and attempting to go to the enemy: 100 lashes. (50)

DOMANACK, Ebenezer. Second Maryland Regiment. Leaving camp without permission, breaking into a house taking a quantity of bacon threatenting the life of an inhabitant: 100 lashes. (115)

DOMINE, _____, Lieutenant. Colonel Livingston's Regiment. Disobedience to orders: acquitted. (128)

DOMINGES, Lewis. First Regiment. Desertion: 100 lashes with switches. (95)

DOMINIQUE, Benjamin. Raising and propagating an impudent and scandalous lie against the character of General Gist: acquitted. (121)

DANAGHY, Thomas, Sgt. Colonel Livingston's Regiment. Getting drunk on post: reduced to the ranks. (94)

DONALDSON, Isaac. Colonel DuBois's Regiment. Sleeping on his post: fifty lashes. (131)

DONALDSON, Thomas, Cpl. Colonel Spencer's Regiment. Stopping Captain Hawkins and Captain Cherry on the road under pretense of authority: reduced to the ranks and 100 lashes. (25) (103) *See* Allen.

DONALDSON, Thomas. Captain Heron's Company. Being drunk on his post: 150 lashes. (93)

DONNALLY, John. Colonel Whitcomb's Regiment. Desertion and enlisting in another regiment: thirty-nine lashes for each offense. (117)

DONNELLY, Patrick, Ens. Seventh Maryland Regiment. Ordering returns to be made of men's names whose terms expired: reprimand. (110)

DONNIT, John, Capt. New Hampshire Regiment. Disobedience to orders, neglect of duty: acquitted. (33)

DONNSIMAN, Daniel. Fourth Georgia Continental Battallion. Desertion: ninety-nine lashes. (90)

DONOHOO, Patrick. Embezzling public stores: fine of thirty dollars and run the gauntlet twice through the whole garrison. (103)

DONOHU, Arthur. Maryland Line. Desertion and joining the enemy: guilty only of joining the enemy—death. (115)

DONOVAN,_____, Lieutenant and Adjutant. Sixth Maryland Regiment. Warning and insisting upon a lieutenant doing duty out of his tour: acquitted, because there was merely a misunderstanding. (110)

DONVERS, William. Captain Moor's Company. Stealing a five dollar bill from Sergeant McCaim: 500 lashes and pay the sergeant the five dollars—300 lashes remitted. (93)

DORAGHTY, Charles, Sgt. Colonel Livingston's Regiment. Getting drunk and leaving his post: reduced to the ranks. (83)

DORCHESTER, Alexander. Breaking open and robbing a store: thirty-nine lashes and a fine of thirty shillings—remitted. (91)

DORMAN, Thomas. Maryland Line. Desertion: 100 lashes. (21)

DOUGHERTY, Francis. Being insolent, drunkenness: fifty lashes. (93)

DOUGHERTY, James. Second New Jersey Regiment. Desertion: 100 lashes. (101)

DOUGLAS, George, Lt. Col. McDougall's Regiment. Mutiny and sedition: acquitted. (1) (132)

DOUGLASS, Jon. Captain Moody's Company. Absent from camp, abusing the inhabitants: guilty only of the first charge — stand on a picket with his bare feet for fifteen minutes. (125)

DOUTTY, Ichabod. Desertion: 100 lashes. (42)

DOW, Abner. Ninth Massachusetts Regiment. Not joining his regiment when ordered to do so by the commanding officer: cashiered. (44)

DOW, Nathan. Killing an ox belonging to an inhabitant: acquitted. (39) *See* Brooks, Carey, Dupee, Holmes, Hunsberry, Jackson.

DOWD,_____, Sergeant. Burning a tent: acquitted because the fire was an accident. (93)

DOWLEY, Joseph. Stealing bread from a corporal: fifty lashes. (23)

DOWNER, Ezra. Desertion: fifty lashes. (41)

DOWNING, Timothy. Desertion: thirty-nine lashes and drummed out of the army, "as he is worthless and incorrigible." (136)

DOWNS, Thomas. General Patterson's Brigade. Desertion, after breaking away from the guard: 100 lashes. (75) *See* Poor.

DOWRY, Joseph. Captain Carr's Company. Stealing and wasting public stores when on sentry: sixty lashes. (75)

DOWZICK, Goshen. Colonel Gallup's Regiment. Neglecting to join his company when detached for one month's service: released because he had been engaged on board the ship *Trumbull* prior to being detached. (82)

DOYLE, Matthew. Colonel Crane's Regiment. Drunkenness on duty: fifty lashes. (12)

DOYLE, Thomas. Colonel Webb's Regiment. Desertion: thirty-nine lashes. (131)

DOYLE, Thomas. Desertion: 100 lashes. (131)

DRAKE,_____, Lieutenant. Colonel Phillips' Regiment. Leaving his regiment without permission, absent twenty days: acquitted. (7) (118)

DRAKE, Benjamin. Colonel Livingston's Regiment. Desertion: fifty lashes. (131)

DRAKE, Seth. Selling his blanket: thirty lashes—pardoned, because of his former good behavior. (23) *See* Richards, Rhodes.

DRESHALL, Jeremiah. Fourth Maryland Regiment. Desertion to the enemy in March 1777, bearing arms against the United States: 100 lashes—remitted. (110) *See* Price.

DRESKELL, Timothy. Second Virginia Regiment. Mutiny and desertion: 100 lashes—remitted. (134)

DREW, Levi. Colonel Cotton's Regiment. Desertion: fifteen lashes—pardoned. (120)

DRIEL, John. Colonel Arnold's Regiment. Refusing to obey Colonel Arnold's order: fined one month's pay and immediately to join Captain Smith's company, according to Colonel Arnold's order. (128)

DRINKWATER, Ebenezer. Second Connecticut Regiment. Desertion on two occasions: 200 lashes, with 100 lashes administered at two different times. (48)

DRISKELL (DRESKELL), Timothy. Second Virginia Regiment. Attempting to desert to the enemy: 100 lashes. (134)

DRIVER, Edward. Second Virginia Regiment. Mutiny and desertion: reprimand. (134)

DRYASE,_____. Colonel Jackson's Regiment. Desertion: thirty-nine lashes—remitted. (23)

DUBEE, John, Capt. Canadian Old Regiment. Striking a lieutenant of that regiment: death. (44)

DUFFEY (DUFFY), John. Delaware Regiment. Desertion to the enemy: 100 lashes. (69) (103)

DUFFY,_____. Breaking his arrest and going six miles from camp without leave: pardoned. (134)

DUFFY,_____, Captain. Fourth Regiment of Artillery. Scandalous and infamous behavior by drawing a sword on Captain Ballard and attempting to stab him, firing a pistol at him when unarmed, seizing from Lieutenant Blewer a loaded pistol, snapping the same at him when he tried to intervene: dismissed from the service. (44)

DUFFY,_____, Captain. Aiding and abetting a riot, insulting and abusing Major Howard in the execution of his office: reprimand. (88) *See* Howard.

DUFFY, James. Desertion: released when no evidence was presented. (93)

DUGGAN, James. Third Connecticut Regiment. Desertion and attempting to go to the enemy: not guilty of the first charge but guilty of the second charge—100 lashes. (50)

DULHAGEN (DULHAGER), Frederick. Colonel McDougall's Regiment. Desertion: thirty-nine lashes, with thirteen lashes administered on three successive days. (132) (136)

DUMMING, William. Sixth North Carolina Battalion. Desertion: 100 lashes. (95)

DUN,_____, Corporal. Maryland Detachment. Having premeditated a plan to desert and endeavoring to get others to go with him: acquitted. (78)

DUN, David. Supplying the enemy with cattle: 250 lashes. (14)

DUNBAR, Charles. Sleeping on his post when a sentinel: fifteen lashes. (123)

DUNBAR, John, Sgt. Colonel Greene's Regiment. Raising a mutiny and behaving in a disorderly manner: not guilty of the first charge but guilty of the second charge—suspended and reprimand. (131) *See* Baptist, Brown, Buck, Cary, Davis, Goold, Hardin, Lane, Luis, Park, Peterson, Tabor.

DUNCAN, George. Colonel McDougall's Regiment. Disobedience to orders of his officers and issuing threats: twenty-one lashes—pardoned. (118)

DUNHAM, John. Stealing and being an accessory to stealing several articles of clothing and silver spoons from an inhabitant of Danbury: fifty lashes. (53) *See* Clements, Perry, Wilton.

DUNIVAN, Antony. Captain Anson's Company. Absenting himself from camp and selling his regimental arms (?) and ammunition: 100 lashes. (89)

DUNKIN, Daniel. Eighty lashes. (42)

DUNLEY, Edward. Theft. (1)

DUNN,_____, Lieutenant. Colonel Patton's Regiment. Striking Lieutenant Street: acquitted. (9) (134)

DUNN, David, civilian. Trying to supply the enemy with cattle: 200 lashes. (134)

DUNN, John, Sailor on board the sloop *Enterprise*. Mutinous behavior: acquitted. (99)

DUNN, Joseph, Cpl. Colonel Topham's Regiment. Playing cards: reduced to private. (98)

DUPEE, Anthony. Killing an ox belonging to an inhabitant: acquitted. (39) *See* Brooks, Cary, Dow.

DURANT, Benjamin. Colonel Bailey's Regiment. Drunk on guard: thirty lashes. (132) (136)

DURNIER,_____, Lieutenant. Colonel Patton's Regiment. Striking and acting in an ungentlemanly manner: acquitted. (15)

DUST, John. Desertion: thirty lashes. (77)

DUTTON, M. Second Connecticut Regiment. Desertion: 100 lashes. (46)

DYAR, Samuel. Rhode Island Regiment. Desertion and joining the enemy: death. (58)

DYERS, James. Desertion: 100 lashes. (42)

EARL, John, Sgt. Major. Colonel Topham's Regiment. Disobedience to orders: reduced to the ranks—restored to his rank later. (98)

EATON,_____, Lieutenant. Third Regiment of Artillery. Exceeding his furlough six days: acquitted. (124)

EATON,_____, Sergeant. Abusing and striking a soldier: reprimand. (23)

EATON,_____, Sergeant. Disobedience to orders, sneaking out of camp: reduced to private. (23) *See* Nichols, Rolf, Whitney.

EDGECOMB, Ezra. Captain Walker's Company. Absenting himself without leave: twenty-seven lashes and a fine of forty shillings to pay for the clothes which he lost. (91)

EDGELL, George. Colonel Ritzema's Regiment. Getting drunk and damning his officers: thirty-nine lashes. (36)

EDMONSON, William, Wagonmaster. Maryland Division. Defrauding the wagoners by neglecting to pay them for the month of August, when he had drawn money for that purpose: acquitted. (28)

EDMUNDS,_____, Sergeant-Major. Mutiny: acquitted of mutiny but guilty of behavior contrary to good order and military discipline—reduced to the ranks. (90)

EDWARDS, Joseph, inhabitant of Pennsylvania. Attempting to drive cattle to the enemy: fine of 100 pounds and confined to the provost guard till the sum is paid; also pay twenty dollars to each of the light horsemen who apprehended the prisoner as an encouragement of their activity and their good conduct, the residue of the sum to be applied for the use of the sick at camp. (14) (134)

EDWARDS, Josiah. Theft and desertion: death. (26)

EDWARDS, Robert. Second Virginia Regiment. Mutiny and desertion: 100 lashes—remitted. (134)

EDWARDS, William. General Stark's Brigade. Riding public horses, plundering: eighty-five lashes. (100)

EGANS, Joshua. Third Regiment. Desertion: acquitted. (111)

EGGES, Elijah. Second New Jersey Regiment. Desertion: 100 lashes. (25)

EGGLESTON, Azeriah, Ens. and Q.M. Colonel Vose's Regiment. Fraud: acquitted. (24)

EGINS, Joshua. Third New York Regiment. Repeated desertions: death. (108)

ELEY, Samuel, Capt. Actions unbecoming an officer: acquitted. (14)

ELIOT, William, Superintendent and director of pack horses. Neglect of duty: acquitted. (96)

ELISS,_____, Light Artillery. Contemptuous behavior toward Captain Jackson of the Third Regiment of Artillery: reprimand. (43)

ELLIOT, Henry. Second New York Regiment. Desertion: acquitted. (25)

ELLIS, Francis. Mutiny, riot, and disobedience to orders: fine of twenty shillings. (135)

ELLIS, Joseph. Fifth New York Regiment. Desertion: 100 lashes. (111)

ELLIS, William. Leaving his detachment, taking the property of other soldiers: guilty of the first charge but not guilty of the second charge. (42)

ELLWILL, O. Fifth Connecticut Regiment. Desertion: 100 lashes. (48)

ELMER, Moses, Dr. Second New York Regiment. Scandalous and disorderly conduct: reprimand. (51)

ELSWORTH, Henry. Captain Burns's Company. Desertion: thirty-nine lashes—pardoned. (118) (123)

EMERSLY, John. Stealing and selling clothing belonging to Catherina Gastner: 100 lashes and pay for the clothing in the amount of forty-five dollars for the stockings and sleeve buttons not yet found. (103)

EMERY, Wesley. Colonel Arnold's Regiment. Refusing to obey Colonel Arnold's order: fined one month's pay and immediately to join Captain Smith's company, according to Colonel Arnold's order. (128)

ENCE, David. Sixth Virginia Regiment. Letting four prisoners escape from the guard house: acquitted. (21)

ENGLISH,_____, Adjutant. Ordering and warning Lieutenant Troy for duty when it was not his tour: reprimand. (11)

ENGLISH, John. Thirty-fourth Regiment of Foot Soldiers. Mutiny and encouraging mutiny: fine of fifteen shillings and fifteen days fatigue duty. (3) (133) (136) *See* Huntington.

ENGLISH, John. Colonel Arnold's Regiment. Absenting himself from his regiment and enlisting in another regiment: ten lashes and repay the advance pay given him. (136)

ENGLISH, Joseph. Tenth Pennsylvania Regiment. Attempted desertion to the enemy: death. (112)

ENGLISH, Patrick. Delaware Regiment. Changing his clothes and name, and reenlisting in one of the New Jersey regiments: 100 lashes. (21)

ENGLISH, Robert, Gunner. Captain Moody's Company. Straggling from camp: reprimand. (125)

ENGLISH, William. Maryland Line. Desertion: 100 lashes. (21)

ENOS, Colonel. Leaving his commanding officer without permission or orders, and returning to Cambridge: acquitted. (133)

ENSLIN,_____, Lieutenant. Colonel Marcum's Company. Attempting to commit sodomy, perjury in swearing to a false account: dismissed from the service with infamy and drummed out of camp. (14) (134) *See* Maxwell.

ERSKINE,_____, Lieutenant. Striking a wagoner: acquitted. (93)

ESSEX, James, Batteauman. Disobedience to orders: twenty lashes. (111)

EVANS, Abel. First Pennsylvania Regiment. Desertion: fifty lashes. (97)

EVANS, Abel. Desertion: 100 lashes. (129)

EVANS, Benjamin. Insolent behavior to Lieutenant Randall: fatigue duty till such time as it shall appear to Captain Gridley that there is a reformation in him and he has asked the pardon of Lieutenant Randall. (104)

EVANS, Emanual. Third New Jersey Regiment. Desertion to the enemy: death. (26)

EVANS, John. Colonel Ritzema's Regiment. Desertion: thirty-nine lashes. (1)

EVANS, John. Colonel McDougall's Regiment. Desertion: thirty-nine lashes. (132)

EVANS, John, inhabitant of Pennsylvania. Attempting to send provisions into Philadelphia: sent to Carlisle to be employed in some work for the benefit of the public during the continuance of the enemy in the state. (9)

EVANS, Nathaniel. Third New Jersey Regiment. Desertion to the enemy, and taking up arms against the States: death. (27)

EVANS, Samuel, Foragemaster. Making false charges regarding forage, forging receipts: forfeit three months' pay. (62)

EVENDON, Edward. Second New Jersey Battalion. Desertion: twenty-five lashes. (101)

EVINS,_____, Lieutenant. Colonel Morrow's Regiment. Alarming the camp by firing guns: reprimand. (96)

EWELL,_____, Captain. First Virginia Regiment. Embezzling money, property of several soldiers; embezzling clothing, the property of the public: not guilty of the first charge but guilty of the second charge and reprimanded – sentence disapproved by the commander-in-chief. (72)

EWELL, Thomas, Capt. Second Virginia Regiment. Maliciously, basely, and falsely traducing officers of the regiment and afterwards acknowledging before several officers that what he had said were palpable lies and without foundation, endeavoring an officer to conceal and support a calumny by offering to secure a loan of money for the said officer: reprimand. (21)

EWING,_____, Captain. Misbehaving before the enemy: reprimand. (93)

EWING,_____, Foragemaster. Having three horses and collars, and other articles, the property of the public: dismissed from the service. (115)

FABRO, Joseph. Striking and threatening the lives of Lt. Charles F. Weissenfels in the Fourth New York Regiment and Ens. Daniel D. Danston: acquitted. (26) *See* Slater, Thorn.

FAIRES,_____, Sergeant. Delaware Regiment. Fighting and abusing Sergeant McGinnis: acquitted. (93) *See* McGinnis.

FARBEN, John. Second New Jersey Battalion. Desertion: pardoned. (112)

FARMER,_____, Ensign. Striking Thomas Allen, a soldier: acquitted with honor since Allen was insolent and disobedient to his order. (93)

FARMER, James. First New Jersey Regiment. Straggling from camp, killing a number of hogs: twenty-five lashes—pardoned. (20)

FARREL, James. Seventh Maryland Regiment. Intention to desert: death. (21)

FARRELL, George. Desertion: 100 lashes. (102)

FARRIS, William. Ninth Pennsylvania Regiment. Drinking, threatening the life of a soldier, striking the corporal of the guard after being confined: thirty lashes. (14)

FASSETT, Amos. Mutiny: thirty-nine lashes. (84)

FASSETT, Jonathan, Capt. Deserting his post without orders or without being attacked or forced by the enemy: cashiered and pay damages to the inhabitants of Onion River due to his unofficerlike retreat. (84) *See* Lyon, Perry, Wright.

FATHOM,_____, Ensign. Virginia Line. Sleeping on guard and suffering a captain to take him and his guard prisoners without discovery of him, suffering part of his guard to go into the country plundering: not guilty of the last charge but guilty of the other charges—cashiered. (115)

FAY, Micijah. Fifth Massachusetts Regiment. Desertion: 100 lashes. (44)

FAY, Patrick. Colonel McDougall's Regiment. Running away supposing he was pursued by the enemy, throwing away his firelock: kept at fatigue continually during the campaign. (99)

FAY, William. Captain Walker's Company. Absent without leave: twenty lashes—pardoned. (91)

FELTON, John. Colonel Hardenburgh's Regiment. Desertion: thirty-nine lashes. (123)

FENAN, Richard. Light Company. Fifty lashes. (53)

FENEY, John. Tenth Pennsylvania Regiment. Desertion: acquitted. (14)

FENNER, Antram. The General's Guard. Out at an unreasonable time of night, abusing a lieutenant: 100 lashes—pardoned because of former good conduct. (19) *See* Quimble.

FENWICK, Baptist. *See* Benick, Baptist.

FEOTHE, John. First New Jersey Regiment. Straggling from camp and killing a number of hogs, the property of the inhabitants: acquitted. (103)

FERREL, Patrick. Captain McConnell's Company. Being drunk and attempting to desert: 200 lashes. (93)

FERRICK, John. Third New York Regiment. Desertion: 100 lashes. (111)

FERRIS, Henry. Colonel Jackson's Regiment. Plundering the inhabitants while near Paramus: acquitted. (33)

FERRIS, Nathan, Lt. Colonel Swift's Regiment. Drunk and incapable of doing his duty when the army engaged the enemy: cashiered. (134)

FERRIS, Sam. Colonel Holmes's Regiment. Sleeping on his post: fine of four shillings – pardoned. (118)

FESSENDEN (TRESANDER), Joseph. Mutiny, riot, and disobedience to orders: fine of twenty shillings – remitted. (135)

FEYNER, Edward. Maryland Line. Plundering: acquitted. (49)

FICKLIN, William. Second Georgia Continental Battalion. Desertion: 100 lashes – pardoned. (90)

FIELD,_____, Sergeant. Colonel McDougall's Regiment. Pardoned. (118)

FIELD, Oliver. Neglect of duty: acquitted for want of evidence. (91)

FINDAMS, John, Ens. Colonel Hartley's Regiment. Desertion to the enemy and enlisting with them: guilty of desertion but not enlisting with them – death. (93)

FINDLY, John. Fourth South Carolina Battalion. Desertion: 100 lashes with switches, at four different times. (108)

FININGHAM, John. Getting drunk when ordered on duty, leaving the ranks when marching to the parade: twelve lashes. (118) (123)

FINLEY, James, Sgt. Captain Price's Company of Riflemen. Expressing himself disrespectfully of the Continental association and drinking General Gage's health: deprived of his arms and accouterments, put on a horse cart with a rope around his neck and drummed out of the army; rendered forever incapable of ever serving in the Continental Army. (135)

FINN, Henry. Colonel Jackson's Regiment. 100 lashes. (23)

FINNAY, Whitey. Massachusetts Regiment. Desertion: fifty lashes. (44)

FINNY, Jasper. Seventh Regiment. Exciting mutiny and speaking disrespectfully of an ensign: reduced to a private and ask the ensign's pardon. (125)

FISH, Benjamin. Ninth Massachusetts Regiment. Desertion: 100 lashes. (86)

FISHER, Bartholomew, Foragemaster. Defrauding the officers of the army in general, and General Putnam in particular, of part of their allowance of grain for the month of April: acquitted. (64)

FISHER, George. Disobedience to orders: fifty lashes – pardoned. (23)

FISHER, Henry. Maryland Line. Desertion: 100 lashes. (49)

FISHER, Richard. Fourth Regiment of Light Dragoons. Robbing money from a house in the State of New Jersey: 100 lashes. (21) *See* Gray, Zimmerman.

FISK,_____, Sergeant. Colonel Lamb's Regiment. Acquitted. (85)

FISK (FISH), Joseph, Lt. Colonel Durkee's Regiment. Leaving the regiment he belongs to while on march toward the enemy, being disguised much with liquor: not guilty of the first charge but guilty of the second charge – reprimand. (134)

FISK (FISH), Joseph, Lt. Colonel Durkee's Regiment. Squandering away public stores: return the stores to the public warehouse and forfeit pay for the damages. (13)

FITCH, Caleb. Second Connecticut Regiment. Desertion: 100 lashes, with twenty-five lashes being administered on four successive mornings. (56)

FITCH, William. Death – pardoned. (95)

FITZGERALD, Cornelius. First Georgia Continental Battalion. Desertion: death by hanging. (90)

FITZGERALD, Nichols. Seventh Maryland Regiment. Desertion and attempting to go to the enemy: death. (69)

FITZGERALD, Thomas. Desertion: 100 lashes – pardoned. (85)

FITZGERALD, Thomas. Attempting to desert to the enemy and enticing others to do the same. (42) *See* Bingham, Price, Van Wert, Walden.

FITZGERALD, Thomas, inhabitant of Pennsylvania. Attempting to relieve the enemy with provisions: 100 lashes. (9)

FITZPATRICK,_____, Captain. Fourth Virginia Regiment. Stealing a horse and detaining a stray horse without advertising him: acquitted. (110)

FLAC, Benjamin. Captain Dusten's Company. Disobedience to orders, absenting himself from camp without leave, taking his firelock to pieces and losing part of it: forty lashes. (43)

FLAGG,_____, Captain. Neglect of duty, suffering the Marquis de Lafayette to pass without being stopped or challenged: acquitted. (13) *See* Laird.

FLECHER, John, Sgt. Light Infantry. Getting drunk on duty: reduced to rank of sentinel. (91)

FLEMING, Samuel, Foragemaster. Neglect of duty in not furnishing the horses with forage sufficient, disobeying orders, refusing to look out for any more forage, making the horses unfit for service: guilty only of disobeying an order—dismissed from the service. (21)

FLEMMING, Jeremiah, Wagonmaster. Desertion: acquitted. (108)

FLETCHER, Duncan. First North Carolina Regiment. Attempting to desert to the enemy: death—pardoned, upon a plea from a "Mrs. Rutledge and other ladies" in Charleston, South Carolina. (94)

FLITCHER, John. Colonel Wyllys's Regiment. Desertion: 100 lashes. (131)

FLORANCE (FOURANCE), Philip. Mutiny, riot, and disobedience to orders: thirty lashes and drummed out of the army. (135)

FLOWER,_____, Captain. Permitting a party under his command to abuse or sell the property of the inhabitants of Ballstown: acquitted. (88)

FLOWERS, Ellis. Captain Hazzard's Company. Deserting twice: 100 lashes and pay for the cost of his apprehension. (93)

FLOWERS, Ithuriel, Sgt. Neglect of duty when on guard some time last month: acquitted. (91)

FLYCH, John. Colonel Wyllys's Regiment. Desertion: sent to the regiment to which he belongs in irons. (9)

FOOT, Ebenezer. Colonel Burrell's Regiment. Leaving his post when on sentry and going to sleep: twenty lashes. (84)

FORA, John. Colonel Bartam's Company. Desertion: forty lashes—pardoned. (98)

FORBES,_____, Ensign. Colonel Shepard's Regiment. Neglect of duty and cowardly behavior: dismissed from the service, with the punishment to be published in the newspapers near the camp and in the state where he resides. (14)

FORBES, Daniel. Colonel Paterson's Regiment. Desertion: acquitted. (101)

FORBES, Rios. Massachusetts Regiment of Artillery. Desertion: 100 lashes. (56)

FORCE, Jeremiah. First Company. Selling or otherwise disposing of his arms and accouterments: pay for the articles. (18)

FORD,_____, Lieutenant. Fourth Virginia Regiment. Disobedience to orders by firing a gun without proper permission in camp: reprimand. (101)

FORD,_____, Ensign. Second Maryland Regiment. Disobedience to orders, marching the Second Maryland Regiment from the parade when directed to the contrary; relating general orders different than those he received, by which he obtained his permission to march; contempt of orders and subverting and subordination in executing the orders of a colonel: acquitted with honor. (26)

FORD, Abel. Ninth Massachusetts Regiment. Stealing rum from an inhabitant's barn: fifty lashes and a fine of ten dollars to pay his share of the rum. (47) *See* Annis, Cruett, Pense, Tucker.

FORD, Dunham, Commissary. General Greene's Division. Theft: pay $200 to the victim and "thereafter to be brought before the provost guard mounted on a horse, back foremost, without a saddle, his coat turned wrongside-out, his hands tied behind him, and be drummed out of the army (never more to return) by all the drums in the regiment; and the above sentence to be published in the newspapers." (13) (134)

FORD, Dunham, Sgt. First South Carolina Battalion. Desertion: acquitted. (108)

FORD, James. Colonel Harrison's Regiment. Desertion and attempting to go to the enemy: death. (21)

FORD, Richard. Colonel Putnam's Regiment. Desertion: 100 lashes — remitted, in consideration of his having enlisted "during the war." (75)

FORESIDES (FORSY), Henry. Colonel Greene's Regiment. Deserting his regiment and enlisting again: 100 lashes and sent on board the Continental guard ship, there to be kept to hard labor during the war. (131)

FOREST, Henry. Being repeatedly drunk, striking Corporal Smith: fifteen lashes. (128)

FORNOKES, Francis. Colonel Moylan's Regiment. Mutiny and desertion: twenty-five lashes. (12) *See* Hows.

FORREST,_____, Major. Colonel Proctor's Regiment of Artillery. Neglect of duty, disobedience to orders, breaking his arrest: reprimand. (93)

FORREST, Thomas. Writing an improper letter: acquitted. (15)

FORSYTHE, William. Delaware Regiment. Mutiny and disobedience: 100 lashes. (64)

FOSDICK,_____, Ensign. Colonel Webb's Regiment and a detachment of Rangers. Abusive language to his officer, mutiny, and disobedience to orders: guilty of abusive language—reprimand. (118)

FOSDICK,_____. Absenting himself from the main guard: fifty lashes. (23) *See* Bloomer, Brown, Conoly.

FOSDICK, Samuel. Colonel Livingston's Regiment. Desertion: fifty lashes. (131)

FOSGATE, Ebenezer. New Hampshire Line. Going below the lines without permission, stealing from and plundering the inhabitants: acquitted. (38) *See* Phillips.

FOSGOOD, Ebenzer. First New Hampshire Regiment. Deserting and forging a discharge in the name of General Poor: run the gauntlet through 500 men in open order with a bayonet at his breast to regulate the pace. (111) *See* Allen, Critchet.

FOSS, John. Losing a gun, the property of John Frazier: acquitted, "the complaint being groundless and vexatious." (133)

FOSTER,_____, Ensign. Sixth Pennsylvania Regiment. Challenging Captain Cruse: dismissed from the service—pardoned and restored to his former rank, "because of the circumstances." (13) (134)

FOSTER,_____, Sergeant. Making an escape from the guard: reduced in rank and do the duty of a sentinel for one week. (23)

FOSTER,_____, Corporal. Seventh Company. Disobeying a captain's order by coming to the parade in a very dirty fashion: reduced to the duty of a private sentinel. (53)

FOSTER, Andrew. Sixth Maryland Regiment. Desertion: death. (41)

FOSTER, Francis. Colonel Swift's Regiment. Desertion and enticing one of his fellow soldiers to desert, threatening to desert to the enemy should he be punished: 100 lashes and return to his station on board the galley from which he had come. (125)

FOSTER, James. Colonel Nixon's Regiment. Robbing Dr. Foster, surgeon of the general hospital: thirty-nine lashes. (135)

FOSTER, John. Captain Malcom's Regiment. Desertion to the enemy: "In consideration of his youth, sentenced to only 100 lashes." (9)

FOSTER, John. Mutiny, riot, and disobedience to orders: fine of twenty shillings—remitted. (135)

FOSTER, Smith. Colonel Carne's Regiment of Artillery. 100 lashes. (124)

FOULER, Michael. Desertion and persuading others to desert: 100 lashes. (85)

FOWLER, Benjamin. 100 lashes. (23)

FOY, Micajah. Colonel Putnam's Regiment. Threatening to desert: thirty-nine lashes. (131)

FRAZIER, Charles. Colonel Crane's Regiment. Desertion. 100 lashes. (24)

FRANCIS, _____, Fife-major. Defrauding an inhabitant: 100 stripes— pardoned because this was his first offense. (23)

FRANCIS, John. Eighth Company. Stealing a board from the commissary: acquitted. (66)

FRANCIS, Nicholas. Colonel Hazen's Regiment. Deserting and reenlisting: 100 lashes. (93)

FRANDON, John. Colonel Hartley's Regiment. Desertion to the enemy and enlisting with them: death. (134)

FRANK, James. Fifth Massachusetts Regiment. Desertion: 100 lashes. (53)

FRANKLIN, Joseph. Second Company. Absent from camp without permission, stealing corn: fifty lashes. (66)

FRANKLIN, William. Colonel Shepard's Regiment. Quitting his command at Newton without leave: 100 lashes and pay the cost of apprehending him. (24) *See* Mayberry.

FRAZIER, John. Colonel Lamb's Regiment of Artillery. Enlisting into the Rhode Island Regiment without obtaining a discharge from his own unit, and afterwards deserting from the Rhode Island Regiment: 100 lashes. (44)

FREDERICK,_____, Corporal. Reduced in rank and run the gauntlet three times. (25)

FREELOVE, David. Second Massachusetts Regiment. Absenting himself from his post without leave: acquitted. (42)

FREEMAN,_____, Captain. Massachusetts Regiment of Artillery. Not attending roll call notwithstanding a positive order: acquitted. The commander-in-chief disagreed with the judgment but did not overturn it. (51)

FREEMAN,_____, Sergeant. Insulting and using abusive language to Sergeant Sullings, being intoxicated: do the duty of a private sentinel. (23) *See* Sullings.

FREEMAN, Cato. Ninth Massachusetts Regiment. Stealing and killing a cow belonging to an inhabitant: 100 lashes and a fine of forty shillings to pay for the cow. (48) *See* Barton, Sweat.

FREEMAN, Cato. Second Company. Losing his shirt: acquitted. (46)

FREEMAN, Ceaser. Plundering the inhabitants of money, and other offenses: acquitted. (33)

FREEMAN, Charles. Captain Allen's Company. Desertion: 100 lashes — pardoned in consideration of his former good conduct. (30)

FREEMAN, Coff. Second Company. Entering another's tent at midnight: acquitted. (46)

FREEMAN, Fortune. Fourth Company. Threatening and attempting to stab Abraham Babcock: acquitted. (63)

FREEMAN, Jack. First Company. Overstaying his furlough: fifty lashes. (91)

FREEMAN, Jack. Colonel Sherburne's Regiment (and the Ninth Connecticut Regiment). Absent without leave: 100 lashes. (91)

FREEMAN, Peter. Plundering the inhabitants of money, and other offenses: fifty lashes. (33)

FREEMAN, Thomas. Colonel Parson's Regiment. Being a confederate with James Convesson, in Colonel Danielson's Regiment, for voluntarily stealing or taking a shirt out of the house of Thomas Shea: acquitted. (105)

FRENCH,_____, Lieutenant. Refusing to do his duty when properly warned: acquitted. (14) (134)

FRENCH, William. Sixth Massachusetts Regiment. Desertion: 100 lashes. (34)

FISCHE, Cato. Second Company. Overstaying his pass and being absent from roll call: twenty lashes. (46)

FRISER, Emanual. Delaware Regiment. Stealing clothes from Johnson Fleetwood: acquitted. (93)

FROTHINGHAM, Thomas, Commissioner of Military Stores. Disobedience to orders given him by General Poor: acquitted. (31)

FRY, George. Colonel Jackson's Regiment. Threatening to take the life of an officer: twenty-five lashes on each of four successive mornings. (24)

FRY, Timothy. Breaking open and robbing the store: thirty-nine lashes and a fine of thirty shillings — remitted. (91)

FRY, Windsor. Colonel Greene's Regiment. Plundering the commissary store and stealing a quantity of beef, candles, and rum; breaking open two windmills and stealing a quantity of meal: death. (28)

FRYE, Ebenezer, Capt. First New York Regiment. Absenting himself from his regiment beyond his furlough, neglecting to join his regiment after being notified to do so: cashiered. (56) (86)

FRYE, Pickman. "Having earlier been sentenced to death, the General now finds him to be insane, and a free pardon was granted." Punishment remitted. (9)

FRYOR, William. Absenting himself from camp without leave, abusing the inhabitants, speaking threatening words respecting the commander of the garrison, speaking words having a tendency to injure the cause of the United States: 100 lashes. (75) *See* Hewes (Hughes).

FULLAN, John. Stealing and concealing a barrel of flour: acquitted. (91)

FULLER,_____, Captain. Fourth Massachusetts Regiment. Abusing and threatening the officers under his command, illegally confining a wagoner: reprimand. (46)

FULLER, Joel (Josiah), Lt. Colonel Durkee's Regiment. Absent from camp for more than a month, being innoculated for the small pox contrary to general orders: acquitted. (106) (132) (136) *See* chapter three.

FULLER, Richard. Selling a pair of shoes: fifty lashes. (28)

FULLER, Simeon. Absent from roll call and exceeding his pass: acquitted. (47)

FULLFORD, James. Second Regiment of Light Dragoons. Desertion: 100 lashes. (46)

FULSOME, Peter. Desertion: 100 lashes. (42)

FULTON, John. Colonel DuBois's Regiment. Desertion, theft: 100 lashes. (85)

GAGE, Thomas. Second Massachusetts Regiment. Desertion: 100 lashes. (85)

GALE, Nathan. Colonel Greene's Regiment. Repeated desertion: death. (41)

GALE, Nathaniel. Colonel Angell's Regiment. Desertion to the enemy: twenty-five stripes on his naked back for four days, and put on board a Continental frigate during the present war and not to be suffered to come on shore the whole time. The court noted that, "upon the examination of Sergeant Wibore and Sergeant Alford, who were prisoners in New York when Gale was with the enemy, find he was anxious to return to his regiment, that he endeavored to facilitate the escape of his American prisoners, that he shew many marks of friendship by furnishing them with money when in confinement." (24)

GALE, William. Captain Gale's Company. Abusing Adjutant Day in a most scandalous and abusive manner and shamefully abusing his character in writing the scandalous letters detected by Captain Ely: make a public confession to Adjutant Day at the head of the regiment and dismissed from the service—"and rendered unworthy to serve as a soldier in so glorious a cause as the United Colonies are engaged in, and if said Gale shall refuse to make his confession as above ordered, to said Day, he is to be drummed out of camp two miles from the regiment, and there let go where he pleases, provided he return not to camp." (105)

GALLING,_____, Lieutenant. Second North Carolina Battalion. Neglect of duty and disobedience to orders: dismissed from the service. (72)

GALLUP, John. Colonel Patterson's Regiment. Absenting himself from 27 June to 27 September, carrying off and disposing of a colony gun: fifteen lashes and pay for the gun. (136)

GAMBLE, David. Eighth Pennsylvania Regiment. Desertion and having counterfeit money in his possession: death. (36)

GAMBOL, George. Seventh Massachusetts Regiment. Behaving in a riotous and mutinous manner in disobeying and actually opposing the orders of an officer: 100 lashes. (64)

GAMEN,_____. Captain Oldham's Company. Theft: acquitted. (115)

GARDINER, Christopher, Capt. Colonel Varnum's Regiment. Deserting his post: cashiered. (2) (135) *See* chapter one.

GARDINER (GARDNER), John. Colonel Huntington's Regiment. Desertion: thirty-nine lashes. (132) (136)

GARDNER, Noah. Light Company, Massachusetts Regiment. Killing a cow and seven geese: seventy-five lashes. (61) *See* Abram, Brayton, Carliss, Cook, Cowell, Jinks, Shea, Wood.

GARDNER, Sharps. Desertion: 100 lashes. (41)

GARNER, Jonathan. Fourth Regiment of Light Dragoons. Robbing money from two houses in the state of New Jersey: 100 lashes. (21) *See* Lankford.

GARNER (GANO), Lee, Capt. Colonel Lamb's Regiment of Artillery. Insulting Lieutenant Colonel McCoughey by confining his waiter and making use of his property: acquitted. (125) (131)

GARNICK, George. Sixth Virginia Regiment. Robbing a house: 100 lashes. (21)

GARRET, Richard. Delaware Regiment. Drunkenness: pardoned. (93)

GARRISON, Paul. Second Regiment. Desertion, encouraging soldiers to desert and enlist in another regiment: guilty only of desertion – fifty lashes with switches – remitted because he had already been punished in the Third Regiment. (95)

GARRISON, Samuel. Absenting himself from guard and being drunk: 100 lashes. (23)

GARRISON, Samuel. Colonel Clinton's Regiment. Desertion: fine of one month's pay – pardoned. (118)

GARRISON, William. Desertion: 100 lashes. (42)

GARTHON, Joseph. Fourth Regiment of Light Dragoons. Robbing two houses, one in New York and one in Pennsylvania: 200 lashes. (21)

GARVEY, Samuel, inhabitant of Pennsylvania. Endeavoring to supply the enemy with provisions: acquitted. (9)

GARVIN, Isaac. Virginia Line. Absent without leave, plundering the inhabitants: run the gauntlet through the whole army. (115)

GARY, Junius. Colonel Hand's Regiment. Leaving camp without leave and riotous drunken behavior. (106)

GASKINS, William. Desertion, making away with his arms and accouterments taken. (109) (121)

GASSWAY,_____, Ensign. Third Maryland Regiment. Disobedience to orders and absent without leave. (69)

GATES, Nathaniel. Embezzling public stores: fine of $130 and run the gauntlet three times. (103)

GATTLING, Lou, Lt. Second North Carolina Regiment. Neglect of duty and disobedience to orders: dismissed from the service. (113)

GAY, John. Colonel Webb's Regiment. Stealing sheep from Mr. Deines, an inhabitant of Bristol: thirty stripes – pardoned. (91) *See* Brown, Merrills, Olmstead.

GAY, Joseph, Lt. Second New Jersey Regiment. Scandalous neglect of duty by absenting himself without leave, gambling and gaming: dismissed from the service. (16)

GAYLORD, Ambrose. First Connecticut Regiment. Desertion from his guard: 100 lashes – remitted. (52)

GAYLORD, Ambrose (Lue), Sgt. First Connecticut Regiment. Endeavoring to excite a mutiny in the Connecticut Line, not discussing with his officers an intended mutiny when he knew a plan was laying: death. (52) *See* Bunce, Parker, and chapter five.

GAYLORD, Josiah. Breaking open and robbing the store: thirty-nine lashes and fine of thirty shillings—fine remitted. (91)

GAYNER, James. Colonel Webb's Regiment. Threatening and challenging to fight: acquitted. (133)

GEELE,_____, Captain. Fifth Pennsylvania Regiment. Leaving his guard before he was properly relieved: reprimand. (103)

GEER, James. Colonel Jackson's Regiment. Being several miles distant from camp without permission, sleeping out of camp: fifty lashes. (23)

GEER, James. Colonel Jackson's Regiment. Absenting himself from camp several miles: 100 lashes—remitted because of his long confinement. (23)

GEOPHREY, Peter. First Regiment. Desertion: 100 lashes with switches. (95)

GEORGE, America. Captain Singleton's Company. Desertion: 100 lashes. (115)

GEORGE, David. Colonel Arnold's Regiment. Refusing to obey Colonel Arnold's order: fined one month's pay and immediately join Captain Smith's company, according to Colonel Arnold's order. (128)

GEORGE, Reuben, civilian express rider. Delaying $300,000 on the road, which he was to deliver to the deputy quartermaster for pay, spending part of it himself. 100 lashes and repay that which he had spent; dismissed from his employment. (35)

GERRISH,_____, Captain. Misbehavior upon the approach of the enemy: acquitted. (74) (92) (94)

GERRISH, Samuel, Col. Massachusetts Forces. Breach of the forty-ninth Article of the Rules and Regulations of the Massachusetts Army: dismissed from the service. (2) (135) *See* chapter four.

GERSHON,_____, Major. Sixth Regiment. Desertion from the North Carolina Levies: returned to duty in the North Carolina Continental Battalion. (95)

GERSON,_____, Major. Fourth North Carolina Regiment. Desertion: 100 lashes with switches. (95)

GEST, Robert, Drummer. Colonel Lamb's Regiment of Artillery. Attempting to desert to the enemy: fifty lashes only, because of his youth. (134)

GIBBONS, Jacob, civilian. Selling sheep to a butcher in Philadelphia: acquitted. (14) (134)

GIBBS,_____, Corporal. First New Jersey Regiment. Desertion and selling and spoiling some of his regimental clothes, forging a discharge: death by hanging. (57) *See* Young.

GIBBS, Timothy. Loading his piece repeatedly and saying that he would kill Ephraim Cohorse: twenty lashes. (22)

GIBBS, Williams, Cpl. First New Jersey Regiment. Marauding: death – pardoned. (44) *See* Davis.

GILCHRIST,_____, Corporal. Disobedience to orders: reduced to the rank of private – retained his rank because of his former good conduct. (23)

GILCHRIST, Charles. Ninth Massachusetts Regiment. Desertion: 100 lashes and serve out his three years. (41)

GILES,_____, Corporal. Absent from roll call and exceeding his pass: reduced to private. (47)

GILES, Thomas. Selling a shirt given to him by John Blake: thirty lashes. (93) *See* Blake.

GILL, John. Colonel Maxwell's Regiment. Defrauding the Continent: thirty-nine lashes. (84)

GILL, William. Disobedience to orders and neglect of duty relative to the public stores: acquitted. (46) *See* Harton.

GILLARD (GARLAND), John. Mutiny, riot, and disobedience to orders: thirty lashes and drummed out of the army. (135)

GILLEY, Elijah. Massachusetts Line. Desertion: 100 lashes. (52)

GILLINGS, Jonathan. Colonel Crane's Regiment. Desertion: fifty lashes. (24)

GILMAN, David, Lt. Second New Hampshire Regiment. Ungentlemanlike behavior in associating with private soldiers, and assuring them a reward of twenty dollars, and engaging to secure them from harm in case any should arise in consequence thereof, if they should bring to him a horse; taking two horses, the property of private persons: cashiered and forfeit all pay due him. (75)

GILMORE, David, Sgt. *See* chapter five.

GIST, Robert. *See* Gest.

GLADDING, Ebenezer. Burning his clothes and accouterments: pay for the articles burned. (23)

GLADDING, William. Captain Bates's Company. Suffering liquor under his charge to be drawn: thirty-nine lashes. (43) *See* Ballard.

GLEASON, Thomas. Desertion: 100 lashes. (42)

GLINN, Hugh. Eighth Pennsylvania Regiment. Absent three weeks without leave: 100 stripes. (11)

GODDARD, Elia. Repeated disobedience to orders, abusing the adjutant: guilty of the first charge but not guilty of the second charge — fine of one month's pay. (128) *See* Balls.

GOINS, William. Going into the country without a pass: fifty lashes — pardoned because of his former good behavior. (50)

GOODLEY, Scarborough, Maj. Deficient in his duty at the battle at Bunker Hill: dismissed from the service, "but on account of his inexperience and youth, and the great confusion which attended that day's transaction in general, they do not consider him uncapable of a Continental commission, should the general officers recommend him to his Excellency." (135)

GOODMAN,_____, Captain Lieutenant. Artillery. Willfully misapplying and embezzling property of the United States: dismissed from the service and pay for the property. (110)

GOODRICH, Daniel, Wagonmaster. First Massachusetts Brigade. Not properly sending horses to pasture: discharged from his office as wagonmaster. (48)

GOODRICH, James. Captain Wyllys's Company. Neglect of duty when on sentinel: forty stripes. (91)

GOODRICH, Levi, Ens. Fourth Connecticut Regiment. Absent without leave 150 days: cashiered. (47)

GOODRICH, Noah. First Massachusetts Regiment. Killing a cow and stealing eleven geese: seventy-five lashes and pay fifteen dollars to the owner. (86)

GOODRICH, Solomon. Absent without leave: fine of eight shillings and reprimand. (91)

GOODYEAR, William, Ens. Dismissed from the service. (94)

GOOKIN, Thomas. Colonel Marshall's Regiment. Desertion in the late retreat from Ticonderoga: returned to his regiment in irons. (9)

GOOLD, John, Cpl. Colonel Greene's Regiment. Raising a mutiny and behaving in a disorderly manner: not guilty of the first charge but guilty of the second charge—suspended and reprimand. (131) *See* Baptist, Brown, Buck, Cary, Davis, Dunbar, Hardin, Lane, Park, Peterson, Tabor.

GORCE, Thomas. Delaware Regiment. Deserting and reenlisting in the Third Maryland Regiment: 100 lashes. (109)

GORDAN, John. Twelfth Massachusetts Regiment. Stealing salt: 100 lashes. (111)

GORDEN, Samuel. Second New Hampshire Line. Carelessly firing a gun which killed Captain Kemble and wounded another man: acquitted, since the gun went off accidentally. (89)

GORDON, Cornelius. Colonel Lamb's Regiment of Artillery. Striking Captain Archibald when in the execution of his duty: 100 lashes and sit on the gallows with a rope around his neck for the space of half an hour. (37)

GORDON, William. Colonel Livingston's Regiment. Desertion and enlisting into another regiment: 100 lashes. (131)

GORE, Alfred. Colonel Thompson's Battalion. Desertion: pardoned. (90)

GORGE, John. Fourth Regiment. Desertion and repeated desertion: 100 lashes. (125)

GOSNELL,_____, Sergeant. Pennsylvania Line. Inciting to mutiny: death. (49) *See* chapter five.

GOULD, Thomas, Sgt. Colonel Arnold's Regiment. Refusing to obey Colonel Arnold's order: reduced to private, fined one month's pay, and immediately join Captain Smith's company, according to Colonel Arnold's order. (128)

GOURMANE, William. Colonel Clinton's Regiment. Desertion: fine of one month's pay—pardoned. (118)

GRAFTON, Joshua, Capt. Colonel Sherburne's Regiment. Abusing Dr. Wardsworth's character in saying he was lazy and indolent, and striking him with a large stick: reprimand and ask the doctor's pardon in front of the regiment. (24) *See* Wardsworth.

GRAHAM,_____, Colonel. Misbehavior upon the approach of the enemy: acquitted. (74) (92) (94)

GRAHAM, Alexander. Desertion: released when no evidence was presented. (93)

GRAHAM, Alexander. Colonel Holmes's Regiment. Mutiny, disobedience to orders, striking officers: thirty-nine lashes and drummed out of the regiment. (118)

GRAHAM, Alexander (alias Smith). Colonel Meig's Regiment. Desertion: death by shooting. (69) (103)

GRANBURY,_____, Captain. Third Carolina Battalion. Neglecting his duty and quitting his command, misdemeanors unbecoming the character of an officer: acquitted. (88)

GRANIER,_____, Lieutenant Colonel. Leaving his regiment when alarmed by the firing of the patrols on the lines and not joining it again till the alarm was over, purchasing a horse from a soldier which belonged to the Continent, treating Adjutant Sackett in an unofficerlike and ungentlemanlike manner: acquitted with honor, the charges being "groundless and dictated by private pique and malice." (103)

GRANT, Azaria. Overstaying his furlough: acquitted. (91)

GRANT, Charles. Third Regiment of Artillery. Desertion and attempting to go to the enemy, stealing a boat: death. (46) *See* Carman, Parsells.

GRANT, Duncan. Colonel Nixon's Regiment. Desertion: thirty-nine lashes. (134)

GRANT, George, Sgt. *See* chapter five.

GRANT, James. Colonel Parson's Regiment. Destroying his arms, abusing his sergeant, insolently affronting his officers: twenty lashes and pay for his arms. (136)

GRANT, Joseph. Corps of Sappers and Miners. Robbing a boy of a bottle of geneva, and threatening to drown him: acquitted. (66)

GRANT, Samuel. Mutiny, riot, and disobedience to orders: thirty lashes and drummed out of the army. (135)

GRANT, Thomas. Massachusetts Line. Desertion: 100 lashes. (57)

GRANVILLE, Sampson. Colonel Parsons's Regiment. Stealing timber from a batteau: fined eight shillings. (118)

GRASS, John. Fourth Company. Insulting Corporal McCullock: reprimand and ask the corporal's pardon at the head of the regiment. (45)

GRASS, John. Fourth Company. Intoxicated on parade: acquitted. (56)

GRATES (GREATY), Philip. Mutiny, riot, and disobedience to orders: fine of twenty shillings. (135)

GRAVES, John. Captain Wahers's Company. Taking boards from the barracks and cutting them up for his own use: fine of twenty shillings to pay for the boards. (91)

GRAY,_____, Lieutenant Colonel. Twelfth Pennsylvania Regiment. Entering into private contracts with the soldiers of his regiment for the deficiencies of rations, by which means and other unwarrantable practices, soldiers were defrauded of a considerable sum of money: cashiered, and the crime published in the newspapers near the camp and the state in which he usually resides. (17)

GRAY,_____, Captain. Colonel Brewer's Regiment. Dissuading soldiers enlisting and therein acting the part of a Tory and enemy to his country: acquitted. (3) (133)

GRAY,_____, Sergeant. Colonel Bradley's Regiment. Desertion to the enemy, and enlisting with them, stealing a dragoon's horse and carrying it to the enemy: death by shooting—remitted upon a finding that he was subject to bouts of insanity and when his brother agreed to pay the cost of the stolen horse. (21)

GRAY, Alexander. Fifth Pennsylvania Regiment. Desertion: fifty lashes. (101)

GRAY, Andrew, Sailor on board the sloop *Enterprise*. Mutinous behavior: acquitted. (99)

GRAY, James. Theft: acquitted. (77)

GRAY, John. Sixteenth Massachusetts Regiment. Absent without leave for more than a year: 100 lashes. (34)

GRAY, Lynch, Sgt. Fourth Regiment of Light Dragoons. Robbing a house in the state of New Jersey: reduced to the ranks and 100 lashes. (21) *See* Fisher, Zimmerman.

GRAY, Robert, Lt. Colonel Hazen's Regiment. Repeated disobedience to orders: acquitted. (3)

GRAY, Samuel, Cpl. First Connecticut Regiment. Desertion and reenlisting in the Massachusetts Line: 100 lashes. (44)

GRAY, Samuel. Colonel Douglass's Regiment. Desertion: be led from the gallows with a rope around his neck, there to receive 100 lashes on his naked back and drummed out of the garrison—the drumming out was amended in favor of being put under confinement on board a ship. (131)

GRAY, William. Fifth Massachusetts Regiment. Desertion and attempting to go to the enemy: 100 lashes. (50)

GRAYHAM (GRAHAM), William, Matross. Captain Moody's Company. Straggling from camp: reprimand. (125)

GREATON (GRATTON), Peter. Mutiny, riot, and disobedience to orders: fine of twenty shillings. (135)

GREEN, Calvan. Light Dragoons. Desertion to the enemy and suspicion of being a spy: guilty only of desertion; death. (100) (111)

GREEN, Jedediah. Colonel Crane's Regiment. Desertion and enlisting twice: fifty stripes and repayment of the bounty—stripes remitted. (9)

GREEN, John, Lt. Eighth Massachusetts Regiment. Exceeding the limits of his furlough by twenty-nine days: dismissed from the service—pardoned and restored to his former rank. (50)

GREEN, John. Colonel McDougall's Regiment. Breaking out of his quarter-guard and being absent two days: thirty-nine lashes. (136)

GREEN, John. Colonel McDougall's Regiment. Desertion: thirty-nine lashes. (79) (136)

GREEN, John. Colonel Angell's Regiment. Selling his uniform coat: 100 lashes. (28)

GREENLEAF, Elijah. Colonel Lee's Regiment. Taking flour from the public store and selling it: thirty lashes. (9)

GREENLEAF, Henry. Disobedience: pardoned. (11)

GREENLEAF, Henry. Captain Drown's Company. Imposing on Anderson, commissary, for rum he had no right to: thirty lashes—remitted. (11) *See* Harton.

GREENLIEF,_____, Captain. Colonel Tupper's Regiment. Unofficerlike behavior at the action at Monmouth: acquitted. (75)

GRESS, Thomas, Third New York Regiment. Desertion: 100 lashes. (100)

GRESSUT, Edward. Going into Philadelphia: 100 lashes. (134)

GRIDLEY, John. Third Regiment of Artillery. Exceeding the limits of his furlough by twenty-five days: acquitted. (50)

GRIDLEY, Judah. Colonel Felson's Regiment. Extorting money from Jonathan Thompson, refusing to give himself up, attempting to escape from Captain Richard Francis, attempting to draw his sword: run the gauntlet through 100 (200) men of the Brigade of Horse. (3) (136)

GRIFFIN,_____, Ensign. Fourth New York Regiment. Disobedience to orders: reprimand. (100)

GRIFFIN, Anthony. Plundering the inhabitants of money, and other offenses: fifty lashes. (33)

GRIFFIN, John. Absent without leave: reprimand. (125)

GRIMES, Daniel. Colonel Maxfield's Regiment. Desertion: punishment remitted, "some favorable circumstances appearing on the prisoner's behalf." (132) (136)

GRIMES, Joseph, Sgt. Light Infantry. Dressing himself like a girl and absenting himself from camp after retreat beat: reduced to the ranks and reprimand. (95)

GRISWOLD, Moses. Major Meggs's Company. Firing his gun and insolent language: fined one shilling and make a humble confession to the sergeant for disobeying his order. (105)

GROSHALL, William. Fifth Massachusetts Regiment. Desertion: 100 lashes. (53)

GROSS, John. Ninth Massachsuetts Regiment. Absent from his regiment without permission: wear a log for a term of four days, during which time he is to remain in confinement but to attend all regimental parades. (42)

GROSSEY, Michael. Fourth Georgia Battalion. Desertion: 100 lashes. (90)

GROVES,_____, Lieutenant. Second Regiment. Insulting Captain Wilkinson, disobeying his orders, given him insolent and abusive language: mulcted of half-month's pay. (120)

GUARDIAN, John. First South Carolina Regiment. Desertion: 100 lashes. (95)

GUILE, Nathan. Desertion: 100 lashes. (42)

GULLY, Daniel. Disobedience to orders: fifty lashes. (103)

GUSTIN, Ebenezer. Light Company. Absenting himself without leave, attempting to steal provisions from the commissary: fifty lashes. (52) *See* Negus, Parker, Toward.

GUSTIN, Ezra. Second Massachusetts Regiment. Desertion: 100 lashes. (42)

GUTHRIE, Abel. Accessory to the killing of a hog: fifty lashes. (91)

GUY,_____, Lieutenant. Colonel Lamb's Regiment of Artillery. Absent from camp without leave, theft: have his sword broken over his head on the grand parade at guard mounting, and discharged from the regiment; that it be deemed a crime of the blackest dye in officers or even soldiers to associate with him after the execution of this just and mild punishment. (14) (134)

GWIN, William. Fifth South Carolina Battalion. Desertion: 100 lashes. (95)

HAASS,_____, Lieutenant. Second Maryland Regiment. Swearing that he would not do another tour of duty as a subaltern, claiming to be sick to escape duty, going to Morristown without leave: acquitted. (28)

HABY, Isaac. Colonel Maxwell's Regiment. Leaving the main guard without permission: thirty-nine lashes. (84)

HACK, Joseph. New Hampshire Troops. Bayoneting two soldiers belonging to the North Carolina Troops: acquitted—"he did his duty as a soldier." (26)

HACKLEIN, Peter. Colonel Macklin's Battalion. Cowardice and shamefully abandoning his post on Long Island: acquitted. (7)

HACKNEY, John. Disposing of a horse, the property of Lieutenant Mangers: acquitted. (121)

HADLEY, Bishop. Sleeping on his post: 100 lashes. (89)

HAIGNEY, Cornelius. Delaware Regiment. Drinking and fighting: acquitted. (93) *See* McCann.

HALE, Samuel. Colonel Crane's Regiment. Desertion: 100 lashes. (24)

HALL,_____, Sergeant. Overstaying his furlough: acquitted, because he was lame and unable to join his regiment. (91)

HALL, Franklin. Colonel Poor's Regiment. Desertion: because of some unfavorable circumstances, be stripped at the post as if to be whipped, and then severely reprimanded. (117)

HALL, David. Colonel Stewart's Battalion of Infantry. Plundering an inhabitant of money: death. (33)

HALL, Edwin. Fifteenth Pennsylvania Regiment. Gaming: reprimand. (16)

HALL, John, Boatman. Quartermaster Department. Stealing liquor and rum while enroute from Windsor to Peekskill: thirty-nine lashes—remitted. (46) *See* McMullin.

HALL, Jonas (Josiah) Carvel. General Smallwood's Regiment. Refusal to comply with a general order issued in an emergency, unofficer-like behavior in threatening to blow out the brains of any officer who should lead a party to execute the same: because of the emergency, not guilty and acquitted with honor. (9)

HALL, Samuel. Cutting a board in pieces belonging to the barracks and burning it for fuel: acquitted. (91)

HALL, Stephen. Captain Heart's Company. Disobedience of orders in neglecting to join a fatigue party: ten lashes – remitted. (91)

HALL, Thomas. North Carolina Troops. Desertion and joining the enemy: 100 lashes and make up the time he was absent from the service. (115)

HALL, Thomas. Seventh Maryland Regiment. Intended desertion: death. (21)

HALLET,_____. Colonel Jackson's Regiment. Drunk on the parade, abusing his officers: lashes – remitted. (10)

HALSTON,_____, Adjutant. First Pennsylvania Brigade. Making a false return, disobedience to orders, breaking his arrest: dismissed from the service. (93)

HAMBELTON, James. Absent from roll call and drunk at the same time: twenty lashes. (43)

HAMBLETON, John, inhabitant of Pennsylvania. Attempting to carry provisions into Philadelphia: acquitted. (14)

HAMILTON, George. Colonel Woodbridge's Regiment. Stealing a blue greatcoat, the property of Solomon Lathrop: thirty lashes and drummed out of the army; fined ten shillings for the coat. (3) (135)

HAMLIN, Joel. Tapping, or suffering to be tapped, a cask of whiskey when on sentinel at the commissary: acquitted, as no evidence was presented. (91)

HAMMEL, James. Fifth Pennsylvania Regiment. Robbery: death by hanging. (26)

HAMMON,_____, Sergeant Major. Neglect of duty in not apprehending a prisoner in his power, abusive language to sergeants for doing their duty: reduced to private – pardoned because of his former good conduct. (23)

HAMMON, Jonathan, Bombardier. Captain Moody's Company. Absent from camp, abusing the inhabitants: guilty only of the first charge – reduced to a matross and stand on a picket with his bare feet for fifteen minutes. (125)

HAMMON, Zebidia, Matross. The Fleet. Mutiny, whereas the enemy might come, and saying he would not fight against them on board the vessel: reduced in rank and returned to his former regiment. (117) *See* Colbert, Powell, Trip.

HANCOCK, John. Fourth Connecticut Regiment. Repeated desertion: 100 lashes. (46)

HAND, Domenic. Third Pennsylvania Regiment. Desertion: acquitted. (21)

HANDLEY, Stephen. Delaware Regiment. Exciting and promoting desertion: acquitted. (109)

HANDMAN, David, Matross. Captain Moody's Company. Straggling from camp: reprimand. (125)

HANDY,_____, Captain. Abusing his tour of duty: acquitted. (21)

HANDY, Russell. Desertion: 100 lashes. (28)

HANE, John. First New York Regiment. Desertion: 100 lashes. (89)

HANES,_____. Colonel Hazen's Regiment. Attempting to desert to the enemy: 100 lashes and discharged from his company and sent to Philadelphia for confinement. (93)

HANEY, Gideon. Desertion and stealing public property from his care when on guard over it: 100 lashes. (41) *See* Chapman, Phay.

HANLEY, James. Fourth New York Regiment. Attempting to desert to the enemy with the arms and accouterments of another soldier: death by shooting. (112) *See* Bell, Lighthall.

HANNON, George, Batteauman: Mutinous behavior: acquitted. (111)

HANSBERRY, William. Conspiring with Baker to spike the cannon at Fort Schuyler, desertion: 100 lashes. (100)

HANSLEY, Jesse. Fourth Regiment of Light Dragoons. Robbing the house of widow Sarah Sanford: 100 lashes. (33) *See* Bourke.

HANTON,_____, Captain. Second Regiment of Light Dragoons. Cowardice and shamefully refusing a command when ordered by Colonel Sheldon, suffering a subaltern officer to take it, requesting leave to return to the rear of the regiment at a time when action was expected: acquitted. (59)

HAPPLE, Adam. Third New York Regiment. Desertion: 100 lashes. (111)

HARCOURT, Charles. Second Pennsylvania Regiment. Attempting to go to the enemy: 100 lashes. (21)

HARD, Dingham, Commissary. General Greene's Division. Theft: Pay Mr. and Mrs. Hallaway $200 and then be mounted on a horse, back foremost, without a saddle, his coat turned wrongsideout, his hands tied behind him, and be drummed out of the army, nevermore to return, and that the sentence be published in the newspapers. (88)

HARDEN, Samuel. Ninth Regiment. Desertion: 100 lashes. (129)

HARDIN, William. Colonel Greene's Regiment. Raising a mutiny and behaving in a disorderly manner: not guilty of the first charge but guilty of the second charge—suspended and reprimand. (131) *See* Baptist, Brown, Cary, Davis, Dunbar, Goold, Louis, Park, Peterson, Tabor.

HARENDON, Thomas. Colonel Angell's Regiment. Desertion: 100 lashes. (26)

HARGRES, Christopher. Colonel Wind's Battalion. Desertion: thirty-nine lashes. (5)

HARGY, John, Sgt. Seventh Regiment. Disobedience to orders, refusing to give up a shirt lent him to appear clean on the parade: reduced to the ranks and return the shirt to Captain Parker. (129)

HARKLEY, Arunah. Captain Buckley's Company. Retailing liquor: acquitted. (91)

HARLEY, Benjamin, Matross. Third Regiment of Artillery. Desertion and reenlisting: death—pardoned. (42)

HARLING, John. Second Pennsylvania Regiment. Desertion and joining the enemy: death. (50)

HARMON, Palatiah. Colonel Jackson's Regiment. Desertion: 100 lashes—remitted. (26)

HARMON, William, Fifer. Colonel Jackson's Regiment. Desertion: 100 lashes—remitted. (26)

HARPER, Christopher. Colonel Wind's Battalion. Desertion: thirty-nine lashes. (134)

HARPER, John. Colonel Malcolm's Regiment. Drunk on his post: thirty lashes. (67)

HARPER, Joseph. Colonel Morrow's Regiment. Shooting on the lines: acquitted. (96)

HARPER, William, Capt. Colonel Wyman's Regiment. Enlisting one James Marston, knowing him to be a deserter from Colonel Poor's Regiment, and detaining him in "number four" to save him from punishment; dismissed from the service. (94) (117)

HARPER, William. Fourth New York Regiment. Desertion and absent for twelve months: run the gauntlet. (26)

HARRIDEN, William. Colonel Reed's Regiment. Desertion: thirty-nine lashes. (134)

HARRIS, James. Captain Cole's Company of Batteaumen. Desertion: fine of four dollars. (83) (84)

HARRIS, Samuel. Mutiny, riot, and disobedience to orders: thirty lashes and drummed out of the army. (135)

HARRIS, Wallis. Captain Whiting's Company. Taking boards from the barracks and cutting them up for his own use: fine of twenty shillings to pay for the boards. (91)

HARRISON, George. Mutinous expressions on the parade: acquitted. (90)

HARRISON, Robert, Wagonmaster. Georgia Brigade. Disobedience to orders; detaining the wagons in Savannah, and upon the road, when the service required dispatch; bringing rum in the public wagons and selling it out of them; transporting property of his own and of other people; letting a wagoner have rum until he was drunk. (9)

HART, Moses, Capt. Twentieth (Twenty-Eighth) Regiment of Foot Soldiers. Drawing more provisions than he was entitled to receive, unjustly confining and abusing his men: cashiered. (81) (104)

HARTHORNE, Nathaniel. Colonel Vose's Regiment. Desertion and enlisting in the Maryland Line: 100 lashes, with twenty-five lashes administered on each of four successive mornings. (44)

HARTHY, William. Desertion: 100 lashes. (42)

HARTNETT, Thomas. Second Pennsylvania Regiment. Desertion to the enemy: death by hanging. (16) (134)

HARTON, B. Disobedience to orders and neglect of duty relating to the public stores: acquitted. (46) *See* Gill.

HARTON, Samuel. Captain Drown's Company. Imposing on Anderson, commissary, for rum he had no right to: thirty lashes. (11) *See* Greenleaf.

HARTSTONE (HOUSTON), John, Capt. Colonel Gansevoort's Third New York Battalion. Deserting to the enemy, receiving $500 recruiting money and taking it to the enemy, forging a pass signed by General McDougall: dismissed from the army. (131)

HARVEY, Jacob. 100 lashes. (42)

HARVEY, William, Sgt. Fourth Company. Permitting a Joseph Wing to absent himself and cross the river while on guard: reduced to a private sentry. (66)

HARWOOD,_____, Corporal. Colonel Gerrish's Regiment. Mutiny: reduced to the ranks and a fine of forty-eight shillings, and thirty-nine lashes. (39) (133) *See* Laraby, North, Putney, Rawlins (Rollins), Williams.

HASPER, Christopher. Colonel Wind's Regiment. Desertion: thirty-nine lashes. (132)

HASS, David. Colonel Shepard's Regiment. Desertion: acquitted. (131)

HATTFIELD, Thomas, Cpl. Captain Craft's Company. Drunk on guard: reduced to do the duty of a matross. (104)

HATTON, W., Capt. Invalid's Regiment. Disobedience of a general order in not joining his brigade until thirty-one days after he had enlisted: acquitted. (54)

HAUGHTEN, John. Massachusetts Line. Desertion: 100 lashes. (53)

HAUZIE, Peter. Colonel Arnold's Regiment. Refusing to obey Colonel Arnold's order: fined one month's pay and immediately join Captain Smith's company, according to Colonel Arnold's order. (128)

HAVEN,_____, Sergeant. Sixth Company. Bringing a man onto the parade for duty with dirty _____: reduced to the rank of a private sentinel for the fortnight. (53)

HAVERBURGH,_____, Ensign. Colonel Livingston's Regiment. Quitting his post in action and hiding behind a log: reprimand only, because of many circumstances in his favor. (88)

HAWK, John Warren. First Yorkers. Stealing shirts from the bales committed to his charge when on sentry, being privy to the theft committed by others, selling some regimental shirts to a Frenchman: thirty-nine lashes and return to the Frenchman the sum he received for the blanket and shirt. (128)

HAWKE, John Warren. Colonel McDougall's Regiment. Mutiny: fine of eight shillings – pardoned. (118)

HAWKINS, Edward. Second New Jersey Regiment. Desertion and exciting others to desert to the enemy, being drunk and absent from his quarters after tattoo, abusing and attempting to fire on an inhabitant in the night: death. (21)

HAWKINS, James. Colonel Thompson's Battalion. Desertion: pardoned. (90)

HAWKINS, John. Colonel Sargent's Regiment. Theft: thirty-nine lashes and repay the money stolen. (104)

HAWLEY,_____, Sergeant. Overstaying his furlough: reprimand. (91)

HAWLEY,_____, Corporal. Seventh Company. Disobedience to orders in staying from the regiment after the expiration of his pass: acquitted. (91)

HAWLEY, Abraham, Sgt. Seventh Company. Neglect of duty when sent on command by Captain Peay: acquitted. (91)

HAWLEY, John. Seventh Massachusetts Regiment. Desertion: 100 lashes. (41)

HAY,_____, Lieutenant Colonel. Granting an unlegal permit to four soldiers to go into the town of Burlington and to return a lady, unmolested; insulting Ensign Rogers in execution of his duty: reprimand – released when the commander-in-chief stated that the lady in question, on her way to New York, needed the protection and required assistance. (28)

HAY,_____, Sergeant. Breaking a window and attempting to break into Colonel Bowen's house: acquitted. (19) *See* Stokes.

HAYLEY, Peter. Colonel Craft's Regiment of Artillery. Abusing several inhabitants of the town: acquitted. (19) *See* Jones.

HAYMOND, Samuel. Presenting a loaded musket to a lieutenant: reprimand. (16)

HAYNES, William. Colonel Ritzema's Regiment. Desertion: twenty-five lashes. (136)

HAYS,_____, Lieutenant. Twelfth Pennsylvania Regiment. Breaking open officers' chests at Bethlehem: acquitted of breaking open the chests, but guilty of ungentlemanlike behavior: dismissed from the service. (13)

HAYS, John. Fourth Maryland Regiment. Desertion: forty lashes. (121)

HAYTON, John. Fourth Maryland Regiment. Desertion: branded on his right cheek with the letter "R." (121)

HAZARD, Peter. Plundering the inhabitants of money, and other offenses: fifty lashes. (33)

HAZARD, Raymond. Desertion: 100 lashes. (42)

HAZARD, Stephen. Colonel Angell's Regiment. Defrauding another soldier of money which was due him: twenty-four stripes and repay the $240 to the victim. (35)

HAZEL, Henry. Desertion and bearing arms against the United States: death by hanging. (115)

HAZEN, Moses, Col. Disobedience to orders, unmilitary conduct on the march from Tappan to the Liberty Pole, halting the brigade under his command without any orders, falsely asserting that he had such orders from General Stark: acquitted when it was determined that he did have such orders. (53) *See* chapter four.

HAZEN, Moses, Col. Refusing to receive into the store the goods General Arnold sent to Chamblee by Major Scott, and not placing proper guards and suffering them to be plundered: acquitted with honor. (61) *See* chapter four.

HEAD, Jonathan. Maryland Line. Leaving camp without leave, plundering the inhabitants: 100 lashes. (115)

HEALY, Daniel. Third Virginia Regiment. Desertion: twenty lashes. (101)

HEANEY, Barney. Desertion: 100 lashes. (129)

HEART, Ebenezer. 100 lashes. (122)

HEATER, Jacob. Desertion: 100 lashes. (42)

HEATH, Sterling. Second New Hampshire Regiment. Desertion and attempting to go to the enemy: 100 lashes. (44)

HEFFLIN, John, Q.M. Sgt. Colonel Nichols's Regiment. Fighting, cursing, damning, challenging to imprison and using menacing words and gestures to Lieutenant Rust: reduced to the ranks and a fine of one-sixth of a dollar for swearing, and ask the lieutenant's pardon. (118) (123)

HELSMAN,_____. Theft: lashes (unspecified number) and drummed out of the army with infamy—lashes were remitted. (94)

HENBY, Lucas. Colonel Bland's Regiment. Plundering William Laurence: run the gauntlet through a detachment of fifty men of the Brigade of Horse. (93)

HENDERSON,_____, Captain. Ninth Pennsylvania Regiment. Fraudulently extorting a sum of money from Alexander Bayard (Baird), an inhabitant of the state, as a fine for having purchased a horse from one John Welch: acquitted of fraud but guilty of extortion: reprimand and refund the money. (17)

HENDERON, Josiah, Noah, Cpl. Colonel Poor's Regiment. Neglect of duty when corporal of the guard, in suffering the prisoners to go at large and permitting one (Samuel Roswell) to escape: reduced to a private. (84)

HENDERSON, William. Colonel Clinton's Regiment. Stealing: acquitted. (118)

HENDRICKS, John, Drummer. Fifth Connecticut Regiment. Desertion, stealing a horse: 100 lashes. (31)

HENING,_____, Ensign. First New York Regiment. Embezzling and misapplying part of the rum: acquitted. (64)

HENLEY,——, Lieutenant Colonel. Non-attendance on the grand parade: reprimand. (134)

HENLEY, Archer. Colonel Bland's Regiment. Plundering: run the gauntlet. (134) *See* Laurence.

HENLY, John. Seventh Massachusetts Regiment. Desertion: death — pardoned. (78)

HENNESSEY, John. Fourth New York Regiment. Desertion and endeavoring to go to the enemy: death. (42)

HENNESSY, William. First Virginia Regiment. Desertion and joining the enemy: death by hanging. (115)

HENNY, Michael. Third New York Regiment. Theft and desertion: death by shooting. (89)

HENNY, Philip. First Regiment. Plundering the inhabitants: 100 lashes. (116)

HENRY,_____, Major. Light Dragoons. Several instances of poor military leadership, involving eight counts of wrongdoing: acquitted of all charges with honor. (110)

HENRY,_____, Sergeant. Fourth Massachusetts Regiment. Repeated desertions: reduced to a private and 100 lashes. (54)

HENRY, Hugh. *See* Renny.

HENSLEY, John. Fourth Regiment of Light Dragoons. Robbing the house of widow Mary Landsford of sundry valuable articles: 100 lashes. (111) (129) *See* Barck.

HERBERT, Thomas. Colonel Sargent's Regiment. Theft: thirty-nine lashes. (106)

HERBERT, Thomas. Captain Wyllys's Company. Convictions of theft and punishment of thirty-nine lashes reversed and acquitted. (132)

HERONDER, William. Colonel Reed's Regiment. Desertion: thirty-nine lashes. (106)

HERRISON, Thomas (alias Williams). Desertion: death by shooting — escaped, recaptured and resentenced to death by shooting. (77)

HERTHER, James. Third Massachusetts Regiment. Desertion: 100 lashes. (61)

HESALL,_____, Drummer. Overstaying his furlough: acquitted. (91)

HEWES (HUGHES), Charles. Absenting himself from camp without leave, abusing the inhabitants, speaking threatening words respecting the commander of the garrison, speaking words having a tendency to injure the cause of the United States: guilty only of the last charge: 100 lashes. (75) *See* Fryor.

HEWSON, Jeremiah. Colonel McDougall's Regiment. Desertion: released with no evidence being presented. (136)

HIBBING,_____, Ensign. Permitting party under his command to abuse or sell the property of the inhabitants of Ballstown: acquitted. (88)

HICKEY, Thomas. Commander-in-Chief's Guard. Exciting and joining in a mutiny and sedition, treacherously corresponding with, enlisting among, and receiving pay from the enemies of the United American Colonies: death by hanging. (1) (136) *See* chapter four.

HICKS, John. Colonel Porter's Regiment. Desertion: thirty-nine lashes. (84) (117)

HIER,_____, Sergeant. Sixth Company. Neglect of duty: reprimand. (23)

HIGGINS, James. Captain Stevens's Independent Company of Riflemen. Striking and abusing several officers of the Twentieth Regiment: thirty-nine lashes. (136) *See* Steel.

HIGGINS, Robert. Colonel Sargent's Regiment. Theft: acquitted. (104)

HIGGINS, William. Captain Hamilton's Company of Artillery. Plundering and stealing: thirty-nine lashes. (7)

HILBART, Jedediah. Stealing: acquitted. (43)

HILBURN, Hezekiah, Sutler. Selling liquor to a soldier: acquitted. (41)

HILERY,_____, Ensign. Drunkenness, profane swearing: reprimand. (93)

HILL, Ebenezer. First Connecticut Regiment. Stealing a barrel of flour from the commissary: 100 lashes. (30) (97) *See* Wardon.

HILL, Nathan. Twenty lashes. (42)

HILL, Silas. Twenty lashes. (42)

HILL, William, Sgt. Colonel Jackson's Regiment. Desertion and attempting to persuade others to desert: reduced in ranks and 100 stripes. (33)

HILLARD, Thomas. Colonel Dayton's Regiment. Stealing leather and insulting Sergeant Brown: fifty lashes. (103)

HILLS, George. Fighting: thirty stripes with rods. (91) *See* Smith.

HILLS, George. Breaking open and robbing the store: thirty-nine lashes and a fine of thirty shillings—fine remitted. (91)

HILMESS, Will. First New York Regiment. Desertion: fifty lashes. (59)

HILTON,_____, Captain. Colonel Paterson's Regiment. Neglect of duty: reprimand. (114)

HILTWATER, Thomas. Ninth Virginia Regiment. Desertion and attempting to go to the enemy: 100 lashes. (101)

HINDEL, James. Desertion: 100 lashes. (42)

HINDS, Ebenezer. Colonel Nixon's Regiment. Stealing two horses and riding them off: fine of forty shillings for damages, and twenty stripes. (133) *See* Stocks.

HINGHAM, Alexander. Stealing rum at the commissary store: acquitted. (69) *See* Bryant, Rockwood, Woodbury.

HINTON, James. Colonel Morrow's Regiment. Insolence to Ensign Hight, of the same regiment: ask the ensign's pardon at the head of the regiment. (96)

HITCHBURN, Gilsbury, Cpl. Absenting himself without leave: reduced to a private sentinel and fifty lashes. (42)

HITCHCOCK, William. Colonel Gist's Regiment. Breaking into a house: 100 lashes. (21) *See* Carson, Garnick, Johnson, Lane.

HOBBS, John. Colonel Porter's Regiment. Desertion: thirty-nine lashes. (117)

HOBBY,_____, Lieutenant. Colonel McDougall's Regiment. Misbehavior in leaving one of the hulks in the North River: complaint adjudged to be groundless – discharged. (71)

HOBBY, Joseph. Connecticut Line. Desertion: fifty lashes. (42)

HODGE, George. Colonel Willy's Regiment. 100 lashes. (130)

HODGE, Joseph. Desertion: 100 lashes. (42)

HODING, Jacob. Colonel Topham's Regiment. Being intoxicated with liquor and abusing the inhabitants, abusing a sergeant: forty-five lashes. (98)

HOFF, Henry Hercules. Colonel Livingston's Regiment. Desertion: 100 lashes. (131)

HOFFENBERGER, George. German Battalion. Mutiny and desertion: death by shooting. (25) *See* Alexander, Bottemer, Cook, Kurts.

HOGAN, Edward. Colonel Marshall's Regiment. Desertion in the late retreat from Ticonderoga: returned to his regiment in irons. (9)

HOGAN, John. Desertion: 100 lashes. (42)

HOGG, Ebenezer, Sgt. Colonel Nixon's Regiment. Absent without leave: ten lashes and not permitted to do the duty of a sergeant during this campaign. (133)

HOLCOMB,_____, Lieutenant. Colonal Johnston's Regiment. Assuming the rank of a captain and wearing a yellow cockade, and mounting guard in that capacity: acquitted. (132) (136)

HOLDEN, Jacob. Colonel Topham's Regiment. Getting intoxicated with liquor, abusing one of the inhabitants, abusing Sergeant Bliss: forty-five lashes—pardoned. (68)

HOLDEN, Joseph. Stealing port and oatmeal from the commissary: acquitted. (48)

HOLDNES, Thomas. Colonel Scammell's Regiment. 100 lashes. (130)

HOLDRIDGE,_____, Lieutenant Colonel. Taking a schooner captured from the enemy, diverting it and part of the goods therein to his own property: acquitted. (21)

HOLE, James. Desertion: 100 lashes. (42)

HOLLAND, George. Third Massachusetts Regiment. Desertion and attempting to go to the enemy: not guilty as charged but guilty of being absent without leave—forty lashes. (54) *See* Cooper.

HOLLAND, Tony, Lt. Colonel Putnam's Regiment. Encouraging a prisoner at Tarrytown to make his escape: acquitted with honor. (22)

HOLLEY, B. North Carolina Line. Desertion: fifty lashes. (115)

HOLLEY, Benjamin. Third South Carolina Line. Desertion: 100 lashes with switches. (95)

HOLLOWAY, Richard. Colonel Malcolm's Regiment. Absent from duty: acquitted. (118)

HOLLOWELL, Richard. Ninth Pennsylvania Regiment. Deserting with his arms and accouterments, forging a pass, stealing, attempting to go to the enemy: death. (21)

HOLMES,_____, Lieutenant. Colonel Sherburne's Regiment. Being acquainted with the circumstances of robbing a house, conniving at and concealing the same, receiving part of the goods, knowing them to be stolen: cashiered. (85)

HOLMES,_____, Corporal. Disobedience to orders: acquitted. (91)

HOLMES, Benjamin, Lt. Second Virginia Regiment. Behavior unbecoming an officer and gentleman: acquitted. (134)

HOLMES, Benjamin. Mutiny: twenty lashes. (84)

HOLMES, Cyprian. Captain Hart's Company. Taking boards from the barracks and cutting them up for his own use: fine of twenty shillings to pay for the boards. (91)

HOLMES, Isaac. Second Massachusetts Regiment. Desertion: acquitted, because he had surrendered himself in accordance with a proclamation by the commander-in-chief granting amnesty for returned deserters. (50)

HOLMES, James. Killing an ox belonging to an inhabitant: acquitted. (39) *See* Brooks, Carey, Dow, Dupee, Hunsberry, Jackson.

HOLMES, Stephen. Mutiny: thirty-nine lashes. (84)

HOLMES, William. Embezzling whiskey: acquitted. (103)

HOLMES, Zepariah. Mutiny: twenty lashes. (84)

HOLT, John. Colonel Porter's Regiment. Desertion: thirty-nine lashes. (84)

HOMER,_____, Sergeant. General Varnum's Guard. Insulting a number of officers, attempting with an iron ramrod to strike a lieutenant, causing and exciting a mutiny: reduced to the ranks and fifty lashes. (9)

HONEYCUTT, Bowlin. Desertion: 100 lashes and make up the time he was absent from the service. (115)

HOOPER, John. Colonel Malcolm's Regiment. Drunk on his post: thirty lashes. (72)

HOOPER, Robert. Mutiny, riot, and disobedience to orders: fine of twenty shillings. (135)

HOOPS, Adam, Lt. Fourth Maryland Regiment. Swearing when he came off of camp guard he would not do another tour of duty as a subaltern, telling the adjutant he would return himself unfit for duty in the next weekly return, returning himself sick and refusing to do duty on that account, absent without leave two days: acquitted. (28) *See* Haass.

HOPE, William. Maryland Line. Leaving camp without leave, plundering the inhabitants: 100 lashes. (115)

HOPKINS,_____, Captain. Fourth Regiment of Light Dragoons. Repeatedly selling public horses and applying the money to his own use: acquitted. (55)

HOPKINS, Binon. Second Brigade of Artillery. Desertion from a party at Danbury: 100 lashes. (54)

HOPPER, John. Colonel Malcolm's Regiment. Drunk on his post: thirty lashes. (132)

HORSTFULL, Caleb. Colonel Arnold's Regiment. Refusing to obey Colonel Arnold's order: fined one month's pay and immediately join Captain Smith's company, according to Colonel Arnold's order. (128)

HORVAN, Jesse, inhabitant of Pennsylvania. Supplying the enemy with provisions: pay fifty pounds for the use of the sick at camp. (15)

HOSKINS, Robert. Delaware Regiment. Plundering a house of an inhabitant near Prospect Hill: fifty lashes and a fine of one-half month's pay. (93)

HOULAD, William. Mutiny: twenty lashes. (84)

HOUSON, Andrew. Colonel Clinton's Regiment. Desertion: fine of one month's pay—pardoned. (118)

HOUSTON, David. Colonel Silliman's Regiment. Breaking open a store and stealing molasses and fish: thirty-nine lashes. (132)

HOW, Moses, Ens. Colonel Brewer's Regiment. Contempt of the service: acquitted. (135)

HOWARD,_____, Major. Wounding Lieutenant Duffy with his sword, abetting a riot in camp, attempting the life of Lieutenant Duffy with a loaded firelock and fixed bayonet: guilty of the second charge but not guilty of the other charges—reprimand. (134)

HOWARD, John Eager, Lt. Col. Maryland Line. Disobedience to orders by not parading his battalion and remaining with it, not furnishing the morning reports and returns of his battalion, errors in those returns: guilty of the first and third charges—reprimand. The commander-in-chief spoke of him in flattering terms and released him. (26)

HOWARD, Jonathan. Colonel Vose's Regiment. Attempted desertion: 100 stripes. (88)

HOWARD, Jonathan. Colonel Vose's Regiment. Desertion and enlisting twice: not guilty of desertion but guilty of enlisting twice—refund the bounty received. (88)

HOWE, David. Colonel Poor's Regiment. Desertion and enlisting with the militia, deserting again: thirty-nine lashes. (117)

HOWE, Joshua. Plundering the inhabitants of money, and other offenses: fifty lashes. (33)

HOWE, Robert, Maj. Gen. An acquittal with the highest honors from a previous court-martial was approved. (124)

HOWEL, Thomas. Colonel Courtland's Regiment. Deserting to the enemy, returning and deserting again, persuading others to desert: death by shooting. (125)

HOWELL, William. Captain Hazard's Company. Abusing Sergeant Thompson, calling him a "chuckleheaded son of a bitch": twenty lashes for abusing the sergeant and ten lashes for being disguised in liquor. (93)

HOWLEY, Grant. Seventh Regiment. Desertion: 100 lashes. (130)

HOWLEY, James. Seventh Massachusetts Regiment. Desertion: death— pardoned because of his recent good behavior. (44)

HOWS, George. Colonel Moyland's Regiment. Mutiny and desertion: twenty-five lashes—remitted. (10) *See* Fornokes.

HOWS, William. Twice deserting: 100 lashes. (121)

HUBBARD, Abner. Colonel Shepherd's Regiment. Desertion: fifty lashes. (88)

HUBBARD, Stephen. Captain Whiting's Company. Taking boards from the barracks and cutting them up for his own use: fine of twenty shillings to pay for the boards. (91)

HUBBARD, Thomas. Colonel Sargent's Regiment. Desertion: thirty-nine lashes—acquitted after an appeal. (136)

HUBBARD, Titus. Captain Whiting's Company. Taking boards from the barracks and cutting them up for his own use: fine of twenty shillings to pay for the boards. (91)

HUBBART, Joseph. Colonel Learned's Regiment. Desertion: thirty-nine lashes. (106)

HUBBELL, William, Capt. Colonel Webb's Regiment. Low, scandalous, and unofficerlike manner: acquitted. (3) (133) (136)

HUBERT, John. Second Virginia Regiment. Desertion: 100 lashes. (21)

HUBLEY,_____, Lieutenant Colonel. Tenth Pennsylvania Regiment. Malicious behavior when Colonel Nagle signed a false return to the injury of his honor, contrary to good order: acquitted. (17)

HUDSON,_____, Ensign. Sixth Virginia Regiment. Embezzling the effects of a dead soldier, theft: acquitted. (134)

HUDSON, George. Colonel Vose's Regiment. Attempted desertion: 100 stripes. (88)

HUFF, David. Second Brigade of Artillery. Desertion: 100 lashes. (54)

HUFNER, Hendrick. Conspiring to desert to the enemy: 100 lashes— remitted. (89)

HUGHES, Bordwill. Captain Douglass's Company. Using insulting language to Sergeant Orcutt, getting drunk and refusing to go on duty when warned: guilty only of the last charge: thirty lashes. (91)

HUGHES, George. Colonel Angell's Regiment. Threatening and attempting to desert to the enemy: acquitted. (24)

HUGHES, Thomas, Paymaster. Seventh Virginia Regiment. Neglect of duty and disobedience to orders, leaving camp with intention not to return without settling his accounts: dismissed from the service, but to continue in camp till he settled his accounts. (14)

HUGHES, William. Third Connecticut Regiment. Carrying a soldier across the river by which means the soldier deserted: acquitted. (54)

HUGO,_____, Captain. Maryland Line. Forcibly taking from Mr. Gamble, assistant quartermaster at Salisbury, soldiers' shoes and other apparel belonging to the United States: not guilty of forcibly taking the clothing, but taking it without authorization, such behavior justified because of the state of their soldiers—acquitted. (115) *See* Pendergast, Williams.

HUGO,_____, Captain Lieutenant. Barbarously striking and cutting a soldier named Catoo, of the Maryland Line, with a sword, disabling him from doing the duties of a soldier: acquitted. (115)

HUGO,_____, Lieutenant. Fifth Maryland Regiment. Beating, wounding, and abusing in a cruel manner sundry soldiers belonging to the Second Maryland Regiment: acquitted. (26)

HULABERT, Christopher. Embezzling public stores: fine of $130. (103)

HULBERT, Joseph. Colonel Reed's Regiment. Desertion: thirty-nine lashes. (1) (136)

HULL, Samuel. Colonel Webb's Regiment. Absent without leave and lodging out of camp: 100 lashes. (91) *See* Clarke.

HULLOWAY, Richard. Absent from duty: acquitted. (123)

HUNDALL, Oliver. Third Massachusetts Regiment. Desertion and selling his firelock and accouterments, reenlisting under the name of Amos Blodgett: 100 lashes, with twenty-five lashes administered at four different times, and fined for the stolen articles. (46)

HUNLEY, Richard. Seventh Pennsylvania Regiment. Threatening and intending desertion: twenty-five lashes. (101)

HUNSEBERRY, Nathan. Killing an ox belonging to an inhabitant: acquitted. (39) *See* Brooks, Carey, Dow, Dupee, Holmes, Jackson.

HUNT,_____, Lieutenant. Fourth New York Regiment. Marching the main guard in a disorderly manner, permitting the men to straggle: reprimand. (28)

HUNT,_____, Lieutenant. Fourth Massachusetts Regiment. Not attending a parade and pretending to be too lame to march in the parade: reprimand. (58)

HUNT,_____, Sergeant. Colonel Bigelow's Regiment. Using threatening words and raising mutiny: reduced to the ranks and 100 lashes. (122) *See* Pearce.

HUNT, Edward. Theft: acquitted. (23)

HUNT, Joseph. Being a spy: acquitted. (9)

HUNT, Josiah. Acting in a mutinous manner, endeavoring to excite a mutiny: forty lashes. (9)

HUNT, Locke. Colonel Cotton's Regiment. Desertion: fifteen lashes— pardoned. (120)

HUNTINGTON, Samuel. Thirty-fourth Regiment of Foot Soldiers. Assisting and encouraging mutiny: fine of fifteen shillings and fifteen days fatigue due. (3) (133) (136) *See* English.

HUNTON, James. Getting drunk, threatening to desert: twenty-nine lashes. (67)

HURLBURT, John, Lt. Colonel Chester's Regiment. Deserting the camp in time of danger: not guilty of desertion but guilty of being absent without leave for twenty-four days—cashiered and a fine of one month's pay. (74)

HURLBUT, Stephen. Stealing corn from an inhabitant: run the gauntlet twice through the regiment. (91) *See* Thompson.

HURLEY, Arthur. Third New York Regiment. Willfully destroying public property by felling a tree upon the tents and arms of the regiment: acquitted. (111)

HURLEY, Benjamin, Batteauman. Mutinous behavior: acquitted. (111)

HURLEY, Richard. Seventh Pennsylvania Regiment. Desertion: 100 lashes. (101)

HURLEY, William. Colonel Scammons's Regiment. Firing on and wounding, without cause, one John Chit, a citizen: acquitted. (1)

HUSSEY, Peter. Colonel Crane's Regiment of Artillery. Desertion and receiving a bounty three times: guilty of enlisting twice, but because he returned the money on one occasion, and because of his long confinement, no sentence was imposed. (9)

HUTCHINSON, George, Matross. Fourth Regiment of Artillery. Desertion: death by shooting. (33)

HUTCHISON, Jeremiah. Colonel McDougall's Regiment. Desertion: released from confinement for lack of prosecution: (79)

HUTMAN,_____, Ensign. Colonel Henley's Regiment. Appearing on the parade intoxicated and incapable of doing his duty: dismissed from the service. (9)

HUTTON, William, Provost Marshal. Assisting Samuel Harrison in making his escape from the provost guard where he was confined for counterfeiting bills of credit: acquitted. (10) *See* chapter four.

HUTTON, William, Provost Marshal. Refusing to execute the office of the post marshal in the execution of John Walker (alias Robert Maples): dismissed from the service. (41) *See* Walker and chapter four.

HYER, Jacob, Ensign. Second New York Regiment. Scandalous and disorderly conduct: reprimand. (51)

IANGE, Philip. Desertion: 100 lashes. (28)

ICOMS,_____, Sergeant. Cruelly beating Patrick Shea, of the Fourth Regiment: guilty of beating him but not in a cruel manner—reprimand. (110)

INGHAM, Alexander. Stealing rum out of the company's general stores: ten lashes. (136) *See* Bryant, Lockwood, Woodburn.

IRELAND, Jonathan. Delaware Regiment. Desertion: guilty only of absence without leave—fifty lashes. (121)

IRVING, James. Desertion: 100 lashes. (93)

IVORY, Jacobus. Rioting in camp at an unreasonable hour, abusing Captain Elsworth in the execution of his office: acquitted. (111) *See* Bele, Benjamin, White.

IVORY, Patrick, Drum major. First Maryland Regiment. Stealing: reduced to a private and 100 lashes. (93)

IVORY, Patrick. First Maryland Regiment. Desertion from the Monmouth command: 100 lashes. (21)

JACKNER, Isaac, Assistant Commissary for the Northern Department. Eight charges of misapplication and neglect of provisions, and similar offenses: reprimand. (116)

JACKSON, Archibald. First New York Regiment. Threatening the lives of officers and endeavoring to entice others to assist him: 100 lashes and sent on board a Continental frigate to serve to the end of his enlistment. (46)

JACKSON, David. Ninth Massachusetts Regiment. Sleeping on his post: 100 lashes—remitted. (48)

JACKSON, Jacob. Killing an ox belonging to an inhabitant: acquitted. (39) *See* Brooks, Carey, Dow, Dupee, Holmes, Hunsberry.

JACKSON, Nathaniel. Captain Craft's Company. Absenting himself from duty when on guard, being drunk on guard: guilty only of the first charge—fatigue duty for two days with a log of three pounds weight hanging to his neck. (104)

JACKSON, Samuel. Ninth Regiment. Desertion: acquitted. (129)

JACKSON, Thomas, Capt. Third Regiment of Artillery. Cowardice and misbehavior before the enemy at Germantown, by relinquishing his command, by being drunk on duty: acquitted. (48) *See* chapter three.

JAKEL, John. Arrested, but released when no evidence appeared. (93)

JAMES,_____, Ensign. Neglect of duty and disobedience to orders: acquitted. (10) (93)

JAMES, John. Eighth Company. Damaging his bayonet: acquitted. (52)

JARMAN, John. Getting drunk: ten stripes. (67)

JAY, Richard. Stealing a shirt: acquitted. (28)

JEANS, Abel, inhabitant of Pennsylvania. Supplying the enemy with money, trading with them, buying and selling counterfeit Continental money: 100 lashes. (15)

JEFFEREY, James. Mutiny, riot, and disobedience to orders: thirty lashes and drummed out of the army. (135)

JEFFERS, Richard. Maryland Line. Desertion: 100 lashes, with twenty-five lashes administered on each of four successive mornings. (44)

JENKINS,_____, Captain. Colonel Brewer's Regiment. Released from his arrest when no charges were placed against him. (75)

JENKINS, John. Sixth Maryland Regiment. Desertion and attempting to go to the enemy: death. (103)

JENKINS, Jonathan. Colonel Nichols's Regiment. Desertion: twenty lashes. (118)

JENNESON, Robert. Stealing port and oatmeal from the commissary: fifty lashes. (48) *See* Holden.

JENNINGS,_____. Colonel Hunley's Regiment. Abuse and insolent behavior to his sergeant: 150 lashes. (10)

JEPSON, William. Disobedience to orders, threatening the drum major: fifty strokes, with his coat off, with sticks or rods. (91)

JEWELL, Hopewill. Stealing and embezzling a Continental mare: 100 lashes, with twenty-five lashes administered on four successive days, but "should the mare be brought before Monday, he then received the whole at once." (93)

JINKS, Thomas. First Massachusetts Regiment. Killing a cow and stealing seven geese: seventy-five lashes and pay fifteen dollars to the owner. (61) (86) *See* Abram, Brayton, Cook, Cowell, Gardner, Shea, Wood.

JIPES, Joseph. Seventh Maryland Regiment. Desertion to the enemy: 100 lashes. (21)

JOAB, Moses. Taking a wagon and horse: 100 lashes and pay three dollars for the wagon. (93)

JOCELINE, David. Stealing apples from an orchard belonging to Robinson's farm: acquitted. (56) *See* Allen, Penham.

JOHNS, Samuel. Second Company. Losing his hunting shirt: acquitted. (46)

JOHNSON, Daniel. Colonel Chandler's Regiment. Deserting to the enemy: guilty of deserting but not of design to remain with the enemy—100 lashes. (113)

JOHNSON, David. Abuse: fine of eight shillings, New York currency. (128)

JOHNSON, James. Desertion: run the gauntlet frontward and backward. (90)

JOHNSON, James. Colonel Wyllys's Regiment. Desertion: thirty-nine lashes. (1) (132)

JOHNSON, James. Colonel Gist's Regiment. Breaking into a house: 100 lashes. (21) *See* Carson, Garnick, Hitchcock, Lane.

JOHNSON, James. Second New York Regiment. Accessory to stealing rum from Mr. Adams, sutler: acquitted. (111) *See* Ladd, Lester, Rose.

JOHNSON, James. Captain Foster's Company. Absent without leave: ask the officers' pardon and severe fatigue for three weeks. (104)

JOHNSON, James. Massachusetts Line. Desertion: 100 lashes. (56)

JOHNSON, John, Cpl. Captain Brown's Company. Abusing Ensign Brown, treating him with insolent language, charging him with a lie: reduced to the ranks. (88)

JOHNSON, John. Fourth Yorkers. Breaking open a box and stealing rum, being drunk when on sentry: thirty-nine lashes. (128)

JOHNSON, Jonas. 100 lashes. (122)

JOHNSON, Mary. Laying a plot to desert to the enemy: 100 lashes and drummed out of the army by all the drums and fifes in the division. (134)

JOHNSON, Peter. Exceeding the limits of his furlough: acquitted. (91)

JOHNSON, Philip. Colonel Harrison's Regiment of Artillery. Conspiracy to spike the cannon at Fort Schuyler and intending to desert to the enemy: 100 lashes. (37) *See* Amos, Stanberry, Watkins, Wright.

JOHNSON, Richard. Second Virginia Regiment. Mutiny and desertion: 100 lashes—remitted. (134)

JOHNSON, Thomas. First Company. Drunk on the parade: thirty-nine lashes. (42)

JOHNSTON,_____, Sergeant. Insolence to Lieutenant Hudson and breach of orders: reprimand. (93) (103)

JOHNSTON, Crawford. North Carolina Line. Desertion: run the gauntlet. (49)

JOHNSTON, Henry. Colonel Wade's Regiment. Attempting to desert to the enemy: acquitted. (9)

JOHNSTON, James. Colonel Ward's Regiment. Desertion: thirty-nine lashes. (136)

JOHNSTON, John. Sixteenth Massachusetts Regiment. Theft: twenty lashes. (136)

JOHNSTON, Moses. Massachusetts Line. Desertion. (53)

JOHNSTON, Thomas. First Company. Absent without leave, selling two pairs of boots not his own property: eighty lashes and a fine for the boots. (53)

JOHNSTON, Thomas. Fifth Maryland Regiment. Attempting to desert: 100 lashes. (93)

JONES,_____, Captain. Colonel Gist's Regiment. Beating a sentry on his post and a corporal on guard: acquitted—but the sentence was disapproved upon review, "evidence clearly proved that both captains (Jones and Mitchell) did beat the guards. Acknowledging that the men were insolent and merited punishment, but ought to have been confined and punished in a regular way, rather than by beating them." (21) *See* Mitchell.

JONES, Daniel. Colonel Craft's Regiment of Artillery. Abusing several inhabitants of the town: acquitted. (19) *See* Hayley.

JONES, Elija. Colonel Tyler's Regiment. Abusing Dr. Arnold, an inhabitant of the town of Providence: forty-three stripes—pardoned. (23)

JONES, Hugh. Third Regiment of Artillery. Desertion to the enemy: acquitted. (57)

JONES, Jacob. Colonel McDougall's Regiment. Sleeping on his post: thirty lashes. (132) (136)

JONES, Jonathan, Sutler. Purchasing axes from the public stores: forfeit the axes and not allowed in camp in the future. (46)

JONES, Patrick, Matross. Artillery. Repeated desertion: seventy-five lashes. (124)

JONES, Samuel, Capt. North Carolina Line. Scandalous behavior: acquitted with honor. (49)

JONES, Samuel. Colonel Gimato's Regiment of Light Infantry. Desertion and intending to go to the enemy: death – pardoned upon the recommendations of two colonels of his regiment. (36)

JONES, Samuel. Regiment of Light Dragoons. Desertion to the enemy: death – pardoned. (125)

JONES, Samuel. Fifteenth Virginia Regiment. Concealing and denying that he had in his possession a pair of mittens belonging to Captain Hall, gaming, treating Captain Hall with abusive language while under arrest: dismissed from the service. (17)

JONES, Solomon, Cpl. Colonel Bigelow's Regiment. Disobedience to orders: acquitted. (24)

JONES, Thomas, Fife major. Colonel Harrison's Regiment. Drunkenness on parade: fifty lashes. (125)

JONES, William. Delaware Regiment. Exciting and promoting desertion: acquitted. (109)

JONES, William. Captain Sample's Company. Out without a pass, attempting to sell a horse: thirty-nine lashes. (116)

JORDAN, Fountain. North Carolina Line. Desertion: 100 lashes. (49)

JORDAN, James. Second Virginia Regiment. Desertion for the third time, forging a discharge, reenlisting in the Twelfth Pennsylvania Regiment: 300 lashes, 100 on each of three different days. (9)

JULY, Jonathan. Maryland Line. Leaving camp without leave, plundering the inhabitants: 100 lashes. (115)

JULY, Peter. Colonel Pinckney's Battalion. Desertion: death. (90)

JUPITER, Silas. Stealing rum from the quartermaster: seventy lashes. (111)

JURGESON, John. Colonel Baldwin's Regiment of Militia. Demanding and receiving money from the soldiers for writing recommendations for the sick to be discharged: drummed out of the army. (123)

JUSTICE, Jacob. Seventh Pennsylvania Regiment. Plundering Mr. Bogart, an inhabitant, near Paramus: death by hanging – pardoned. (26) *See* Bell, Brown, Powers.

JUSTIN, Charles. Stealing hinges, absent from his quarters at an unreasonable hour of the night: twenty lashes – remitted. (91)

KATOR, James. Third Massachusetts Regiment. Desertion: 100 lashes. (86)

KEARNEY, Thomas, Matross. Colonel Lamb's Regiment of Artillery. Threatening the life of Captain Davis, and sundry other crimes: 100 lashes. (83) (84)

KEITH, James, Major. Eighth Massachusetts Regiment. Detaching a party of men from West Point without the knowledge of the commandant, putting them under the direction of a person not an officer, dealing behind the enemy line, making use of a soldier with a military guard to assist him, purchasing stores from within the enemy lines: dismissed from the service. (58)

KELLERAN,_____, Captain. Captain Willington's Company. Taking a horse belonging to Mr. Price of Albany: acquitted. (88)

KELLEY, David. Captain Munston's Company. Repeatedly attempting to pass the guard in the dark of the evening, with an improper pass: fifty lashes. (100)

KELLEY, Elijah. Massachusetts Line. Desertion: 100 lashes. (76)

KELLEY, John. Colonel Marks's Regiment. Threatening to shoot Captain Richards: thirty-nine lashes and reprimand. (84) (117)

KELLY,_____, Corporal. Second New York Regiment. Willful disobedience to orders: reduced to a private sentinel. (64)

KELLY, Barnabas. Colonel Cortlandt's Battalion. Desertion; forging, and procuring to be forged a pass: 100 lashes for each offense. (83) (84)

KELLY, John. Second Regiment. Enlisting in the Third Regiment: fifty lashes – pardoned. (95)

KELLY, John. Mutiny, riot, and disobedience to orders: thirty lashes and drummed out of the army. (135)

KELLY, Robert. Fourth New York Regiment. Suffering a prisoner under his charge to escape from the guard: acquitted. (111)

KELLY, William. Delaware Regiment. Disobeying orders and insulting Lieutenant Devall, of the Second Maryland Regiment: 100 lashes. (93)

KELTON,_____, Captain. Colonel Paterson's Regiment. Neglect of duty: reprimand. (105)

KEMP, John (Jason). Colonel Learned's Regiment. Desertion: thirty-nine lashes. (136)

KENDRICK, Richard. Mutiny, riot, and disobedience to orders: fine of twenty shillings. (135)

KENNEDY, Dennis. Ninth Pennsylvania Regiment. Attempting to desert and persuading a number of others to desert with him: not guilty of the first charge but guilty of the second charge – 100 lashes. (14) *See* Deland.

KENNERY, Daniel. First Battalion. Theft: 100 lashes. (102)

KENNIS (KAVAS), John. Third Pennsylvania Regiment. Desertion: 100 lashes. (131)

KENNY, Benjamin. Colonel Arnold's Regiment. Refusing to obey Colonel Arnold's orders: fine one month's pay and immediately join Captain Smith's company, according to Colonel Arnold's order. (128)

KENNY, Stephen. Colonel Marshall's Regiment. Desertion in the late retreat from Ticonderoga: returned to his regiment in irons. (9)

KENT, John. Colonel Cilly's Regiment. Sleeping on his post: 100 lashes. (103)

KENT, Simon. First New Jersey Regiment. Repeated desertion: death – pardoned. (78)

KENTFIELD, Shem. First New Hampshire Regiment. Desertion and bearing arms in the service of the King of Great Britain against the U.S.: death by hanging. (51)

KEOGH, William. Sixth Maryland Regiment. Desertion and enlisting in a Virginia state regiment: death by shooting. (121)

KETCHUM,_____, Sergeant. Colonel Varnum's Regiment. Scandalizing the officers of his regiment: acquitted. (126) (132)

KETCHUM, Nathaniel. Being a spy: acquitted. (9)

KETTS, David. Colonel Ward's Regiment. Stealing a shirt: sentence was postponed. (136)

KEYS, William, Deputy Commissary of Forage. Unequal and partial distribution of forage, failure to deliver forage in some cases: dismissed from the service – remitted and restored to his office. (48)

KEYTON, John. Tenth Virginia Regiment. Mutiny and desertion: acquitted. (70)

KIDDER, John. Desertion: ninety-nine lashes. (122)

KIEF, Richard. Colonel Nicholson's Regiment. Stealing a coat and several firelocks: thirty-nine lashes. (136) *See* Cahagan.

KIEL, Christopher. Colonel Thomas's Regiment. Desertion: thirty-nine lashes and dismissed from the service. (118) (123)

KIESENER, Charles. Tenth Regiment. Desertion: 100 lashes. (129)

KILBREATH, Hugh. Colonel Hand's Regiment. Assaulting, beating, and wounding Asa Baker and David Avery, of the artillery: thirty-nine lashes. (136)

KILBURN,_____. Fifth Company. Stealing rum from another person's canteen: acquitted. (23)

KILTON,_____, Captain. Colonel Paterson's Regiment. Neglect of duty: severe reprimand at the head of the regiment. (135)

KINCADE,_____, Corporal. First Regiment. Abusing and disposing of public stores embezzled by another: reduced to the ranks and 100 lashes – remitted. (116)

KINCADE, Joseph, Drummer. First Regiment. Desertion: fifty lashes. (129)

KINCAID,_____, Adjutant and Acting Brigade Major to General Scott. Not bringing his picket on the grand parade on time: acquitted. (93)

KINDAL, Oliver. Eighth Massachusetts Regiment. Desertion, forging his captain's and colonel's name on a pass, selling his blanket: 100 lashes, with twenty-five lashes administered on four different mornings. (50) (124)

KINDERS, John. Commander-in-Chief's Guard. Going out, with others, with sidearms, to do harm to other soldiers: acquitted. (125)

KING, Charles. Robbery, cocking and presenting his piece at an officer, desertion: thirty-nine lashes, followed by thirty-nine lashes one week later, and one month's confinement in irons, and then be drummed out of the service. (128)

KING, James, Sgt. Colonel Paterson's Regiment. Absent without leave, striking Sergeant Goodrich: reduced to the ranks and a fine of twenty shillings. (113) (136)

KING, James (alias McMullen, James). Third Maryland Battalion. Repeated desertions: 100 lashes and a fine of $120, which was the bounty he received at the time of his enlistment. (26)

KING, James. Colonel Angell's Regiment. Threatening to take the life of Lieutenant Peckham and then desert to the enemy: picketed for fifteen minutes and then receive 100 lashes on four different times. (24)

KING, John. First New Jersey Regiment. Desertion: fifty lashes. (101)

KING, Jonah. Being out of camp at unreasonable hours, being drunk: twenty-five lashes. (23)

KING, Josiah, Sgt. Appearing at the weekly inspection with his arms very dirty: reduced to private. (41)

KING, Patrick. Losing his cartridge box and cartridges: acquitted—the decision was disapproved and ordered to pay for the lost articles. (47)

KING, William. Fourth New York Regiment. Desertion: death—pardoned. (42)

KINGHAM, Edward. Fifth Regiment. Enlisting in the Third Regiment: 100 lashes. (95)

KINGSBURY, Richard. Desertion: twenty-five lashes. (124)

KINKEAD,_____. First Pennsylvania Regiment. Desertion: fifty lashes. (97)

KINNER, John. Fourth Regiment. Leaving his post: acquitted. (59)

KINNEY, Abraham, Lt. Sheldon's Light Dragoons. Going below the lines, assisting and conniving in an illicit intercourse and trafficking with the enemy, opposing a lieutenant in the exercise of his duty, leaving his cantonment of General Hazen's Regiment, disobedience to orders: reprimand and ask the pardon of the lieutenant. (64)

KINSEY, Isaac. Third South Carolina Regiment. Desertion: 100 lashes. (95)

KINSEY, James. Colonel Foreman's Regiment. Breaking open a store and drawing rum, or suffering it to be done. (132) See Cock, Relsworth.

KIRK,_____, Ensign. Colonel Grayson's Regiment. Permitting several of his guards to be asleep and not demanding the password and countersign: reprimand. (12)

KIRK, Philip. Supplying the enemy with cattle: confined in some gaol in the state of Pennsylvania during the enemy's engagement, his personal goods and estate to be taken from him for the use of the United States of America—the personal property was not taken, as Washington felt such a punishment was improper. (14) (134) See Williamson.

KIRKHAM (KIRCUM), Benjamin. Captain Williams's Company. Cutting up his blanket and making it into a coat: sixteen stripes—pardoned. (91)

KIRKPATRICK,_____, Captain Lieutenant. Corps of Sappers and Miners. Mutinous behavior and disobedience to orders by bringing his baggage into a captain's quarters contrary to orders and refusing to take it away: reprimand and suspended from the service for three months—remitted, when Washington said, "The commander-in-chief leaves the young gentlemen to the sting of their own reflections as a punishment for what has passed, and only advises them not to be guilty of anything of a similar nature in the future." (63) (87) *See* Taulman.

KIRTHY,_____, Lieutenant. Eighth Virginia Regiment. Disobedience to orders, absenting himself three months beyond the alloted time for him to join his regiment: guilty of the first charge but acquitted of the second charge—dismissed from the service. (101)

KISCUM, Benjamin. Stealing corn from an inhabitant: picketed for ten minutes. (91)

KISSADAY, Allen. Second Pennsylvania Regiment. Drunk on his post: twenty lashes. (94)

KITTON,_____, Captain. Colonel Paterson's Regiment. Neglect of duty: severe reprimand. (2)

KITTS, Daniel. Colonel Ward's Regiment. Stealing a shirt. (106)

KNEELAND, Henry. Eighth Company. Stealing a shirt and other articles of clothing from Asa Kamp: thirty-nine lashes. (65)

KNICKABACKER, Andrew. Second New York Regiment. Desertion: pardoned in compliance with Washington's proclamation granting amnesty to returned deserters. (25) (103)

KNOTT, William. Sixth Massachusetts Regiment. Disobedience to orders and attempting to charge his bayonet upon Captain Haywood when under drill: 200 lashes, with 100 lashes administered at two different times. (53)

KNOWLAND (KNOWLTON), John. Colonel Prescott's Regiment. Plundering a cellar belonging to a citizen of New York: released to his regiment. (7) *See* Butler, McIntire, Webster.

KNOWLTON, Thomas. Colonel Bridge's Regiment. Quitting his post when on duty: fifteen lashes—pardoned. (136)

KOUGH, William. Sixth Maryland Regiment. Desertion and enlisting in a Virginia state regiment: death by shooting. (109)

KURTZ, Frederick. German Battalion. Mutiny and desertion: death by shooting. (25) *See* Alexander, Bottemer, Cook, Hoffenberger.

LABB, James. Colonel Angell's Regiment. Threatening and attempting to desert to the enemy: 100 lashes. (24)

LACEY, Hugh. Captain Steward's Company of Highlanders. Impudence and disobedience to the orders of his captain: twenty lashes — pardoned. (136)

LADD, Joseph, Cpl. Third New York Regiment. Stealing rum from Mr. Adams, sutler: acquitted. (111)

LAFFLIN, John. Absenting himself from his regiment seventeen months without leave: 100 lashes and make good the lost time — lashes remitted because a general order was issued during his confinement pardoning prisoners. (91)

LAINE,_____, Captain. Permitting a party under his command to abuse or sell the property of inhabitants of Ballstown: acquitted. (88)

LAIRD,_____, Captain. Neglect of duty, suffering the Marquis De Lafayette to pass without being stopped or challenged: acquitted. (13) *See* Flagg.

LAKE, Thomas. Colonel Marshall's Regiment. Desertion and enlisting several times: death by hanging. (9)

LAMBERT,_____, Captain. Fourteenth Virginia Regiment. Stealing a hat from Captain Allis: cashiered and pay thirty dollars for the hat, and his name and crime published in the newspapers. (134)

LAMBERT, Arthur. Second New York Regiment. Desertion: 100 lashes. (100)

LAMBERT, Tabor. Fifth Pennsylvania Regiment. Desertion: fifty lashes. (101)

LAMBERTON, Catherine. Abusive language to Lieutenant Hardenburgh: ask the pardon of the lieutenant and reprimand. (111)

LAMBERTON, Symon, Sgt. Being drunk and disturbing the camp at an unreasonable hour, abusive language to Lieutenant Hardenburgh after he was confined: 100 lashes. (111)

LAMONT, W., Lieutenant Corps of Invalids. Behavior unbecoming an officer and a gentleman: dismissed from the service. (51)

LAMPIER, Thomas. Third New York Regiment. Theft, desertion: death by shooting — pardoned. (89)

LANCASTER, Jacob. Colonel Arden's Regiment. Desertion and enlisting twice: 100 lashes. (88)

LANCASTER, Jacob. Colonel Putnam's Regiment. Deserting to the enemy: 100 lashes. (88)

LAND,_____, Captain. Second Massachusetts Regiment. Permitting prisoners to escape from the guard when he commanded: reprimand—pardoned. (48)

LAND, Joseph. First Massachusetts Regiment. Sleeping on his post: fifty lashes. (46)

LANDERS, Phillip. First New Hampshire Regiment. Stealing a boat and deserting to the enemy on Long Island: 100 lashes. (46)

LANDOVERS, George. Stealing money from William Welsh: acquitted. (43)

LANDRESS, Asa, Provost Marshal. Striking and abusing a soldier in the company of invalids when under confinement: acquitted. (50)

LANE,_____, Captain. Colonel Wigglesworth's Regiment. Acting in a cowardly manner when sent on a scouting party, in ordering his men to retreat when he had a considerable advantage over the enemy: dismissed from the service. (14)

LANE,_____, Lieutenant. Second Battalion. Opening a packet from the British Commissioners to Congress while on command at Two Rivers: cashiered. (72) (113)

LANE, John. 100 lashes. (42)

LANE, Joshua. Colonel Marshall's Regiment. Desertion in the late retreat from Ticonderoga: returned to his regiment in irons. (9)

LANE, Samuel. Stealing and concealing a barrel of flour: acquitted. (91)

LANE, Thomas. Colonel Angell's Regiment. Selling his clothes that were delivered him from the Continental store: 100 lashes and pay for the clothing. (131)

LANE, Thomas. Sixth Virginia Regiment. Breaking into a house: 100 lashes. (21) *See* Carson, Garnick, Hitchcock, Johnson.

LANE, William, Drummer. Colonel Greene's Regiment. Raising a mutiny and behaving in a disorderly manner: not guilty of the first charge but guilty of the second charge—suspended and reprimand. (131) *See* Baptist, Brown, Buck, Cary, Davis, Dunbar, Goold, Hardin, Luis, Park, Peterson, Tabor.

LANG, Hugh. The Highlanders. Disobedience to orders: twenty lashes—pardoned. (79)

LANG, Thomas. Stealing. (1)

LANGLEY, Ben. Fifth Company. Forging a pass: seventy-five lashes. (47)

LANGSET, Philip. Fourth Regiment of Light Dragoons. Robbery of sundry articles: 100 lashes. (35)

LANHAM, William. Second Regiment of Artillery. Desertion and attempting to go to the enemy: death — new trial ordered "on account of the illegal construction of the court, being held neither by his (Washington's) order nor by that of a general officer commanding in the State of New Jersey." (55)

LANKFORD, Philip. Fourth Regiment of Light Dragoons. Robbing money from two houses in the state of New Jersey: 200 lashes. (21)

LANSING, Garret. First New York Regiment. Desertion and joining the enemy, changing his name to John Johnson, and reenlisting in the Massachusetts Line: death — remitted. (44)

LARABY, Issac. Colonel Gerrish's Regiment. Mutiny: fine of forty-nine shillings and thirty-nine lashes. (133) (136) *See* Harwood, North, Putney, Rawlins (Rollins), Williams.

LARKIN, Oliver. Sixth Company. Stealing corn: acquitted. (66) *See* Franklin, Harvey, Parker.

LARKINS, Thomas. Desertion: acquitted. (93)

LASH, Elias. Seventh Company. Stealing a pewter teapot from Lee's hut in the Fifth Connecticut Regiment: acquitted. (76)

LASHLY, Adam. Fourth Company. Stealing a hide from the commissary: fifty lashes. (61)

LASHLY (LASHLEY), Thomas. Stealing a piece of linen out of the army's store at Newburgh: 100 lashes. (63)

LATIMER, Levi. Absence without leave, selling his uniform, clothing, arms, and accouterments: not guilty of the first charge but guilty of the other charges — fifty lashes and pay for the lost clothing — payment remitted. (91) *See* Pulford.

LATIMER, Levi. Captain Whiting's Company. Taking boards from the barracks and cutting them up for his own use: thirty lashes, since he and Thomas Ramous were the "first promoters of the crime," there being several others who were fined twenty shillings each. (91) *See* Ramous.

LATTON, John. Colonel Vose's Regiment. Deserting the hospital, abusing Lieutenant Grace: "The Court, considering the flogging Latton had received from Lieutenant Grace, and his long confinement, are of the opinion that he be released from his confinement." (24)

LATY, John. Colonel Ward's Regiment. Desertion: thirty-nine lashes. (136)

LAUDERBACK, John. Second Regiment of Artillery. Desertion: 100 lashes. (53)

LAURENCE, William. Plundering: run the gauntlet. (134) *See* Henley.

LAWLER, Thomas. Fourth Pennsylvania Regiment. Desertion to the enemy: 100 lashes. (14)

LAWRENCE, John, Drummer. Third South Carolina Regiment. Desertion and attempting to escape to the enemy: guilty only of desertion – 100 lashes. (95)

LAWRENCE, Joseph. Mutiny, riot, and disobedience to orders: fine of twenty shillings – remitted. (135)

LAWRENCE, Richard. Colonel Prescott's Regiment. Desertion: thirty-nine lashes. (132) (136)

LAWSON, Richard. Colonel Swarthout's Regiment. Desertion: thirty-nine lashes. (123)

LAYBURN, Bowers (Bowen). Colonel McDougall's Regiment. Desertion: thirty-nine lashes. (1)

LAYS, John. Delaware Regiment. Plundering the house of an inhabitant near Prospect Hill: fifty lashes and a fine of one-half month's pay. (93)

LEADBETTER, George. Desertion and being found in arms with the enemy: death. (44)

LEAMON, John. Colonel Thompson's Battalion. Disobedience and mutinous behavior: fine of twenty shillings and six days imprisonment. (135) Note: along with Leamon, several others were also convicted of the same offense, each being fined, with only Leamon being imprisoned.

LEAUNDEN, Joseph, Capt. Colonel Sargent's Regiment. Drawing more provisions than he had men in his company to consume, taking away a gun, the property of William Turner, threatening the life of Sergeant Conner: cashiered. (2)

LEAVITT, John. Colonel Coffins' Regiment. Drunkenness and absent from the guard: fine of ten shillings – pardoned. (133)

LEE,_____, Lieutenant. Disobedience of orders by Major Taylor: reprimand. (93)

LEE,_____, Ensign. Colonel Maxwell's Regiment. Buying a gun belonging to the regiment, and defacing the name "New Jersey" and the number which was marked on it: reprimand and return the gun. (84) (117)

LEE, Charles, Maj. Gen. *See* chapter four.

LEE, Charles. Colonel Putnam's Regiment (Colonel Ritzema's Regiment). Leaving his regiment in a disorderly manner, absent without leave: acquitted. (113) (125)

LEE, Edward. Desertion: fifty lashes. (77)

LEE, Edward. Leaving the detachment when on the march, disposing of a public firelock: guilty of the first charge but not guilty of the second charge—fifty lashes. (42)

LEE, Henry. Desertion: 100 lashes. (42)

LEE, John. *See* Lis, John.

LEE, Moses. First Massachusetts Regiment. Assisting and conniving in breaking into a clothing store at Newburgh in the night, stealing shoes and boots: acquitted. (62) *See* Blaisdell.

LEE, Troy. Fifth Massachusetts Regiment. Desertion, changing his name and enlisting in the Hampshire Line: death. (42)

LEEDS, Thomas. Lieutenant Colonel Tyler's Company. Profane swearing: fine of one shilling. (105)

LEFFINGWELL, Ebenezer. Colonel Durkee's Regiment. Cowardice and misbehavior before the enemy: death by shooting—pardoned because of his former good character. (7) *See* chapter three.

LEFFINGWELL, Thomas. Colonel Abbot's Regiment. Disobedience to orders in not joining his company when ordered: turned over to the state's attorney for civil trial when the defendant declared at the court-martial that he was a loyal subject of King George III. (82)

LEIGH, Cornelius. Colonel Marshall's Regiment. Desertion and enlisting twice and receiving two bounties: 100 lashes and repayment of the bounties. (11)

LEMOYE, John. Desertion, theft. (1)

LENIOR, Francis. Scandalous and infamous behavior, breaking his arrest, threatening a captain's wife: dismissed from the service. (17)

LENS (?), William. Colonel Topham's Regiment. Profane cussing and abusing the corporal and striking a sentry on his post: seventy-five lashes. (98)

LENT, Elias. Colonel McDougall's Regiment. Desertion: released when no evidence was presented. (13) (136)

LENT, Henrick. Colonel McDougall's Regiment. Desertion: released when no evidence was presented. (13) (136)

LENT, Jacob. Colonel McDougall's Regiment. Desertion: released when no evidence was presented. (13) (136)

LENT, Moses. Third New York Regiment. Theft: acquitted. (111)

LEONARD, Enoch. First New Jersey Regiment. Straggling from camp, killing a number of hogs: twenty-five lashes – pardoned. (20) *See* Farmer, McLaughlin, Mumford, Osborne, Rush, Walker, Whitehead.

LEONARD, James. Desertion. (42)

LEONARD, Patrick. Colonel Hand's Regiment. Leaving the camp without leave, riotous behavior: thirty lashes. (132) (136) *See* Crary.

LEONARD, Roger. Third Maryland Regiment. Desertion and attempting to go to the enemy: death. (22)

LESTER,_____, Sergeant. Second New York Regiment. Neglect of duty, accessory to stealing from Mr. Adams, sutler: guilty of the first charge but not guilty of the second charge – reduced to private sentinel. (111) *See* Johnson, Ladd, Rose.

LESTER, James. Being a spy, desertion, sedition, and enviegling Continental soldiers to desert to the enemy: death by hanging. (90)

LEWIS,_____, Lieutenant. Ninth Virginia Regiment. Disobedience to orders on 27 of June: reprimand. (72)

LEWIS, Anthony. Mutiny, riot, and disobedience to orders: fine of twenty shillings. (135)

LEWIS, John. Colonel McDougall's Regiment. Desertion: thirty-nine lashes. (135)

LEWIS, John. Colonel Ritzema's Regiment. Insulting and striking Lieutenant Cole, of Colonel Wyllys's Regiment when on command: thirty-nine lashes. (135)

LEWIS, John. Colonel Jackson's Regiment. Stealing, drunk on duty: 100 lashes. (26)

LEWIS, Jonathan. Light Company. Stealing a shirt: 100 lashes. (52)

LEWIS, William. Captain Wells's Company. Abusing, calling Captain Peter Perrit a liar: make a public confession to his captain, and upon his refusal to do so, be whipped twenty stripes. (105)

LEWSON, Burrell. Thirty-nine lashes – pardoned. (120)

LIGHT, Ebenezer. Second New Hampshire Regiment. Overstaying his furlough. (31)

LIGHTHALL, Lancaster. Third New York Regiment. Attempting to desert to the enemy with the arms and accouterments of another soldier: death by shooting. (29) *See* Spegy.

LILLIE (LITTLE), John. Colonel Knox's Regiment. Striking Adjutant Henley: thirty-nine lashes. (6)

LINAHAN, Darby. Maryland Line. Plundering: acquitted. (49)

LINCH, Timothy. Second Maryland Line. Desertion: 100 lashes. (103)

LINCOLN, Jeremiah. Desertion: 100 lashes. (41)

LINCOLN, Michael. First Company. Stealing spirits at Newburgh: acquitted. (63)

LINDERBACH, Joseph. Mutiny, abusive language, and striking a captain: not guilty of the first charge but guilty of the other charges—100 lashes. (42)

LINDSEY, Ebenezer, Capt. Colonel Gerrish's Regiment. Absenting himself from his post which was attacked and abandoned to the enemy: dismissed from the service. (2) (135)

LINE, William. First Battalion. Theft: 100 lashes. (102)

LINSEY, Hugh, Cpl. Captain Moody's Company. Absent without leave: reduced to a private. (125)

LINSEY, Jonathan. Maryland Line. Desertion and bearing arms against the United States: 100 lashes. (115)

LION,_____, Lieutenant. Major Johnson's Company. Aiding and countenancing a mutiny: acquitted. (104)

LIPSCOMB,_____, Captain and Acting Quartermaster General. General DeSteuben's Division. Treating the general in a disrespectful manner: acquitted. (17) *See* chapter two.

LIS (LEE), John. Mutiny, riot, and disobedience to orders: fine of twenty shillings. (135)

LITTLE, Pomfrey. Losing his canteen. Acquitted. (46)

LITTLE. *See* Lillie, John.

LIVELY, Abel. Fourth Georgia Continental Battalion. Desertion thirty-nine lashes. (90)

LIVERMORE,_____, Captain. First New Hampshire Regiment. Threatening and insulting Major Murnan, of the Corps of Engineers; striking him, whereby he received a wound and was otherwise injured: dismissed from the service. (44)

LIVINGSTON, Henry, Col. (a) Traducing the conduct of Brigadier General McDougall in ordering a retreat of the Continental troops 23 March, last; (b) neglecting to bring down his regiment on time on that day although ordered in time, when the enemy was near the town and it then was unprovided with ammunition; (c) ordering Mr. Smith, doing the duty of major of brigade for his brigade, not to turn parties out of it unless the orders were directed to him, which is contrary to the usage of the army, by which he embarrassed the service; (d) delaying the returns of his regiment and brigade by orders and whims of his own, contrary to the known rules of the army; (e) abusive language to General McDougall at his own quarters: not guilty of the first three charges but guilty of neglect, and guilty of the last two charges—reprimand in general orders. (131) *See* chapter four.

LLOYD, John. Colonel Livingston's Regiment. Drawing provisions illegally for his regiment: dismissed from the service. (15)

LOCK, Henry. Desertion; 100 lashes. (42)

LOCKWOOD, Joseph. Stealing rum out of the company's stores: ten lashes. (136) *See* Bryant, Ingham, Woodburn.

LOGAN, William. Third Maryland Regiment. Desertion and joining the enemy: death by hanging. (115)

LOGUE, Thomas, Matross. Colonel Proctor's Artillery. Desertion: 100 lashes. (103)

LOISIEN,_____, Captain. Colonel Livingston's Regiment. Threatening to burn the hospital, abusing the priest and superior of the nunnery, threatening the doctors and attendants on the sick; behaving in a riotous, disorderly, and ungentlemanlike manner: reprimand. (128) *See* Batema.

LORD,_____. Desertion: 100 lashes. (42)

LORD,_____, Captain. Second Massachusetts Regiment. Suffering several prisoners to escape from the guard which he commanded: reprimand. (124)

LORD, Roger. Colonel Wigglesworth's Regiment. Leaving his regiment when on the march, absenting himself from camp at an unreasonable time, losing his arms, clothing, and other accouterments: 100 lashes and pay for the lost articles. (9)

LORD, Roger. Captain Cogswell's Company. Cutting up his blanket: fifty lashes. (124)

LORD, William, Sgt. Fifteenth Regiment. Threatening and deserting: reduced to the ranks, ninety-nine lashes, and run the gauntlet— the running of the gauntlet was remitted. (122)

LOSA, Lewis, Sgt. Colonel Hazen's Regiment. Drawing his sword on Lieutenant Sullivan, of the Fourth Regiment of Dragoons, attempting to kill him in the execution of his duty: reduced to a private sentinel and 100 lashes – lashes remitted. (86)

LOU, Jonas. Thirteenth Virginia Regiment. Desertion: 100 lashes. (14)

LOVE, William. Fourth Pennsylvania Regiment. Stealing money from Frederick Buzzard: 100 lashes. (13)

LOVEBY, John, Sgt. Corps of Sappers and Miners. Forging a due bill for thirty pounds of beef and attempting to pass it: not guilty of the first charge but guilty of the second charge – reduced to a private sentinel and twenty-five lashes. (66)

LOVELY, Benjamin. Second Maryland Regiment. Desertion and joining the enemy: 100 lashes only, because of his youth and inexperience. (11)

LOWELL, Barnard. Third Massachusetts Regiment. Desertion and attempting to go to the enemy: 100 lashes. (50)

LOWERY, Patrick. Sixth Pennsylvania Regiment. Disobedience to orders, mutiny: guilty of the first charge but not guilty of the second charge "In consequence of his receiving prompt punishment from Captain Valentine, do sentence him to receive only fifty lashes, and from the above encumbrance of Captain Valentine's punishing the prisoner on the spot, the Court recommends to his Excellency, clemency" – sentence remitted. (21)

LOWERY, William. Second Maryland Regiment. Promoting sedition and inciting mutiny, concealing an intended mutiny after it came to his knowledge: 100 lashes. (40)

LOWRY, John. Damning the general and his orders: thirty-nine lashes. (101)

LUCAS, Thomas, Capt. Colonel Varnum's Regiment. Discharging a soldier and receiving a sum of money for so doing, returning the soldier's name on the muster roll after discharging him: dismissed from the service. (16) *See* chapter two.

LUDD, James. Colonel Shepard's Regiment. Desertion: fifty lashes and forfeit half of the prizes taken by the privateer or privateers on which he served during his absence from his regiment. (11)

LUDLOW, David. Colonel McDougall's Regiment. Desertion: twenty lashes. (132) (136)

LUIS, Asa. Colonel Greene's Regiment. Raising a mutiny and behaving in a disorderly manner: not guilty of the first charge but guilty of the second charge—suspended and reprimand. (131) *See* Baptist, Brown, Buck, Davis, Dunbar, Goold, Hardin, Lane, Park, Peterson, Tabor.

LUKE, Nicholas. Desertion: fifteen lashes and dismissed from the service. (93)

LUKEMAN, John (alias Graham, Alexander). Desertion to the enemy: death. (130)

LULEY, John. Colonel Ward's Regiment. Desertion: thirty-nine lashes. (106)

LUNT, Joseph. Colonel McDougall's Regiment. Disobedience to orders, striking Ensign Young when in the execution of his duty: confined five days on bread and water. Washington said, "The General thought the punishment inadequate to the crimes, that he disapproves the sentence. The General hopes that this kind of admonition will make future courts-martial more particular and severe on the heinous crimes of a soldier striking or attempting to strike his officer or disobey his orders." (106) (136)

LUSK, John. Stealing public rum out of a cask: 100 lashes. (111)

LUTHER, Theopolis. Quarrelling with his messmates, abusive language to Sergeant Raymond: forty lashes. (91)

LUTY, John. Fourth Maryland Regiment. Desertion: 100 lashes. (121)

LYNCH, David. Second Regiment of Artillery. Desertion: acquitted. (50)

LYNCH, Jonathan. Colonel Magaw's Regiment. Striking and wounding an officer: thirty-nine lashes. (1) (136)

LYON,_____, Lieutenant. Thirty-first Regiment (Thirty-fourth Regiment). Aiding and countenancing a mutiny in camp: acquitted. (3) (69)

LYON, Aron. Sleeping on his post: 100 stripes—pardoned, because of extenuating circumstances. (23)

LYON, Galatah. Seventh Massachusetts Regiment. Sleeping on sentry: acquitted. (50)

LYON, Joseph. Third Regiment of Artillery. Desertion, forging a pass in the colonel's name, selling his blanket: 100 lashes. (124)

LYON, Matthew. Deserting his post without orders or without being attacked or forced by the enemy: cashiered and pay damages to the inhabitants on Onion River due to his unofficerlike retreat. (84) *See* Fasset, Perry, Wright.

LYON (LYONS), Patrick. Colonel Learned's Regiment. Sleeping on his post: twenty-five lashes. (68) Thirty-nine lashes. (136)

LYON (LYONS), Patrick. Colonel Learned's Regiment. Being in liquor and sleeping on his post: thirty lashes. (68) Twenty lashes. (136)

LYON, Theopolis, Lt. Thirty-fourth Regiment. Aiding and countenancing a mutiny in camp: acquitted. (3) (133) (136)

LYONS, Solomon. Second Virginia Regiment. Desertion: death. (69) (103

LYTLE, William. Fourth North Carolina Regiment. Disobedience of a repeated order: acquitted. (115)

MacCAIL, William. Fifth Pennsylvania Regiment. Insulting and charging his bayonet on the officer of the Ferry Guard at Trent Town: released when no evidence was presented. (101) *See* McConel.

MacDANIEL (MACK DANIEL), John. Colonel Learned's Regiment. Stealing a pocketbook of money from a soldier in Captain Stephenson's Company: acquitted. (70)

MacDONALD, Alexander. Seventh Pennsylvania Regiment. Desertion: 100 lashes. (101)

MacDONALD, Alexander. Intending and threatening to desert: fifteen lashes. (101)

MACHEM, Justice. Desertion: run the gauntlet. Upon review, it was determined that "the running of the gauntlet being an undetermined mode of punishment not authorized by any Article of War, the General disapproves the sentence. (41) *See* chapter three.

MACHIN,_____, Captain. Second Regiment of Artillery. Enlisting a soldier belonging to the Second Connecticut Regiment, sending him to recruit without the knowledge of the commanding general, enlisting several men unfit for service: guilty only of neglect — reprimand and recalled from the recruiting service. (56) Note: the unfit recruits were Crump, John and Fountain (John and Fincas).

MACINTIRE,_____, Corporal. Colonel Topham's Regiment. Getting drunk and appearing in liquor on parade: reduced to the ranks. (98)

MACINTIRE, Phenis. Conspiring to desert to the enemy: 100 lashes. (89)

MacINTOURS, Jonathan. Maryland Line. Desertion; stealing three blankets, a pair of shoes and knapsack; losing his musket: 100 lashes. (115)

MACKEY,_____, Sergeant. Seventh Pennsylvania Regiment. Leaving the guard without permission: reduced to the ranks. (101)

MACKCARUN (McCARREN), William. Third Pennsylvania Regiment. Stealing horseshoes: 100 lashes. (21)

MAD, William, inhabitant of Pennsylvania. Attempting to drive cattle into the enemy lines: pay ten pounds and confined. (14)

MADDOCK, William, inhabitant of Pennsylvania. Attempting to drive cattle into Philadelphia: fine of £100 and confined in the provost guard till the sum is paid. (7)

MAFFORD, John. Sixth Massachusetts Regiment. Desertion to the enemy: 100 lashes. (46)

MAGALINE, Freeman. Sixth North Carolina Battalion. Desertion: 100 lashes—remitted. (95)

MAHONEY, Patrick. Colonel Holmes's Regiment. Firing his gun: confinement for twenty-four hours in the dungeon—pardoned. (118)

MAKEPEACE, Jason. Fifth Massachusetts Regiment. Desertion: 100 lashes. (57)

MALCOLM, Thomas. Death. (95)

MALLOROY, Philip, Lt. Eleventh Virginia Regiment. Disobedience to orders in not joining his regiment with all possible expedition: acquitted. (21)

MALONY, Timothy. Drunk on his post: forty stripes—pardoned because of his former good character. (10)

MAN, Nathaniel. Colonel Reed's Regiment. Desertion and reenlistment into another corps: thirty-nine lashes. (71)

MAN, Thomas. Delaware Regiment. Beating a number of persons, breaking windows and other abuseful treatment: guilty only of abusive treatment—reprimand. (103)

MANGER (MARGER), Jonathan. Colonel McDougall's Regiment. Sleeping on his post: thirty lashes. (67)

MANNA, Dennis. Captain Holland's Company. Theft: seventy-five lashes for the theft and twenty-five lashes for lying to the court. (93)

MANNERING, Peter. Captain Johnson's Company, Colonel Gallup's Regiment. Neglecting to join his regiment when detached for one month for the defense of the post: take an oath of fidelity and return to duty. (82)

MANSFIELD,_____, Captain. Fourth Regiment of Light Dragoons. Selling a horse: reprimand and replace the horse with one of equal value, in that he had no intent to defraud. (35)

MANSFIELD, James. Massachusetts Line. Desertion: twenty-five lashes. (53)

MANSFIELD, John, Col. Nineteenth Regiment of Foot Soldiers, Massachusetts Forces. Remiss in the execution of his duty in the engagement at Bunker Hill: cashiered. (2) (135)

MAPLES, Robert (alias Walker, John). Enlisting in Colonel Alden's Regiment and deserting therefrom, using another name, taking a bounty of $200 and deserting again: death. (41) *See* Hutton and chapter four.

MARKHAM, John, Lt. Col. Eighth Virginia Regiment. Leaving the regiment in time of action and delay when ordered to support the advance guard: cashiered. (134)

MARNEY,_____, Sergeant. Insolent and abusive language and damning the officers of his regiment: guilty of the first charge but acquitted of the second charge – reprimand. (100)

MARNEY, William. First Massachusetts Regiment. Letting three prisoners escape from the provost: acquitted. (40)

MARRS, John. Second South Carolina Regiment. Desertion: death by shooting. (95)

MARS, William. Colonel Livingston's Regiment. Stealing, insolence, disturbing the camp after tattoo, beating Lieutenant Wallace and attempting to strike him several times, destroying Ensign Cook's commission: death by shooting. (9) (19)

MARSH, Charles. Colonel Hazen's Regiment. Desertion: run the brigade gauntlet once a week for two weeks, from right to left and left to right each time. (112)

MARSHALL, Thomas. Fraudulently reenlisting: acquitted. (42)

MARTIN, Alexander. Second North Carolina Regiment. Cowardice: acquitted. (93)

MARTIN, Gideon. Colonel Jackson's Regiment. Desertion: acquitted. (24)

MARTIN, Gideon. Sixth Massachusetts Regiment (Ninth Massachusetts Regiment). Desertion: 100 lashes – remitted. (47)

MARTIN, Joseph. Colonel Silliman's Regiment. Abusing and robbing a woman in the market: acquitted. (132) (136)

MARTIN, Robert. Delaware Regiment. Exciting and promoting desertion: acquitted. (109)

MARTIN, Samuel. Suffering a prisoner to escape: three days' confinement in the dungeon – pardoned. (118)

MARTIN, Thomas. North Carolina Line. Joining the enemy and bearing arms against the United States: death—remitted, because he said he had been taken prisoner at Charlestown and joined the British to get away from them but had not had such an opportunity. (115)

MARTIN, William. Sixth Pennsylvania Regiment. Housebreaking and robbery: 100 lashes. (21) *See* Terney.

MASON,_____, Lieutenant Colonel and Director, Laboratory at Springfield. Taking Continental stores and property and converting them to his own use, related offenses including the taking of firewood for three fires in unlimited quantity: acquitted because "while the charges were literally true, they did not amount to any criminality or embezzlement of public property, the articles being of no great value." (21)

MASON, James. Third New York Regiment. Desertion from his guard and betraying his trust in carrying off a prisoner entrusted to his care: death by shooting. (89)

MASON, James. Colonel Lamb's Regiment. 100 lashes. (124)

MASON, John. Mutiny. (90)

MASON, Joseph. Desertion: 100 lashes. (42)

MASON, Thomas. Defrauding Rufus Wilson out of a pair of shoe buckles: the charges not fully supported but was found guilty of defrauding him of twenty-four dollars which he received as down payment and which he did not refund—100 lashes and repay the twenty-four dollars. (111)

MASSA,_____. Disobedience to orders, insolence and imprudent behavior: fifty lashes. (10)

MATHEW, John. First New Hampshire Regiment. Desertion: 100 lashes. (41)

MATHEWS, John. Colonel Jackson's Regiment. Desertion: run the gauntlet and confined in the dungeon for one month on bread and water—remitted. (26) *See* Barney, Pierce.

MATHEWS, Joseph. Colonel Doolittle's Regiment. Selling his gun which the selectmen of his town had given him, and receiving pay for a blanket from the said selectmen: ten lashes and twenty shillings for the blanket. (2) (135)

MATIEN (MATIAN), Anthony, civilian. Supplying the enemy with fowls: acquitted. (69) (103)

MATTESON, Benjamin. Colonel Sherburne's Regiment. Stealing a rifle, absenting himself from guard when on duty: 100 lashes. (9) (19)

MATTHEWS, George. Colonel Shepard's Regiment. Quarrelling and fighting with the inhabitants, frequently getting drunk and abusing the barracks master: fifty stripes. (14)

MATTHEWS, James, Lt. Colonel Poor's Regiment. Appearing on parade disguised in liquor, selling liquor to private soldiers in his own tent, associating with persons below the character of an officer: dismissed from the service. (4) (84) (117)

MATTHEWS, James. Colonel Poor's Regiment. Stealing and concealing a sword: not guilty of stealing but guilty of concealing—pay seven pounds to the owner of the sword. (84)

MATTHEWS, Richard. Maryland Line. Desertion: 100 lashes. (21)

MATTHEWS, William. Colonel Wyllys's Regiment. Desertion: 100 lashes. (125)

MATYARD, Thomas. Mutiny, riot, and disobedience to orders: fine of twenty shillings. (135)

MAXFIELD, John. Colonel Huntington's Regiment. Desertion: thirty-nine lashes. (136)

MAXWELL,_____, General. Disguised in liquor in such a manner as to be disqualified in some measure, but not fully from doing his duty. Once or twice besides, his spirits were a little elevated with liquor: acquitted. (93)

MAXWELL,_____, Ensign. Colonel Malcolm's Regiment. Propagating a scandalous report prejudicial to the character of Lieutenant Enslin: acquitted. (14) *See* Enslin.

MAYBERRY, William. Colonel Shepard's Regiment. Quitting his command at Newtown without leave: 100 lashes and pay the cost of apprehending him. (24) *See* Franklin.

MAYES, John. Colonel Hutchinson's Regiment. Stealing ammunition: acquitted. (133)

MAYNARD, Daniel. First New Hampshire Regiment. Desertion: fifty lashes. (46)

MAYSOUNDER, William. First Regiment. Desertion: 100 lashes. (129)

McALBORN, John. Second New Jersey Battalion. Desertion: 100 lashes. (112)

McALLISTER,_____. Disobedience to orders, being out of camp at unreasonable hours: thirty-nine lashes—pardoned. (23)

McALLISTER, Joseph. Plotting and persuading a soldier to desert:

acquitted. (78)

McALLISTER, Randall. Theft, abuse to a corporal: not guilty of the first charge but guilty of the second charge—ask the corporal's pardon at the head of the regiment. (23) *See* Stanford.

McALPHEN (McALPIN), John. Colonel Malcolm's Regiment. Drunk on his post: thirty lashes. (132) (136)

McBRIDE, Daniel. Colonel Lee's Regiment. Absenting himself from quarters without leave: fifty stripes. (10)

McBRIDE, Peter. Second Regiment of Artillery. Mutinous behavior: 100 lashes. (42)

McCAFFERTY, James. Colonel Holmes's Regiment. Mutiny, disobeying orders, striking officers: thirty-nine lashes and drummed out of the regiment. (118)

McCALLA, William, civilian. Selling a batteau, the sails and part of the rigging of a schooner, and four barrels of pork belonging to the Continent: reprimand, because he acted imprudently rather than committing fraud. (84)

McCALLAHAN, Dennis. Desertion and selling his arms: 200 lashes. (93)

McCALLER, James. Desertion: 100 lashes and run the gauntlet—running of the gauntlet remitted. (122)

McCALLOCK,_____, Sergeant. Wantonly breaking a fife: pay for the value of the fife. (50)

McCALVEY, Thom. Fourth Pennsylvania Regiment. Attempting to desert to the enemy with his arms and accouterments: death. (112) *See* Clark.

McCANN, Thomas. Delaware Regiment. Drinking and fighting: acquitted. (32) *See* Haigney.

McCANN, Thomas. Desertion: death—pardoned on condition that he enlist for the duration of the war. (90)

McCARNEY, Edward. Colonel Ritzema's Regiment. Desertion: thirty-nine lashes. (136)

McCARTEE,_____, Doctor. Fourth Pennsylvania Regiment. Scandalous behavior in seizing Captain Pell by forcibly putting him out of a room in a public house, taking his sword from him and breaking it: acquitted. (28) *See* Sparr (Schoon).

McCARTHY, Daniel. Garrison at West Point. Disobedience to several orders: reprimand. (48)

McCARTY, D. Feloniously detained a coat and hat belonging to a lieutenant:

twenty lashes—sentence overturned since the detention was by ignorance and not feloniousness. (128)

McCARTY, Jonathan. Ill treatment of a quartermaster and disrespectful of others: ask the quartermaster's pardon on the parade. (96)

McCAY, John. Second Connecticut Regiment. Desertion and reenlisting: 100 lashes. (59)

McCAY, Lewis. Pennsylvania Line. Desertion: 100 lashes. (78)

McCLAHENING, Patrick. Colonel Hazen's Regiment. Desertion: run the brigade gauntlet once a week for two weeks, from right to left and left to right each time. (112)

McCLELAN, Thomas, Lt. Third New York Regiment. Slandering and defaming the officers of his regiment, and Colonel Grosvert in particular; ungentlemanlike conduct in many respects: dismissed from the service. (89)

McCLELAN, John, Capt. First Pennsylvania Regiment (Fifth Pennsylvania Regiment). Neglect of duty while commanding a Morristown pickett: acquitted. (26) (27)

McCLEMONS (McCLEMENTS), David. Delaware Regiment. Desertion: acquitted. (103)

McCLESSON, David. Delaware Regiment. Desertion: acquitted. (69)

McCLOUD, John. Colonel Lamb's Regiment. Sleeping on his post: fifty lashes—remitted. (125)

McCLURE, Andrew, Sgt. Fourth Regiment. Desertion: reduced to a private sentinel. (112)

McCLURE, John. Sutling in camp contrary to orders: released. (13) (134)

McCONKLIN, William. Sixth Maryland Regiment. Desertion and attempting to go to the enemy: death. (69)

McCOFF, Marcham. Fifteenth Virginia Regiment. Desertion: twenty-five lashes. (101)

McCOLLASTER,_____, Lieutenant. First Maryland Regiment. Leaving his guard on the Haverstraw Road: reprimand. (93)

McCOLLASTER, Patrick. Captain Kirkwood's Company. Delaware Regiment. Stealing a rifle and selling the same: fifty lashes. (93)

McCONEL, James. Fifth Pennsylvania Regiment. Insulting and charging his bayonet on the officer of the ferry guard at Trent Town;

presenting his piece at Lieutenant Smith, of the Fifth Pennsylvania Regiment, in the face of the whole regiment: 100 lashes. (101) *See* MacCail.

McCORDY, Joseph. Colonel Thompson's Regiment. Abusing Lieutenant Cleveland: acquitted. (133) *See* Simpson, White.

McCORMICK,_____, Captain. Thirteenth Virginia Regiment. Laying down in time of action and behaving in a cowardly unofficerlike manner: acquitted with honor. (134)

McCORMICK, Francis. Desertion: serve the time "prescribed by the act of Assembly." (102)

McCORMICK, James. Colonel Woodbridge's Regiment. Leaving camp without permission: thirty-nine lashes. (3)

McCORMICK (McCORNISH), James. Colonel Paterson's Regiment. Striking Colonel Putnam's horse and saying at the same time, "Damn you, who's there, clear the road;" leaving the camp without orders: thirty-nine lashes. (133) (136)

McCORMICK (McCORMACK), James. Colonel Sargent's Regiment. Desertion and mutiny: death by hanging. (136)

McCORNICE, Charles. General Hazen's Regiment. Desertion: 100 lashes. (56)

McCORNICK, James. Colonel Sargent's Regiment. Desertion: thirty-nine lashes. (136)

McCORTEL, John. Colonel Hazen's Regiment. Desertion: run the brigade gauntlet once a week for two weeks, from right to left and left to right each time. (112)

McCOY, Andrew, Sutler. Fraud and extortion: 100 lashes and drummed out of camp and never permitted to sell any more. (93)

McCOY, Malachai. Third South Carolina Regiment. Desertion: 100 lashes and a fine of twenty dollars as a refund of the bounty he received–the lashes remitted. (95)

McCROMEY, Reuben. Second Rhode Island Regiment. Desertion: 100 lashes. (100)

McCULLOCH, Lewis. Captain Bathser's Company, German Battalion. Stealing a pocketbook of money from an inhabitant of the town: 100 lashes and return the money, and pay for any that was missing. (20)

McCUMBER,_____, Ensign. Colonel Sargent's Regiment. Plundering the inhabitants of Harlem: cashiered. (74)

McCUMBER,_____, Ensign. (Orders from Congress regarding his previous trial.) (118)

McCURDY, James. First Pennsylvania Regiment. Desertion to the enemy: 100 lashes. (110)

McDANIEL, James. Forging an order of General Putnam to obtain a quart of rum, abusive language to Colonel Griffith: twenty lashes. (71)

McDANIEL, Michael. Colonel Hazlet's Regiment. Robbing Isaac (Isiah) Ryder: acquitted. (74) (94) *See* Cawley.

McDANNELS, Michael. Sixth Massachusetts Regiment. Desertion: 100 lashes. (50)

McDOHNEL, Daniel. Seventh Massachusetts Regiment. Desertion: 100 lashes. (53)

McDONALD,_____, Lieutenant. Third Pennsylvania Regiment. Absenting himself from his regiment without consent of his commanding officer: acquitted. (17)

McDONALD,_____, Lieutenant. Third Pennsylvania Regiment. Taking two mares and a barrel of carpenter's tools, which mares he conveyed away, and sold the tools at a private sale, insulting behavior by refusing to comply with his arrest: acquitted. (17) *See* chapter two.

McDONALD,_____, Corporal. Asleep on guard: reduced in rank. (10)

McDONALD, Alexander. First Regiment of Artillery. Stealing soap: seventy-five lashes. (95)

McDONALD, James. Colonel Ritzema's Regiment. Threatening the life of Lieutenant Young and others: confined eight days on bread and water. (136)

McDONALD, Michael. Sixth Massachusetts Regiment. Desertion: 100 lashes. (21)

McDONALD, Michael. Colonel McDougall's Regiment. Running away from the enemy's breastwork: released when no evidence was presented. (99)

McDONALD, Philip, Cpl. Desertion and selling his arms: reduced to the ranks and 200 lashes. (93)

McDONNELL, Joel. Sixth Connecticut Regiment (Fourth Connecticut Regiment). Desertion and enlisting in another regiment: not guilty of the first charge but guilty of the second charge—100 lashes. (53)

McDOUGALL, Alexander, Gen. *See* chapter four.

McDOUGALL, James. Twelfth Massachusetts Regiment. Desertion: 100 lashes. (53)

McFARLANE,_____, Sergeant. Wounding William Hartley in a dangerous and insufferable manner: acquitted. (85)

McFARLIN, Andrew, Sgt. Captain Moody's Company. Absent without leave: reduced to a matross. (125)

McFARLIN, James. Second Company. Acquitted. (63)

McFARLIN, John. Colonel Dayton's Regiment. Desertion: acquitted. (136)

McFARLING,_____, Lieutenant. First Pennsylvania Regiment. Unmercifully beating James Welch, a soldier in the Seventh Pennsylvania Regiment: acquitted. (72)

McFRAINE, William. Colonel Sargent's Regiment. Desertion: thirty lashes. (132)

McGEE, Michael. Colonel Burrell's Regiment. Abusing and threatening the life of Allan McDonald, an inhabitant: acquitted. (84)

McGEE, Michael. Colonel Holmes's Regiment. Sleeping on his post: ten lashes – pardoned. (118)

McGIBBONEY (McGIBBENY),_____, Lieutenant. Fourth North Carolina Regiment. Embezzling and misapplying the money with which he was entrusted for enlisting men into the service, and taking bribes to discharge enlisted men from the service: acquitted. (13) (134)

McGINNIS,_____, Sergeant. Delaware Regiment. Fighting and abusing Sergeant Faims (?): acquitted. (93) *See* Faires.

McGLAUGHLIN, Cornelius. Delaware Regiment. Neglect of duty and drunkenness: thirty-nine lashes – pardoned "because of his age." (93)

McGONIGAL, Neal. Seventh Pennsylvania Regiment. Deserting from his post: not guilty of deserting but guilty of absenting himself without leave: 100 lashes. (21)

McGONIGAL, Neal. Seventh Pennsylvania Regiment. Threatening Captain Scott's life, drawing his bayonet repeatedly and stabbing while in the execution of his duty: death. (69) (103)

McGUIGEN,_____, Sergeant. Striking a soldier in the execution of his duty: reduced in ranks. (42)

McGUIRE, Andrew. Disobeying an order: one log on each leg for seven days, and to wear his coat inside-out for those seven days. (10)

McGUIRE, Daniel. Arrested but released when no evidence was presented. (93)

McGUIRE, Daniel. Colonel Sargent's Regiment. Desertion and enlisting in another company, and taking a second bounty: thirty-nine lashes. (132)

McGUIRE, James. Seventh Company. Theft, disturbance at unreasonable hours: fifty lashes. (45)

McGUIRE, Philip. Death. (95)

McGUYER, James. Striking and abusing: reprimand and beg the pardon of his victim. (42)

McGUYER, James. Seventh Company. Frequently absent from roll call: ten lashes. (46)

McGWIN,_____. Colonel Thayer's Regiment. Desertion and enlisting himself in another corps and taking a second bounty: thirty-nine lashes. (136)

McINTIRE, Alexander. Colonel Prescott's Regiment. Plundering a cellar belonging to a citizen of New York: released to his regiment. (7) *See* Butler, Knowland, Webster.

McINTIRE, William. Seventh Pennsylvania Battalion. Robbing a load of wheat from one of Colonel Spencer's wagoners: thirty lashes. (13) (134)

McINTOSH, Ann. Mutiny and desertion: acquitted. (134)

McINTOSH, William. Second Virginia Regiment. Mutiny and desertion: acquitted. (134)

McKAY, Alexander, Bombardier. Captain Moody's Company. Absent without leave: reduced to a matross. (125)

McKAY, Daniel. Fourth Georgia Continental Battalion. Desertion: death by shooting. (90)

McKEENAN,_____, Lieutenant. Using insolent language to Lieutenant Gooding: fine of two shillings and reprimand. (70)

McKEY, John. Continental Line. Desertion: 100 lashes – remitted. (53)

McKINDREY,_____, Ensign. Sixth Massachusetts Regiment. Absenting himself from the regiment when called to action on 29 August, last: acquitted with honor. (89)

McKINNEY,_____, Lieutenant. Colonel Scrivener's Battalion. Scandalous abuse of a lady of distinction: dismissed from the service. (90)

McKINNEY, Charles, Lt. and Assistant Deputy Q.M. Taking fifteen dollars from Patterson and Fisher, wagoners in the public service; paying the accounts improperly; offering to discharge Graham, wagoner, for a sum of money: dismissed from the service and the crime published in the gazette of the state in and about the camp, and pay the money he received from the wagoners. (95)

McKINNEY, Daniel. Endeavoring to seduce soldiers to desert: 100 lashes and drummed out of the camp. (89)

McKNIGHT, Charles, Doctor, Surgeon, and Physician in the General Hospital. Converting fatted oxen to his own use, also a large quantity of Indian meal which was obtained for the hospital, also other items converted to his own use, using public horses and wagons to work his own farm which was a private business, drawing large quantites of wood for the hospital but using it for his own purposes: acquitted. (50) *See* chapter four.

McNIGHT, Robert. Colonel Sherburne's Regiment. Desertion and twice enlisting: 100 lashes. (85) (113) (125)

McLAIN, Charles. Third Pennsylvania Regiment. Desertion: 100 lashes. (26)

McLAIN, Oliver. Acting in a mutinous manner, endeavoring to excite a mutiny: fifty lashes. (9) *See* Askin, Hunt, Trasson, Wilson.

McLANE, Daniel. Corps of Artillery. Cashiered. (130)

McLOED, Daniel. Captain Chessman's Company. Abuse and refusing to do his duty: thirty-nine lashes. (128)

McLAUGHLIN, Charles. First New Jersey Regiment. Straggling from camp, killing a number of hogs: twenty-five lashes – remitted. (20) *See* Farmer, Leonard, Mumford, Osborne, Rush, Walker, Whitehead.

McLAUGHLIN, P. Fifth Company. Drunk and abusing a sergeant: fifty lashes – pardoned, in consideration of his good character and behaving like a good soldier in general. (23)

McLEAN, John. Fourth New York Regiment. Desertion and absent for twelve months: 100 lashes, with twenty-five lashes on four successive days. (26)

McMANUS, Barney. Colonel Gunby's Regiment. Absenting himself from camp all night: 100 lashes. (93)

McMANUS, Henry. Sixth Maryland Regiment. Desertion to the enemy and attempting to carry off several soldiers with him: death. (21)

McMARCH (McMARTH), William. Captain Lee's Company of Artillery. Desertion, stealing a horse from General McIntosh: not guilty of the first charge but guilty of the second charge – 100 lashes and pay for the horse, lashes remitted because of his former good conduct. (13) (134)

McMARRAN, Barney. Colonel Hitchcock's Regiment. Sleeping on his post, abusing and insulting the captain of the guard: thirty-nine lashes and drummed out of the army. (136)

McMEATH, William. Colonel Lamb's Regiment of Artillery. Desertion to the enemy: death by hanging. (9)

McMICHAEL,_____, Lieutenant. Seventh Pennsylvania Regiment. Disobedience to orders, neglect of duty, releasing a prisoner from the guard, stating that he did little duty in the regiment and would do no duty so long as it was commanded by Major Moore: acquitted of all except the last charge: reprimand. (26)

McMICHAEL,_____, Lieutenant. Pennsylvania State Regiment. Ungentlemanlike behavior: dismissed from the service. (14)

McMULLIN, Robert, Boatman. Quartermaster Department. Stealing liquor and rum while enroute from Windsor to Peekskill: thirty-nine lashes—remitted. (46) *See* Hall.

McMURRY, Samuel. Delaware Regiment. Being drunk and offering to sell a razor belonging to Ensign Purnell: guilty of the first charge but acquitted of the second charge—reprimand. (93)

McMURRY, Samuel. Getting drunk and stealing a pair of shoes: guilty of the first charge but acquitted of the second charge—fifteen lashes. (93)

McNAMARRA,_____, Lieutenant. Colonel Harrison's Regiment of Artillery. Speaking disrespectfully of the commander-in-chief and treating Lieutenant Hill in a scandalous manner, contemptuous of Colonel Harrison after being arrested: reprimand. (72) *See* Warters.

McNEIL, Adam. Colonel Livingston's Regiment. Not joining the regiment and enlisting twice: fifty lashes. (131)

McNULTY, John. Being drunk when paraded for duty, having previously been warned: acquitted. (91)

McOWEN,_____, Mrs. Obtaining public stores and selling them to the inhabitants: fifteen lashes and be drummed from the whipping post—remitted, because of the delicacy of her sex, and permitted to live with her husband in the regiment during her good behavior. (116)

McOWEN, Edward. Captain Sample's Company. Out without a pass, attempting to sell a horse: fifty lashes. (116)

McPHERSON, Murdock, Ens. Colonel Hazen's Regiment. Neglect of duty by leaving the guard under his command, having prisoners in charge, permitting a number of prisoners to escape: reprimand. (42)

McSTRAIN (McSTORIN), William. Colonel Thayer's Regiment (Colonel Sargent's Regiment). Desertion: thirty lashes. (136)

McVICKERS, Daniel, Wagoner. Georgia Brigade. Neglect of duty, drunkenness. (90)

MEACHEM,_____, Lieutenant. Third Massachusetts Regiment. Absenting himself beyond the limits of his furlough and neglecting to return after being notified: cashiered. (58)

MEAD,_____, civilian. Colonel Flower's Regiment. Selling meat, flour, spirits, and salt out of the public stores without proper authority, delivering a quantity of butter and coffee drawn for the brigade: acquitted. (129)

MEADOWS,_____, Corporal. Eighth Massachusetts Regiment. Mutinous conduct: reduced to a private sentinel, and 100 lashes. (64) *See* Barnes, Birch.

MEALY, Edward. Captain Blair's Company. Desertion: acquitted. (70)

MEASH, Elhaja. Desertion: run the gauntlet. (41)

MECAN, Daniel. Captain Gale's Company. Swearing and striking Alexander Keene and others: ten stripes. (105)

MECHAM,_____, Lieutenant. Third Massachusetts Regiment. Overstaying his furlough and neglecting to join it when notified: cashiered. (86)

MECHAN, Daniel. Advising and inviting John Smith to defect to the enemy: fifteen stripes and one year in confinement at the New Gate Prison—sentence overturned for lack of proof, but since it was felt he was not a fit person to remain in the company, was ordered out of camp, not to return on threat of receiving thirty-nine lashes. (4) *See* Smith, John.

MEDLING,_____, Corporal. Plundering and encouraging his guard to do the same: reduced to the ranks. (115)

MEERS, Abram. Delaware Regiment. Striking and abusing a drummer for doing his duty and accusing him of whipping a convicted soldier in too severe a manner the day perviously: ask the drummer's pardon in the presence of his commanding officer. (93)

MEGUIN, Henry. Disobedience to orders: thirty lashes—pardoned. (23)

MELANBERGER, Michael, inhabitant of Pennsylvania. Attempting to carry provisions to the enemy at Philadelphia: acquitted. (14)

MELANY, John. Third Company. Disobedience to orders: twenty-five lashes—pardoned, because of extenuating cicumstances. (23)

MEREDITH, Peter. Colonel Crane's Brigade of Artillery. Desertion: fifty lashes. (54)

MERNON, James. Second Company. Losing his blanket: acquitted. (44)

MERRICK, William, Capt. St. John's Company. Attempting to desert to the enemy: fifty lashes. (22)

MERRILL, William. First New York Regiment. Being concerned with mutinous libel and threatening the lives of others: acquitted. (46)

MERRILLS, Aaron. Captain Wyllys's Company. Fighting with his messmates, abusive language to Sergeant Phillips, threatening his life: thirty-nine lashes. (1)

MERRILLS, Ephraim. Colonel Webb's Regiment. Stealing sheep from Mr. Deines, an inhabitant of Bristol: thirty stripes – pardoned. (91) *See* Brown, Gay, Olmstead.

MICHAEL, Robert. Colonel Hazen's Regiment. Desertion: run the brigade gauntlet once a week for two weeks, from right to left and left to right each time. (112)

MIEN, Nathaniel. Colonel Read's Regiment. Desertion and enlistment into another corps. (5)

MIERS, John. Third Massachusetts Regiment. Desertion: 100 lashes. (47)

MILDENBERGER, Oliver, Lt. Colonel Lasher's Regiment. Leaving the regiment without permission: cashiered and mulcted of one month's pay. (74) (118) (123)

MILES, William. Third South Carolina Regiment. Desertion: fifty lashes – remitted because of his debilitated body. (95) Note: soon after this, he was discharged from the army "being unfit for service."

MILIKEN, Nathaniel. Colonel Jackson's Regiment. Desertion: 100 lashes – remitted. (36)

MILLER, B., Lieutenant. Colonel St. Clair's Regiment. Possessing himself of parts of the hangings of Lieutenant Christie's swords, having secreted some effects of the late Captain Watson: acquitted with honor. (84)

MILLER, Charles, Ens. Colonel Wyllys's Regiment. Leaving his guard at the city hall and suffering a prisoner to be absent: acquitted. (1) (136)

MILLER, Charles. Second Pennsylvania Regiment. Attempting to go to the enemy: 100 lashes. (21)

MILLER, John. Colonel Stewart's Battalion of Light Infantry. Robbery: death. (36)

MILLER, Lawrence. Death. (103)

MILLER, Peter. Desertion: 100 lashes and drummed out of the army. (63)

MILLIMAN, George. Colonel Angell's Second Rhode Island Battalion. Mutiny: death. (23)

MILLS, Isrel. First New Jersey Regiment. Desertion: 100 lashes. (25)

MILLS, William, Lt. Regiment of Light Infantry. Disobedience to orders: acquitted. (35)

MILTON, William. Desertion: 100 lashes. (42)

MIND, Adam. Pennsylvania Regiment. Desertion: 100 lashes. (97)

MINDETH, Peter. Colonel McDougall's Regiment. Desertion: thirty lashes. (1)

MINET, Joseph. Third New York Regiment. Neglect of duty, disobedience to orders by not keeping in confinement a prisoner: reprimand. (28)

MINN, John. Maryland Line. Desertion: 100 lashes. (21)

MINOIS, Pere. Desertion: serve the time "prescribed by the act of Assembly." (102)

MISSICK, Joseph (Joshua). Firing of guns contrary to general orders: fatigue duty of two days and do his back duty for the time he had been confined, and to lay every other night in the guardhouse till the punishment is fulfilled. (104) *See* Baxter.

MISSICK, Joseph (Joshua). Captain Craft's Company. Sleeping when on sentry: six day's fatigue with his coat wrongside-outward, and do his back duty in the company. (104)

MITCHEL, John. Seventh Regiment. Desertion: 100 lashes. (130)

MITCHELL,———, Captain. Fourth New Jersey Regiment. Disobedience to orders on the night of 6 September: acquitted with honor. (172)

MITCHELL,_____, Captain. Maryland Line. Taking the artificers from their work and keeping them from their duty, and related misbehavior: acquitted. (49)

MITCHELL,_____, Captain. Colonel Gist's Regiment. Beating a sentry on his post and a corporal on guard: acquitted. The general disapproved the sentence since "the evidence clearly proved that both captains (Mitchell and Jones) did beat the guards. Acknowledging that the men were insolent and merited punishment, but ought to have been confined and punished in a regular way, rather than by beating them." (21) *See* Jones, Captain.

MITCHELL,_____, Lieutenant. Third Georgia Battalion. Refusing to do duty under pretense of sickness: acquitted. (90)

MITCHELL, M. Massachusetts Regiment. Desertion: 100 lashes, with twenty-five lashes administered on four successive days. (53)

MITCHELL, Richard. Colonel Brewer's Regiment. Desertion and enlisting twice and receiving two bounties: 100 lashes for each offense, and repayment of the bounty. (9)

MITCHELL, William. Colonel Bradley's Regiment. Desertion: 100 lashes. (131)

MIX, Thomas. Stealing and concealing a barrel of flour: acquitted. (91)

MOFFET, Joseph. Desertion: 100 lashes. (42)

MOFFETT, Alexander. Captain Moody's Company. Absent from camp, abusing the inhabitants: guilty only of the first charge—stand on a picket with his bare feet for fifteen minutes. (125)

MONEY, John. Colonel McDougall's Regiment. Desertion: confined five days on bread and water only, because of unfairness in enlisting him, and his being very ignorant. (106)

MONHANT, Stephen, Sgt. Sixth Continental Regiment. Desertion: 100 lashes—remitted upon presentation of a member of the Eastern Navy Board. The prisoner had claimed he had previously been placed in command of a Continental vessel of war, *The Black Prince*, and that Dr. Franklin (presumably Benjamin Franklin) had employed him. However, he could not prove his claim. (31)

MONTGOMERY, Alexander. Third New Jersey Regiment. Fifty lashes—remitted. (25)

MONTGOMERY, Alexander. Third New Jersey Regiment. Desertion and forging a pass: 100 lashes for each offense. (25)

MONTGOMERY, Mathew. Embezzling public stores: fine of forty dollars and run the gauntlet twice. (103)

MOON, Jacob, Paymaster. Fourteenth Virginia Regiment. Defrauding the soldiers out of their pay: reprimand. (134)

MOON, Michael. Theft: acquitted. (115)

MOONES, James. Stealing a piece of check linen: thirty-nine lashes and pay for the linen. (93)

MOORE, Alexander, Sgt. Colonel Wind's Battalion. Desertion: thirty-nine lashes. (5) (132) (136)

MOORE, Burgess. Neglect of duty while a sentinel: pardoned. (90)

MOORE, James. Colonel Stewart's Battalion of Light Infantry. Robbery: death. (36)

MOORE, John. Captain Jackson's Regiment. Desertion from his post while on sentry duty: death by hanging. (17)

MOORE, Peter. Colonel Crane's Regiment of Artillery. Stealing two guineas and a silver watch from a French soldier when he was asleep: acquitted. (44)

MOORE, Thomas, Lt. Thirteenth (Fifteenth) Virginia Regiment. Encouraging the men to breed a mutiny: acquitted. (134)

MOORE, Thomas. Third Pennsylvania Regiment. Behaving in a scandalous manner, beating a number of persons, breaking windows and other abusive treatments: guilty only of abusive behavior—reprimand. (69) *See* Armstrong, Christy.

MOOSEMAN, Timothy, Lt. "Released from his arrest, as there was something in the manner of his being arrested unprecendented." (88)

MORAND, Edmund, Lt. Sixth Maryland Regiment. Neglecting to join his corps at the expiration of his furlough and after orders to rejoin it: dismissed from the service. (121)

MORE, Davis. Commander-in-Chief's Guard. Going out, with others, with sidearms, to do harm to other soldiers: acquitted. (125)

MORE (MOORE), John. Colonel Ritzema's Regiment. Absenting himself from camp without leave, forging a pass: thirty-nine lashes and confined seven days upon bread and water—confinement remitted. (136)

MORE, Jonathan. Commander-in-Chief's Guard. Going out, with others, with sidearms, to do harm to other soldiers: acquitted. (125)

MORE (MOORE), William. Third Massachusetts Regiment. Repeated desertion and attempting to go to the enemy: not guilty of the first charge but guilty of the second charge—100 lashes. (54)

MORGAN, James. Colonel Hazen's Regiment. Desertion: run the brigade gauntlet once a week for two weeks, from right to left and left to right each time. (112)

MORGAN, John. Colonel McDougall's Regiment. Sleeping on his post: thirty lashes. (132) (136)

MORGAN, Simon, Lt. Thirteenth Virginia Regiment. Cowardice: acquitted with honor. (134)

MORGAN, Thomas. First New Jersey Battalion. Desertion: 100 lashes. (25)

MORGAN, Thomas. Captain Wyllys's Regiment. Absent from roll call, being intoxicated with liquor, endeavoring to impose a falsehood on Lieutenant Colonel Huntington: fifty stripes. (91)

MORGAN, William, inhabitant of Pennsylvania. Stealing a horse and attempting to carry him back to the city of Philadelphia: hard labor during the contest with Great Britain, "not less than thirty miles from the enemy's camp, and if he is caught making his escape, shall suffer death." (15)

MORNEY, Barney. First Pennsylvania Regiment. Desertion: fifty lashes. (97)

MORREL, John. Colonel Jackson's Regiment. Desertion from his post while on sentry duty: death by hanging. (16) (134)

MORRELL, Phillip. Colonel Wheelock's Regiment. Refusing to do his duty, threatening the life of a sergeant: thirty-nine lashes for the first charge and thirty lashes for the second charge. (84) (117)

MORRILL, John. Absent from camp without leave: thirty lashes. (43)

MORRILLS, Cyprian. Captain Williams's Company. Taking boards from the barracks and cutting them up for his own use: fine of twenty shillings to pay for the boards. (91)

MORRIS, Francis. First Pennsylvania Regiment. Repeated desertions: death. (13)

MORRIS, Hugh, Clerk to the Commissary Marshal. Insulting and abusive language to a lieutenant; refusing to answer him to civil questions; damning him and saying he was a damned rascal and scoundrel; ordering him out of doors, to his quarters: acquitted, and the court believed there was indecent language on both sides. (75)

MORRISON,_____, Captain. First New Jersey Battalion. Selling as substitutes men who were enlisted: acquitted. (16)

MORRISON, Claudius. Fourth Georgia Continental Battalion. Desertion: death by shooting. (90)

MORRISON, Richard. Colonel Whitcomb's Regiment. Desertion and enlisting into another company: repay the $330 paid to him as a bounty, since the action was done out of ignorance rather than by design. (84) (117)

MORRISON, Samuel. Colonel Nixon's Regiment. Enlisting twice and receiving two bounties: returned to his unit without conviction, because of lack of evidence and his long confinement. (9)

MORTON, James. Colonel Poor's Regiment. Desertion: thirty-nine lashes. (84)

MOSELY, James. Stealing or being concerned in stealing a shirt, a pair of linen overalls, and a black handkerchief belonging to another soldier: acquitted. (66) *See* Baily.

MOSER, Henry. Reduced in ranks and run the gauntlet three times. (25)

MOYLAN,_____, Colonel. Disobedience to the orders of General Pulaski; striking a gentleman and officer in the Polish service when disarmed, and putting him under guard; giving irritating language to General Pulaski: acquitted. (134)

MOZAIS, Lewis. Pennsylvania Line. Desertion: 100 lashes. (86)

MUCHINSON, George, Matross. Fourth Regiment of Artillery. Desertion: death by shooting. (97)

MUCKFORD, James. Colonel Wind's Battalion. Desertion and enlistment into another corps: thirty-nine lashes. (5)

MUGRIDGE, Samuel. Colonel Jackson's Regiment. Breaking into the hospital store at sundry times and stealing wine: thirty lashes. (77) *See* Woodman.

MULFORD, James. Colonel McDougall's Regiment. Desertion and reenlistment into another corps: thirty-nine lashes. (71)

MULLEN, William. First North Carolina Regiment. Assaulting the house of Mr. Uriah McKeel, firing several shots through it, wounding Thomas Brown and robbing him, plundering a house of several articles of wearing apparel: death – pardoned. (26) *See* Borough, Burger, Rickets.

MUMFORD, Benjamin. Losing his new regimental hat: thirty-nine stripes and a fine to pay for the hat. (52)

MUMFORD, Benjamin. Colonel Bond's Regiment. Theft: acquitted. (136)

MUMFORD, David. Second New Jersey Regiment. Straggling from camp, killing a number of hogs: twenty-five lashes – pardoned. (20)

MUMFORD, James. Second New York Regiment. Desertion: 100 lashes. (36)

MUNDAY,_____, Lieutenant. Second New York Regiment. Falsely accusing others of fraud: reprimand. (25)

MUNDAY,_____, Lieutenant. Second New York Regiment. Sending an insulting and abusing note while under sentence to Captain Joseph Wright, leaving his arrest before being set at liberty: acquitted. (25)

MUNDAY,_____, Lieutenant. Second New York Regiment. Disobedience to orders and neglect of duty: dismissed from the service. (4)

MUNFORD, James. Colonel McDougall's Regiment. Desertion and reenlisting in another corps: thirty-nine lashes. (132) (136)

MUNN, Leonard, Cpl. Desertion: reduced in ranks and a fine of one pound two shillings. (70)

MUNN, Nathaniel. Colonel Budd's Regiment. Desertion and reenlisting in another corps: thirty-nine lashes. (132) (136)

MUNNS, Richard. Second Massachusetts Regiment. Desertion: 100 lashes. (46)

MUNROE,_____, Corporal. Being from his quarters at an unreasonable hour of the night, attempting to cross the river: reduced to a private sentinel.

MUNROE, John. Maryland Line. Desertion: 100 lashes. (21)

MUNSON, John. Massachusetts Line. Desertion: 100 lashes. (38)

MURMAN,_____, Major. Corps of Engineers. Taking possession of the quarters of the Reverend David Jones in his absence, and similar behavior to him in quarters: acquitted. (36) (116)

MURPHEY, Edward. Colonel Olney's Regiment (Colonel Angell's Regiment). Desertion: 100 lashes. (131)

MURPHEY, Edward. Colonal Angell's Regiment. Deserting the second time: 100 lashes and be put on board one of the Continental ships and serve during the war. (125)

MURPHEY, James. Colonel Livingston's Regiment. Endeavoring to persuade Negroes to enlist in order to join Roger's Rangers, getting drunk, suspected of going to the enemy: fifty lashes. (131)

MURPHY, James. Desertion: fifty lashes. (93)

MURPHY, James. Stealing: thiry-nine lashes and fourteen days' confinement in the guardhouse. (118)

MURPHY, John. Second Maryland Regiment. Housebreaking, stealing, and beating the inhabitants: death by hanging. (93) *See* Bay, Brown.

MURPHY, John, Sailor on board the sloop *Enterprise*. Mutinous behavior: acquitted. (99)

MURPHY, Patrick. First Company. Stealing another person's coat: acquitted. (56)

MURRAY, Abraham. Overstaying his furlough: acquitted. (91)

MURRAY, John. Colonel McDougall's Regiment. Desertion: confined to bread and water for five days only, "as much unfairness has been in enlisting the prisoner, and his being very ignorant." (136)

MURRAY, Lawrence. Maryland Line. Desertion: 100 lashes. (21)

MURREY, Clement. Colonel Hazen's Regiment. Desertion: run the brigade gauntlet once a week for two weeks, from right to left and left to right each time. (112)

MURREY, Francis. Fifth Pennsylvania Regiment. Desertion to the enemy: death. (72)

MURROW, Daniel. Captain Majors's Company. Absconding from duty six days: twenty lashes. (22)

MURROW, John. Ninth Massachusetts Regiment. Desertion: 100 lashes, with twenty-five lashes on four successive mornings. (78) (86)

MURRY, Bartlett. Conspiring to desert to the enemy: 100 lashes—remitted. (89)

MURRY, Samuel. Delaware Regiment. Being drunk: released when no evidence was presented. (93)

MURTON, James. Colonel Poor's Regiment. Desertion: thirty-nine lashes. (117)

MUZZY,_____, Lieutenant. Second Massachusetts Regiment. Exceeding his furlough by eighty days: lose pay for the days of absence. (50)

MYERS,_____, Lieutenant. German Battalion. Scandalous and infamous manner unworthy the character of a gentleman, in getting drunk and abusing the colonel and the rest of the officers of the regiment: acquitted—the commander-in-chief dissented from the verdict and ordered a reconsideration of the matter. Upon reconsideration, the court still felt that an acquittal was proper—acquitted and approved by commander-in-chief. (101)

MYERS, Christian. Colonel Jackson's Regiment. Desertion: 100 lashes—remitted. (26)

MYERS, Conrad. Second Regiment. Enlisting in the Third Regiment: released as no evidence was presented. (95)

MYERS, Dennis. Sixth Massachusetts Regiment. Desertion: not guilty of desertion but guilty of absence without leave—fifty lashes. (64)

NAGLE, George, Col. Tenth Pennsylvania Regiment. Associating with a sergeant in company with women who had bad reputations, in the sergeant's hut: acquitted. (17) *See* Stake.

NAIRN, William, Cpl. Colonel McDougall's Regiment. Leaving his post and attempting the life of Major Sedwitz: acquitted. (99)

NEAL, Richard. Captain Thompson's Independent Company of Riflemen. Striking and abusing several officers of the Twentieth Regiment: thirty-nine lashes. (1)

NEFF, John. Desertion: 100 lashes. (40)

NEGUS, William. Light Company. Breaking into a cellar and stealing cider: acquitted. (50)

NEGUS, William. Light Company. Absenting himself without leave, attempting to steal provisions from the commissary: 100 lashes. (52)

NEIGLE, James. Fourth Georgia Continental Battalion. Desertion: death by shooting. (90)

NESSHOND, Daniel. Ninth Massachusetts Regiment. Desertion and carrying his arms and ammunition with him: fifty lashes and a fine to pay for the stolen articles. (53)

NEWBERRY, Jeremiah. Fourth Regiment. Desertion and repeated desertion: 100 lashes. (125)

NEWEL,_____. First Virginia Regiment. Embezzling money, property of several soldiers, embezzling clothing belonging to the public: acquitted of the first charge but guilty of the second charge—released without punishment. (113)

NEWELL, Farrow. Second Company. Overstaying his pass and being absent from roll call: reprimand. (46)

NEWELL, Jonas. Second Company. Absenting himself without leave for four days: 100 lashes, "50 with hickory sticks and 50 with the bats." (53)

NEWELL, Peter. Mutiny, riot, and disobedience to orders: fine of twenty shillings. (135)

NEWLAND,_____, Captain. Damning and abusing Colonel Stark: guilty, but the satisfaction given by Colonel Stark at the time of the abuse was sufficient, and therefore was acquitted. (84)

NEWMAN, Benjamin. Colonel Arnold's Regiment. Refusing to obey Colonel Arnold's order: fined one month's pay and immediately join Captain Smith's company, according to Colonel Arnold's order. (128)

NEWMAN, John. Captain Hunt's Company. Mutinous conversation and advising a soldier to strike a sergeant: fifty lashes. (27)

NEWMAN, Jonathan. Fourth Massachusetts Regiment. Desertion to the enemy with a horse: acquitted. (56)

NEWN, John. Leaving his guard and going into town to sleep: acquitted. (23) *See* Clear.

NEWT,_____, Lieutenant. Fourth Regiment of Light Dragoons. Disobedience to orders: reprimand. (35)

NEWTON, Caleb. Captain Bates's Company. Stealing: fifty lashes. (43)

NEVILLE, Marc. Colonel Harrison's Regiment of Artillery. Desertion and attempting to go to the enemy: death – remitted. (21)

NIA, Cornelius. Deserting to the enemy twice and endeavoring to do so a third time, piloting a British prisoner of war through their lines: death. (28)

NICCOLOS, William, Sgt. Captain Moody's Company. Absent without leave: reduced to a matross. (125)

NICE, Richard. Captain Stephenson's Company of Riflemen. Striking and abusing an officer: thirty-nine lashes. (106)

NICHOL, James. Second New Hampshire Regiment. Overstaying his furlough. (31)

NICHOLAS, Hugh. First New Jersey Battalion. Desertion: 100 lashes. (112)

NICHOLAS, Jacob. Colonel Nixon's Regiment. Sleeping on his post: fifty lashes. (88)

NICHOLAS, Thomas. Fourth Georgia Continental Battalion. Desertion: 100 lashes. (90)

NICHOLS, John. Twelfth Regiment. Desertion: 100 lashes. (122)

NICHOLS, Lewis, Col. Depriving a captain of being assigned to a company, misassigning soldiers, false return, drawing pay for absentees and deserters, illegally removing prisoners from the guardhouse, and other charges: acquitted with honor. (46)

NICHOLS, Thomas, Sgt. Colonel Topham's Regiment. Disobedience to orders, sneaking out of camp: reduced to private. (23) *See* Eaton, Rolf, Whitney.

NICHOLS, William, Cpl. Desertion: 100 lashes. (101)

NICHOLS, William. Sixth South Carolina Regiment. Desertion: death. (115)

NICHOLSON,_____, Lieutenant. First North Carolina Regiment. Making out and repeatedly filing false returns: reprimand. (21)

NICHOLSON, William. Fifteenth Virginia Regiment. Desertion: twenty-five lashes. (101)

NIMES, Ebenezer. Desertion: three months in confinement. (41)

NINHAM, Daniel. Losing his canteen: ten lashes—pardoned. (44)

NOBLE, Mark. Desertion from the Massachusetts Regiment and reenlisting in the Rhode Island Regiment: 100 lashes. (44)

NOCK, Nicholas. Colonel Reed's Regiment. Desertion, enlisting in another regiment and receiving a bounty: thirty-nine lashes for each of the two offenses and a fine of thirty dollars. (84) (117)

NORCROSS, Aaron. General Hand's Brigade. Disobedience to orders, partial distribution of public stores, particularly in issuing of rum, not issuing provisions to the brigade agreeable to orders: guilty of the charges—reprimand. (32)

NORRIS, Henry, inhabitant of Pennsylvania. Supplying the enemy with provisions: pay fifty pounds for the use of the sick at camp. (15)

NORTH, Gab. Absenting himself from the main guard when on duty: twenty-five lashes—pardoned. (91)

NORTH, Samuel. Colonel Gerrish's Regiment. Mutiny: fine of forty-eight shillings and thirty-nine lashes. (3) (133) (136) *See* Harwood, Laraby, Rawlins (Rollins), Putney, Williams.

NORTON,_____, Lieutenant. Second Pennsylvania Regiment (Fourth Pennsylvania Regiment). Entering the encampment of the Third Pennsylvania Regiment with several others in a mutinous manner, attempting to enter Colonel Craige's house between the hours of twelve and one o'clock in the morning on 9 June, with a drawn sword: acquitted. (69) (103)

NORTON, G. Colonel Shepard's Regiment. Desertion: 100 stripes. (88)

NORTON, Jabez. Captain Wyllys's Company. Sleeping out of camp: thirty-five lashes—remitted. (91)

NORWOOD,_____, Captain. Fourth Maryland Regiment. Two charges of disrespect to the commander-in-chief and General Smallwood: reprimand—sentence disapproved because all the charges had not been tried by the court; continued confinement until he was tried further. (72)

NORWOOD,_____, Captain. Fourth Maryland Regiment. Refusal to comply with a general order: reprimand. (18)

NOTANS, Thomas. Colonel Bridges's Regiment. Quitting his post when on duty: fifteen lashes – pardoned, because of his youth and ignorance of his duty. (133) *See* Davison.

NOYES, Nathaniel. Being a spy: acquitted. (9)

NY, Joseph. Taking and killing a cow: 200 lashes and a fine of fifty pounds, New York currency, to pay the owner of the cow. (122) *See* Pardee, Pindar.

OAKLEY, Elijah, Lt. Colonel McDougall's Regiment. Assaulting and beating without provocation one Mr. Patterson, an inhabitant of the city of New York: cashiered and a fine of twenty dollars to pay to the victim. (1) (136)

OAKLEY, John, Sgt. Second New York Regiment. Leading, promoting, and being principal in a mutiny: 100 lashes and drummed out of the army with a label on his back with the word, "Mutiny" on it. (64)

OAKMAN, Onesinus. Colonel McDougall's Regiment. Desertion: released when no evidence was presented. (136)

OATES, John. 100 lashes – pardoned. (90)

O'BRIAN, Cornelius. Colonel Henman's Regiment. Locking and snapping a loaded musket at a lieutenant and a sergeant, cutting another lieutenant: thirty-nine lashes, confined on bread and water until the lashes are administered over a period of four days, drummed out of the regiment handcuffed with a halter about his neck, and be sent to Fort George in irons and handcuffs. (118)

O'BRIAN, John, Sutler. Striking Ensign Jenkins of the Third Massachusetts Regiment: 100 lashes and drummed out of the garrison – seventy of the lashes remitted. (124)

O'BRIAN, John. Colonel McDougall's Regiment. Sleeping on his post when on sentry: twenty lashes. (106) (136)

O'BRIAN, John. Getting drunk: ten stripes. (67)

O'BRIAN, John. Colonel Courtland's Regiment. Stealing liquor and being drunk, sleeping on his post, absenting himself from his guard: not guilty of the first charge but guilty of the second charge – fifty lashes. (131)

O'BRIAN, Matha, Bombardier. Colonel Crane's Regiment. Disobedience to orders and insolent language to an officer: reduced to a matross and fifty lashes. (125)

O'BRYAN, John. Massachusetts Line. Desertion: remitted. (53)

O'BRYAN, Thomas. Third Regiment of Artillery. Desertion and disposing of his clothing: 100 lashes. (52)

OGDEN,_____, Colonel. Neglect of duty, repeated fraud against the public, cowardice, gaming: acquitted of the first three charges but guilty of the last charge – reprimand. (21)

OGDEN, David. Colonel Sullivan's Regiment. Breaking open a store and stealing rum, fish, and molasses: thirty-nine lashes. (79)

OGLEBY, Nicholas. Mutiny, riot, and disobedience to orders: fine of twenty shillings. (135)

OLDHAM,_____, Captain. Third Virginia Regiment. Ordering a soldier not to comply with the orders of Lieutenant Colonel Campbell, and two related charges: acquitted with honor. (115)

OLDS, George. Mutiny: thirty-nine lashes. (94)

OLDS, Zebulon. Colonel Shepard's Regiment. Enlisting twice: fifty lashes. (88)

OLIVER,_____, Lieutenant. Fourteenth Virginia Regiment. Sending a corporal and a file of men into Colonel Stewart's Regiment to seize a keg of whiskey belonging to one of his officers, without consulting Colonel Stewart or any of his officers: acquitted. (15) (134)

OLMSTEAD, Francis. Colonel Webb's Regiment. Stealing sheep from Mr. Deines, an inhabitant of Bristol: thirty stripes – pardoned. (91) *See* Gay, Brown, Merrills.

O'NEAL,_____, Doctor. Tenth Pennsylvania Regiment. Cruel treatment of the sick of the regiment so much that they were really afraid to apply to him when they were really sick, embezzling the hospital stores, giving an unjust forage account and drawing money for the same, refusing to discharge the expenses of his house at Millstone when at quarters and making his mate pay an equal expense for the state stores, and selling the greater part of the stores in the country: dismissed from the service. (110)

O'NEALE, Peter. Seventh Pennsylvania Regiment. Threatening to desert: fifty lashes. (101)

O'NEIL,_____, Sergeant. Second George Continental Battalion. Insolence to Lieutenant Dunbar: reduced to the ranks and 100 lashes. (90)

O'QUIN, Daniel. Captain Oldham's Company. Forcibly taking a quantity of bacon under pretense of doing it for his officers: 100 lashes. (115) *See* Young.

ORANGE, Jacob. Colonel Morrow's Regiment. Firing his gun contrary to orders: fifteen lashes – pardoned, but forfeit one month's pay. (96)

ORANGE, James. Colonel Mott's Battalion. Desertion, and other offenses: 100 lashes for each of the two offenses, to be administered at two different days. (90)

ORR,_____, Lieutenant. Tenth Pennsylvania Regiment. Conniving and secreting stolen food, carrying off and offering for sale a Mulatto slave belonging to Major Shaw, ungentlemanlike behavior: guilty only of the last charge – dismissed from the service. (9)

ORR, Samuel. Colonel Jackson's Regiment. Disobeying orders: thirty-nine lashes. (9)

ORR, Samuel. Captain Major's Company. Theft: acquitted. (23)

ORR, Samuel. Attempting to pick a man's pocket: acquitted. (23)

ORR, Samuel. Falsehood and disobedience to orders: wear the log one week and attend the parade with it on. (23)

OSBORNE, Joseph. First New Jersey Regiment. Straggling from camp, killing a number of hogs: twenty-five lashes. (20) *See* Farmer, Leonard, McLaughlin, Mumford, Rush, Walker, Whitehead.

OSBURN,_____, Lieutenant. Disobedience to orders: acquitted. (84)

OSLERY, Laughlin. Second Georgia Battalion. Abusive language to Lieutenant Turner: 100 lashes, but Colonel Elbert was "empowered to remit any part of the sentence he may think proper." (90)

OTIS, Robert. Fifth Connecticut Regiment. Pardoned. (124)

OWEN, Elliott. Colonel Holmes's Regiment. Absent without leave: confined seven days in the dungeon and a fine of one month's pay. (118)

OWEN, John. North Carolina Line. Desertion: 100 lashes. (49)

OWEN, William. Insolence and abuse of a sergeant: ask the pardon of the sergeant at the head of the regiment. (23)

OWEN, William, Fifer. Eighth Company. Stealing a blanket from a sergeant: acquitted. (63)

OWENS, Maberny. Second New York Regiment. Desertion to the enemy, and taking up arms against the United States. (110)

OWENS, Terrence, Fife Major. Colonel McDougall's Regiment. Mutiny: fine of four shillings – pardoned. (118)

PAGE,_____, Corporal. Captain Walker's Company. Neglect of duty: reduced to the ranks. (91)

PAGE, Levi. Losing or wasting musket cartridges: thirty lashes. (91) *See* Stannard.

PAHNER, Nathaniel, Sgt. Colonel Topham's Regiment. Playing cards with Joseph Fortin and taking his money which he won at the game: reduced to the ranks and repay the money. (98)

PAINT, John. Colonel Prescott's Regiment. Desertion: thirty-nine lashes. (136)

PAINTER, Elisha. Artificers. Absent without leave, neglect of duty: dismissed from the service. (125)

PALMENTIER, Isaac, Drummer. Third New York Regiment. Robbing William Richardson and Benjamin Brooks, soldiers in the Sixth Massachusetts Regiment, threatening their lives: 100 lashes and pay for the articles robbed. (111) *See* Burnett.

PALMER, Edmund. Plundering, robbing, and carrying off cattle, etc. from the inhabitants, being a spy for the enemy: death by "hanging him up by the neck till he is dead, dead, dead." (131)

PALMER, Jabez. Colonel McDougall's Regiment. Desertion: thirty lashes. (132) (136)

PALMER, Ladian. First Massachusetts Regiment. Desertion: 100 lashes. (54)

PALMER, Samuel. Fifth Connecticut Regiment. Desertion: 100 lashes—remitted. (46)

PARALL, Charles. *See* Pearce.

PARDIS, John. Pennsylvania Regiment. Getting drunk on his post: twenty lashes. (117)

PARENTS, John. Colonel Prescott's Regiment. Desertion: thirty-nine lashes. (126)

PARK,_____, Captain. Fraudulent behavior with an inhabitant: reprimand. (44)

PARK, Theopolis, Lt. Defrauding his men of their pay and bounties, repeated forgeries: cashiered with infamy, by having his sword broken over his head on the public parade in front of the regiment, and his punishment published in the newspapers of Pennsylvania. (27)

PARK, William, Sgt. Colonel Greene's Regiment. Raising a mutiny and behaving in a disorderly manner: not guilty of the first charge but guilty of the second charge—suspended and reprimand. (131) *See* Baptist, Brown, Buck, Cary, Davis, Dunbar, Goold, Hartin, Lane, Luis, Peterson, Tabor.

PARKER,_____, Captain. Seventh Massachusetts Regiment. Repeatedly overstaying the limits of his furlough: dismissed from the service. (39)

PARKER,_____, Captain. Disobedience to orders: acquitted with honor. (84)

PARKER,_____, Lieutenant. Permitting a party under his command to abuse or sell the property of the inhabitants of Ballstown: acquitted. (88)

PARKER,_____, Ensign. Striking and abusing Lieutenant Henshaw and Lieutenant Craige, keeping Lieutenant Craige in the meeting house under guard all night: dismissed from the service. (113) (136) *See* Soper.

PARKER, Benjamin. Eighth Massachusetts Regiment. Exceeding the limits of his furlough by 485 days: cashiered. (56)

PARKER, Daniel. Colonel Clinton's Regiment. Desertion: fine of one month's pay—pardoned. (118)

PARKER, David. Absent from camp without permission, stealing corn: fifty lashes. (66) *See* Harvey, Franklin, Larkin, Wing.

PARKER, Levi. Light Company. Absenting himself without leave, attempting to steal provisions from the commissary: fifty lashes. (52) *See* Gustin, Negus, Toward.

PARKER, Moses. Desertion: eighty lashes. (42)

PARKER, Moses. Captain Blandard's Company. Theft: acquitted. (43)

PARKER, Oliver, Capt. Colonel Prescott's Regiment. Defrauding his men of their wages by false returns, imposing on the commissary and drawing supplies for more men than were in the company, and for selling these: cashiered. (2) (135) *See* chapter two.

PARKER, William. Desertion: 100 lashes. (42)

PARKER, Wyman, Sgt. Third Connecticut Regiment. Endeavoring to excite a mutiny in the Connecticut Line, not discussing with his officer an intended mutiny when he knew a plan was laying: death. (52) *See* Bunce, Gaylord, and chapter five.

PARKS,_____, Captain. Tenth Massachusetts Regiment. Unofficerlike and ungentlemanlike behavior in the seige of Yorktown in Virginia: dismissed from the service. (48)

PARMER, Farbes. Colonel McDougall's Regiment. Desertion: thirty lashes. (79)

PARREE, Nathan. Taking and killing a cow: 200 lashes and a fine of fifty pounds, New York currency, to pay the owner. (122) *See* Ny, Pindar.

PARSELLS, John. Third Regiment of Artillery. Desertion and attempting to go to the enemy, stealing a boat: death. (46) *See* Carman, Grant.

PARSONS, Samuel. Mutiny, riot, and disobedience to orders: fine of twenty shillings. (135)

PARSONS, William. Captain Wing's (Winder's) Company. Desertion with intention of going to the enemy, persuading others to go along with him: death – pardoned, because of his generally good character. (21) *See* Williams.

PASSON, Thomas. Seventh Massachusetts Regiment. Desertion: 100 lashes. (111)

PATTEN, James. Second New Hampshire Regiment. Absenting himself and reenlisting in the Massachusetts Line: 100 lashes. (78)

PATTEN, Nathaniel. Colonel Prescott's Regiment. Attempting to pass the low guards and making a disturbance on Cobble Hill, contrary to orders: acquitted. (3) (133) (136)

PATTEN (PATTON), William. Colonel Gridley's Regiment. Leaving his post while on guard. (1)

PATTEN (PATTON), William. Colonel Gridley's Regiment. Threatening and assaulting a number of persons while a prisoner in the guardhouse: ride the wooden horse fifteen minutes. (1) (135)

PATTERSON, Assistant Commissary of Hides. Forging a pass to a soldier in the Maryland Line without authority: released when he confessed his wrongdoing. (110)

PATTERSON, David, Lt. Disobedience to orders when on the lines near King's Point, going without the guards and patrols, and staying till an unreasonable hour in the night, suffering a small scout to break into the house of Mr. John Barker and take provisions from him, disposing of a number of horses without their being condemned: dismissed from the service. (116)

PATTERSON, William. Colonel Sheldon's Regiment. Plundering: run the gauntlet through a detachment of fifty men. (134)

PAYNE, Anthony. Sixteenth Virginia Regiment. Desertion: twenty lashes. (101)

PEARCE,_____, Sergeant. Colonel Bigelow's Regiment. Using threatening words and raising mutiny: reduced to the ranks and 100 lashes. (122) *See* Hunt.

PEARCE (PARALL), Charles. Mutiny, riot, and disobedience to orders: thirty-nine lashes, and drummed out of the army. (135)

PEARCE, Isaac, Capt. Colonel Stephenson's Regiment. Dealing with the Indians contrary to general orders, by giving an Indian a shirt and three dollars for two deer skins: reprimand—sentence disapproved and ordered to remain in confinement. (96)

PEARL,_____, Captain. Colonel Woodbridges' Regiment. Defrauding his men of their pay: acquitted, the charges being vexatious—the chief complainant, Daniel Davids, to be confined. (81)

PEASE, James. Desertion: 100 lashes. (42)

PEAT, William. Delaware Regiment. Various charges, including the abuse of a sergeant: 100 lashes. (93)

PEDLEY, William. Colonel Jackson's Regiment. Desertion: 100 lashes. (23)

PELTON, Daniel, Lt. Colonel Ritzema's Regiment. Leaving camp two days without leave: fine of one month's pay. (74) (107) (118) (123)

PELTON, Thomas. Second Virginia Regiment. Mutiny and desertion: 100 lashes—remitted. (134)

PELTROW (PETERS), John. Mutiny, riot, and disobedience to orders: thirty lashes and drummed out of the army. (135)

PEMBERTON, John. Delaware Regiment. Stealing a watch: acquitted. (93)

PENDERGAST,_____, Lieutenant. Maryland Line. Forcibly taking from Mr. Gamble, Assistant Quartermaster at Salisbury, soldiers' shoes and other apparel belonging to the United States: not guilty of forcibly taking the clothing but taking it without authorization, and such behavior justified because of the state of their soldiers—acquitted. (115) *See* Hugo, Williams.

PENDERGRASS, Thomas. Colonel Jackson's Regiment. Desertion: acquitted. (29)

PENDERGRASS, Thomas. Colonel Jackson's Regiment. Desertion from his regiment, and attempting to go to the enemy on Rhode Island: death. (23)

PENDLETON,_____, Captain. Corps of Artificers. Neglect of duty: mulcted of one month's pay for the use of the prisoners in the garrison who do not draw pay. (72) (125)

PENDLETON, Daniel. Regiment of Artificers. Defrauding the U.S. by "dating men back to the time of their enlistment" and discharging two men, one of which was a deserter and the other never joined, taking money for such discharges and reporting them as present: acquitted. (36)

PENDLETON, Samuel (Solomon), Lt. Colonel DuBois's Regiment. Acting in a manner unbecoming an officer and a gentleman: acquitted with honor. (83) (84)

PENHAM, Joseph. Stealing apples from an orchard belonging to Robinson's farm: acquitted. (56) *See* Allen, Jocelin.

PENNEL, William. Captain Gorven's Regiment. Desertion and intending to go to the enemy: 100 lashes. (101)

PENSE, Joel. Ninth Massachusetts Regiment. Stealing rum from an inhabitant's barn: fifty lashes and a fine of ten dollars to pay his share of the rum. (47) *See* Annis, Cruett, Ford, Tucker.

PERHAM, Francis. Seventh Company. Disobedience to orders, absent from camp without leave: thirty-nine lashes. (45)

PERO, John. Fifth Maryland Regiment. Desertion: 100 lashes. (46)

PERO, William. Colonel Topham's Regiment. Profane swearing and damning the general, abusing the corporal, striking the sentinel on his post: seventy-five lashes. (68)

PERRIS, Thomas. Second Maryland Regiment. Desertion: 100 lashes. (103)

PERRY,_____, Captain. Colonel Walker's Regiment. Permitting persons to pass the lines at Boston Neck: reprimand. (114)

PERRY,_____, Sergeant. Colonel Putnam's Detachment. Getting drunk, defrauding his detachment of beef and selling it to the inhabitants: fifty lashes and reduced to the ranks—lashes remitted, because of his former good conduct. (46)

PERRY,_____, Sergeant. Delaware Regiment. Frequent drunkenness: reduced to the ranks. (93)

PERRY, Constant. Stealing and being an accessory to stealing several articles of clothing and silver spoons from an inhabitant of Danbury: fifty lashes. (53) *See* Clements, Durham, Wilton.

PERRY, Foster. Ninth Regiment. Stealing sheep: acquitted. (46) *See* Baker, Clemons.

PERRY, John. Captain Cogswell's Company. Disposing of his arms and accouterments when on the lines: acquitted. (129)

PERRY, Joseph. Corps of Sappers and Miners. Threatening to desert the corps and treating his officers with language abusive and unbecoming a soldier: thirty-nine lashes. (54)

PERRY, Robert. Second Virginia Regiment. Attempting to go to the enemy, persuading a number of men to go with him: death. (21)

PERRY, Rufus. Deserting his post without orders or without being attacked or forced by the enemy: cashiered and pay damages to the inhabitants on Onion River due to his unofficerlike retreat. (94) *See* Fasset, Lyon, Wright.

PERRY, Thomas. Colonel McDougall's Regiment. Desertion: thirty-nine lashes. (1)

PERRY, Thomas. Maryland Line. Plundering: acquitted. (49)

PERSON,_____, Lieutenant. Sixth Virginia Regiment. Absent from his patrol, and thereby suffering the enemy to surprise and take his men at Woodbridge: reprimand. Upon review, Washington said, "The General is sorry he is obliged to declare that he thinks the sentence inadequate to the offense." (21)

PETERS, Jonathan. Stealing or attempting to steal from the garden of Lieutenant Colonel Huntington: thirty lashes – punishment postponed during good behavior. (91)

PETERSON, David, Lt. Massachusetts Regiment. Disobedience to orders when on the line near King Street, going without the guard and patrols at unreasonable hours of the night in contempt of orders delivered him, suffering others to break into the house of Mr. John Barkin and take provisions from him, disposing of a number of horses without their being condemned by civil or military authorization: dismissed from the service. (35)

PETERSON, John, Sgt. Colonel Greene's Regiment. Raising a mutiny and behaving in a disorderly manner: not guilty of the first charge but guilty of the second charge – suspended and reprimand. (131) *See* Baptist, Brown, Buck, Cary, Davis, Dunbar, Goold, Hardin, Lane, Luis, Park, Tabor.

PETTINGIL, Jacob. Second Company. Attempting to steal from a soldier of the Seventh Company: thirty lashes. (91)

PETTIS,_____, Corporal. Colonel Wigglesworth's Regiment. Out at an unreasonable time of night, attempting to strike Ensign Webb: reduced to a private and fifty lashes – pardoned due to his former good conduct. (19)

PETTON, Daniel. Colonel Ritzema's Regiment. Absent two days without leave: fine of one month's pay. (7)

PEVEY, Ichabod. Colonel Topham's Regiment. Desertion: 100 lashes. (68)

PHALON, Detrick, Lt. Ninth Massachusetts Regiment. Cowardly behavior at Yorktown in Virginia by not leading his company into the enemy's ranks, suffering a sergeant to command the company while taking cover for himself: acquitted. (50)

PHANSON, Thigham. Fifth Company. Going into the country without a pass and taking property from the inhabitants: fifty lashes. (46)

PHAY, N. Desertion and stealing public property from his care when on guard over it: fifty lashes. (41) *See* Chapman, Haney.

PHEAS, Jonas. First Continental Regiment. Desertion, enlisting a second time: fifty lashes. (31)

PHILLIPS,_____, Sergeant. Colonel Siliman's Regiment. Cowardice and leaving his post: acquitted. (7) (118) (123)

PHILLIPS, Abraham. Desertion: death by shooting. (93)

PHILLIPS, Anderson. Absent from roll call and exceeding his pass: acquitted. (47)

PHILLIPS, Anderson. Desertion: 100 lashes. (42)

PHILLIPS, George. Stealing: 100 lashes. (93)

PHILLIPS, Neamiah. New Hampshire Line. Going below the lines without permission, stealing, and plundering the inhabitants: acquitted. (38) *See* Fosgate.

PIALY, E. Conspiring to desert to the enemy: 100 lashes. (89)

PICKERTON, Andrew. Seventh Pennsylvania Regiment. Robbing a wagon: 100 lashes—thirty of the lashes remitted. (38)

PICKETT, Moses. Colonel Glover's Regiment. Disobedience to orders and damning his officers: thirty lashes and drummed out of his regiment. (71)

PIERRE, Jean. Desertion: serve the time "prescribed by act of Assembly." (102)

PIERCE, Jesse. Colonel Jackson's Regiment. Desertion: confined in a dungeon for one month, on bread and water. (26) *See* Barney, Mathews.

PIKE,_____, Ensign. Permitting a party under his command to abuse or sell the property of the inhabitants of Ballstown: acquitted. (88)

PIKE, Samuel, Cpl. Second Company. Disobedience to orders: reduced to a private sentinel. (53)

PINDAR, James. Taking and killing a cow: 200 lashes and a fine of fifty pounds, New York currency, to pay the owner of the cow. (122) *See* Ny, Pardee.

PINDERSON,_____, Ensign. Plundering in action: acquitted. (88)

PIPER, Thomas. Commander-in-Chief's Guard. Destroying and moving Mr. Thayer's house: guilty of pulling away and carting off some boards from the house—no punishment other than his confinement prior to his trial. (125)

PIPER, Zodiac. Colonel McDougall's Regiment. Being concerned in a riot: six days upon bread and water. (72) *See* Watkins.

PIRKENS, John. Sixth Maryland Regiment. Desertion and attempting to go to the enemy: death. (69)

PITTS, James. Fourth Regiment of Light Dragoons. Robbery: 100 lashes. (35)

PLEASE, Nathaniel. Colonel Shepard's Regiment. Desertion: 100 lashes. (131)

PLOWMAN, William. Drunk on his post, firing two shots, declaring he would be the death of some person, letting no person pass without money: trial deferred to court-martial at a level different from a regimental court-martial. (93)

PLUNKET,_____. Theft: acquitted. (115)

POINTER, Elisha (Stephen), Major. Corps of Artificers. Absenting himself from the garrison, neglect of duty: dismissed from the service. (72)

POLAND, James. Eighth Massachusetts Regiment. Desertion: 100 lashes. (46)

POLAND, William. Maryland Line. Desertion and joining the enemy: death. (115)

POLLARD, Andrew. Delaware Regiment. Burning a tent: acquitted, because the fire was an accident. (93)

POLLARD, Jonathan. Colonel Wigglesworth's Regiment. Enlisting twice: acquitted. (88)

POLLET, James. Desertion and bearing arms against the United States: death. (115)

POLLOCK, Jacob. Colonel Smith's Regiment. Suffering five pairs of shoes to be taken from under his care while on sentry: acquitted. (9) *See* Redford, Steward, Whittam.

POMPEY, Andrew. Losing his canteen: fifteen lashes—remitted. (47)

PONDARS (PENDRICK), Richard. Mutiny, riot, and disobedience to orders: fine of twenty shillings. (135)

POOLE,_____, Captain. Colonel Cary's Regiment. General Fellows's Brigade. Shamefully abandoning his post: cashiered. (92) (94)

POOLES, John. Light Dragoons. Desertion, selling his Continental clothing, stealing a horse: 100 lashes and serve on a frigate during his enlistment—the service on the frigate was remitted. (72)

POOR, John. Mutiny, riot, and disobedience to orders: fine of twenty shillings. (135)

POOR, Michael. Colonel Douglass's Regiment. Getting drunk and endeavoring to force the guard, speaking treasonous language against the states of America: 100 lashes. (131)

POOR, William. General Patterson's Brigade. Desertion, after breaking away from the guard: 100 lashes. (74) *See* Downs.

POPE,_____, Lieutenant Colonel. Defrauding the public of the services of one Joseph Hibbard, a private soldier in the Delaware Regiment, by employing him in his domestic business in the spring of the year 1778: acquitted. (21)

POPE,_____, Ensign. Tenth Virginia Regiment. Not attending his duty on parade: acquitted. (101)

POPE, Samuel. Desertion: fifty lashes and serve the time "prescribed by act of Assembly"—lashes remitted. (102)

PORTER,_____, Major. Sixth Massachusetts Regiment. Taking an action without proper authority from his commanding officer, absenting himself from his regiment beyond the time limited by the commander-in-chief: dismissed from the service. (58)

PORTER,_____. Seventh Maryland Regiment. Robbing and plundering a woman of money: cashiered. (26)

PORTER, Andrew. Artillery. Falsely and maliciously misrepresenting the conduct of Colonel Thomas Proctor in saying he discharged soldiers of his regiment for his private gain: acquitted. (36) *See* Proctor.

PORTER, Anthony. Eleventh Regiment. Availing himself of a forged furlough for desertion: 150 lashes. (112)

PORTER, John. Stealing a forty dollar bill from Sergeant Price, of the German Regiment: acquitted. (103) *See* Price.

PORTER, Moses. Captain Williams's Company. Refusing to do his duty when ordered by Sergeant Boardman: drummed through the ranks from right to left and left to right, with the Rogue's March—pardoned. (91)

PORTER, Nathaniel. Overstaying his furlough five days: acquitted. (91)

POST,_____, Major. Colonel Macklin's Battalion. Cowardice and shamefully abandoning his post on Long Island upon the approach of the enemy: acquitted of cowardice but guilty of misbehavior—dismissed from the service. (6) (107)

POST, James, Batteauman. Disobedience to orders: twenty lashes. (111)

POTTER,_____, Ensign. Permitting a party under his command to abuse or sell the property of the inhabitants of Ballstown: acquitted. (88)

POTTER, James. Second New Hampshire Regiment. Absenting from his regiment and reenlisting in the Massachusetts Line, and deserting from it: 100 lashes. (86)

POTTER, William. Colonel Angell's Regiment. Desertion and reenlisting: 100 lashes.

POTTS, Robert. Desertion: death—pardoned on condition that he enlist for the duration of the war. (90)

POWELL,_____, Captain. Third Virginia Regiment. Insulting Lieutenant Davis when on his guard, arresting him on a groundless foundation: not guilty of the first charge but guilty of the second charge. (13)

POWELL, John. New Hampshire Line. Repeated desertions: death. (42)

POWELL, John. Colonel Poor's Regiment. Desertion: thirty-nine lashes. (84) (111)

POWELL, Joseph. Fourth Georgia Continental Battalion. Desertion: death by shooting. (90)

POWELL, Thomas. Colonel Courtland's Regiment. Deserting to the enemy, returning and deserting again, persuading other soldiers to desert with him: death by shooting. (131)

POWELL, William, Boatman. The Fleet. Mutiny, whereas the enemy might come, and saying that he would not fight against them on board the vessel: seventy-eight lashes and do duty as a private in his former regiment—"the criminals to be whipped from vessel to vessel, receiving a part of their punishment on board each." (117) *See* Colbert, Hammon, Trip.

POWELL, William. Colonel Angell's Regiment. Desertion and reenlisting and perjury: 300 lashes. (17)

POWERS, John, Lieutenant. Fifth Massachusetts Regiment. Not returning to his unit when ordered to do so: cashiered. (46) *See* chapter three.

POWERS, Nathaniel. Colonel Learned's Regiment. Desertion: thirty-nine lashes. (1)

POWERS, Robert. Tenth Pennsylvania Regiment. Plundering Mr. Bogart, an inhabitant, near Paramus: death by hanging – pardoned. (26) (135) *See* Bell, Brown, Justice.

POWERS, Thomas. First Massachusetts Regiment. Desertion: 100 lashes. (47)

PRATT, Allen. Stealing a carpenter's hammer: twenty-five lashes. (91)

PRATT, Allen. Stealing and concealing a barrel of flour: 100 lashes and pay one dollar to the baker – fine remitted. (91)

PRATT, James. Breaking open and robbing the store: thirty-nine lashes and a fine of thirty shillings – fine remitted. (91)

PRATT, L., Captain. Abusing in a wanton and cruel manner, Phillips, a soldier in the Third New Hampshire Regiment: acquitted. (25)

PRAUX, James. Disobedience to orders and kicking Lieutenant Whelp: acquitted. (85)

PREVEAUX,_____, Lieutenant. Reprimand. (90)

PRICE, C_____, Captain. Second Maryland Regiment. Gaming with cards for money, neglect of duty, gambling, striking a lieutenant with a cane: guilty of two of the charges – reprimand. (2)

PRICE, Abraham. German Battalion. Stealing a forty dollar bill from Sergeant Price, of the same regiment: pay back the money stolen. (10) *See* Porter.

PRICE, Daniel. Fourth Maryland Regiment. Desertion to the enemy in March 1777, bearing arms against the United States: 100 lashes – remitted. (110) *See* Dreshall.

PRICE, John. Foragemaster. Not taking measures to forward a boatload of corn, which was in the line of his duty, and being deserted by the boatman, was left to waste: acquitted, because it was an error of judgment only. (115)

PRICE, Thomas. Colonel Marshall's Regiment. Desertion and enlisting twice and receiving two bounties: 100 lashes and repayment of the bounties – lashes remitted. (11)

PRICE, William. Attempting to desert to the enemy, and enticing others to do the same. (42) *See* Binham, Fitzgerald, Walden, Van Wert.

PRIEST, Elizar. Eighth Company. Refusing to clean his clothes when ordered: 100 lashes – remitted. (63)

PRIEST, John. Colonel Prescott's Regiment. Desertion: thirty-nine lashes. (106)

PROCTOR, James (Thomas), Col. Artillery. Mustering men into his regiment as soldiers that were not actually doing the duty of soldiers, enlisting them as being present when they were doing the duty of servants in other families in the city of Philadelphia, discharging soldiers for sums of money, fraud in settlement of his recruiting accounts, sending a false certificate for quartermaster stores, discharging a number of able-bodied men: acquitted with honor. (36) (116) (125) *See* Porter.

PROCTOR, Jonas, Ens. Colonel Doolittle's Regiment. Absenting himself from his regiment from 9 August to 27 September: mulcted of one month's pay. (136)

PROUTTY, John. Sleeping on his post and suffering flour to be taken when left in his charge: acquitted. (50)

PULFORD, Samuel. Captain Whiting's Company. Taking boards from the barracks and cutting them up for his own use: fine of twenty shillings to pay for the boards. (91)

PULFORD, Samuel. Absence without leave, selling his uniform, clothing, arms, and accouterments: not guilty of the first charge but guilty of the other charges—fifty lashes and pay for the lost clothing—payment remitted. (91) *See* Latimer.

PURDY, John. First Pennsylvania Regiment. Drunk on his post: twenty lashes. (84)

PUSSECK, Joseph. Fifth Massachusetts Regiment. Desertion: not guilty of desertion but guilty of absenting himself without leave: fifty lashes. (46)

PUTNAM,_____, Ensign. Colonel Henley's Regiment. Appearing on the parade intoxicated. (19)

PUTNEY, Jonathan, Sgt. Colonel Gerrish's Regiment. Mutiny: reduced to the ranks and a fine of forty-eight shillings and thirty-nine lashes. (3) (133) *See* Harwood, Laraby, Rawlins (Rollins), North, Williams.

PUTNEY, Joseph. Third New York Regiment. Sleeping on his post: 100 lashes. (103)

QUACKENBUSH, Benjamin. Third New York Regiment. Attempting to desert to the enemy without his arms and accouterments: run the gauntlet twice with fixed bayonets at the breast to regulate his pace. (29)

QUALE (QUAIL), John. Fourth Regiment of Light Dragoons. Desertion and taking with him a dragoon horse and accouterments, and a horse belonging to Captain Hurd: guilty of the first charge but not guilty of the other charges – picketed fifteen minutes and 100 lashes. (33) (129)

QUICK, Cornelius. Abusive language and absenting himself from duty: picketed twelve minutes. (111)

QUIGLEY, Thomas. Colonel Webb's Regiment. Attempting to desert to the enemy on Rhode Island: death by hanging. The execution was first ordered for "6 o'clock this evening," and postponed to "2 o'clock tomorrow afternoon." (8/27/78). (9)

QUIM, John. Colonel Ward's Regiment. Desertion: thirty-nine lashes. (136)

QUIMBLE, Joseph. Colonel Vere's Regiment. Out at an unreasonble time of night, abusing a lieutenant: 100 lashes – pardoned due to his former good conduct. (19) *See* Fenner.

QUINA, Patrick. First Regiment. Plundering the inhabitants: acquitted. (116)

RABLY, Michael. Second New York Regiment. Desertion: 100 lashes. (100)

RADBY,_____, Sergeant. Maryland Line. Expressing himself in disaffection in the presence of soldiers; speaking disrespectfully of Colonel Howard, his commanding officer; frequently saying in the presence of the soldiers he would never endeavor to injure the enemy: death. (115)

RADFORD, Daniel. Embezzling public stores: fine of forty dollars and run the gauntlet twice. (103)

RAGAN, William. Giving up all his clothing and blankets – pardoned. (118)

RAINS,_____, Lieutenant. Fifth Virginia Regiment. Sending a soldier (William Bluford) to bring water in a tin cartouche box: acquitted. (134)

RALLYHORN, Samuel. Maryland Line. Repeated desertions: death – pardoned. (49)

RALSTON,_____, Adjutant. First Pennsylvania Battalion. Making a false return, disobedience to orders, leaving his arrest: cashiered. (88)

RAMNANT, Josiah. Colonel Peterson's Regiment. Sleeping on his post: twenty lashes – pardoned. (84)

RAMOUS, Thomas. Captain Whiting's Company. Taking boards from the barracks and cutting them up for his own use: thirty lashes, since he and Levi Latimer were the "first promoters of the crime," there being several others who were fined twenty shillings each. (91) *See* Latimer.

RAMOUS, Thomas. Sleeping on his post when on sentinel: sixty-five lashes. (91)

RAND, David. Colonel Poor's Regiment. Desertion and enlisting with the militia, and deserting again: thirty-nine lashes. (4)

RANDALL, Thomas, Lt. Regiment of Artillery. Stabbing a matross in the Second Regiment: reprimand. (136)

RANDALL, William, State clothier. State of Maryland. Distributing the clothes for the use of the officers in a partial manner, whereby the officers were injured: acquitted. (28)

RANDOM, John. Delaware Regiment. Plundering the house of an inhabitant near Prospect Hill: seventy-five lashes (fifty for the offense and twenty-five for lying to the court), and a fine of one-half month's pay. (93)

RANSDALL, Saul. Sixth Massachusetts Regiment. Desertion: sixty lashes. (53)

RANSOM, Jonathan, Ens. Light Infantry. Disobedience to orders: acquitted. (100)

RASBY, Phillip. Conspiracy with Baker to spike the cannon at Fort Schuyler, desertion: 100 lashes. (100)

RAVEN, James. Desertion: 100 lashes. (42)

RAWLINS (ROLLINS), Thomas. Colonel Gerrish's Regiment. Mutiny: fine of forty-eight shillings and thirty-nine lashes. (133) *See* Harwood, Laraby, North, Putney, Williams.

RAY, Daniel. Thirteenth Massachusetts Regiment (Second Connecticut Regiment). Desertion: 100 lashes—fifty on his bare bottom and fifty on his bare back. (46)

RAYMAND, Zevial, Cpl. Captain Blandard's Company. Violating his trust on guard, stealing liquor: reduced in rank and fifty lashes. (43)

RAYMOND,_____, Lieutenant. Tenth Massachusetts Regiment. Absenting himself from his guard: reprimand. (45)

RAYMOND, William. Sixth Massachusetts Regiment (Ninth Massachusetts Regiment). Desertion: 100 lashes. (48)

RAYMOUR (RAMOUS), Thomas. Ninth Massachusetts Regiment. Carrying off timber belonging to Captain Donnels: acquitted. (48)

REA (RAY), John, Q.M. Sixth Pennsylvania Regiment. Fraudulent practices: dismissed from the service. (13)

READ, Patrick. Maryland Line. Plundering: acquitted. (49)

READING, Samuel. Colonel Maxwell's Regiment. Declaring his intention to desert as soon as possible, persuading others to desert: tied naked to the post for five minutes, and reprimanded. (84) (117)

READMAN, John. Second New York Regiment. Repeated desertions: death. (44)

REDFORD, Edward. Colonel Smith's Regiment. Suffering five pairs of shoes to be taken from under his care while on sentry: acquitted. (9) *See* Pollock, Steward, Whittam.

REDMAN,_____, Captain. Colonel Patton's Regiment. Neglecting to guard the paper by which means Captain Humphrey was surprised, not coming to Captain Humphrey's assistance when he was attacked by the enemy: not guilty of the first charge but guilty of the second charge, but since he had sufficient reason not to come to Captain Humphrey's assistance, he was eventually acquitted with honor. (17)

REED, Amos, Cpl. Colonel Johnson's Company. Speaking disrespectfully and vilifying the commander-in-chief: reduced to the ranks and thirty-nine lashes, with thirteen lashes administered on three successive days. (71) (107)

REED, William, Cpl. Colonel Elliot's Regiment of State Artillery. Stealing corn from an inhabitant: reduced to a matross and do duty accordingly. (91)

REEVES,_____, Lieutenant. *See* Rivvers.

REGINER,_____, Lieutenant Colonel. Disobedience to orders: acquitted. (15)

REGINER (REGNER),_____, Lt. Col. Leaving his regiment when alarmed by the firing of the patrols on the morning of 29 June, last, and not joining his regiment again until the alarm was over; purchasing a horse from a soldier which properly belonged to the Continent; treating Adjutant Sackett in an unofficerlike and ungentlemanlike manner: acquitted with honor. (69)

REID (REED), James, Maj. General Hazen's Regiment. Improprieties in bringing people of his unit to justice in the proper manner, disobedience to orders, defrauding the government by converting money to his own use: acquitted. (41) (62)

REILEY, John. Second Virginia Regiment. Deserting from his guard and taking with him two prisoners in irons: death. (13) (134)

REILEY (RILEY), Thomas. Seventh Pennsylvania Regiment. Desertion to the enemy: death – pardoned. (35) (129)

REILY, John, Capt. Corps of Invalids. Receiving his pay for the month of January, partly in money and partly in orders drawn on the paymaster, and afterwards applying for and receiving the same month's pay from the deputy paymaster: reprimand. (64)

REILY, John. Seventh Maryland Regiment. Desertion, changing his clothes, selling his arms and accouterments: 100 lashes. (21)

RELSWORTH, Jeremiah. Colonel Little's Regiment. Breaking open a store and drawing rum, or suffering it to be done. (132)

RENKIN,_____. Firing on the lines: acquitted. (96)

RENNY (HENRY), Hugh. Mutiny, riot, and disobedience to orders: thirty-nine lashes and drummed out of the army. (135)

REYNOLD, Joseph. Colonel Worthing's Regiment. Using threatening language to Sergeant Wales and denying the same: ten stripes and drummed out of camp. (119)

REYNOLDS, Condant. Mutiny: thirty-nine lashes. (84)

REYNOLDS, Israel. Enticing a soldier to sell his gun: acquitted. (92)

REYNOLDS, John. Major Pottard's Corps. Striking a lieutenant: 100 lashes. (16)

REYNOLDS, Michael. Fifth Pennsylvania Regiment. Deserting toward the enemy: 100 lashes and sent on board one of the Continental frigates to serve during his enlistment. (101)

RHODES, Samuel. Fifth Company. Purchasing a blanket from Drake and Richards: fifty lashes – pardoned because of previous good behavior. (23) *See* Drake, Richards.

RHODES, William. Fourth Massachusetts Regiment. Attempting to desert to the enemy: 100 lashes. (42)

RHYER, Michael. Ninth Pennsylvania Regiment. Being drunk on his post: ninety-five lashes. (101)

RIAC, James, Sgt. Colonel Harrison's Regiment. Desertion. (125)

RICE, Hopkins. Colonel Ritzema's Regiment. Desertion: thirty-nine lashes. (132)

RICE, Jedediah. First New York Regiment. Desertion: 100 lashes. (41)

RICE, Stephen. Eighth Virginia Regiment. Plundering inhabitants of the country: 100 lashes. (13) (134)

RICE, Thomas. Colonel Marshall's Regiment. Desertion and enlisting twice: fifty lashes for each offense, and repayment of the bounty. (9)

RICHARDS, Benjamin. Colonel Baldwin's Regiment. Publishing the countersign and openly proclaiming it in a public house after tattoo beating: twenty lashes. (136)

RICHARDS, John. Colonel Crane's Regiment. Desertion: seventy-five lashes. (46)

RICHARDS, John. Fifth Company. "Being overmuch dirty": thirty-nine lashes—remitted because of extenuating circumstances. (23)

RICHARDS, John. Selling a blanket: fifty lashes—remitted because of his former good conduct. (23) *See* Drake, Rhodes.

RICHARDS, Patrick. Second Regiment. Attempting to desert to the enemy: 100 lashes. (116)

RICHARDS, Peter, Sgt. The General's Guard. Abusing and striking Capt. Caleb Gibbs: reduced in rank and thirty-nine lashes. (7) (136)

RICHARDSON, James. Colonel Lamb's Regiment of Artillery. Desertion and enlisting twice: 100 lashes. (113)

RICHARDSON, Roosevelt. Captain Wooster's Company. Disobedience to orders: drummed through the ranks from left to right and in front of the battalion from right to left, with the Rogue's March. (91)

RICHOSON, Thomas. Twelfth Regiment. Desertion: thirty-nine lashes—remitted. (122)

RICKETS, Patrick. Pennsylvania Regiment. Desertion: 100 lashes. (97)

RICKETS, Reason. First North Carolina Regiment. Assaulting the house of Mr. Uriah McKeel, firing several shots through it, wounding Thomas Brown and robbing him, plundering the house of several articles of wearing apparel: death. (26) *See* Borough, Burger, Mullen.

RICKEY, Andrew, Sutler. Selling liquor to the soldiers: fifty lashes—remitted. (41) *See* Warren.

RICKEY, George. Colonel Marshall's Regiment. Desertion in the late retreat from Ticonderoga: returned to his regiment in irons. (9)

RICKS, Harry. Third New York Regiment. Desertion: acquitted. (27)

RICKY, John. Lieutenant Perkins's Company. Disobedience to orders and abusive language to the captain: ask the captain's pardon at the head of his company, and wear a board of eight inches square one day on his back, with a label on the board saying, "A disobeyer of orders," and ten days' fatigue with the bricklayers. (104)

RIDER, Joseph, Ens. Colonel Sage's Regiment. Going home 120 miles distant from camp when permitted only to leave the camp for convenient quarters to restore his health: dismissed from the service. (92)

RIGGS, John, Lt. Colonel Nixon's Regiment. Counterfeiting; assuming the character of a field officer and under pretense of being a field officer of the day, ordering out one of the principle guards of the army, imposing upon Captain Somner: cashiered. (106) (136)

RILEY, John, Capt. Leaving his regiment for a month, claiming rank in the Third Pennsylvania Regiment upwards of nine months after he had informed the commanding officer that he would not join it: reprimand. (3)

RILEY, Thomas. *See* Reiley.

RIPLEY, Job. Third Massachusetts Regiment. Desertion: 100 lashes. (57)

RIPPEE (RISSEC), Elijah. Colonel Spencer's Regiment. Desertion: 100 lashes. (25) (103)

RIPPLEE, Phineas, Cpl. Mutiny: reduced to the ranks and thirty-nine lashes. (84)

RITTER, G. Colonel Proctor's Regiment. Ungentlemanlike behavior, going into the city of Philadelphia since the enemy had taken possession: not guilty of the first charge but guilty of the second charge—fifty lashes. (9)

RIVVERS (REEVES),_____, Lieutenant. Tenth Pennsylvania Regiment. Granting a pass to Daniel Quinn, a soldier in the Tenth Pennsylvania Regiment: acquitted. (36) (116)

ROACH, Frederick. Regiment of Artillery. Insulting and striking some inhabitants of Long Island. Thirty-nine lashes. (136)

ROACH, Nathaniel. Colonel Peterson's Regiment. Refusing his duty and striking an officer: thirty-nine lashes for each offense. (84)

ROATCH, John, Sgt. Colonel Vose's Regiment. Absent without leave from his company; forging a pass, signing the colonel's name to it: not guilty of forging the pass but guilty of the other charges— reduced to the ranks. (88)

ROBBARTS, David. Absence without cause: acquitted. (91)

ROBBARTS, Stephen. Absence without cause: acquitted. (91)

ROBECHEAU,_____. Colonel Livingston's Regiment. Endeavoring to raise a mutiny while said regiment was under arms: acquitted with honor. (85)

ROBERTS (ROBBINS), Corporal. Delaware Regiment. Promoting and encouraging desertion among the men and declaring he intended to desert himself at the first opportunity, and advising them to go along with him: death. (27)

ROBERTS, Benjamin. Desertion: 100 lashes. (77)

ROBERTS, Daniel. Captain Whiting's Company. Taking boards from the barracks and cutting them up for his own use: fine of twenty shillings to pay for the boards. (91)

ROBERTS, Daniel. Breaking open and robbing the commissary stores: acquitted. (91)

ROBERTS, Ezekial. Captain Pettibone's Company. Loading his gun and threatening the lives of sundry persons: acquitted. (105)

ROBERTS, John. Colonel Arnold's Regiment. Refusing to obey Colonel Arnold's order: fine one month's pay and immediately join Captain Smith's company, according to Colonel Arnold's order. (128)

ROBERTS, John. Second North Carolina Regiment. Absenting himself from camp without leave: acquitted. (17)

ROBERTS, William, Drummer. Maryland Line. Desertion and reenlisting in the cavalry: twenty-five lashes. (49)

ROBERTSON, Andrew. Third New York Regiment. Desertion: 100 lashes. (89)

ROBINSON,_____, Lieutenant Colonel. Pennsylvania Regiment. Absent upwards of twenty days when he had leave for only two days: reprimand. (27)

ROBINSON,_____, Ensign. Thirteenth Virginia Regiment. Encouraging a soldier's wife to sell liquor in General Muhlenberg's Brigade, taking the liquor after they had been seized, repeatedly getting drunk: reprimand. (14) (134)

ROBINSON, Benjamin. Colonel Porter's Regiment. Desertion: thirty-nine lashes. (84) (117)

ROBINSON, James. Arrested but released when no evidence was presented. (93)

ROBINSON, James. Desertion: pardoned, because of his previous good character. (26)

ROBINSON, Peter. Colonel Hazen's Regiment. Leaving his post, desertion: 200 lashes. (93)

ROBINSON, Peter. Colonel Harrison's Regiment of Artillery. Desertion and attempting to go to the enemy: death. (21)

ROBINSON, Sully, Lt. Fourth Virginia Regiment. Absenting himself from his regiment without leave: dismissed from the service and forfeit his pay from 13 December, last, until he joined his regiment. (101)

ROBINSON, William. Desertion: 100 lashes. (42)

ROCH, Richard. Colonel Paterson's Regiment. Refusing his duty and striking his officer: thirty-nine lashes. (117) *See* Roach, Nathaniel.

ROCHE, Thomas, Matross. Colonel Crane's Regiment. Desertion and attempting to go to the enemy: death. (134)

ROCK, Samuel. Absenting himself from his company and engaging in another corps: thirty-nine lashes. (128) *See* Camron.

ROCKWOOD, Joseph. Stealing rum at the commissary store: ten lashes. (69) *See* Bryant, Hingham, Woodbury.

ROE,_____, Captain. Insulting and ill treating Mr. Coldong, conductor of the wagons in the march from Morristown: acquitted. (101)

ROGERS, Amos. Colonel Gallup's Regiment. Refusing to march when ordered by their captain for the defense of New London and places adjacent: ride the wooden horse not exceeding one-half hour. (82) *See* Stewart.

ROGERS, Ebenezer. Colonel Gallup's Regiment. Refusing to march when ordered by their captain for the defense of New London and places adjacent: ride the wooden horse not exceeding one-half hour. (82) *See* Stewart, Rogers.

ROGERS, Silas. Third Massachusetts Regiment. Desertion: 100 lashes, twenty-five on each of four days. (54) (86)

ROLF,_____, Sergeant. Disobedience to orders, sneaking out of camp: reduced to private. (23)

ROLLINS. *See* Rawlins.

ROLSTON, John, Sutler. Selling rum to the soldiers, suffering them to be drunk at his hut at unreasonable hours: ordered off the grounds and prohibited from suttling thereafter to the Northern army. (84)

ROMANDER, John. Colonel Hazen's Regiment. Desertion: run the brigade gauntlet once a week for two weeks, from right to left and left to right each time. (112)

ROOKER,_____, Lieutenant. Fifteenth Virginia Regiment. Being drunk on parade: reprimand. (101)

ROONEY, Peter. Colonel Stewart's Battalion of Light Infantry. Robbery: death. (36) *See* Miller, Moore, Welsh.

ROOT, Stephen. Stealing nineteen quarts and one pint of whiskey belonging to Captain Cogswell's Company: thirty-nine lashes. (124) *See* Crosby.

ROSAN, Jonathan. Disobedience to orders: acquitted. (116)

ROSE, Albert, Cpl. Third New York Regiment. Stealing rum from Mr. Adams, sutler: reduced to private sentinel and 100 lashes and repay Mr. Adams. *See* Johnson, Ladd, Lester. (111)

ROSE, Amos. Colonel Webb's Regiment. Firing a gun loaded with a ball at Lieutenant Elisha Brewster: death by shooting. (131)

ROSE, Benjamin. Eighth Company. Indecent and disorderly behavior on the parade: thirty lashes. (63)

ROSE, Samuel, Sgt. Fifteenth Regiment. Threatening and deserting: reduced to the ranks, 100 lashes, and run the gauntlet – running of the gauntlet remitted. (122)

ROSEBURY, Michael. Death. (25)

ROSS, Major. Leaving his arms in the field in the action of 4 October, near Germantown: acquitted with highest honor. (9)

ROSS, John. Conspiring to desert to the enemy: 100 lashes – remitted. (89)

ROSS, Joseph. Fifth Connecticut Regiment. Desertion and reenlisting in Colonel Sheldon's Regiment of Light Dragoons: 100 lashes. (44)

ROSS, William. Colonel Huntington's Regiment. Attempting to desert to the enemy: 100 lashes. (131)

ROSSER, Jonathan, Ens. Disobedience to orders: acquitted. (129)

ROUNDS,_____, Sergeant. Disobedience to orders: reduced to the rank of private. (22)

ROUNDS, Amos. Colonel Jackson's Regiment. Desertion: death – remitted. (26)

ROUSE, Simeon. Colonel Jackson's Regiment. Desertion: 100 lashes. (24)

ROWE, Jacob. Desertion: 100 lashes. (42)

ROWLANDSON, Joseph. Captain Walker's Company. Disobedience of orders, insulting language to Sergeant Nicholson: thirty-nine lashes. (91)

ROWLING, John. Colonel Paterson's Regiment. Desertion and going to the enemy: guilty only of desertion – 100 lashes and sent on board the Continental frigate to serve during his enlistment. (101)

ROYALL, John. Fourth Georgia Continental Battalion. Desertion: ninety-nine lashes – pardoned. (90)

ROYAN, William, Lt. Cashiered. (104) (114)

ROZAN, John. See Bryan.

ROZIER, Jordan. North Carolina Line. Desertion and joining the Tories, bearing arms against the United States: death. (115)

RUFF, Adam. Tenth Regiment. Desertion: 100 lashes. (116)

RUNDELL, Eli, Sgt. Colonel Waterbury's Regiment. Deserting his post in action: acquitted. (99)

RUSH,_____. Captain North's Company. Stealing rum from a sergeant: 100 lashes. (29) *See* Cole.

RUSH, David, inhabitant of Pennsylvania. Attempting to relieve the enemy with provisions: 100 lashes. (10)

RUSH, John. First New York Regiment. Straggling from camp, killing a number of hogs: twenty-five lashes—pardoned. (20) *See* Farmer, Leonard, McLaughlin, Mumford, Osborne, Walker, Whitehead.

RUSSELL,_____, Lieutenant. Captain Symond's Twenty-first Regiment of Foot Soldiers. Disobedience to orders: acquitted. (135)

RUSSELL,_____, Ensign. Colonel Sherburne's Regiment. Defaming Colonel Sherburne's character by saying he was a damned liar and a rascal: reprimand. (32)

RUSSELL, Andrew. Massachusetts Line. Desertion and enlistment in a fictitious manner: 100 lashes. (63)

RUSSELL, Ceaser. Second Company. Overstaying his pass and being absent from roll call: reprimand. (46)

RUSSELL, Elmer. Second Regiment of Artillery. Desertion: 100 lashes. (42)

RUSSELL, Joseph, Cpl. Sixth Massachusetts Regiment. Desertion while on the march: reduced to the ranks and fifty lashes. (46)

RUSSELL, Oliver. Second New York Regiment. Desertion: 100 lashes. (24)

RUST, John, Lt. Tenth Pennsylvania Regiment (Tenth Virginia Regiment). Aggravating Lieutenant Grubwater (Broadwater) to strike him, playing cards, drunk and beating Captain Laird on the Sabbath while the captain was under arrest: cashiered—reinstated to service. (14) (134)

RUTTLEDGE, William. Colonel Crane's Regiment. Desertion 100 lashes. (24)

RYAN, Thomas, inhabitant of Pennsylvania. In company with Thomas Butler, taking eight quarters of mutton and a bull beef to Philadelphia: fine of fifty pounds and confined in the guardhouse till the sum is paid. (14) (134) *See* Butler.

SABIN, Jonas. North Carolina Line. Desertion and joining the enemy in arms: death by hanging. (115)

SACKET,_____, Doctor, Surgeon's Mate. Fourth Virginia Regiment. Repeatedly neglecting to visit and secure necessities for the sick of the regiment, absenting himself and going to the state of New York without leave: not guilty of the first charge but guilty of the second charge – reprimand. (9)

SADLER, George. Colonel Livingston's Regiment. Attempting to desert to the enemy with his arms: 100 lashes only, "several circumstances appearing in his favor." (112)

SALMON, William. Second Regiment of Artillery. Desertion and attempting to go to the enemy: death. (58)

SAMBERSTEN, Simon, Sailor on board the sloop *Enterprise*: mutinous behavior: acquitted. (99)

SAMPSON, Croker, Lt. Refusing to go on duty in his tour when warned: reprimand. (41)

SAMPSON, CROCKER, Lt. Seventh Massachusetts Regiment. Absent from his company when ordered to parade, and absent from roll call, taking a soldier with him into the country without consent of the commanding officer: reprimand. (51)

SAMSON,_____, Ensign. Defrauding a number of the officers of clothing, making an unequal distribution of goods: guilty only of the second charge – reprimand. (130)

SAMSON,_____, an Indian. Shooting his gun and wounding a soldier: thirty-nine stripes and drummed out of the army. (70)

SANFORD,_____, Lieutenant. Behaving unlike a gentleman and an officer to Captain O'Hara: acquitted. (93)

SARGENT, James. Captain Prince's Company of Riflemen. Drinking General Gage's health: deprived of his arms and accouterments, put in a cart with a rope around his neck and drummed out of the army. (2)

SAUNDERS, Jesse, Capt. Colonel Sargent's Regiment. Frequently drawing more provisions than he had men in his company to consume; forcing the sentries and taking away a gun, the property of William Turner; threatening the life of Sergeant Connor, cocking and presenting his gun at him when in the execution of his duty: cashiered. (2) (135)

SAUNDERS, John. Colonel Jackson's Regiment. Desertion: 100 lashes. (27)

SAUNDERS, John. Captain Burns's Company. Desertion: thirty-nine lashes – pardoned. (118) (123)

SAUNDERS, William. Second Connecticut Regiment. Desertion: acquitted. (46)

SAVAGE, Richard. Fourth Georgia Continental Battalion. Desertion: death by shooting. (90)

SAVIER, Robert. Colonel McDougall's Regiment. Mutiny and sedition: twenty lashes. (1)

SAWYER, Ebenezer. Colonel Prescott's Regiment. Desertion: thirty-nine lashes. (136)0

SAWYER, Robert. Colonel McDougall's Regiment. Mutiny and sedition: twenty lashes. (132)

SCAMMONS,_____, Colonel. Massachusetts Forces. Disobedience to orders, backwardness in the execution of duty: acquitted. (1) (134)

SCHIELD, William (Richard), Wagonmaster. North Carolina Brigade. Exchanging a horse as one of his own, stealing forage, selling other horses and fodder: dismissed from the service. (22)

SCHOOLEY, Michael. Abuse of a commissary official: released from confinement when complaint was found to be groundless. (8)

SCHUYLER, Phillip, Gen. *See* chapter four.

SCOTT, Gabriel. Colonel Pinckney's Battalion. Desertion: ninety-nine lashes and picketed for one and one-half hours, with parts of his punishment to be inflicted at different times. (90)

SCOTT, Henry. Colonel Sherburne's Regiment. Desertion: 100 lashes. (113)

SCOTT, Henry. Colonel Sherburne's Regiment. Desertion: fifty lashes and confined in some jail till he can be put on board the Continental navy, there to remain during the war. (69) (103)

SCOTT, John. Colonel Nixon's Regiment. Insulting the country and attempting to pass the guard at Boston. (1)

SCOT, John. Desertion: ninety-nine lashes and stand on the picket for one-quarter hour. (90)

SCOTT, Thomas. Taking forage contrary to general orders: acquitted. (13) (134)

SCOTT, Thomas. Fifth Pennsylvania Regiment. Desertion: acquitted. (14)

SCOTT, Timothy. Second Massachusetts Regiment. Stealing two chests and their contents out of a covered wagon in the night time: 100 lashes. (38)

SCRIBNER, Job, Conductor of Wagons. Neglect of duty and disobedience to orders: dismissed from the service and pay $150. (26)

SCULLY, William. First Pennsylvania Regiment. Forcibly entering the house of Robert Dennis, and robbing it of sundry goods, stabbing William Cox with a bayonet: 100 lashes. (21)

SEABURN, Frederick. Colonel McDougall's Regiment. Cowardice: acquitted. (99)

SEARLS, Josiah. Mutiny, riot, and disobedience to orders: thirty-nine lashes and drummed out of the army. (135)

SEARY, Kedy, Sailor on board the sloop *Enterprise*. Mutinous behavior: acquitted. (99)

SECOR, Issac. Colonel Clinton's Regiment. Desertion: fine of one month's pay—pardoned. (118)

SEDAM, Richer. First New Jersey Battalion. Seizing a cow belonging to the husband of Catherine Leggett under pretense of its being designed for the enemy, and afterwards carrying the same cow below the enemy lines and selling it there: acquitted. (60)

SEDENIER, John. Second Massachusetts Regiment. Desertion: 100 lashes. (53)

SEELBY,_____, Captain. Fifth Pennsylvania Regiment. Leaving his guard before he was regularly ordered: reprimand. (69)

SEELY, Gideon. Colonel Webb's Regiment. Drunk and disobedience to orders; insulting and striking Mr. Webb, aide-de-camp to General Putnam: thirty-nine lashes. (136)

SEELY, Lewis, Matross. Second Regiment of Artillery. Desertion and reenlisting: death. (78)

SELISWAY, Reuben. Desertion: thirty lashes. (42)

SELMAN, William. New York Regiment of Artillery. Deserting from his quarters at Brunswick with intention of going to the enemy: death. (86)

SETTLES, Isack. Fifth New York Regiment. Desertion: 100 lashes. (28)

SEWONS,_____, Lieutenant. Third Maryland Regiment. Absent without leave: reprimand. (103)

SEYMOUR, John. Colonel Gridley's Regiment. Desertion, theft. (1)

SCHACKHORNE, Morris. Theft: 100 lashes. (90)

SHADDOCK, William. Ninth Pennsylvania Regiment. Twenty-five lashes. (101)

SHANKS, Thomas, Ens. Tenth Pennsylvania Regiment. Stealing two pairs of shoes from Lieutenant Adams, regimental quartermaster: dismissed from the service. (93)

SHANNON,_____, Lieutenant. First Virginia Regiment. Putting the paymaster of the regiment in the guardhouse: ask the paymaster's pardon in the presence of the officers of the regiment. (101)

SHANNON, Thomas. First New York Regiment. Leaving his post and attempting to go to the enemy: acquitted. (37)

SHANWAY, Whitney. Eighth Massachusetts Regiment. Desertion: fifty lashes. (44)

SHARP, James, Dr. Disobedience to orders: reprimand. (36)

SHARP, John. Mutiny, riot, and disobedience to orders: fine of twenty shillings. (135)

SHARP, Jonathan. Colonel Phinney's Regiment. Stealing cartridges from the commissary: acquitted. (3) (135)

SHATFORT, William. Colonel Arnold's Regiment. Refusing to obey Colonel Arnold's order: fined one month's pay and immediately join Captain Smith's company, according to Colonel Arnold's order. (128)

SHAW, David. First Connecticut Regiment. Desertion: fifty lashes. (124)

SHAW, David. Second New York Regiment. Desertion: 100 lashes, with twenty-five lashes administered on each of four successive mornings. (44)

SHAW, James. Colonel Palding's Regiment of Levies of New York. Desertion: 200 lashes, to be administered at two different times. (48)

SHAW, John. Colonel Marshall's Regiment. Sleeping on his post and suffering a prisoner to escape who was under his care: thirty-nine lashes—pardoned. (75)

SHAW, William. Colonel Jackson's Regiment. Desertion: death—remitted. (26)

SHAY,_____, Captain. General Schuyler's Brigade. Released when no evidence was presented. (88)

SHEA, David. First Massachusetts Regiment. Killing a cow and stealing eleven geese: 100 lashes and pay fifteen dollars to the owner. (86)

SHEA, David. Light Company, Massachusetts Regiment. Killing a cow and seven geese: 100 lashes. (61) *See* Abram, Brayton, Carliss, Cook, Cowell, Gardner, Jinks, Wood.

SHELDON, Elisha, Col. Second Regiment of Light Dragoons. Discharging a number of enlisted men without proper authority, defrauding the public by selling and exchanging regimental horses, converting avails to his own use, defrauding his soldiers of plunder taken in action, offensive and ungentlemanlike behavior: acquitted with honor. (36)

SHEPARD, Amos. Stealing boards: reduced to the ranks. (91)

SHEPPARD, George. Stealing from and abusing one Patten Russell: acquitted. (133)

SHERLOCK, Christopher, Sailor on board the sloop *Enterprise*. Mutinous behavior: acquitted. (99)

SHERMAN, John. Sleeping on his post: 100 lashes. (25)

SHERRILL, Jacques. Fifty stripes. (10)

SHIPMAN,_____, Ensign. Colonel Webb's Regiment and Detachment of Rangers. Abusive language to his officer, mutiny, and disobedience to orders: guilty of abusive language—reprimand. (118)

SHIPPEN, William, Dr. Acquitted by Congress. (111)

SHIPPEY, Abram. Desertion: 100 lashes and picketed for ten minutes. (28)

SHIRE, Sylvanus. Desertion: fifteen lashes only, because of his youth and disposition. (123)

SHIREN, Thomas. First New York Regiment. Desertion and attempting to go to the enemy: acquitted. (100)

SHORT, Jonathan. Colonel Sage's Regiment. Leaving his company and regiment and being absent more than forty days without leave: fine of twenty shillings and reprimand. (92)

SHUGART,_____, Lieutenant. German Battalion. Challenging Lieutenant Laudermick: cashiered—pardoned. (134)

SHURLOCK, Ichabod. Stealing provisions from his messmates: twenty-five lashes. (42)

SICKLES,_____, Lieutenant. Disobeying general orders by loading a wagon with goods not the proper baggage of the regiment: cashiered. (94)

SIEGLER,_____, Lieutenant. Striking and wounding inhumanely with his sword, James Quinn, a soldier belonging to the Seventh Pennsylvania Regiment, of which wound he died: acquitted becuase the act was justified as being in the line of duty. (13)

SILY (SELY), Jesse. Colonel McDougall's Regiment. Desertion: twenty lashes. (72)

SIMMONDS, Thomas. Fourth Massachusetts Regiment. 100 lashes. (42)

SIMMONS, Ephraim. Colonel Gansevort's Regiment. Desertion: 100 lashes and put on board a Continental ship to serve during the war. (125)

SIMMONS, Silas. General Cilley's Regiment. Straggling from camp and killing a number of hogs, the property of an inhabitant: acquitted. (103)

SIMMONS, William. First Battalion. 100 lashes. (90)

SIMMS, Hugh. Fourth Georgia Continental Battalion. Desertion: picketed one-half hour. (90)

SIMONS, John. Colonel Cotton's Regiment. Desertion: fifteen lashes — pardoned. (120)

SIMONS, Joseph. Captain Williams's Company. Leaving his post when on sentinel: forty stripes only, because of his youth and inexperience. (91)

SIMPSON, Richard. Colonel Little's Regiment. Abusing Lieutenant Cleveland: acquitted. (133) *See* McCordy, White.

SIMS, Micajah. Sixth Virginia Regiment. Losing his arms, equipment, and accouterments: reprimand. (134) *See* Consolven, Talbot.

SIMSON, James. Delaware Regiment. Promoting and encouraging discontent among the men, making use of language intended to countenance desertion: death. (28)

SIPPLE, Martinius. Delaware Regiment. Abusing Sergeant Johnson when he ordered him on duty: ask the sergeant's pardon in the presence of his commanding officer. (93)

SKINNER, William. Delaware Regiment. Plundering a house of an inhabitant near Prospect Hill: thirty-nine lashes and a fine of half-month's pay — remitted because of his youth. (93)

SLACK, James, Sgt. Captain Moody's Company. Absent without leave: reduced to a matross. (125)

SLATER, David. Striking and threatening the lives of Lt. Charles F. Weissenfels, in the Fourth New York Regiment, and Ens. Daniel D. Denston: acquitted. (26)

SLAUGHTER, Jacob. Third New York Regiment. Stealing a knapsack with sundry articles in it: acquitted. (111)

SLOAN (SLOWN), David. Light Company. Robbing John Bemus of a shirt and overalls: 100 lashes, with twenty-five lashes administered on four successive days. (53)

SLOAN, David. Third Company. Abusing a sergeant: acquitted. (50)

SLOAN (SLONE), David. Light Company. Absenting himself from his guard without leave, stealing from an inhabitant: fifty lashes – pardoned. (40)

SLOCUM, Solomon. Second Maryland Regiment. Attempting to desert, persuading others to desert: 100 lashes – pardoned. (109) (121)

SMALL, Jonathan. Colonel Reed's Regiment. Selling spirituous liquors when expressly forbidden by the commanding officer: thirty-nine lashes. (84) (117)

SMALLEY, Thomas. Desertion: 100 lashes. (85)

SMALLWOOD,_____. 100 lashes. (129)

SMALLWOOD, Jacob. Mutiny, riot, and disobedience to orders: thirty lashes and drummed out of the army. (71)

SMALLWOOD, Joseph, civilian wagoner. Insulting and knocking Lieutenant Beard off his horse: 100 lashes. (35)

SMART, John. Eighth Massachusetts Regiment. Desertion: 100 lashes. (50)

SMEDES, Abraham, Lt. Colonel Hardenborough's Regiment. Spreading a false and malicious report concerning Colonel Hardenborough's conduct on the day of the retreat from New York, absenting himself from his regiment without leave: ask the colonel's pardon and admit he lied – cashiered and fined one month's pay. (74)

SMITH,_____, Lieutenant Colonel, Deputy Quartermaster. Supplying Captain Pyncheon's house and the family with their necessary firewood amounting sometimes to three fires, in unlimited quantity from the public stores; laid out large sums of public money to build boats without orders; established a Continental ferry across the Connecticut River where the country ferry has for ages been established; enlisted a number of men for one year with Continental pay and rations at great expense while the country ferryman offered to supply the Continental ferry for the sum of £200 a year: acquitted. (21) *See* chapter four.

SMITH,_____, Lieutenant. Sixth Massachusetts Regiment. Drinking and gaming with the soldiers and causing them to miss roll call: acquitted. (63)

SMITH,_____, Ensign. Permitting a party under his command to abuse or sell the property of the inhabitants of Ballstown: acquitted. (88)

SMITH,_____, Sergeant. Colonel Topham's Regiment. Remaining at his guard post at Stubb's Wharf when he ought to have been out on the night: reduced to private and to do private sentinel duty. (68) (98)

SMITH,_____. Colonel Jackson's Detachment, Colonel Smith's Regiment. Stealing a pair of breeches: 100 lashes. (9)

SMITH, Alexander. Colonel Greaton's Regiment. Desertion: 100 lashes. (85)

SMITH, Arthur. Cursing and swearing and refusing to do his duty, sleeping on his post: reprimand. (136)

SMITH, Charles. First New Jersey Regiment. Desertion and enlisting again as a substitute: acquitted. (14) (134)

SMITH, Christian. Desertion: 100 lashes. (42)

SMITH, Christopher. 100 lashes. (42)

SMITH, David. Third Continental Regiment. Fraudulently hiring a substitute and obtaining a discharge: acquitted, but ordered to pay the amount of pay received by the substitute after he then deserted. (31)

SMITH, David. Colonel DuBois's Regiment. Desertion: fifty lashes. (131)

SMITH, Ebenezer. Colonel Webb's Regiment. Attempting to desert to the enemy: acquitted. (9)

SMITH, Eleazer. Counterfeiting the currency of the Massachusetts Bay: thirty-nine lashes. (84)

SMITH, Elias. Maryland Line. Desertion and reenlisting in the cavalry: 100 lashes. (49)

SMITH, Elisha. Second Regiment of Light Dragoons. Desertion to the enemy, defrauding the public by selling his horse, arms, and accouterments; mutiny in insulting and menacing his officers while a prisoner with them: death. (72) (125)

SMITH, Ephraim. Mutiny: twenty lashes. (84)

SMITH, Francis. Virginia Line. Absence without leave, plundering the inhabitants: run the gauntlet through the whole army. (115)

SMITH, Francis. Desertion: forty lashes. (42)

SMITH, Francis. Tenth Massachusetts Regiment. Desertion and attempting to join the enemy: guilty of the first charge but not guilty of the second charge—100 lashes. (42)

SMITH, Foster. *See* Foster, Smith.

SMITH, Henry. Seventh Massachusetts Regiment: 100 lashes—remitted. (124)

SMITH, Hugh. Pennsylvania Line. Using traitorous and disrespectful language against the U.S., intending to encourage desertion among the soldiers: 100 lashes. (50)

SMITH, Ichabod. Colonel Gallup's Regiment. Neglecting to join his company when detached for one month's service: released, because he had been engaged on board the ship *Trumbull* prior to being detached. (82)

SMITH, James. New Hampshire Line. Desertion: 100 lashes. (63)

SMITH, James. South Carolina Regiment of Artillery. Desertion: 100 lashes. (95)

SMITH, Job. Colonel Lee's Legion. Desertion: 100 lashes. (57)

SMITH, John, Sgt. Colonel Angell's Regiment. Desertion and attempting to go to the enemy, stealing and embezzling cartridges, carrying off his arms and accouterments belonging to the Continent: reduced to the ranks and 100 lashes, and be sent on board the *Man-of-War* immediately upon receiving the punishment at Fort Montgomery. (131)

SMITH, John. First New Hampshire Regiment. Desertion and attempting to go to the enemy: 100 lashes. (44)

SMITH, John. Desertion: 100 lashes. (42)

SMITH, John. Fourth Massachusetts Regiment. Desertion and enlisting with the York troops: 100 lashes. (52)

SMITH, John. Massachusetts Line. Desertion and enlistment in a fictitious manner: 100 lashes. (63)

SMITH, John. Colonel Lamar's Regiment. Attempting to defraud: six month's imprisonment and a fine of eight shillings. (4) *See* Mechan.

SMITH, John. Second Brigade of Artillery. Desertion: 100 lashes. (53)

SMITH, John. Maryland Line. Desertion: 100 lashes. (121)

SMITH, John. Colonel Holmes's Regiment. Stealing pork out of the commissary stores: seven days' confinement in the dungeon. (118)

SMITH, John. German Battalion. Desertion and attempting to go to the enemy: 100 lashes. (103)

SMITH, John. Fifth Regiment. Attempting to desert from Fort Johnston: acquitted. (95)

SMITH, John. First Virginia Regiment. Robbing Jacob Hopkins of his hat: fifty lashes. (103)

SMITH, John. Seventh Pennsylvania Regiment (formerly in the Sixth Pennsylvania Regiment). Enlisting in the Ninth Pennsylvania Regiment with a discharge: twenty-five lashes and repay the twenty dollars bounty he received. (101)

SMITH, Jonathan. Lieutenant Erwine's Company. Absent without leave: 100 lashes. (115)

SMITH, Jonathan. Colonel Drake's Regiment. Stealing a pocket book from Thomas Sinnet, containing many papers of value: acquitted. (74)

SMITH, Joshua. Absenting himself from camp without leave, forging a pass: twenty lashes and confined seven days upon bread and water—the bread and water provision and the imprisonment were remitted. (136)

SMITH, Michael. First Massachusetts Regiment. Breaking open the home of a citizen and insulting and abusing the inhabitants, attempting to kill Captain Frye and Captain Ellis in execution of their office, robbing them of a hat: acquitted. (64) *See* Blake, Curtis.

SMITH, Peter. Colonel Tyler's Regiment. Desertion: acquitted. (23)

SMITH, Samuel. Colonel Holmes's Regiment. Sleeping on his post: fine of four shillings—pardoned. (118)

SMITH, Samuel. Mutiny: thirty-nine lashes. (84)

SMITH, Samuel. Fighting, stabbing George Hills with a knife in the arm, threatening to kill him: forty stripes with rods. (91) *See* Hills.

SMITH, Samuel. Colonel Webb's Regiment. Neglect of duty in sitting on post when sentinel: twenty-five lashes—pardoned. (91)

SMITH, Solomon. Conspiring to desert to the enemy: 100 lashes. (89)

SMITH, Stokely. Colonel Smith's Regiment. Stealing a pair of breeches: 100 lashes. (19)

SMITH, Thomas, Cpl. Stealing and plundering a yoke of oxen and a horse from an inhabitant in Bridgefield, Connecticut: 100 lashes and a fine to pay for the oxen and the horse. (48)

SNOW, Benjamin, Ens. Colonel Sargent's Regiment. Leaving his guard when on duty and absenting himself from camp without leave: acquitted. (74) (123)

SNOW, Isaac (Asa). Nineteenth Massachusetts Regiment. Disobedience to orders, attempting the life of Captain Allen by jabbing him with a fixed bayonet: 100 lashes. (35)

SNOWDEN,_____, Lieutenant. New Jersey Brigade. Disobedience to orders, neglect of duty: acquitted. (21)

SNYDER, Philip, Cpl. German Battalion. Absent without leave, mutiny: reduced to private and 100 lashes. (25)

SODER, Isaac. Captain Dutcher's Company. Drunkenness, desertion: fifteen lashes. (118) (123)

SOGUE, Thomas. Colonel Proctor's Regiment of Artillery. Desertion: 100 lashes. (25)

SOLDIER, Austin. Colonal Silliman's Regiment. Breaking open a store and stealing rum, molasses, and fish: thirty-nine lashes. (136)

SOMAN, Peter. Sleeping on his post: 100 lashes. (89)

SOPER, Oliver, Capt. Colonel Reed's Regiment. Defrauding the public by drawing pay for more men than he had in his company: acquitted. (136)

SOPER (SOAPER),_____, Lieutenant. Abusing Lieutenant Stephens and Lieutenant Craige, keeping Lieutenant Craige in the meeting house under guard all night: dismissed from the service. (3) (133) (136) *See* Parker.

SOSE (?), Louis, Sgt. General Hazen's Regiment. Drawing his sword on Lieutenant Sullivan, of the Fourth Regiment of Light Dragoons, and attempting to kill him when in the execution of his duty: reduced to private and 100 lashes. (78)

SOUDINEER, John. Second Massachusetts Regiment. Desertion: 100 lashes. (50)

SOW, Nicholas. Colonel Morrow's Regiment. Alarming the camp by firing guns: reprimand. (96)

SPALDING, Edward. Second Company. Absent from roll call: thirty lashes. (56)

SPANGENBERG, John, Adjutant. Colonel Macklin's Battalion. Cowardice and shamefully abandoning his post on Long Island upon the approach of the enemy: acquitted. (7)

SPEGHY, Frederick. Third New York Regiment. Attempting to desert to the enemy with the arms and accouterments of another soldier: death by shooting. (29) *See* Lighthall.

SPENCER, James. Captain Williams's Company. Taking boards from the barracks and cutting them up for his own use: fine of twenty shillings and pay for the boards. (91)

SPENCER, Thomas. Colonel Prentice's Regiment. Desertion: fifty lashes. (131)

SOINIEACE, F. Desertion: serve the time "prescribed by act of Assembly." (102)

SPINKHOUSE, Anthony. Seventh Pennsylvania Regiment. Desertion to the enemy: death. (36)

SPOOR, John, Ens. Third New York Regiment. Scandalous behavior toward Capt. Treadwell Pell, of the Second New York Regiment, and several others by putting them out of a room of a public house: dismissed from the service. (27)

SPRIGG, Abraham. Colonel Hazen's Regiment. Suffering prisoners to escape while he was sentinel at the guardhouse: acquitted. (112)

SPRINGER,_____, Lieutenant. Colonel Elliot's Regiment of Artillery. Absent from his post without leave: acquitted. (98)

SPRINGER, John. Colonel Sherburne's Regiment. Drinking the health of King George and challenging Corporal Taylor to fight a duel: guilty of the first charge but acquitted of the second charge — released, recause he was a British prisoner and unworthy of a fight under the standard of the United States. (113)

SPRINGSTEAD, Abraham. Captain Graham's Company. Striking and abusing Sergeant Dunn in the execution of his office: sixty lashes. (111)

SPROUT, James. Fourth Connecticut Regiment. Desertion: 100 lashes and a fine of two pounds and eight shillings for the expense of taking him into custody. (47)

STAFFORD, Thomas. Second Georgia Continental Battalion. Desertion: death — pardoned. (90)

STAKE,_____, Captain. Tenth Pennsylvania Regiment. Propagating a report that Colonel Nagle was seen drinking either tea or coffee in Sergeant Howcraft's tent with his whore, her mother, and his family: acquitted. (170 *See* Nagle.

STANBERRY, William. Colonel Harrison's Regiment of Artillery. Conspiracy to spike the cannon at Fort Schuyler and intending to desert to the enemy: 100 lashes. (37) *See* Amos, Johnson, Watkins, Wright.

STANBURY, Elijah. Colonel Nichols's Regiment. Desertion: twenty lashes. (118)

STANFORD,_____. Theft: acquitted. (23)

STANFORD, James. Theft, abuse to a corporal: acquitted. (23) *See* McAllister.

STANFORD, James. Colonel Jackson's Regiment. Insolence and abusing a sergeant: twenty-five lashes. (23)

STANFORD, Moses. Captain Hastings's Company. Breaking his furlough: forfeit one month's pay. (11)

STANFORD, William. Speaking disrespectfully to the officers: 100 lashes. (23)

STANLEY, Nathaniel. Colonel Wyllys's Regiment. Absenting from and refusing to join his company after he had received a month's pay and blanket money: thirty-nine lashes and confined on bread and water for seven days. (106)

STANNARD, Seth. Losing or wasting musket cartridges: thirty lashes. (91) *See* Page.

STANNARD, Seth. Breaking open and robbing a store: thirty-nine lashes and a fine of thirty shillings—remitted. (91)

STANTON,_____, Captain. Second Regiment of Light Dragoons. Cowardice and refusing a command in the line of duty: acquitted. (58)

STANWOOD, Steven. Desertion: 100 lashes. (42)

STARKWEATHER,_____. Mutiny: twenty lashes. (84)

STARNES, Increase. 100 lashes. (122)

STATT, Moses. Desertion: 100 lashes. (42)

ST. CLAIR, Arthur, Gen. *See* chapter four.

ST. CLAIR, Francis. Third Company. Losing his canteen: acquitted. (46)

STEARN, John. Disobedience to orders and insolence: wear a log chained to his right leg with a lock to the same for a term of seven days. (77)

STEEL,_____, Ensign. Colonel Burrell's Regiment. Leaving the army and going on to Crown Point with a battalion of men, contrary to orders: cashiered. (84)

STEEL, Danille. Colonel DuBois's Regiment. Robbing and plundering a house of Mrs. Marline: 100 lashes and pay Mrs. Marline twenty-four pounds, to be taken from his pay. (69)

STEEL, James. Colonel Ritzema's Regiment. Sleeping on his post: twenty lashes. (132)

STEEL, Richard. Captain Stevens's Independent Company of Riflemen. Striking and abusing several officers of the Twentieth Regiment: thirty-nine lashes. (134) *See* Higgins.

STEEL, William. Fifth Maryland Regiment. Attempting to desert: 100 lashes. (93)

STEEL, William, Colonel and Deputy Quartermaster Corps. Neglect of duty and incapacity for his office, delay in transporting provisions and other stores for an expedition until it was too late, spending the time which should have been employed for the public upon his private concerns, embezzlement and suffering others to embezzle the public property, repeated disobedience and insulting his commanding officer: acquitted. (21)

STEND, James. Pennsylvania Regiment. Desertion: 100 lashes. (97)

STENSON,_____, Sergeant. Insolence and breach of orders: reduced to the rank of a private sentinel. (93)

STEPHEN,_____, General. Unofficerlike behavior in the retreat from Germantown owing to inattention or want of judgement, frequently intoxicated since in the service to the prejudice of good order, unmilitary discipline: dismissed from the service. (9) (134)

STEPHEN,_____, Lieutenant. Acquitted. (113)

STEPHENS, Benjamin, civilian. Refusing to deliver provisions to the hospital to which he had been ordered, other improprieties concerning provisions: acquitted. (39)

STEPHENS (STEVENS), John. Second New York Regiment. Desertion: 100 lashes. (20 (2)

STEPHENS, Thomas. Colonel Holmes's Regiment. Deserting his post: fine of four shillings—pardoned. (118)

STEPHENSON, Jonathan. Third Massachusetts Regiment. Desertion: 100 lashes. (54)

STETSON, Isiah, Capt. Colonel Bradford's Regiment. Forgery: acquitted with honor. (75)

STEVANS, Francis. Third Regiment. Desertion: 100 lashes. (95)

STEVENS, Adam. Third Virginia Regiment. Desertion to the enemy: 100 lashes. (210

STEWARD,_____, Corporal. Selling his shoes: acquitted. (23)

STEWARD, John. Desertion: 100 lashes. (11)

STEWARD, Jonathan, Foragemaster. Disobedience to orders by leaving camp with his accounts not settled, issuing forage without instructions and contrary to the resolves of Congress: dismissed from the service and fined—fine remitted. (115)

STEWARD, Wentworth, Capt. Colonel Phinney's Regiment. Disobedience to orders and gross abuse of Lieutenant Colonel March: reprimand and ask Colonel March's pardon. (133)

STEWARD, William. Colonel Smith's Regiment. Suffering five pairs of shoes to be taken from under his care while on sentry: acquitted. (9) *See* Pollock, Redford, Whittam.

STEWART,_____, Lieutenant. Striking Sergeant Phillips and threatening the life of Colonel Silliman: acquitted. (7) (118)

STEWART, Elisha. Colonel Gallup's Regiment. Refusing to march when ordered by their captain for the defense of New London and places adjacent: ride to wooden horse not exceeding one-half hour. (82) *See* Rogers.

STEWART, Joseph. Stealing and concealing a barrel of flour: acquitted. (1)

STILLER, Lawrence. Death. (25)

STINSON, James. Delaware Regiment. Promoting and encouraging discontent among the men, making use of language that tended to countenance desertion: death. (136)

ST. LUKE, Landon. Theft, other misdemeanors: acquitted. (100) *See* Winning.

STOCKER, Christopher. Ninth Massachusetts Regiment. Repeated desertion and reenlisting, changing his name: 100 lashes, with twenty-five lashes administered on each of four successive mornings. (46)

STOCKS, Peter. Colonel Nixon's Regiment. Stealing two horses and riding them off: fine of forty shillings for damages, and twenty stripes. (133) *See* Hinds.

STODDARD, Ebenezer, Sgt. Illegal purchasing of Continental clothing: reduced to a private. (39)

STOKES,_____, Sergeant. Breaking a window and attempting to break into Colonel Bowen's house: reduced in rank. (19) *See* Hay.

STONE, Joseph. Colonel Thompson's Battalion. Desertion: pardoned. (90)

STONER, John, Capt. Leaving the regiment in a cowardly manner in the action at Chad's Fort on Brandywine, on 11 September, last: reprimand. (134)

STRIDDLE, Edward, Helmsman. Embezzling whiskey: fine of sixty dollars and run the gauntlet three times. (103)

STRINY, Solomon. Colonel Marshall's Regiment. Desertion: fifty lashes—remitted. (75)

STRIPE, Devall. Desertion from the detachment: thirty-nine lashes. (134)

STUBBS, Robert. Eleventh Pennsylvania Regiment. Desertion: 100 lashes. (112)

STURD, John. Colonel Jackson's Regiment. Desertion, disobeying an order, threatening to stab a sergeant: 100 lashes. (9)

STURDAVENT, Samuel. Enlisting in Captain Granger's Company after he had enlisted in Colonel Swift's Regiment, after he had received the bounty: 100 lashes, administered over a period of three days, and then sent on board one of the Continental guard ships to be kept at hard labor during the present war. (131)

SUGARS,_____,Lieutenant. German Battalion. Challenging Lieutenant Lowden, of the same battalion: cashiered—remitted. (13)

SULIVAN, Denis. Third New York Regiment. Encouraging soldiers to desert: acquitted. (89)

SULLINGS,_____, Sergeant. Striking and insulting Sergeant Freeman: reprimand. (23) *See* Freeman.

SULLIVAN,_____, Captain. Fourth New York Regiment. Calling Adjutant Sackett a liar and drawing a sword on him when unarmed, insinuating that he was a coward and challenging him to fight a duel: acquitted. (103)

SULLIVAN, John, Bombardier. Captain Moody's Company. Straggling from camp: reprimand. (125)

SULLIVAN, Jonathan. Mutiny. (90)

SULLIVAN, Jonathan. North Carolina Line. Desertion: "Being detained by his master, the court are of opinion will be a sufficient punishment." (115)

SUMMERS, John, Capt. First North Carolina Regiment. Entering the tent of Lieutenant Richard Dickerson whilst he was in bed, disarming and striking him; acting in a disorderly manner; playing cards in camp: reprimand. (26) *See* Baccart, Craven, Dickerson.

SUR, Joseph. Colonel Learned's Regiment. Insulting and abusing Lieutenant Lyman, profane swearing: ten stripes and a fine of one shilling. (70)

SUTER, Samuel. Conspiring to desert to the enemy: 100 lashes. (89)

SUTTON, John. Colonel Hardenbergh's Regiment. Desertion: thirty-nine lashes. (118)

SWAIN,_____, Brigade Major. Repeated neglect of duty, particularly in not attending to orders in proper time, which resulted in not properly taking care of his soldiers: reprimand. (134)

SWAIN, John. Captain Foster's Company. Absent three days without leave: ask the officers' pardon and severe fatigue for three weeks. (104)

SWANY,_____, Clothier for the State of Pennsylvania. Absenting himself from camp without leave, neglect of duty: dismissed from the service. (30)

SWARTOUT,_____, Ensign. Second New York Regiment. Disobedience to orders: reprimand. (100)

SWEAT, Cicero. Sixth Massachusetts Regiment (Ninth Massachusetts Regiment). Stealing and killing a cow belonging to an inhabitant: 100 lashes and a fine of forty shillings to pay for the cow. (28)

SWEDEN, Castries. Drunk and sleeping on his post: 100 lashes. (25)

SWEETLAND, William, Conductor of Military Stores. Breach of a garrison order: acquitted. (124)

SWIFT, John. Captain Spalding's Independent Company. Aiding and abetting and clandestinely conveying away a mare found in the woods to defraud the owner of the property: fifty lashes and pay for the mare. (20) *See* Baldwin.

SYKES, Sampson. North Carolina Line. Desertion and forging a colonel's name: 100 lashes. (115)

SYMAN, William. Colonel Lamb's Regiment of Artillery. Insolent behavior toward Lieutenants Webb and Allen: forty lashes — pardoned. (113) *See* Winkelman.

SYTZ, Frederick. Third _____. Desertion: 100 lashes. (53)

TABOR, Noel, Sgt. Colonel Greene's Regiment. Raising a mutiny and behaving in a disorderly manner: not guilty of the first charge but guilty of the second charge — suspended and reprimand. (131) *See* Baptist, Brown, Buck, Cary, Davis, Dunbar, Goold, Hardin, Lane, Luis, Park, Peterson.

TACK, Forbes. Colonel Shepard's Regiment. Desertion: 100 lashes. (24)

TAGGART,_____, Lieutenant. Third South Carolina Regiment. Using traitorous and disrespectful words against the legislative body of the state: cashiered – quashed, since it was felt that he was in no way traitorous to the legislature and the words were uttered in the heat of passion and intoxication. (95)

TAGGART, William, Lt. Challenging Lieutenant Richard Jones to a duel: reprimand. (95)

TAILOR, Jonathan. Maryland Line. Leaving camp without leave, plundering the inhabitants: 100 lashes. (115)

TALBOT,_____, Sergeant. Sixth Virginia Regiment. Losing his arms, equipment, and accouterments: reprimand. (134) *See* Consolven, Sims.

TANNEN (TANNER), Zebulon. Colonel Topham's Regiment. Stealing meat and bread from the soldiers: thirty-nine lashes. (98)

TANNEN (TANNER), Zebulon. Colonel Topham's Regiment. Stealing a pair of buckles and stealing rice: not guilty of the first charge but guilty of the second charge – twenty-five lashes – pardoned. (68) (98)

TARCARE, Benjamin, Sgt. Exciting mutiny and speaking disrespectfully of an ensign: reduced to the ranks and ask the ensign's pardon. (125)

TAULMAN,_____, Captain Lieutenant. Corps of Sappers and Miners. Disobedience to orders, improper returns, mutinous behavior, particularly in commanding soldiers to disobey Captain Bushnal's orders: reprimand and suspended for three months. (87)

TAULMAN,_____, Captain Lieutenant. Corps of Sappers and Miners. Mutinous behavior and disobedience to orders by bringing his baggage into a captain's quarters contrary to orders and refusing to take it away: reprimand and suspended for three months – remitted when Washington said, "The commander-in-chief leaves as a punishement to the sting of their own reflections as a punishment for what has passed, and only advises them not to be guilty of anything of a similar nature in the future." (62) *See* Kirkpatrick.

TAYLOR,_____, Captain. North Carolina Brigade. Drunkenness and abusive language to the commanding officer of the regiment: acquitted of the first charge but guilty of the second charge – released since he had already served considerable time in confinement. (95)

TAYLOR, Edward. Second New York Regiment. Desertion: run the gauntlet of three regiments, with a sentinel at his breast to regulate the pace. (20) (25)

TAYLOR, George. Drunkenness, repeated absence from roll call: fifty lashes. (23)

TAYLOR, George. Absent from roll call without permission: thirty lashes. (45)

TAYLOR, George. Third Company. Stealing corn belonging to an inhabitant, absconding from camp without leave: forty lashes for each crime. (56) *See* Bradbury.

TAYLOR, George. Seventh Massachusetts Regiment. Desertion: 100 lashes. (64)

TAYLOR, George. Losing his knapsack, clothing, and shoes: fifty lashes and pay for the shoes—lashes remitted. (30)

TAYLOR, Hanna. Persuading the soldiers to desert: acquitted. (93)

TAYLOR, James. Stealing: acquitted. (93)

TAYLOR, Thornton, Conductor of Military Stores. General Woodford's Brigade. Striking a soldier, abusing and swearing a falsehood: dismissed from the service—sentence disapproved for lack of proper evidence. (110)

TAYLOR, Wiliam. Provost Marshal. Disobeying general orders by riding wagon horses belonging to the army: acquitted. (131)

TAYLOR, William. Pennsylvania Line. Desertion and forgery: death. (59)

TEEKLIN, William. Fifth Regiment. Desertion: death by shooting. (95)

TEMPLE, Stephen. Fifth Massachusetts Regiment. Desertion: 100 lashes. (50)

TEMPLETON, John. Fourth Massachusetts Regiment. Desertion: acquitted. (130)

TENNIT, John. Colonel McDougall's Regiment. Desertion: thirty-nine lashes. (136)

TENNY, David. Third Company. Absent from roll call: twenty lashes. (136)

TENNY, Peter. Massachusetts Regiment. Threatening to desert to the enemy and trying to persuade others to do the same: 100 lashes. (56)

TERMETON, Evan. Inciting to mutiny: acquitted. (49)

TERN, Joseph. Third Virginia Regiment. Deserting from the Provost's guard, taking prisoners with him: 100 lashes. (13)

TERNEY, Roger. Sixth Pennsylvania Regiment. Housebreaking and robbery: 100 lashes. (21) *See* Martin.

THAYME, Caleb. Fifth Massachusetts Regiment. 100 lashes. (63)

THEMES, John. Spencer's Regiment. Stealing hogs: fifty lashes and pay for the hogs. (20)

THOMAS, C. Colonel Cotton's Regiment. Desertion: fifteen lashes—pardoned. (120)

THOMAS, Charles. Third Maryland Regiment. Desertion and attempting to go to the enemy: death. (22)

THOMAS, Dennsey. Third South Carolina Regiment. Desertion: 100 lashes. (95)

THOMAS, George. Colonel DuBois's Regiment. Attempting to persuade others to desert: 100 lashes and confined in gaol at Poughkeepsie until he can be put on board the Continental navy during the war. (85)

THOMAS, Jacob. Desertion: 100 lashes. (42)

THOMAS, James. Seventh Massachusetts Regiment. Desertion: 100 lashes. (41)

THOMAS, John. Sixteenth Massachusetts Regiment. Theft: twenty lashes. (34)

THOMAS, John. Spencer's Regiment. Stealing hogs: fifty lashes and return the money. (25)

THOMAS, Michael. First Virginia Battalion. Desertion: acquitted of desertion but guilty of absence without leave—fifty lashes. (108)

THOMAS, Peter. Selling his ammunition, neglecting to clean his arms when ordered: twenty-five lashes. (41)

THOMAS, Peter. Sixteenth Massachusetts Regiment (Colonel Jackson's Regiment). Absent from his regiment for more than one year without leave: 100 lashes, with fifty lashes administered at two different times. (33) (34)

THOMPSON,_____, Adjutant. Ninth Pennsylvania Regiment. Refusing to come when called for by his commanding officer, treating him with ill language when he did come to him: not guilty of the first charge but guilty of the second charge—reprimand. (16)

THOMPSON, Daniel. Commander-in-Chief's Guard. Going out, with others, with sidearms, to do harm to other soldiers: acquitted. (125)

THOMPSON, John. Disobedience to orders, forcing the guard with clubs: thirty-nine lashes. (118)

THOMPSON, John. Colonel Webb's Regiment. Deserting from and enlisting into three different regiments and taking Continental money: 100 lashes and drummed out of camp with a halter about his neck as a rogue and a rascal. (131)

THOMPSON, Joseph. Captain White's Company. Absent without leave: 100 lashes. (100)

THOMPSON, Matthew. Stealing corn from an inhabitant: run the gauntlet twice through the regiment. (91) *See* Hurlbut.

THOMPSON, Nathaniel. Colonel Reed's Regiment. Desertion: thirty-nine lashes. (1) (136)

THOMPSON, Richard. Colonel Webb's Regiment. Desertion: not guilty of desertion but guilty of being absent without leave—reprimand. (113) (133)

THOMPSON, Richard. Colonel Webb's Regiment. Desertion a second time: twenty lashes and pay a victim of a theft an amount of four dollars. (133)

THOMPSON, Samuel, Ens. First New Hampshire Regiment. Overstaying his furlough upwards of fifteen months: cashiered. (44)

THOMPSON, Thomas, Foragemaster. General Hand's Brigade. Exchanging public oats for bribes: pay for the damage and dismissed from the service. (36)

THOMPSON, William. Desertion and attempting to go to the enemy: guilty of the first charge but not guilty of the second charge—100 lashes. (38)

THOMSON, George. Desertion: acquitted. (95)

THORN, Daniel. Striking and threatening the lives of Lt. Charles F. Weissenfels, of the Fourth New York Regiment, and Ens. Daniel D. Denston: acquitted. (26) *See* Fabro, Slater.

THORP, Etephalet, Capt. Abusing the person and plundering the property of Margaret Wayman: not guilty of abusing Margaret Wayman by words or actions, but guilty of taking from her about twenty shillings and about five yards of cloth in a manner not to be justified, but that Wayman, the husband of said Margaret is a vile Tory, and had taken from said Thorp a vessel of considerable value, and that Captain Thorp supposed it lawful to take the property of Tories as well as enemies—return the cloth in addition to the money which had already been returned. Sentence disapproved and further steps ordered to be taken by his commanding officer. (73)

THRALL, William. Killing a hog: fifty lashes. (91)

THRASHER, Anthony. Desertion: 100 lashes. (63)

THRASHER, Arthur (alias Allen, James). Massachusetts Regiment. Desertion: 100 lashes. (53)

THRASHER, Joseph. Colonel Angell's Regiment. Desertion: 100 lashes. (23)

THRASHER, Noah. Lieutenant Colonel Smith's Regiment. Stealing and disobedience to orders: thirty-nine lashes. (10) *See* Cole.

THRIPPS, Benjamin. Colonel Lamb's Regiment of Artillery. Desertion: fifty lashes. (125)

THURSTON, Thomas, Drummer. First Regiment. Stealing a gun: acquitted. (95)

TIBBOTS, Job. Being a spy: acquitted. (9)

TICHENER, Isaac, civilian. Mishandling his authority with regard to provisions for the army in several instances at several times, defrauding the army for his own personal gain: acquitted of most of the charges and it was determined that he did not incur any personal benefit—reprimand. (36)

TILLOTSON, Jacob, Jr. Colonel Gallups' Regiment. Neglecting to join his company when detached for one month's duty: continue in service for one month from the date of his confinement and pay charges. (82)

TILSTON,_____, Captain. Colonel Paterson's Regiment. Neglect of duty: severe reprimand. (2)

TIPTON,_____, Lieutenant. Twelfth Virginia Regiment. Gaming: acquitted—the general disapproved of the sentence, but did not overturn it. (14) (134)

TIPTON,_____, Lieutenant. Twelfth Virginia Regiment. Embezzling the clothing drawn for the soldiers, taking a blanket from William Smith: acquitted. (134)

TIRN, Joseph. Third Virginia Regiment. Desertion from the provost guard, and taking a prisoner with him: 100 lashes. (134)

TITSWORTH, Thomas. Second New York Regiment. Desertion: 100 lashes. (25)

TOBIAS, Job. Desertion: 100 lashes. (41)

TOBMAN (TOLMAN), Samuel. Colonel Topham's Regiment. Stealing cartridges from soldiers' boxes on guard and burning them under the pots of the men cooking: acquitted. (68) (98)

TODD, Thaddeus. Stealing and concealing a barrel of flour: acquitted. (91)

TOMKINS, Francis. Third Regiment. Stealing a gun: fifty lashes—remitted because he was a new recruit and never had the Articles of War read to him. (95)

TOOMEY,_____, Lieutenant. Colonel Gist's Regiment. Detached to the Third Maryland Regiment. Disobedience to orders: reprimand. (17)

TOROND, Timothy. Colonel Clinton's Regiment. Desertion: fine of one month's pay – pardoned. (118)

TOVAS, Amos. Captain Prentice's Company. Neglect of his duty: ride the wooden horse fifteen mintues. (80)

TOWARD, John. Light Company. Absenting himself without leave, attempting to steal provisions from the commissary: 100 lashes. (52) *See* Gustin, Negus, Parker.

TOWER, Asoph. Colonel Cotton's Regiment. Desertion: fifteen lashes – pardoned. (120)

TOWLES, John. Colonel Nixon's Regiment. Deserting from his guard and being absent three days without leave: twenty lashes. (136)

TOWLES, John. Colonel Nixon's Regiment. Desertion: 100 lashes. (72) (113)

TOWN, John, Sgt. Colonel Waterbury's Regiment. Deserting his post in action: acquitted. (99)

TOWNE,_____, Captain. Colonel Woodbridge's Regiment. Suffering a soldier to escape: reprimand and a fine of three pounds. (133) (136)

TRASON, George. Colonel Burrell's Regiment. Leaving his post when on sentry and going to sleep: twenty lashes. (84)

TRASTON, Abiel. Acting in a mutinous manner, endeavoring to excite a mutiny: acquitted. (9) *See* Askin, Hunt, McLain, Wilson.

TRASTON (TROFTON), Joshua, Ens. Thirtieth Regiment of Foot Soldiers. Offering to strike his colonel, disobedience to orders: confined to his tent for three days. (135)

TRENGTORY, John. Colonel Barton's Corps. Desertion: forty lashes – pardoned because he was a Frenchman and did not understand the regulations. (68)

TRENT,_____, Lieutenant. Fourth Regiment of Light Dragoons. Disobedience to orders: reprimand. (35)

TRESANDER, Joseph. *See* Fessenden.

TRIM, Ezra. Colonal Lamb's Regiment of Artillery. Desertion from the wagon service: fifty lashes. (125)

TRIP, William, Seaman. The Fleet. Mutiny, whereas the enemy might come, and saying that he would not fight against them on board the vessel: seventy-eight lashes and return to duty on board, "the criminals to be whipped from vessel to vessel, receiving a part of their punishment on board each." (117) *See* Colbert, Hammon, Powell.

TRIPLETT,_____, Lieutenant. Second Virginia Regiment. Drinking and carousing with the common soldiers: reprimand. (21)

TRIPLETT, Rozier, Lt. Second Virginia Regiment. Appearing on the brigade parade and taking charge of a platoon when so drunk as to be incapable of doing his duty: cashiered. (110)

TRIPPS, Reuben. Third Massachusetts Regiment. Desertion: not guilty of desertion but guilty of being absent without leave—100 lashes—remitted. (46)

TRISCOT, Thomas. Neglect of duty, insolent language: 100 lashes. (125)

TRUEBRIDGE, Luther, Sgt. Colonel Arnold's Regiment. Refusing to obey Colonel Arnold's order: reduced to a private, fined one month's pay, and immediately join Captain Smith's Company, according to Colonel Arnold's order. (128)

TRUMAN, Jonathan. Lieutenant Ewing's Company. Absent without leave: 100 lashes. (115)

TRUSDALE, Darius. Second Company. Overstaying his furlough: ten lashes. (91)

TUCKER,_____, Sergeant. Ninth Massachusetts Regiment. Stealing rum from an inhabitant's barn: reduced to the ranks and a fine of ten dollars to pay for the rum, and fifty lashes. (47) *See* Annis, Cruett, Ford, Pense.

TUCKER, Joseph. Cilley's Regiment. Straggling from camp, killing a number of hogs: acquitted. (20) *See* Coburn.

TUCKER, Joseph. Eighth Massachusetts Regiment. 100 lashes. (124)

TUO, Peter. Colonel Jackson's Regiment. Breaking into another soldier's tent and taking a gun and bayonet, using threatening language: thirty-nine lashes. (10)

TURNER,_____, Lieutenant. Permitting a party under his command to abuse or sell the property of the inhabitants of Ballstown: acquitted. (88)

TURNER, Edward. Mutiny: twenty lashes. (84)

TURNER, Nichols. Colonel Hazen's Regiment. Attempting to seduce soldiers to desert and join the enemy, holding a secret correspondence with fifty-eight who had deserted and supplying them with arms, ammunition, provisions, etc.: released when no evidence was produced against him. (83) (84)

TUTTLE, Jacob. Second New York Regiment. Desertion: 100 lashes. (28)

TUTTLE, John. *See* chapter five.

TWEDY, Thomas, Gunner. Colonel Proctor's Regiment of Artillery. Desertion: fifty lashes—remitted because of his former good behavior. (25)

TWITCHEL, Benjamin. Mutiny: death—pardoned, "upon the presentation of Brigadier General Stark." (23)

TYRREL,_____, Sergeant. Fourth Georgia Continental Battalion. Mutiny and attempting to seduce and enveigle the party under command of Lieutenant Frazer to desert: death. (90)

TYSON, Matthew, inhabitant of Pennsylvania. Supplying the enemy with provisions: pay fifty pounds for the use of the sick at camp. (15)

TYTUS, James. Fourth New York Regiment. (89)

URANN, James. First Massachusetts Regiment. Killing a cow and stealing eleven geese: 100 lashes and pay fifteen dollars to the owner. (86)

VACHE,_____, Doctor. Fourth Virginia Regiment. Neglect of duty, disobedience, using menacing language to his colonel, spreading false reports: acquitted with honor. (12)

VAIL, Michael. Second New Hampshire Regiment. Overstaying his furlough. (31)

VAN, Jeremiah, Artificer. Insolence, threatening the life of McCoy: guilty of the first charge only—reprimand and the appropriate Article of War read to him. (95)

VANANGLAN,_____, Captain of Commissary. General Hand's Brigade. Cruelly beating and abusing a sergeant of the German Battalion: reprimand. (103)

VAN CLEAF, Laurence. Conspiring to desert to the enemy: 100 lashes—reprimand. (89)

VANDENBURGH,_____. Fifth New York Regiment. Disobedience to orders on the grand parade: acquitted. (100)

VANDENBURGH, Peter. Colonel Graham's Regiment. Desertion: thirty-nine lashes. (118) (123)

VANDERGRIFT, Jacob. First Pennsylvania Regiment. Desertion: 100 lashes. (97) (129)

VAN DEURSEN, William. Colonel McDougall's Regiment. Mutiny: fine of twelve shillings—pardoned. (118)

VAN GILDER, Benjamin. Desertion: 100 lashes. (42)

VAN GUILDER, David. Desertion: fifty lashes – remitted. (124)

VAN GUILDER, Isaac. New York Line. Desertion: 100 lashes. (42)

VAN GUILDER, John. Colonel Porter's Regiment. Desertion: thirty lashes. (84) (117)

VAN GUILDER, Reuben. Desertion: fifty lashes – remitted. (124)

VAN GUILDER, Stephen. Desertion: fifty lashes – remitted. (124)

VAN HERE,_____, Captain. Abusing David Parks, an inhabitant of Pennsylvania, ordering said Parks, wagoner, to be whipped; defrauding the United States in converting two public horses to his own private property: acquitted. (110)

VAN WERT,_____. Attempting to desert to the enemy, enticing others to do the same: acquitted. (42) *See* Bingham, Fitzgerald, Price, Walden.

VANY, Benjamin. Colonel Crane's Regiment of Artillery. Desertion: 100 lashes – remitted. (9)

VARNHAM, Gorden. Sixth Massachusetts Regiment. Desertion: 100 lashes. (56)

VARNIER,_____, Lieutenant. First North Carolina Regiment. Playing cards repeatedly in camp, conniving and encouraging the same practice amongst the soldiers, playing cards in camp since his arrest, breaking his arrest: cashiered. (110)

VAUGHAN, John. Eighth Massachusetts Regiment. Neglect of duty when on sentry at the public store at Newburgh: acquitted. (64)

VEAL (VAIL),_____, Captain. Second Carolina Battalion. Cowardice at the battle of Germantown, not taking his post when ordered: guilty of the first charge but not guilty of the second charge – dismissed from the service, the charge to be published in the newspapers in and about the camp and in the particular state he belongs to or in which he usually resides, "after which it shall be deemed scandalous for any officer to associate with him." (134)

VERIER,_____, Adjutant. Colonel Paterson's Regiment. Cruelly beating the fife major of the same regiment: reprimand. (82)

VIBBARD,_____, Corporal. Disobedience to orders: acquitted. (91)

VIBBARD,_____, Corporal. Captain Wyllys's Company. Absenting himself from the regiment without leave: reduced to the ranks. (91)

VIBBARD, John. Captain Whitney's Company. Playing cards: picketed for ten minutes. (91) *See* Ward.

VOCAN, Conrad. Third Regiment. Desertion: acquitted. (111)

VOSE, Joseph L., Col. Commander of the Fourteenth Massachusetts Regiment. Charged with nine counts: acquitted. (23) *See* chapter four.

VOSS,_____, Lieutenant. Invalid Regiment. Repeatedly drunk for two or three days at a time, treating the officers with very abusive and insolent language: not guilty of the first charge but guilty of the second charge—dismissed from the service. (58)

WABBY, Roger. Conspiring to desert to the enemy: fifty lashes—remitted. (89)

WADDEN, Thomas, Drummer. Abusing a soldier and insulting a sergeant: thirty lashes. (52)

WADDY, Peter. Colonel Vose's Regiment. Absenting himself without leave, attempting to desert: guilty of absenting himself only—thirty lashes. (88)

WADER, Joseph. Colonel Graham's Regiment. Desertion: thirty-nine lashes. (118)

WAID, Patrick. Sixth Maryland Regiment. Desertion and attempting to get to the enemy: death. (103)

WAILY, William, Sgt. Sixth South Carolina Battalion. Desertion: death by hanging. (108)

WALDEN, Nathan. Attempting to desert to the enemy and enticing others to do the same: acquitted. (42) *See* Bingham, Fitzgerald, Price, Van Wert.

WALES,_____, Lieutenant. Fourth Connecticut Regiment. Absenting himself from camp from 18 September 1778 to 20 May 1780, without liberty, also absent another time when he had liberty for only five days: acquitted. (38)

WALES,_____. Virginia Line. Absence without leave, plundering the inhabitants: run the gauntlet through the whole army. (115)

WALKER,_____, Lieutenant. Colonel Nixon's Regiment. Maliciously and falsely accusing Captain Butler of high crimes and misdemeanors which led to his arrest and court-martial, at which time he was honorably acquitted. (1) (136) *See* Butler.

WALKER, Francis. First New Jersey Regiment. Straggling from camp, killing a number of hogs: twenty-five lashes. (20) *See* Coburn, Farmer, Leonard, McLaughlin, Mumford, Rush, Whitehead.

WALKER, John (alias Maples, Robert). Enlisting in Colonel Alden's Regiment and deserting therefrom, using another name, taking a bounty of $200 and deserting again: death. (41) *See* Hutton and chapter four.

WALKER, Zacharia, Lt. Cowardice in the action at Bunker Hill: acquitted. (136)

WALLACE, Benjamin. Captain Stewart's Independent Company, New York Forces. Desertion and enlisting in another company: thirty-nine lashes. (67) (79)

WALLACE, Hugh. Colonel Hazen's Regiment. Desertion and joining another Maryland regiment into which he had previously enlisted: refund the money received – upon review, the sentence was deemed too lenient and he was held pending further investigation. (93)

WALLACE, John. Desertion: 100 lashes. (41)

WALLACE, Jonathan. Colonal Drayton's Regiment. Robbing the quartermaster-general's store: ten lashes. (133)

WALLINGS,_____, Lieutenant. Colonel Wingate's Regiment. Complaining that Captain Badger had cheated his men, encouraging the desertion of Daniel Rand, leaving his arrest: dismissed from the service. (84)

WALTER, Elijah. Third Connecticut Regiment. Pardoned. (124)

WALTON, Henry. Captain Warner's Company. Playing and gambling contrary to general orders: reprimand – pardoned but required to dig the first two vaults (latrines) that the regiment needed. (136) *See* Wilham.

WALTON, Thomas. Seventh Company. Theft: fifty lashes. (53)

WAMLY, James. Losing his canteen: ten lashes – remitted. (47)

WARD, Abner. Colonel Shepard's Regiment. Desertion: fifty lashes. (88)

WARD, Daniel. Captain Whitney's Company. Playing cards: picketed for ten minutes. (91) *See* Vibbard.

WARD, Daniel. Breaking open and robbing the commissary store: acquitted. (91)

WARD, Daniel. Colonel Webb's Regiment. Wounding Daniel Tucker of the same regiment: guilty of shooting and mortally wounding the victim, but not of design – acquitted. (85) (113) (125)

WARD, Francis. Attempting to desert to the enemy: death. (93)

WARD, John. Cavalry. Desertion: pardoned because of his previous good character.

WARD, Steven. Desertion: 100 lashes. (42)

WARD, Zachariah. Sixth Maryland Regiment. Desertion and attempting to go to the enemy: death. (69)

WARDEN, William. First Connecticut Regiment. Stealing a barrel of flour from the commissary: 100 lashes. (30) (97)

WARDER, Joseph (alias Weeker). Colonel Graham's Regiment. Desertion: thirty-nine lashes. (123)

WARDSWORTH, Joseph, Dr. Surgeon to Colonel Sherburne's Regiment. Abusing, striking, and damning Captain Grafton: acquitted because he acted in self-defense. (24) *See* Grafton.

WARNER, Nathaniel, Sgt. Third Massachusetts Regiment. Desertion: reduced to the ranks only because "there are many circumstances in his favor." (47)

WARREN, John. *See* Hawk.

WARREN, Samuel, Sutler. Selling liquor to the soldiers: fifty lashes. (41) *See* Rickey.

WARREN, Thomas. Invalid Corps. Leaving his post when a sentinel, theft: death by shooting—pardoned. (26)

WARTERS,_____, Lieutenant. Colonel Harrison's Regiment of Artillery. Speaking disrespectfully of the commander-in-chief and treating Lieutenant Hill in a scandalous manner, contemptuous of Colonel Harrison after being arrested: reprimand. (72) *See* McNamarra.

WASHBURN,_____, Ensign. Colonel Bigelow's Regiment. Leaving his area: reprimand. (13)

WASHBURN, Reuben. Ninth Massachusetts Regiment. Desertion: reduced to a private sentinel and fifty lashes. (42)

WASSON, John. Fifth Regiment. Desertion: 100 lashes. (129)

WASSON, Levi. Colonel Cotton's Regiment. Desertion: fifteen lashes—pardoned. (120)

WATERHOUSE, Joseph. Colonel Jackson's Regiment. Desertion: death—remitted. (26)

WATERMAN, John, Lt. Colonel Durkee's Regiment. Scandalous and cowardly manner before the enemy on a scouting party near the White Plains, making a false alarm in quarters at the same time: guilty of the first charge but not guilty of the second charge—cashiered, and his crime, name, place of abode, and punishment be published in newspapers in and about the camp and in that state from whence he came and where he usually resides. (131)

WATERS, Elisha. Raffling: reprimand. (91)

WATERS, John. Seventh Company. Losing his gun: acquitted. (47)

WATKINS,_____. Colonel McDougall's Regiment. Being concerned in a riot: six days upon bread and water. (136)

WATKINS, Benjamin. Colonel Harrison's Regiment of Artillery. Conspiracy to spike the cannon at Fort Schuyler and intending to desert to the enemy: 100 lashes. (37) *See* Amos, Johnson, Stanberry, Wright.

WATSON, Alexander, civilian. Retailing spirituous liquor to the soldiers contrary to general orders: released when no evidence was presented. (117)

WATSON, Jonathan. Pennsylvania Regiment. Desertion: 100 lashes. (97)

WATSON, William. Mutiny and drawing his sword on Lieutenant Bowman: 400 lashes. (93)

WATTS, Charles. Tenth Regiment. Absenting himself from his assignment without leave, attempting to go to the enemy: death—pardoned at the intercession of the officers of his regiment. (40)

WATTS, James, Sutler. Attempting to take the life of a sergeant, and threatening the lives of two others: license forfeited. (41)

WAYNE, Anthony, Gen. *See* chapter four.

WEARING, James. Second Regiment of Light Dragoons. Forcing a guard, stealing a horse from one of his officers, desertion and attempting to go to the enemy: guilty of the first two charges and the latter part of the third—death. (100)

WEATHERWAX, William. Desertion: fifty lashes. (42)

WEAVER, Henry. Third New York Regiment. Desertion: fifty lashes. (100)

WEAVER, Samuel. Colonel Sargent's Regiment. Desertion: thirty lashes. (132)

WEAVER, Samuel. Colonel Thayer's Regiment. Desertion and enlisting himself in another corps and taking a second bounty: thirty lashes. (136)

WEBB,_____, Lieutenant. Seventh Virginia Regiment. Disobedience to orders by going on duty with a hunting shirt, confessing he had a coat, after being warned that if he had no regard for his own appearance to have some for the credit of his own regiment, and therefore not to appear so unofficerlike: reprimand. (17)

WEBB, David. Colonel Gridley's Regiment. Plundering an inhabitant of money: death. (1)

WEBB, Thomas. Colonel Jackson's Regiment. Repeatedly getting drunk: twenty-five lashes. (15)

WEBB, Thomas. Stealing a Continental shirt and selling it: not guilty of intentional theft, but ordered to return the shirt to its rightful owner and to return the money from its sale—thirty-nine lashes only because he was known to be a notorious drunkard. (10)

WEBSTER, Benjamin. Second South Carolina Regiment. Desertion: 100 lashes—remitted because he was constantly employed in the service during his absence and his good character. (95)

WEBSTER, Benjamin. Absenting himself from the main guard when on duty: twenty-five lashes—pardoned. (91)

WEBSTER, John. Colonel Wyllys's Regiment. Desertion: thirty-nine lashes. (71)

WEBSTER, Levi. Colonel Wyllys's Regiment. Desertion: thirty-nine lashes. (107)

WEBSTER, Levi. Colonel Wyllys's Regiment. Plundering a cellar belonging to a citizen of New York: released to join his regiment. (6) *See* Butler, Knowland, McIntire.

WEED, Israel. General Hand's Brigade. Selling flour, meat, and fruits out of the public stores without difficulty, not delivering a quantity of butter and coffee drawn for the brigade: acquitted with honor. (35)

WEISELS, James. 100 lashes. (35)

WELBIERS, B. Escape: acquitted. (41)

WELCH,_____, Lieutenant. Colonel Putnam's Regiment. Challenging Captain Barnes to a duel, insulting and abusive language offered to him: cashiered—remitted and restored to his command. (72) (113)

WELCH, James. Colonel Stewart's Battalion of Light Infantry. Robbery: death. (36) *See* Miller, Moore, Rooney.

WELCH, John. First New York Regiment. Desertion: no punishment because of his long confinement and because he voluntarily had returned to his regiment. (100)

WELLS, David. Colonel Gridley's Regiment. Sleeping on his post when on sentry: acquitted. (71)

WELLS, Richard. Colonel Gallup's Regiment. Challenging an officer and sundry other abuses: ten stripes. (82)

WELSH,_____, Lieutenant. Ninth Massachusetts Regiment. Absenting himself from the regiment without leave, leaving his company without an officer in charge: dismissed from the service. (33)

WELSH, James. Colonel Marshall's Regiment. Desertion in the late retreat from Ticonderoga: returned to his regiment in irons. (9)

WELSH, John. Tenth Regiment. Deserting from the guard when on command, enlisting in another regiment: guilty of the first charge but acquitted of the second charge—100 lashes. (116)

WELSH, John. Mutiny: twenty lashes. (84)

WELSH, Lawrence. Second Massachusetts Regiment. Neglect of duty by sleeping on his post: 100 lashes. (41)

WELSH, Michael. Desertion: 100 lashes. (42)

WELTON, Joel. First Connecticut Regiment. Desertion: fifty lashes—remitted. (46)

WENTWORTH,_____, Captain. Colonel Poor's Regiment. Refusing to do his duty when properly called on: cashiered. (84)

WENTZ,_____, Sergeant. German Battalion. Complained of being unjustly detained in the service contrary to his enlistment: acquitted and given his discharge. (103)

WESLEY, Robert. Colonel Arnold's Regiment. Refusing to obey Colonel Arnold's order: fine of one month's pay and immediately join Captain Smith's Company, according to Colonel Arnold's order. (128)

WESSELLS,_____, Sergeant. Colonel McDougall's Regiment. Pardoned. (118)

WEST,_____, Lieutenant. Colonel Angell's Regiment. Plundering the property of a citizen: dismissed from the service. (17)

WEST, James, Dr. Surgeon of the Third Connecticut Regiment. Exceeding his furlough forty days: acquitted. (124)

WEST, Joseph. Breach of trust and selling a shirt which was committed to his care: seventy-five lashes. (24)

WESTBROOK, John. Second Battalion. Desertion: serve the time "prescribed by act of Assembly." (102)

WESTON, Asa. Colonel Cotton's Regiment. Desertion: fifteen lashes—pardoned. (120)

WESTON, Thomas. Colonel Cotton's Regiment. Desertion: fifteen lashes—pardoned. (120)

WESTON, William. Colonel Cotton's Regiment. Desertion: fifteen lashes – pardoned. (120)

WHALAND, Joseph. Theft: acquitted. (23)

WHALEN, John (alias Goodwin, John). Massachusetts Line. Desertion: 100 lashes and serve out his terms as a recruit after completion of his first enlistment. (56)

WHEELER, Abner. Massachusetts Line. Desertion and enlistment in a ficticious manner: 100 lashes. (63)

WHEELER, Elias. Colonel Graham's Regiment. Desertion: thirty-nine lashes. (118)

WHEELER, James. Fourth Maryland Regiment. Using words tending to mutiny: acquitted. (121)

WHIT, Stephen. Fifth Massachusetts Regiment. Desertion: acquitted. (50)

WHITBEE, Richard, Lt. Encouraging theft in the army: acquitted. (70)

WHITCOMB, Abel. Colonel Bailey's Regiment. Desertion and taking a second bounty from Colonel Cilley's Regiment: 100 lashes and repay the illegal bounty received. (75)

WHITCOMB, Abel. Colonel Bailey's Massachusetts Regiment. Desertion and changing his name and enlisting again: death. (124)

WHITE,_____, Lieutenant. Eleventh Regiment. Absenting himself from his guard at night, notwithstanding his being positively ordered to the contrary: dismissed from the service. (130)

WHITE, John. Colonel Thompson's Regiment. Abusing Lieutenant Cleveland: acquitted. (133) *see* McCordy, Simpson.

WHITE, John. Massachusetts Line. Desertion: acquitted because he had already been discharged from the army. (50)

WHITE, Thomas, Capt. North Carolina Brigade. Disobedience to orders to report for his duty: acquitted. (95)

WHITE, Thomas (alias Jones, Thomas). Colonel Hurthy's Company. Desertion: fifty lashes. (101)

WHITE, William. Colonel Angell's Regiment. Desertion and attempting to go to the enemy, stealing and embezzling cartridges, carrying off his arms and accouterments belonging to the Continent: reduced to the ranks, 100 lashes, and be sent on board the man-o-war, immediately upon receiving the punishment at Fort Montgomery. (131) *See* Smith.

WHITE, William. Captain Hazlet's Company. Absconding from his regiment: reprimand. (111)

WHITE, William. Frequently absenting himself from roll call: 100 lashes. (111)

WHITE, William. Rioting in camp at an unreasonable hour, abusing Captain Elsworth in the execution of his office: acquitted. (25) *See* Bele, Benjamin, Ivory.

WHITEHEAD, James. Second New Jersey Regiment. Straggling from camp, killing a number of hogs: twenty-five lashes—pardoned. (2) *See* Coburn, Farmer, Leonard, McLaughlin, Mumford, Osborn, Rush, Walker.

WHITEHEAD, William. Third Georgia Battalion. Desertion: 100 lashes—remitted. (95)

WHITING, John (alias Wright, Jo). Colonel Wigglesworth's Regiment. Enlisting twice: 100 lashes. (131)

WHITING, Justice, Gunner. Colonel Lamb's Regiment of Artillery. Sleeping on his post: reduced to a matross. (125)

WHITLEY,_____, Corporal. Mutiny: reduced to the ranks and thirty-nine lashes. (84)

WHITMARCH,_____, Lieutenant. Permitting a prisoner to escape the provost guard while he was officer of said guard: acquitted. (92) (94)

WHITMORE, Ernest, Cpl. Insolent behavior and insulting language to an ensign: reduced to the ranks. (42)

WHITMORE, James. First New Hampshire Regiment. Desertion: 100 lashes. (24)

WHITMORE, John. Third Maryland Regiment. Desertion and attempting to go to the enemy: death. (22)

WHITNEY,_____, Lieutenant. Colonel Wheelock's Regiment. Neglect of duty while on guard: cashiered. (84)

WHITNEY,_____, Sergeant. Fifteenth Regiment. Threatening and deserting: reduced to the ranks, ninety-nine lashes, and run the gauntlet—running of the gauntlet remitted. (122)

WHITNEY,_____, Corporal. Disobedience to orders, sneaking out of camp: reduced to private. (23) *See* Eaton, Nichols, Rolf.

WHITNEY, Benjamin. Eighth Massachusetts Regiment. Desertion: 100 lashes. (50)

WHITNEY, James, Cpl. Colonel Jackson's Regiment. Desertion: reduced to do the duty of a private sentinel and 100 lashes—the lashes remitted. (26)

WHITNEY, Thomas. Captain Bowman's Company of Artillery. Desertion: 100 lashes. (14)

WHITTAM, Jeremiah. Losing his arms and accouterments: fifty stripes. (23)

WHITTAN, Jeremiah. Colonel Smith's Regiment. Suffering five pairs of shoes to be taken from under his care while on sentry: acquitted. (9) *See* Pollock, Redford, Steward.

WHITTIER, Daniel. Fifth Company. Theft: acquitted. (23)

WHITTON,_____. Colonel Hunley's Regiment. Drunk on duty and disobedience to orders: fifty lashes. (10)

WHITTON, Thomas. Losing his knapsack and clothing: pay for the lost articles. (27)

WHITNELL,_____, Doctor. Third Massachusetts Regiment. Repeatedly and publicly defaming the characer of Lieutenant Flower, of the Sixth Massachusetts Regiment, for saying he was a damned rascal and would kick him out of the company when he found him: acquitted. (124)

WICKAM, Isaac. Suffering prisoners to escape from the guard: acquitted. (130)

WIESNER,_____, Captain. Misbehavior before the enemy in the attack on Montreal Island: cashiered with infamy. (94)

WIGGANS, Archibald, Capt. Colonel Morrison's Regiment. Absent from his guard and suffering about one-half of his men to be absent at the same time: acquitted. (96)

WILCOX, Job. Neglect of duty when on sentinel in suffering a public building to be destroyed, refusing to keep a prisoner when directed by Captain Hart: fifty lashes—remitted. (91)

WILD, Philip. Colonel Jackson's Regiment. Allowing a prisoner to escape from his guard at Fort Hill, in Boston: reprimand. (10)

WILD, Philip. Colonel Jackson's Regiment. Desertion: 100 lashes—remitted. (26)

WILDS, John. Colonel McDougall's Regiment. Desertion the second time: 100 lashes. (67)

WILHAM, Samuel. Captain Jacob Gerrish's Company. Playing and gambling contrary to general orders: reprimand – pardoned, but to dig the first two vaults (latrines) that the regiment wanted.(136) *See* Walton.

WILKIN,_____, Captain. Colonel Stewart's Battalion, Pennsylvania Line. Riotous behavior: acquitted. (44)

WILKINS, Jonathan, Sgt. Colonel Woodbridge's Regiment. Attempting to steal, insolent language to the quartermaster general: fine of twenty shillings. (133) (136)

WILKINSON, David. Desertion: fifty lashes. (41)

WILLAR, John. Pennsylvania Line. Mutiny and speaking disrespectfully of his Excellency George Washington and Congress, drinking to the health of King George: 100 lashes and drummed out of the army with a halter around his neck. (64)

WILLEY, Benjamin. Colonel Poor's Regiment. Desertion: thirty-nine lashes. (117)

WILLHEAD, James. First New Jersey Regiment. Straggling from camp and killing a number of hogs, the property of the inhabitants: twenty-five lashes – remitted. (103)

WILLIAMS,_____, Lieutenant. Second Regiment of Artillery. Imposing a falsehood, drawing a sword on a captain while unarmed, writing a challenge to another captain and leaving it in a barroom in a public tavern, unsealed: reprimand. (62)

WILLIAMS,_____, Sergeant. Third New York Regiment. Theft, abusive behavior: acquitted. (27)

WILLIAMS, Charles. Fourth New York Regiment. Desertion and forging a pass to effect the same: run the gauntlet. (28)

WILLIAMS, Charles. Captain Gale's Company, Sixth Regiment. Desertion: thirty-nine stripes and drummed out of the camp. (105)

WILLIAMS, Daniel, Capt. Third North Carolina Battalion. Disobedience to orders to attend the inspection parade: acquitted. (95)

WILLIAMS, Daniel. Arrested, but released when no evidence appeared. (93)

WILLIAMS, Easton. Virginia Line. Forcibly taking from Mr. Gamble, assistant quartermaster at Salisbury, soldiers' shoes and other apparel belonging to the United States: not guilty of forcibly taking the clothing, but taking it without authorization; such behavior justified because of the state of their soldeirs – acquitted. (115) *See* Hugo, Pendergast.

WILLIAMS, Ebenezer. Colonel Gerrish's Regiment. Mutiny: fine of forty-eight shillings and thirty-nine lashes. (3) (133) See Harwood, Laraby, North, Putney, Rawlins (Rollins).

WILLIAMS, Edward. Colonel Crane's Battalion of Artillery. Enlisting twice and receiving two bounties: 100 lashes and repayment of the bounty, in the amount of fifteen pounds and ten shillings. (9)

WILLIAMS, Elijah. Fourth Massachusetts Regiment. Desertion: 100 lashes—remitted. (47)

WILLIAM, Henry, Lt. Second Regiment of Artillery. Arrested and confined till eventually released for lack of prosecution. (124)

WILLIAMS, Henry. Unofficerlike and ungentlemanlike behavior: reprimand and suspended for three months. (87)

WILLIAMS, Henry. Colonel Shephard's Regiment. Desertion: thirtynine lashes. (136)

WILLIAMS, Henry. Colonel Swift's Regiment. Persuading soldiers to desert: 100 lashes. (131)

WILLIAMS, James. Mutiny, riot, and disobedience to orders: thirty lashes and drummed out of the army. (135)

WILLIAMS, John. Sixth Massachusetts Regiment. Desertion: death. (41)

WILLIAMS, John. Desertion to the enemy: death—pardoned because of his youth and former good conduct. (32)

WILLIAMS, John (alias Foster, John). Colonel Nixon's Regiment. Desertion, enlisting in Colonel Lamb's Regiment of Artillery, reenlisting in Colonel Nixon's Regiment, forging a pass in the name of Colonel Nixon: guilty of all but the last charge—300 lashes and lose pay from the time of his enlistment in 1777 to 21 July 1780, and a fine of fifty dollars to repay his bounty. (122)

WILLIAMS, Jonathan. Captain Winder's Company (Captain Wing's Company). Desertion with intention of going to the enemy: death—pardoned because of his generally good character. (21) *See* Parsons.

WILLIAMS, M., Cpl. Beating a wagoner: acquitted. (95)

WILLIAMS, Peter. Captain Sacket's Company. Stealing shirts when on guard: released when no evidence was presented. (128)

WILLIAMS, Richard. Desertion: 100 lashes. (42)

WILLIAMS, Rowland. First South Carolina Regiment. Desertion: 100 lashes with switches. (95)

WILLIAMS, Rowland. First South Carolina Regiment. Desertion: acquitted. (95)

WILLIAMS, Samuel. Attempting to desert to the enemy: acquitted. (9)

WILLIAMS, Solomon. Conspiring to desert to the enemy: 100 lashes — remitted. (89)

WILLIAMS, Thomas. Colonel Sargent's Regiment. Desertion: thirty-nine lashes. (136)

WILLIAMS, Thomas. Colonel Reed's Regiment. Impeaching and falsely asserting that Captain Soper did knowingly and designedly defraud the public: cashiered. (136) *See* Soper.

WILLIAMS, William, Lt. Thirteenth Virginia Regiment. Buying a pair of Continental shoes from a soldier and thereby rendering the soldier unfit for service; messing and sleeping with the soldiers, taking their bread and not returning it, by which the soldiers suffered from hunger: not guilty of taking the bread but guilty of the other charges — dismissed from the service. (14) (134)

WILLIAMS, William. Attempting to desert to the enemy with his arms: acquitted. (112)

WILLIAMSON, Daniel, civilian. Attempting to take a number of sheep into Philadelphia: 200 lashes. (14) (134)

WILLIAMSON, John, civilian. Supplying the enemy with cattle: 250 lashes. (14) (134)

WILLIAMSON, Reuben. North Carolina Brigade. Forging an order with a major's name to the quartermaster to obtain forage to be used in his private business: dismissed from the service. (49)

WILLIS, Gideon. Captain Hart's Company. Taking boards from the barracks and cutting them up for his own use: fine of twenty shillings to pay for the boards. (91)

WILLIS, Josua. Captain Walker's Company. Defaming the character of Sergeant Nicholson: run the gauntlet twice through the regiment. (91)

WILLISON, John. Colonel Marshal's Regiment. Desertion: eighty lashes. (75)

WILLY, Benjamin. Colonel Poor's Regiment. Desertion: thirty-nine lashes. (84)

WILSON,_____, Corporal. First New Jersey Regiment. Using the state stores of liquor. (25) *See* Albuy.

WILSON,_____, Corporal. Disobedience to orders: not guilty. (10)

WILSON, Abraham. Second Massachusetts Regiment. Disorderly conduct: 100 lashes. (63)

WILSON, Alexander. Seventh Massachusetts Regiment. Desertion: 100 lashes. (111)

WILSON, George. Twelfth Massachusetts Regiment. Desertion: pardoned in compliance with the proclamation of the commander-in-chief granting amnesty to returned deserters. (52)

WILSON, Isaac. Captain Allen's Company. Offering to sell his gun: fined and reprimand. (70)

WILSON, John. Colonel Clinton's Regiment. Desertion: fine of one month's pay—pardoned. (118)

WILSON, Thomas. Acting in a mutinous manner, endeavoring to excite a mutiny: 100 lashes. (9) *See* Askin, Hunt, McLain, Trasson.

WILSON, William. Disobedience: reprimand. (11)

WILTLOW, John. Losing his gun: acquitted. (111)

WILTON, Thomas. Defrauding an inhabitant, being out of camp at unreasonable hours: 100 lashes. (23)

WILTON, Thomas. Intoxicated when on guard and leaving his post: fifty lashes—pardoned. (45)

WILTON, Thomas. Stealing and being an accessory to stealing several articles of clothing and silver spoons from an inhabitant in Danbury: 100 lashes. (53) *See* Clements, Dunham, Perry.

WINDOR, William. Discharged from confinement and join his regiment. (130)

WING, Joseph. Sixth Company. Stealing corn: acquitted. (66) *See* Franklin, Harvey, Larkin, Parker.

WINKLEMAN, John. Colonel Lamb's Regiment of Artillery. Insulting behavior toward Lieutenants Webb and Allen: sixty lashes. (113) *See* Syman.

WINNING, William. Theft and other misdemeanors: not guilty of the first charge but guilty of the second charge—twenty-five lashes—remitted. (100) *See* St. Luke.

WINSLOW, Jacob. Colonel Lamb's Regiment of Artillery. Selling or losing his clothing: acquitted. (125)

WINSLOW, William. Captain Perkins's Company of Artillery. Stealing a cartridge of powder: acquitted. (135)

WINSLOW, William. Colonel Cotton's Regiment. Desertion: fifteen lashes—pardoned. (120)

WITESKAY, John. Pennsylvania Line. Desertion: 100 lashes—remitted because of his former good behavior. (64)

WITT, Stephen. Desertion and reenlisting in the Massachusetts quota and then reenlisting again in Massachusetts: 100 lashes and a fine of fourteen pounds eleven shillings, four pence for the cost of bringing him to trial. (57)

WITTON, Thomas. Striking a corporal and other disorderly conduct: acquitted. (23) *See* Bourk.

WOLF, Adam. Desertion: ten lashes. (96)

WOLFE, Ludwick, Trumpeteer. Massachusetts Forces. Consorting a plot to desert to the enemy and carry with him two horses, the property of Captain Von Heer: 100 lashes. (21)

WOOD, Clement, Ens. Fourth New Jersey Regiment. Absence without leave and disobedience to orders: dismissed from the service. (93)

WOOD, Francis. Third New Jersey Regiment. Desertion and forging a pass: death. (25)

WOOD, Jonathan. Absent without leave: fine of eight shillings and reprimand. (91)

WOOD, Joseph. Stealing nine stamped handkerchiefs: 150 lashes. (93)

WOOD, Joseph. Colonel Clinton's Regiment. Desertion: fine of one month's pay—pardoned. (118)

WOOD, Joseph. Seventh Massachusetts Regiment. Desertion: 100 lashes. (54)

WOOD, Levi (Lewis). Colonel Prescott's Regiment. Absent without leave, refusing to take the oath and threatening to leave the army: pardoned upon a promise of future obedient behavior. (105) (114)

WOOD, Peter. First New York Regiment. Robbery and desertion: acquitted of the first charge but guilty of the second charge—100 lashes. (72) (113)

WOOD, Samuel. Light Company, Massachusetts Regiment. Killing a cow and seven geese: seventy-five lashes. (61) *See* Abram, Brayton, Carliss, Cook, Cowell, Gardner, Jinks, Shea.

WOOD, Thomas. Fifth Carolina Regiment. Desertion and joining the enemy: death by hanging. (115)

WOOD, William. Stealing: fifty lashes. (93)

WOODBORNE, George. Massachusetts Line. Desertion: 100 lashes. (56)

WOODBURY,_____, Captain. Colonel Stark's Regiment. Keeping a soldier of his company out of his pay and denying that he had drawn it: acquitted with honor. (84) (117)

WOODBURY (WOODBURN), Francis. Stealing rum at the commissary store: acquitted. (133) *See* Bryant, Hingham, Rockwood.

WOODCOCK, John. Mutiny. (90)

WOODMAN, John. Colonel Hensley's Regiment. Breaking into the hospital store at sundry times and stealing wine: thirty lashes (77). *See* Mugridge.

WOODRACK, Benjamin. Ninth Massachusetts Regiment. Not coming out to join the working party when ordered: acquitted. (48)

WOODS, Samuel. First Massachusetts Regiment. Killing a cow and stealing eleven geese. Seventy-five lashes and pay fifteen dollars to the owner. (86)

WOODWARD, Elijah. Colonel Shepard's Regiment. Desertion and enlisting twice and receiving two bounties: 100 lashes for each offense and repay the bounties received. (9)

WOODWARD, Elijah. Colonel Shepard's Regiment. Using many names and enlisting many times: death by shooting—the order to be executed "on Thursday, the 11th day of September, next, between the hours of 8 and 11 o'clock in the morning, on the bottom of the Common in Boston." (9)

WOODWARD (WOODARD), Richard, Lt. Colonel Gridley's Regiment of Artillery. Cowardice at the battle of Bunker Hill, mutiny: cashiered. (134)

WOODWORTH, Zebediah. Getting drunk, fighting, and making a disturbance in camp at unreasonable hours of the night: one day's fatigue—the general thought the punishment in no way adequate to the crime. (91)

WOOLENT, Joseph. Absent without leave: acquitted. (91)

WORDEN, Nathaniel. Conspiracy to desert to the enemy: 100 lashes—remitted. (89)

WORRELL, Joseph, inhabitant of Pennsylvania. Giving intelligence to the enemy, acting as a guide to pilot the enemy: not guilty of the first charge but guilty of the second charge—death. (14)

WORTERS, Benjamin, Ens. Fourth Connecticut Regiment. Exceeding his furlough three days: acquitted. (124)

WORTMAN, Samuel. Commander-in-Chief's Guard. Going out, with others, with sidearms, to do harm to other soldiers: acquitted. (125)

WRIGHT,_____, Lieutenant. First North Carolina Regiment. Drunkenness and disobedience to orders: acquitted. (75)

WRIGHT,_____, Corporal. Colonel Topham's Regiment. Getting drunk and appearing in liquor on parade: reduced to the ranks. (98)

WRIGHT, Anthony. Colonel Flower's Regiment of Artillery. Going into debt with a private and refusing to pay him, drinking at public houses with private soldiers at their expense, going to a dance at night at the soldiers' houses without their invitation and playing cards with them, beating and abusing, borrowing a pair of shoes and not returning them: guilty of a portion of the charges—dismissed from the service. (27)

WRIGHT, Daniel. Stealing and concealing a barrel of flour: acquitted. (91)

WRIGHT, James (Jonathan). Colonal Hazen's Regiment. Suffering a prisoner to escape: acquitted. (93)

WRIGHT, Job. Colonel Harrison's Regiment of Artillery. Conspiracy to spike the cannon at Fort Schuyler and intending to desert to the enemy: 100 lashes. (37) *See* Amos, Johnson, Stanberry, Watkins.

WRIGHT, John. Massachusetts Line. Desertion: acquitted, since he had previously been discharged. (124)

WRIGHT, Jonathan, Lt. Deserting his post without orders or without being attacked or forced by the enemy: cashiered and pay the damages to the inhabitants on Onion River due to his unofficerlike retreat. (94) *See* Fasset, Perry, Lyon.

WRIGHT, Jonathan. Colonel Paterson's Regiment. Desertion: thirty-nine lashes. (47) (48)

WYLEY, John, Capt. Fraud, in several counts: acquitted. (130)

WYMAN,_____, Colonel. Receiving and clandestinely carrying off the ration money of Colonel Marks and his officers at Cambridge the last campaign, and not settling his accounts: acquitted with honor. (94) (117)

WYMAN, Abel, Capt. Second New Jersey Regiment. Scandalous and disorderly conduct: acquitted. (51)

WYMAN, Dean. Fifth Massachusetts Regiment. Desertion and attempting to go to the enemy: 100 lashes. (50)

WYMAN, Walter, Sgt. Maj. Colonel Elliot's Regiment. Striking and abusing Gabriel Conner, of the same regiment: acquitted and commended for doing his duty. (98) *See* Conner.

YHOWAN, Ahimaz. Colonel Nixon's Regiment. Desertion: thirty-nine lashes. (106)

YONGS, John. Absent from his fatigue party without leave: 100 lashes. (111)

YOUNG, Alexander, Matross. Captain Moody's Company. Absent from camp, abusing the inhabitants: guilty only of the first charge — stand on a picket with his bare feet for fifteen minutes. (125)

YOUNG, John. Colonel Graham's Regiment. Desertion from the advance guard, getting drunk: twenty-four lashes for the first offense and twenty lashes for the second offense. (123) *See* Dennis.

YOUNG, John. Captain Stanburgh's Company. Drunk on guard, breaking his firelock: reprimand. (118) (123)

YOUNG, Jonathan. Captain Oldham's Company. Forcibly taking a quantity of bacon under pretense of doing it for his officers: 100 lashes. (115) *See* O'Quin.

YOUNG, Sylvester. First New Jersey Regiment. Desertion and spoiling regimental clothes: death by hanging — pardoned. (57) *See* Gibbs.

YOUNG, William, Sgt. Colonel Crane's Regiment. Desertion and taking a soldier with him, forging a pass: 100 lashes. (125)

YOUNGMAN, Thomas, Lt. Colonel Hallet's Regiment. Absenting himself from his regiment without leave: cashiered. (74) (118) (123)

YOUNT,_____, Captain. Colonel Bedel's Regiment. Deserting his post at St. Anns, on the Island of Montreal: acquitted. (84)

ZANE,_____, Captain. Thirteenth Virginia Regiment. Acting in a cowardly manner when sent out on a scouting party, by ordering his men to retreat when he had a considerable advantage over the enemy: dismissed from the service. (13) (134) *See* chapter three.

ZANK (ZANKS), Jacob, Lt. Colonel Hand's Regiment. Insulting and abusing Lieutenant Zeigler, adjutant of said regiment: ask the pardon of Lieutenant Zeigler. (136)

ZIMMERMAN, William. Fourth Regiment of Light Dragoons. Robbing money from a house in the state of New Jersey: reduced in rank and 100 lashes. (21) *See* Fisher, Gray.

ZUFFEN, Stephen, Sgt. Colonel Wheelock's Regiment. Leaving his guard without orders: acquitted. (84)

ZUGLIN,_____, Lieutenant. Striking and wounding with his sword James Quin, a soldier in the Seventh Pennsylvania Regiment, of which wound he died: acquitted, since the action was done in the line of duty and was justified. (88)

# Source Documents – Orderly Books

*The numbers in parentheses at the end of each court-martial entry in chapter 6 refer to the orderly books similarly numbered in the list below.*

## PART ONE – MICROFILM SERIES M853 – NUMBERED RECORD BOOKS, National Archives, Washington, D.C.

1. Roll 2. Vol. 12: George Washington's Headquarters, Cambridge, Massachusetts: Orderly Book #1: 23 June 1775 – 18 July 1775 Orderly Book #2: 4 July 1775 Orderly Book #3: 15 June 1776 – 9 July 1776.

2. Roll 2. Vol. 196: William Hawk's Quarterly Book; George Washington's Orderly Book, Cambridge, Massachusetts, 29 July 1775 – 2 August 1775.

3. Roll 2. Vol. 195: Colonel Edmund Phinney's Massachusetts Regiment. (Maine); George Washington, Boston, Massachusetts, 1 August 1775 – 18 December 1775.

4. Roll 2. Vol. 13: Second Pennsylvania Regiment; Second New Jersey Regiment, 17 January 1775 – 2 February 1777.

5. Roll 2. Vol. 13: Second Pennsylvania Regiment; Second New Jersey Regiment, 22 February 1776 – 11 September 1776.

6. Roll 2. Vol. 194: Samuel Drake's New York Regiment, 18 August 1776 – 12 March 1777.

7. Roll 2. Vol. 15: George Washington's Headquarters, Cambridge, Massachusetts, 21 August 1776 – 4 October 1776.

8. Roll 2. Vol. 197: Colonel Ezra Woods's Massachusetts Regiment, George Washington's Headquarters. 27 December 1776 – 10 December 1778.

9. Roll 3. Vol. 16: General Heath, Boston, Massachusetts, 23 May 1777 – 20 October 1778.

10. Roll 3. Vol. 17: Colonel Smith's Regiment, Boston, Massachusetts, 1 June 1777 – 25 March 1780.

11. Roll 3. Vol. 18: Boston, Massachusetts. 22 June 1777 – 10 December 1779.

12. Roll 3. Vol. 19: Payne Downs. 11 June 1777 – 25 April 1778.

13. Roll 3. Vol. 20: Valley Forge Camp. 1 January 1778.

14. Roll 3. Vol. 21: Valley Forge Camp. 1 February 1778.

15. Roll 3. Vol. 22: Valley Forge Camp. 25 March 1778 – 23 April 1778.

16. Roll 4. Vol. 23: General Muhlenberg's Regiment, Valley Forge. 18 April 1778 – 21 July 1778.

17. Roll 4. Vol. 24: Valley Forge Camp. 24 April 1778 – 23 July 1778.

18. Roll 4. Vol. 25: Valley Forge Camp. 5 June 1778 – 21 August 1778.

19. Roll 4. Vol. 26: Colonel Jackon's Regiment, Providence (orderly book #6). 5 September 1778–22 October 1778.

20. Roll 4. Vol. 27: Albany, New York. 20 October 1778–25 June 1779.

21. Roll 4. Vol. 28: Adjutant General Scammell, Middlebrook. 22 February 1778–2 June 1779.

22. Roll 4. Vol. 29: General McDougall's Regiment, Peekskill. 4 August 1779.

23. Roll 5. Vol. 32: Providence. 20 February 1779–4 December 1779.

24. Roll 5. Vol. 30: Providence. 15 May 1779–4 July 1779.

25. Roll 5. Vol. 31: General Hand's Regiment, Wyoming. 23 June 1779–23 August 1779.

26. Roll 5. Vol. 33: Adjutant General Scammell, Morristown. 17 October 1777–22 March 1780.

27. Roll 6. Vol. 35: 20 February 1780–15 May 1780.

28. Roll 6. Vol. 36: Morristown. 22 March 1780–15 May 1780.

29. Roll 6. Vol. 37: Morristown. 21 May 1780.

30. Roll 6. Vol. 38: General Lord Stirling. 23 May 1780–27 July 1780.

31. Roll 6. Vol. 39: First Connecticut Regiment, 4 June 1780–24 July 1780.

32. Roll 6. Vol. 40: 7 June 1780–8 August 1780.

33. Roll 6. Vol. 41: 1 August 1780–20 September 1780.

34. Roll 6. Vol. 42: 1 August 1780–20 September 1780.

35. Roll 7. Vol. 43: 9 August 1780–20 September 1780.

36. Roll 7. Vol. 46: Orangetown. 28 August 1780–14 June 1781.

37. Roll 7. Vol. 45: West Point. 21 September 1780–25 November 1780.

38. Roll 7. Vol. 47: 16 November 1780–10 January 1781.

39. Roll 7. Vol. 48: West Point. 29 November 1780–8 February 1781.

40. Roll 8. Vol. 49: West Point. 15 January 1781–16 February 1781.

41. Roll 8. Vol. 50: 16 February 1781–1 July 1781.

42. Roll 8. Vol. 51: West Point; New Windsor. 26 April 1781–1 July 1781.

43. Roll 8. Vol. 52: Dobbs Ferry. 7 June 1781–2 October 1781.

44. Roll 8. Vol. 53: New Windsor. 19 June 1781–2 November 1781.

45. Roll 8. Vol. 54: Phillipsburg. 4 July 1781–20 August 1781.

46. Roll 9. Vol. 55: Continental Village. 22 August 1781–17 October 1781.

47. Roll 9. Vol. 56: Continental Village. 13 October 1781–6 December 1781.

48. Roll 9. Vol. 57: 7 December 1781–21 January 1782.

49. Roll 9. Vol. 58: General Gist, South Carolina. 13 March 1782–12 May 1782.

50. Roll 9. Vol. 59: West Point; Highlands. 24 March 1782–26 May 1782.

51. Roll 9. Vol. 60: Newburgh. 27 April 1782–9 August 1782.

52. Roll 10. Vol. 61: Highlands. 7 May 1782–13 June 1782.

53. Roll 10. Vol. 62: Highlands. 14 June 1782–2 August 1782.

54. Roll 10. Vol. 63: Highlands. 24 July 1782–2 August 1782.

55. Roll 10. Vol. 64: Newburgh. 2 August 1782–14 November 1782.

56. Roll 10. Vol. 65: Dobbs Ferry. 3 August 1782–4 September 1782.

57. Roll 10. Vol. 66: Newburgh. 10 August 1782–7 September 1782.

58. Roll 11. Vol. 67: Verplank's Point. 8 September 1782–20 December 1782.

59. Roll 11. Vol. 68: 30 September 1782–1 November 1782.

60. Roll 11. Vol. 70: Newburgh. 21 December 1782–9 February 1783.

61. Roll 11. Vol. 71: 8 January 1783–11 February 1783.

62. Roll 11. Vol. 72: Newburgh. 10 February 1783–28 March 1783.

63. Roll 11. Vol. 73: Newburgh. 19 March 1783–17 May 1783.

64. Roll 11. Vol. 74: 29 March 1783–22 June 1783.

65. Roll 11. Vol. 75: 11 June 1783–12 August 1783.

66. Roll 11. Vol. 76: West Point. 13 August 1783–27 September 1783.

## PART TWO—MANUSCRIPT DIVISION, LIBRARY OF CONGRESS, Washington, D.C.

67. Adams, Ebenezer: Attached to Colonel Durkee's Twentieth Continental Infantry, Connecticut. 25 July 1776–12 October 1776.

68. Alger, Nicholas, Sgt. Colonel John Topham's Rhode Island Regiment, 10 May 1779–26 November 1779.

69. Boynton, Caleb, Jr., Pvt. Captain Thomas Wiliams's Company, Massachusetts Militia, 1775. Captain David Batchellor's Company, 1778. 2 Vols: 5 September 1775–12 November 1775; 16 July 1778–17 August 1778. 16 July 1778–17 August 1778.

70. Briggs, James, Capt. Colonel John Bailey's Regiment, Massachusetts Militia. 14 December 1775–13 January 1776.

71. Brown, Robert, Capt. Colonel William Douglas's Connecticut State Regiment. 16 August 1776–14 September 1776.

72. Buckmaster, Richard, Lt.-Adjutant, Sixth Massachusetts Continental Regiment. 7 August 1778–1 February 1779.

73. Burnham, John, Capt. Eighth Massachusetts Continental Regiment. 14 January 1777–25 February 1777.

74. Butts, Sherebiah, Capt. Colonel John Douglas's Regiment, Connecticut Militia. 19 September 1776–8 November 1776.

75. Clap, Caleb, Lt.-Adjutant. Ninth Massachusetts Continental Regiment. 24 September 1778–9 July 1779.

76. Clift, Lemuel, Capt. First Connecticut Continental Regiment. 10 May 1782–20 September 1782.

77. Cole, Thomas, Sgt. Colonel Jacob Gerrish's Regiment of Guards, Massachusetts Militia. 1 July 1778–1 October 1778.

78. Dexter, John Singer, Maj. Assistant to the Adjutant General. 2 Vols.: 22 April 1781–2 August 1781; 26 November 1782–17 January 1783.

79. Dolson, Peter, Sgt. Third New York Continental Regiment. 29 July 1776–12 September 1776.

80. Douglas, William, Col. Connecticut State Regiment. 10 July 1776–13 December 1776.

81. Fenno, John, Secretary to General Artemus Ward, Massachusetts Militia. 20 April 1775–6 September 1775.

82. Gallup, Nathan, Lt. Col. Connecticut Militia. 16 July 1779–22 August 1779.

83. Gates, Horatio, Maj. Gen. Continental Army. 19 April 1777–2 June 1777.

84. Gates, Horatio, Orderly Book—Horatio Gates Papers—New York Historical Society. 10 July 1776–3 June 1777. Microfilm at Library of Congress.

85. Gates, Horatio, Orderly Book, Highlands—Horatio Gates Papers—New York Historical Society. 20 August 1777–16 July 1778. Microfilm at Library of Congress.

86. Gates, Horatio, Orderly Book, Newburgh—New Windsor. Horatio Gates Papers—New York Historical Society. 31 October 1782–31 January 1783. Microfilm at Library of Congress.

87. Gates, Horatio. 1 February 1778–8 April 1783.

88. Clover, John, Brig. Gen. Continental Army. 24 August 1777–18 January 1778.

89. Gregg, James, Capt. Third New York Continental Regiment. 24 April 1779–14 October 1779.

90. Howe, Robert, Brig. & Maj. Gen. Continental Army. 25 June 1776–14 July 1776.

91. Huntington, Ebenezer, Lt. Col. Colonel Samuel Webb's Regiment. 9 September 1778–8 October 1783.

92. Johnson, Obadiah, Maj. Third Connecticut Continental Regiment. 22 July 1775–22 September 1775.

93. Kirkwood, Robert, Capt. Delaware Regiment. 1 March 1777–21 December 1777.

94. Lee, Charles, Maj. Gen. Continental Army. 26 January 1775–17 November 1775; 30 March 1776–6 August 1776; 12 October 1776–17 November 1776.

95. Mayson, John, Lt. Col. (unit unknown). South Carolina. 23 June 1778–1 May 1779.

96. McCready, Robert, Sgt.-Adjutant. Colonel Jonathan Stephenson's Regiment. Pennsylvania Militia. 17 October 1778–8 December 1778.

97. McLean, James, Adj. Tenth Pennsylvania Continental Regiment. 24 July 1780–23 August 1780.

98. Miller, James, Lt. First Rhode Island State Regiment. 17 March 1779–1 March 1780.

99. Montgomery, Richard, Brig. & Maj. Gen. Continental Army, Expedition to Canada. 5 June 1775–6 October 1775.

100. Mooers, Benjamin, Lt.-Adjutant. Second Canadian Regiment. 16 September 1780–19 November 1780.

101. Morgan, Daniel, Col. Eleventh Virginia Continental Regiment. 15 May 1777–1 July 1777.

102. Muhlenberg, Peter, Maj. Gen. Continental Army. 25 October 1780–18 April 1781.

103. Myers, Christian, Capt. German Regiment of Pennsylvania. June 1779–March 1780.

104. Niles, Jeremiah, Adj. Cambridge, Massachusetts. Colonel Richard Gridley's Artillery Regiment, 1775: Colonel Henry Knox's Artillery Regiment, 1775-76. 2 Vols.: 10 August 1775–15 November 1775; 18 November 1775–5 January 1776.

105. Orderly Book, Sixth Connecticut Regiment. 3 June 1775–5 August 1775.

106. Orderly Book, Continental Army–New York. 19 May 1776–5 August 1776.

107. Orderly Book, Continental Army–New York. 30 August 1776–4 October 1776.

108. Orderly Book, Siege of Savannah. 18 September 1779–14 October 1779.

109. Orderly Book, Sixth Maryland Regiment. 4 April 1780–11 August 1780.

110. Orderly Book, Morristown, New Jersey and New York Highlands; Sixth Maryland Regiment. 15 August 1779–24 December 1779.

111. Orderly Book, New York Highlands. 8 July 1780–12 October 1780.

112. Orderly Book, Fourth Pennsylvania Regiment. 7 April 1780–6 June 1780.

113. Parsons, Samuel H., Brig. & Maj. Gen. Continental Army 2 Vols.: 18 April 1778–16 July 1778; 31 July 1778–15 September 1778.

114. Patterson, John, Col. Massachusetts Militia. 19 July 1775–22 September 1775.

115. Pendleton, Nathaniel, Aide-de-camp to Maj. Gen. Nathanael Greene. 18 July 1781–1 January 1782.

116. Reeves, Enos, Quartermaster-Adjutant. Tenth Pennsylvania Regiment. 3 Vols.: 7 July 1780–20 July 1780; 25 August 1780–10 October 1780; 14 October 1780–23 November 1780.

117. Roberts, James, Lt. Col. Colonel Edward Wigglesworth's Regiment, Massachusetts Militia–Ticonderoga. 30 October 1776–24 November 1776.

118. Schulyer, Phillip, Maj. Gen. Continental Army. 22 September 1775–6 October 1776.

119. Scranton, Abraham, Capt. Captain Josiah Baldwin's Company, Connecticut Militia. 8 September 1778–20 September 1778.

120. Simmons, Peter, Col. South Carolina Militia. 13 June 1776–1 August 1776.

121. Smallwood, William, Brig. & Maj. Gen. Continental Army. 3 July 1780–2 October 1780.

122. Sprout, Ebenezer, Lt. Col. Twelfth Massachusetts Continental Regiment. 17 January 1780–13 February 1780.

123. Thomas, Thomas, Col. New York Militia. 17 August 1776–5 October 1776.

124. Tufts, Francis, Lt.-Adjutant. Eighth Massachusetts Regiment. 10 January 1782–8 April 1782.

125. Walker, Robert, Capt. Second Artillery Regiment, New York. 3 Vols.: 12 July 1777–4 June 1778; 13 September 1778–24 November 1778; 18 October 1780–24 November 1778 (orderly book kept by John Smith).

126. Walton, William, Sgt. Captain John Henderson's Company, New Jersey Militia. 10 July 1776–18 July 1776.

127. Waterbury, David, Col. Fifth Connecticut Regiment; Brigadier General Connecticut State Line. 6 June 1775–22 June 1775; 25 September 1775–7 October 1775; 26 May 1781–26 July 1781.

128. Weissenfels, Frederick, Brigadier Major. Fifth Connecticut Regiment. 8 November 1775–26 February 1776.

129. Wilson, James, Capt. First Pennsylvania Continental Regiment. 14 August 1780–23 September 1780.

130. Young, Nathaniel, Second Lieutenant. First New York Continental Regiment. 23 February 1780–28 May 1780.

## PART THREE—PUBLISHED ORDERLY BOOKS

131. *General Orders Issued by Major General Israel Putnam, When in Command of the Highlands, in the Summer and Fall of 1777.* Editor: Ford, Worthington C. Brooklyn: Historical Printing Club, 1893. Reprinted, Boston: Gregg Press, 1972. (Library of Congress: E233 .A5)

132. *Order Book Kept by Peter Kinnan, 7 July–4 September 1776.* Princeton, New Jersey: Princeton University Press, 1931. (LOC: E232 .K65)

133. *Order Book Kept by Jeremiah Fogg, Colonel Enoch Poor's Second New Hampshire Regiment. Winter Hill during the Siege of Boston, 28 October 1775 to 12 January 1776.* Exeter, New Hampshire: reprinted from the Exeter News Letters, 1903. (LOC: E231 .N54)

134. *Valley Forge Orderly Book of General George Weedon.* New York: New York Times and the Arno Press, 1971. (LOC E231 .W54)

135. *Orderly Book of Colonel William Henshaw, 20 April–26 September 1776.* Boston: Press of John Wilson & Son, 1877. (LOC: E 231 .H542)

136. *The Orderly Books of Colonel William Henshaw, 1 October 1775 through 3 October 1776.* Worcester, Mass.: American Antiquarian Society, 1948. Reprinted from the *Proceedings* for April, 1947. (LOC: E231 .H543)

# ORDERLY BOOKS NOT USED

In addition to the 136 sets of orderly books from which court-martial entries were extracted for use in chapter six, thirty-three others were examined but not used. The reasons for the exclusions were (a) they contained no court-martial entries; (b) they were entirely duplicative of entries extracted from other orderly books; or (c) they were too faint to read. Those who wish to make further searches on their own may well examine these excluded sources.

Of the seventy microfilmed orderly books at the National Archives, abstracts of courts-martial were made from sixty-six, the others being duplicative or almost illegible.

Of the ninety-three sets of orderly books at the Manuscript Division of the Library of Congress, abstracts of courts-martial were made of sixty-four. The remaining twenty-nine sets contained no court-martial entries, or were duplicative of records extracted from other orderly books. For reference only, a list of those orderly books housed in the Manuscript Division but not used follows.

Brown, John, Capt. First North Carolina Regiment. 21 May 1777–3 January 1778.

Clinton, James, Gen. Continental Army. 4 May 1779–23 August 1779.

Eddy, Jonathan, Col. Massachusetts Militia. 1 August 1777–25 August 1777.

Fourth Virginia Regiment. 13 May 1776–20 September 1776.

Gates, Horatio, Gen. Orderly Book while commanding the Southern Army.

Gates, Horatio, Gen. Horatio Gates Papers–New York Historical Society. 26 July 1780–4 December 1780.

Gates, Horatio, Gen. New Hampshire Brigade; Newburgh. 6 January 1783–15 February 1783. Horatio Gates Papers–New York Historical Society.

Grosvenor, Thomas, Lt. Connecticut Militia. 3 July 1775–30 December 1775.

Hazen, Moses, Col. Second Canadian Regiment, Continental. 1 January 1780–27 April 1780.

Heath, William, Gen. Continental Army. 31 March 1776–13 August 1776.

Hubley, Adam, Capt. First Pennsylvania Battalion. 11 May 1776–10 June 1776

Hyatt,_____, Captain. Third Regiment, New York Militia. 14 May 1776–24 June 1776.

Johnson, Obadiah, Lt. Col. Colonel Andrew Ward's Connecticut State Regiment. 3 November 1776; 9 February 1777–18 March 1777.

Lining, John, Capt. South Carolina Militia. 4 April 1776–30 April 1776.

Orderly Book, Continental Army–New York City and vicinity. 30 August 1776–4 October 1776.

Orderly Book, Harlem Heights, New York. 8 September 1781–21 September 1781.

Orderly Book, Orangetown, New York. 24 September 1781–1 October 1781.

Orderly Book, Pennsylvania Militia. 18 June 1777–20 July 1777.

Orderly Book, Valley Forge, Pennsylvania. 1 January 1778–23 April 1778.

Piper, John, Adjutant. Virginia Militia. 4 March 1781–1 April 1781.

Reed, William, Capt. Colonel John Thomas's Regiment, Massachusetts Militia. 12 May 1775–25 August 1775.

Shepard, _____, Colonel. Fourth Massachusetts Regiment. 1 September 1777–27 September 1777.

Stephen, Adam, Col. Fourth & Fifth Virginia Regiments. 13 May 1776–20 September 1776.

Torrey, William, Adjutant. Second Massachusetts Regiment. 24 Vols.: 1 August 1776–5 October 1776; 16 September 1777–16 February 1783.

Walker, William, Adjutant. Colonel John Peterson's Regiment, Massachusetts Militia. 8 July 1775–9 October 1775.

Ward, Andrew, Lt. Col. Connecticut Militia. 22 February 1776–23 March 1776.

Ward, Artemus, Gen. Continental Army. 7 June 1776–1 August 1775.

Warner, Daniel, Capt. Colonel Jonathan Homan's Regiment, Massachusetts Militia. 30 July 1776–16 October 1776.

## BIBLIOGRAPHY

Billias, George A., ed. *George Washington's Generals.* New York: William Morrow and Company, 1964. (Library of Congress: E206 .B5)

Boatner, Mark M. *Encyclopedia of the American Revolution.* New York: David McKay Company, Inc., 1966. (Library of Congress E208 .B68)

Bowman, Allen. *The Morale of the American Revolutionary Army.* Washington, D.C.: American Council on Public Affairs, 1943. (Library of Congress: E255 .E76)

Callan, John F. *The Military Laws of the United States.* Baltimore: John Murphy & Company, 1858. (Library of Congress: KF7250 .A3)

Calvert, Michael and Peter Young. *A Dictionary of Battles.* New York: Mayflower Books, 1979. (Library of Congress: D25 .A2C34)

Commager, Henry S., and Richard B. Morris, eds. *The Spirit of Seventy-Six,* 2 Vols. Indianapolis–New York: Bobbs-Merrill Company, Inc. 1958. (Library of Congress: #203 .C69)

DeHart, William C. *Observations on Military Law and the Constitution and Practice of Courts-martial.* New York: Wiley and Putnam, 1846. (LOC: UB500 .D4)

Dupuy, R. Ernest and Trevor N. Dupuy, *The Compact History of the Revolutionary War.* New York: Hawthorne Books, Inc., 1963. (LOC: E230 .D8)

Fitzpatrick, John C., ed. *The Writings of Washington,* 26 Vols. Westport Conn.: Greenwood Press, 1970. (Library of Congress: E312.)

Fleming, Thomas J. *1776, Year of Illusions.* New York: W. W. Norton & Company, Inc., 1975. (Library of Congress: E232 .F57)

Freeman, Douglas S. *George Washington, A Biography,* 4 Vols. New York: Charles Scribner's Sons, 1951. (Library of Congress: E312 .F83)

Godfrey, Carlos E. *The Commander-in-Chief's Guard, Revolutionary War.* Washington, D.C.: Stevenson-Smith Company, 1904. (Library of Congress: E260 .G58)

Hatch, Louis C. *The Administration of the American Revolutionary Army.* New York: Longmans, Green & Company, Inc., 1904. (LOC: E255 .H36)

Heitman, Francis B. *Historical Register of Officers of the Continental Army during the War of the Revolution, April 1777 to December 1783.* Washington, D.C.: Rare Book Shop Publishing Company, 1914. Reprinted, Baltimore: Genealogical Publishing Company, 1969. (Library of Congress: E255 .H48)

Higginbotham, Don. *The War of American Independence, Military Attitudes, Policies and Practices; 1783-1789.* New York: MacMillan, 1971. (Library of Congress: E210 .H63)

Karsten, Peter. *The Military in America: From the Colonial Era to the Present.* New York: Free Press, 1980. (Library of Congress: UA25 .M5626)

Lancaster, Bruce. *From Lexington to Liberty.* New York: Doubleday & Company, Inc., 1955. (Library of Congress: 208 .L25)

Lee *Proceedings of a General Court-martial . . . for the Trial of Major General Lee.* New York: privately printed, 1864. (Library of Congress: E241 .M7L4)

Martin, James and Mark Lender *A Respectable Army—The Military Origins of the Republic, 1763-1769.* Arlington Heights, Illinois: Harlan Davidson, 1982. (Library of Congress: E230 .M34)

Middlekauff, Robert. *The Glorious Cause.* New York–Oxford: Oxford University Press, 1982. (Library of Congress: E173 .094)

Neagles, James and Lila. *Locating Your Revolutionary War Ancestor.* Logan, Utah: The Everton Publishers, Inc., 1983 (1985)

Preston, John H. *A Short History of the American Revolution.* New York: Harcourt Brace & Company, 1933. (Library of Congress: E208 .P952)

Royster, Charles. *A Revolutionary People at War, The Continental Army and American Character, 1775-1783.* Chapel Hill, North Carolina: University of North Carolina Press, 1979. (Library of Congress: E259 .R69)

Sellers, John R., et al. American Revolutionary Bicentennial Office. *Manuscript Sources in the Library of Congress on the American Revolution (The Bicentennial Index).* Washington, D.C.: The Library of Congress, 1975. pp 141-150: Orderly Books—American.

Stille, Charles. *Major General Anthony Wayne and the Pennsylvania Line in the Continental Army.* Philadelphia: J.B. Lippincott Company, 1893. (Library of Congress: E207 .W35S8)

Svejda, George. *Quartering, Disciplining, and Supplying the Army at Morristown, 1779-1780.* Washington, D.C.: U.S. Department of the Interior, Division of History, 1970. (Library of Congress: E255 .S9)

Thompson, Ray. *Benedict Arnold in Philadelphia.* Fort Washington, Pennsylvania: Bicentennial Press, 1975. (Library of Congress: E236 .T45)

United States Army. Courts-martial, U.S. Army. *General Court-martial of Benedict Arnold.* New York: privately printed, 1865. (Library of Congress: E278 .A7U48)

United States Continental Congress, 1775. *Rules for Better Government of Troops.* (Library of Congress: UB501–1776)

Van Doren, Carl. *Secret History of the American Revolution.* New York: The Viking Press, 1941. (Library of Congress: E255 .V26)

Wallace, Willard. *Appeal to Arms; A Military History of the American Revolution.* New York: Harper, 1951. (Library of Congress: E230 .W3)

White, Lee. *The American Revolution in Notes, Quotes, and Anecdotes.* Fairfax, Virginia: L.B. Price & Company, Inc. 1975. (Library of Congress: E296 .248)

Wright, John Womack, Col. *Some Notes on the Continental Army.* Cornwallville, New York: Hope Farm Press, 1963. (Library of Congress: E255 .W7)

# Index

This index does not repeat the names of court-martialed persons since they are listed in alphabetical order in chapter six; nor does it contain the names of their commanding officers as shown in that chapter. For this latter purpose, reference is made to the *Historical Register of Officers of the Continental Army during the War of the Revolution*, by Francis B. Heitman.

All other persons named in chapter six, such as victims and others associated with a court-martial; as well as persons, places, and subjects mentioned in the other chapters, are included in this index.

## A

absence without leave, 7-8
alcohol
    use of, 8, 22
Allen, Thomas, 131
Arnold, Benedict, 18, 41, 46
    charges against, 45
court-martial of, 44-46
    trial of Moses Hazen, 47
Articles of War, 5-7, 35-37, passim
assault, 34
Avery, Richard, 75

## B

Babcock, Abraham, 139
Baker, Hugh, 26
Baley, Captain, 25
Barker, John, 218
Barkin, John, 221
Bayard (Baird), Alexander, 158
Beall, Captain Thomas, 26
Beatty, John, 27
Beebe, Dr., 28
Bemus, John, 244

Bettin, Captain Adam, 60
Blackmore, Sergeant Amaziah, 25
Blake, John, 144
Blodgett, Amos, 166
Board of War, 47
Bogley, Ensign Josiah, 94
bounty land, 33
Bowser (Bowzar), William, 59
Brandywine, Pennsylvania, 41
    battle of, 18-19
brigade court-martial, 5
British deserters, 34
British military justice, 5
British spies, 42, 59
Brooks, Benjamin, 94, 216
Brouty, Luther, 120
Brown, Jacob, 69
Brown, James, 6
Brown, Thomas, 94, 207
Bunker Hill (Breed's Hill)
    battle of, 18
Butler, Lieutenant Colonel William, 60-61
Buzzard, Fred, 120

# C

Callender, Captain John, 97
Camden, South Carolina
 battle of, 20-21
Campbell, Captain Joseph, 60
Campbell, Isiah, 109
Carlton, Ens. Moses, 112
cat-o'-nine-tails, 35
Charleston, South Carolina
 battle of, 19-20
Charlottesville, Virginia
 mutiny at, 58
Chit, John, 167
Collins, John, 55
colonials
 loyalty of, 15
Commander-in-Chief's Guard, soldiers
 in, 69, 90, 108, 160, 175, 205, 223,
 257, 278
 plot to kill George Washington, 42
confinement, 35
Connecticut Line
 mutiny of, 58
Connell, Daniel, 59
Continental Army, 6, 15, 17, 27, 58-59
Continental Congress, 57, 60, 62-63
 deals with mutiny, 61
 enlistment bonuses, 33
 on desertion, 32
 outlaws gambling, 7
 pay for troops, 24
 trading with enemy, 27
Continental Line officers, 29
Cornwallis, General, 20
countersign, 10
court-martial
 congressional review, 5
 procedure, 5
 types of, 5
cowardice, 7, 31, 54
Cowpens, South Carolina
 battle of, 20
crime, situational, 15-16
Crosby, Reuben, 108
Crump, John, 188

# D

Dantson, Ens. Daniel D., 131
Davids, Daniel, 219
Davis, Israel, 26
death sentence, 6, 37
Dennis, Robert, 240
Denston, Ens. Daniel D., 243, 258
depreciation lands, 24

desertion, 7-8, 32-34, 57, passim
Dickerson, Lt. Richard, 74
dismissal
 of officers, 32
 with infamy, 37
Donovel, Daniel, 72
drum-head justice, 36
drumming out of the army, 32, 37
dueling, 7
dysentery, 18, 21, 23

# E

Edwards, Joseph, 27
embezzlement, 7, 17, 26
Eustis, Doctor William, 43-44
Eutaw Springs, South Carolina
 battle of, 20

# F

fear of death, 16-17
File, Peter, 108
financial opportunity, 24
First New York Regiment
 mutiny of, 58, 63
Fishing Creek, South Carolina
 battle of, 20
flogging, 35-36
food, scarcity of, 21
Forbes, Gilbert, 42
Fort Stanwix, 18
Fort Ticonderoga, 49-51
Fort Washington, New York
 battle of, 18
Fortin, Joseph, 216
Fountain, John and Fincas, 188
Fourteenth Massachusetts Regiment, 54
Francis, Captain Richard, 149
fraud, 7, 17, 26
French and Indian War, 5
Fry, Windsor, 26
Fuller, Lieutenant Josia, 31

# G

gambling, 7
Gardener, Captain Christopher, 13
Garner, Andrew, 94
garrison court-martial, 5
Gastner, Catherina, 129